ROWLATT ON PRINCIPAL
AND SURETY

CANADA and USA
Carswell
Toronto

NEW ZEALAND
Brookers
Auckland

SINGAPORE and MALAYSIA
Thomson Information (S.E. Asia)
Singapore

AUSTRALIA
LBC Information Services
Sydney

CANADA and USA
Carswell
Toronto

NEW ZEALAND
Brooker's
Auckland

SINGAPORE and MALAYSIA
Thomson Information (S.E. Asia)
Singapore

ROWLATT ON PRINCIPAL AND SURETY

[FIFTH EDITION]

GABRIEL MOSS Q.C. AND DAVID MARKS

LONDON
SWEET & MAXWELL
1999

[First edition 1898, second edition 1926, third edition 1936, fourth edition 1982]

Published by
Sweet & Maxwell Limited of
100 Avenue Road,
Swiss Cottage, London NW3 3PF
http://www.smlawpub.co.uk
Typeset by Interactive Sciences Ltd, Gloucester
Printed and bound in Great Britain by Butler & Tanner of Frome
and London

A C.I.P. catalogue record for this book
is available from the British Libray

ISBN 0421 39090 5

10014 96 166

No natural forests were destroyed to make this product,
only farmed timber was used and replanted.

©
Sweet & Maxwell
1999

PREFACE

In many ways there has been an inordinate delay in the preparation of a fifth edition of this work. On the other hand, the passage of time has allowed certain radical developments relating to guarantees to be considered and refined in the case law, the most notable area being in connection with undue influence and misrepresentation as exemplified in the House of Lords' decision in *Barclays Bank Plc v. O'Brien* [1994] 1 A.C. 180 and *CIBC Mortgages Plc v. Pitt* [1994] 1 A.C. 200. Even in the relatively settled area of the Statute of Frauds the House of Lords has to some extent redefined the law in *Elpis Maritime Co. v. Manti Chartering Co.* [1992] 1 A.C. 21.

The flow of judicial decisions has not abated since the last edition particularly in the Commonwealth where this work is cited with increasing frequency. However, we have not for the moment thought it possible or desirable to quote Commonwealth authorities in full although we have tried to highlight and note decisions which we feel deserve comment and due consideration. There still remain areas within this field where the views of Commonwealth courts and English courts are not entirely at one. Even with regard to English decisions, there are now so many reported and unreported cases that it has not been thought practical or sensible to cite every single one.

As in the last edition, we have regarded our task as striking a balance between the preservation of the principles put in place by the author on the one hand and on the other a fair rendition of the existing law. This has necessitated a re-working principally of Chapters 6, 11 and 14 but there are many other passages which for the time being have been grafted on to the earlier text in an attempt to sound what we believe to be the appropriate note. We have no doubt that there will be extensive rewritings of other areas of this work in the next and subsequent editions. To give but one example, the impact of European Directives such as the Unfair Contract Terms in Consumer Contract Regulations 1994 remains fraught with both promise and uncertainty.

We wish to thank the substantial and invaluable assistance of all those whose names appear at the beginning of this edition whilst of course accepting for ourselves sole and final responsibility for the views expressed. The law is stated as at October 1998.

Gabriel Moss Q.C. and David Marks
3/4 South Square
Gray's Inn
London

October 23, 1998

CONTRIBUTORS TO THE DRAFTING OF THE FIFTH EDITION

The authors wish to acknowledge the substantial and invaluable assistance received from the following, whilst accepting for themselves final responsibility for the views expressed and for errors and omissions in the text of this edition:

Chapter

2	Samantha Knights, BA (Oxon.), Barrister, 3–4 South Square, Gray's Inn, WC1R 5HP
3	Adam Goodison, BA (Dunelm.), Barrister, 3–4 South Square, Gray's Inn, WC1R 5HP
10	Lucy Frazer, MA (Cantab.), Barrister, 3–4 South Square, Gray's Inn, WC1R 5HP
13, 16	Jeremy Goldring, BA (Oxon.), MA (Yale), Barrister, 3–4 South Square, Gray's Inn, WC1R 5HP
17	Lucy Frazer, MA (Cantab.), Barrister, 3–4 South Square, Gray's Inn, WC1R 5HP
18	Philip Ridgway, BA (Hons), LL M (Cantab.), ATII, Barrister, principal with Deloitte & Touche, Chartered Accountants, Hill House, 1 Little New Street, EC4A 3TR
19	Felicity Toube, BA, BCL (Oxon.), Barrister, 3–4 South Square, Gray's Inn, WC1R 5HP

DM

GM

Contents

TABLE OF CASES

TABLE OF STATUTES

STATUTORY INSTRUMENTS

EUROPEAN MATERIAL

TREATIES & FOREIGN STATUTES

ICC UNIFORM RULES FOR DEMAND GUARANTEES

CHAPTER 1

SCOPE OF THE LAW OF PRINCIPAL AND SURETY

Definition

A surety may be defined as one who contracts with an actual or **1–01** possible creditor of another to be responsible to him by way of security, additional to that other, for the whole or part of the debt.

The obligation of a surety is thus necessarily a collateral obligation, postulating the principal liability of another, the principal debtor.[1] A person is not, therefore, a surety who either (a) in order to procure an advantage for another becomes bound upon any other basis than that that other shall also become liable,[2] or (b) becomes bound instead of a person already bound who is released by the substitution.[3]

Principal under disability

In view of the necessity of a principal debtor a difficulty arises **1–02** where a person purports to become surety for one who is under disability. It seems clear that this does not prevent the so-called surety from being liable to the creditor where there is no fraud or misrepresentation. In nearly every instance it will be found that the proper inference from the facts is that the intention of the parties was that the so-called surety should be liable as principal, *i.e.*

---

[1] See *Re Royal Albert Life Assurance Company* (1870) L.R. 11 Eq. 164 at 177. *Cf. Nicholas v. Ridley* [1904] 1 Ch. 192 at 209, 210. If the promisor has himself an interest in the transaction, the proper inference is often that he is more than a surety and is a principal debtor: *Huggard v. Representative Church Body* [1916] 1 I.R. 1 at 13. *Cf.* below, pp. 32 *et seq.* and the cases there cited.

[2] See *Mountstephen v. Lakeman* (1871) L.R. 5 QB 613; 7 QB 196; 7 HL 17.

[3] Despite the definition in the text, there have been occasional judicial comments to the effect that "collateral" does not sufficiently convey the accessory character of suretyship see, *e.g. National Telephone Co. v. I.R.C.* [1899] 1 QB 250, 258 *per* A. L. Smith L.J. affd. [1900] A.C. 1. *Cf. Re Athill, Athill v. Athill* (1880) 16 Ch D 211 at 222. The definition and discussion contained in the 2nd edition of this work was cited in *Re Conley* [1938] 2 All E.R. 127 where Lord Greene M.R. saw no distinction between the giving of personal credit and the giving of a pledge or security for the purpose of rendering the giver a surety. One of the leading American treatises on principal and surety, Simpson, *Handbook on the Law of Suretyship* (West Publishing Co., 1950) makes a further distinction between suretyship, which in its narrow sense entails a primary, though still accessory obligation on the part of the surety, and guarantee, which is entirely secondary in nature (see pp. 6 to 11 and 16 to 23 inclusive). For an American judicial discussion see *W. T. Rawleigh Co. v. Overstreet*, 32 S.E. 2d 574; 71 Ga.App. 873 (1944). For judicial and practical illustrations of the differences between guarantes and indemnities see, *e.g. Yeoman Credit Ltd v. Latter* [1961] 1 W.L.R. 828; *Unity Finance Ltd v. Woodcock* [1963] 1 W.L.R. 455; *Goulston Discount Co. Ltd v. Clark* [1967] 2 QB 493; *Stadium Finance Co. Ltd v. Helm* (1965) 109 S.J. 471; *Goulston Discount Co. Ltd v. Sims* (1967) 111 S.J. 682; *Ralli Brothers Ltd v. Cooper* (1968) 112 S.J. 67. See also *Argo Caribbean v. Lewis* [1976] 2 Lloyd's Rep. 288 at 296.

whether the principal could be liable or not.[4] Thus, although a promise that a company or corporation shall do something beyond its legal powers is void,[5] a surety for the repayment of money borrowed by a company *ultra vires* may be liable on his guarantee if the transaction was entered into in good faith.[6] However, in the case of a loan made to a minor which is made void by statute,[7] it has been held that the guarantors of a loan where the fact of the minority is known to all parties, cannot be liable on the guarantee.[8] But a contract to repay money lent to an infant will, it seems, be enforceable if on its proper construction it is a contract of indemnity.[9]

Liability of surety collateral not necessarily conditional

1–03   The liability of a surety is often spoken of as a liability to pay "if the principal does not." This does not mean that his liability is necessarily only conditionally enforceable[10] but merely that it is collateral. Being collateral, the liability of a surety is in substance, from the surety's point of view, certainly contingent, because if the principal pays, the debt is satisfied, and the surety is free.[11] What is contemplated is that the principal shall pay. This may be so, although the undertaking of the surety is as absolute as that of the principal. To say, therefore, that a debtor is surety only does not necessarily imply more than that he has become bound as an additional party, and only as security for another, the principal debtor, who alone has enjoyed or is to enjoy the consideration,[12] and upon the terms, express or implied, of being indemnified by

---

[4] *Heald v. O'Connor* [1971] 1 W.L.R. 497; *Wauthier v. Wilson* (1912) 27 T.L.R. 582, 28 T.L.R. 238; *Cf. Maggs v. Ames* (1828) 4 Bing. 470; *White v. Cuyler* (1795) 1 Esp. 200. Also *ex p. Chippendale* (1853) 4 De. G.M. & G. 19; *Chambers v. Manchester and Milford Railway* (1864) 5 B. & S. 588, 612; *Yorkshire Railway Wagon Co. v. Maclure* (1881) 19 Ch D 478; 21 Ch D 309; and *Garrard v. James* [1925] Ch. 616.

[5] *McGregor v. Dover and Deal Railway Co.* (1852) 18 QB 618.

[6] See *Garrard v. James* [1925] Ch. 616, and also *Coutts & Co. v. Browne-Lecky* [1947] K.B. 104 at 111 where it was suggested that this type of case may be different in its consequences from voidness brought about by the express provisions of a statute. See also *Heald v. O'Connor* [1971] 1 W.L.R. 497.

[7] Infants Relief Act 1874, ss.1 and 2; Betting and Loans (Infants) Act 1892, s.5. See also *Steyn* (1974) 90 L.Q.R. 246.

[8] *Coutts & Co. v. Browne-Lecky*, above, following *Swan v. Bank of Scotland* (1836) 10 Bli. (N.S.) 927, HL where a bank was precluded by statute from recovering against a principal debtor because it had knowingly honoured unstamped drafts. *Wauthier v. Wilson*, above, was not followed.

[9] See *Harris v. Huntbach* (1757) 1 Burr. 373; *Duncomb v. Tickridge* (1648) Alleyn 44; *Yeoman Credit Ltd v. Latter* [1961] 1 W.L.R. 828. *Cf. Western Credit Ltd v. Alberry* [1964] 1 W.L.R. 945. In the 3rd edition of this work it was suggested that in some such cases the liability is here more accurately explicable as that of suretyship by estoppel. As to guarantees by minors, see further Chap. 4. There are interesting articles touching on guarantees by infants by Steyn, *op. cit.*, and Else Mitchell (1947) 63 L.Q.R. 355 and Cohn (1974) 10 M.L.R. 40.

[10] *cf. Amott v. Holden* (1852) 18 QB 593 at 607, 608; *White v. Corbett* (1859) 1 E. & E. 692. And see below, p. 108.

[11] *ibid.* and see *ex p. Whittaker* (1891) 63 L.T. 727.

[12] See *per* Stuart V.-C., in *Wright v. Sandars* (1857) 3 Jur. (N.S.) 504 at 507; *Re Keily* (1856) 6 Ir.Ch.R. 394. In the latter case the question was whether a son, entitled in remainder, who had joined with his father, the tenant for life, in mortgaging the property, was in the position of a surety. It was held under the circumstances there existing that he was. Contrast *Huggard v. Representative Church Body* [1916] 1 I.R. 1.

him. The rights which a surety can claim at the hands of a creditor depend not upon any term in the contract between them but upon an equity arising out of the knowledge of the creditor of the relation between the surety debtor and the principal debtor, which binds him to respect, subject to his own right to exact payment from either, the right of surety to have the money found by the principal.[13]

Surety need not expressly contract as such

This being the basis of the rights of a surety, it follows that he   **1–04** need not be expressed to contract as surety, inasmuch as his admission to the rights of one will not vary or add to his written contract. A typical example is where a person gives another his promissory note to secure an advance to a third person.[14] Here the legal right of the creditor is to demand payment from the maker unconditionally according to the tenor of the note.[15] The equitable right of the maker is, without limiting that legal right of the creditor,[16] to have the creditor respect in his dealings with the principal the right of the maker to be indemnified by the principal. This is not contradicting or modifying the terms of the note. The unconditional promise to pay does not import that the maker gives up equities which introduce no conditions. Similarly an IOU can be given as a guarantee.[17]

Rights of surety depend not on contract but on notice

In strictness perhaps, no-one under a liability *ex facie* absolute   **1–05** should be described as a surety, unless that liability was from the first, to the knowledge of the creditor at that time, only undertaken for the purpose of affording security for the payment of the principal debt.[18] On the other hand, the rights of a surety depend not upon contract but upon notice. Accordingly, a person whose liability is *ex facie* that of a principal may acquire the equitable rights of a surety by notice to the creditor, even after such person has become liable.[19] It also follows that such a person may acquire the rights of a surety if either at the time of his becoming liable or since[20] it was agreed between him and the other debtor that the latter should

---

[13] See *Pooley v. Harradine* (1857) 7 E. & B. 431; *Greenough v. McLelland* (1860) 2 E. & E. 424; *Leicestershire Banking Co. v. Hawkins* (1900) 16 T.L.R. 317.

[14] See cases cited in the previous footnote.

[15] For an attempt to impose conditions, see *Abrey v. Crux* (1869) L.R. 5 C.P. 37; and compare *Hitchings v. Northern Leather Co.* [1914] 3 K.B. 903. See generally Chap. 13.

[16] See *Ewart v. Latta* (1865) 4 Macq. HL 903. The discussion here does not deal with the question of whether there are special cases where the surety may have an equity against the creditor to compel him to go first against the principal or against some fund: see the discussion in Chap. 7.

[17] *R. v. Chambers* (1871) L.R. 1 C.C.R. 341.

[18] See *Duncan Fox & Co. v. North & South Wales Bank* (1880) 6 App. Cas. 1 *per* Lord Selborne at 11 where at least three different kinds of suretyship were listed.

[19] *Oriental Finance Corporation v. Overend, Gurney & Co.* (1871) L.R. 7 Ch. App. 142; 7 HL 348; *Duncan Fox & Co. v. North & South Wales Bank* (1880) 6 App. Cas. 1.

[20] *Rouse v. Bradford Banking Co.* [1894] A.C. 586.

assume the whole interest in the consideration and the whole duty of discharging the liability.

This proposition itself was conclusively established by the decision of the House of Lords in *Rouse v. Bradford Banking Co.*[21] The doctrine at common law was (except in two decisions by Lord Ellenborough, which were later overruled) never extended beyond the case where the creditor, at the time of taking an instrument not under seal, actually agrees to regard as surety only who one who by the instrument contracts in form as principal.[22] In equity though, the wider rule always prevailed that the creditor was constrained to regard the position of the surety not by contract but by notice only,[23] and that notice given after the contract has been entered into was sufficient.[24]

1–06   Furthermore, there was no difficulty, in equity, in applying this principle to instruments under seal[25]; and consequently an obligor in a bond by which he appeared to be principal could show that he became bound as surety only, and from the date of notice of that circumstance to the obligee, claim the rights of a surety.[26]

The decision in *Rouse v. Bradford Banking*[27] finally settled the question of whether a notification to the creditor, after the contract, of the fact that one of a number of debtors had since the contract become, as between himself and the others, a surety only, would bind the creditor. It was held that the creditor was obliged to respect his position as a surety, even if the creditor had not consented to a modification of the original position, and agree to regard him as surety.[28] On this principle it was held in that case that a partner retiring with the ordinary provision for indemnity had the rights of a surety as against the creditor of the old firm having notice of that provision, and that no assent of the creditor to the change of the relation between the parties was necessary.[29]

---

[21] *ibid.*

[22] *Manley v. Boycot* (1853) 2 E. & B. 46 (decided just before the introduction of equitable pleas); following *Kerrison v. Cooke* (1813) 3 Campbell 362; *Fentum v. Pocock* (1813) 5 Taunt 192; *Price v. Edmunds* (1829) 10 B. & C. 578; *Nichols v. Norris* (1831) 3 B. & Ad. 41, note; *Harrison v. Courtauld* (1832) 3 B. & Ad. 36; and overruling *Laxton v. Peat* (1809) 2 Camp. 185 and *Collott v. Haigh* (1812) 3 Camp. 281, the decisions of Lord Ellenborough referred to in the text. And see *Mutual Loan Fund v. Sudlow* (1858) 5 C.B. (N.S.) 449.

[23] *Bank of Ireland v. Beresford* (1818) 6 Dow 233; *ex p. Glendinning* (1819) 8 Buck. 517; *Oakeley v. Pasheller* (1836) 4 C. & F. 207; *Hollier v. Eyre* (1840) 9 C. & F. 1; *Wythes v. Labouchere* (1859) 3 De G. & J. 593; *Davies v. Stainbank* (1855) 6 De G. M. & G. 679; *Pooley v. Haradine* (1857) 7 E. & B. 431; *Greenough v. McLelland* (1860) 2 E. & E. 424; *Wright v. Sandars* (1857) 3 Jur. (N.S.) 504; *Rayner v. Fussey* (1859) 28 L.J. Ex. 132.

[24] *Oriental Financial Corporation v. Overend, Gurney & Co.*, above, but see *Ex p. Graham* (1854) 5 De G.M. & G. 356.

[25] See *per* Lord Loughborough in *Rees v. Berrington* (1795) 2 Ves. 540; 2 W. & T.L.C. Eq. (8th ed.), p. 571 and compare (*Davey v. Prendergrass* (1821) 5 B. & Ald. 187.

[26] *Wythes v. Labouchere* (1859) 3 De G. & J. 593; *Wright v. Sandars* (1857) 3 Jur. (N.S.) 504, and see *Wyke v. Rogers* (1852) 1 De G.M. & G. 408; *Tucker v. Laing* (1856) 2 K. & J. 745; *Oakeley v. Pasheller*, above; *Hollier v. Eyre*, above.

[27] [1894] A.C. 586.

[28] See *Swire v. Redman* (1876) 1 Q.B.D. 536; *Rouse v. Bradford Banking Co.* [1894] A.C. 586.

[29] *Rouse v. Bradford Banking Co.*, above; *Goldfarb v. Bartlett* [1920] 1 K.B. 639. As to the liability of retired partners see also *Stevens v. Britten* [1954] 1 W.L.R. 1340.

Cases analogous to suretyship—"quasi-sureties"

There lies beyond the borderline of suretyship a class of cases in **1–07** which, without any contract between the debtors, there is a primary and a secondary liability of two persons for one and the same debt. In such a case, the debt is, as between the two, that of one of those persons only, and not equally of both; so that the other, if he should be compelled to pay it, would be entitled to reimbursement by the person by whom, as between the two, it ought to have been paid.[30] Such persons, when both have become liable to the creditor, and it is within his choice upon which to put the burden, do stand in a relation to one another which gives rise to an equity identical with one which exists between principal and surety—namely, that securities given by the primary debtor are attributable in the hands of the creditor to the satisfaction of the debt, and do not go back to that debtor or his general creditors.[31]

This relation is not, however, genuinely that of principal and surety.[32] Thus the drawer of a bill of exchange is not in the complete sense a surety for the acceptor.[33] This is even though (on grounds independent of suretyship):

   (i) he is discharged by time being given to the acceptor,

  (ii) he is only liable on his default,

 (iii) he is, after the bill has been dishonoured, entitled as against the acceptor to securities covering the bill given by the acceptor and in the hands of the holder,[34] and

 (iv) he can, even if not the holder of the bill, recover over against the acceptor any sum paid by him in his exoneration.[35]

But an accommodation party to a bill of exchange known to be such is a surety in every sense[36] inasmuch as his liability upon the bill was only undertaken to afford security for the debt of the party accommodated.

Again,   **1–08**

   (i) the transferor of shares, who is liable by statute under certain circumstances to pay calls if the transferee does not,[37]

---

[30] See *Duncan Fox & Co. v. North & South Wales Bank* (1880) 6 App. Cas. 1 *per* Lord Selborne at 11.

[31] *ibid.*

[32] *Duncan Fox & Co. v. North & South Wales Bank* (1880) 6 App. Cas. 1.

[33] *ibid.*; *Ex p. Yonge* (1814) 3 Ves. & B. 31 at 40. See generally Chap. 13.

[34] *Duncan Fox & Co. v. North & South Wales Bank* (1880) 6 App. Cas. 1.

[35] *Pownal v. Ferrand* (1827) 6 B. & C. 439.

[36] See below, Chap. 13.

[37] Companies Act 1985, s. 502(2)(c); *Hudson's Case* (1871) L.R. 12 Eq. 1; *Helbert's Case* (1871) L.R. 5 HL 28; *Roberts v. Crowe* (1872) L.R. 7 C.P. 629.

(ii) the owner of goods which by the law of distress may become liable for the rent of the premises upon which they are,[38]

(iii) a lessee liable for the covenants in a lease assigned,[39]

(iv) a mortgagor liable for the mortgage money after the sale of the equity of redemption,[40]

can none of them be classed as sureties. This is so even though in each case the liability is a secondary one, and in each case the person secondarily liable has upon payment the right to be reimbursed[41] by the person primarily liable, founded upon the same principle as the right of the surety to sue the principal for the money paid by him.[42]

Suretyship by pledge or mortgage[43]

1–09   A person may also become a surety by pledging, mortgaging or charging his property for the debt of another as by pledging his personal credit: in fact he may well become a surety in both ways at once[44]; and he will be entitled to the same remedies for his indemnity and to have security released upon the same grounds in the one case as the other.[45] Thus a wife charging her own property

---

[38] See *Exall v. Partridge* (1799) 8 Term. Rep. 308.

[39] See *Re Russell, Russell v. Shoolbred* (1885) 29 Ch D 254; *Baynton v. Morgan* (1888) 21 Q.B.D. 101; 22 Q.B.D. 74. The covenant of the lessee is not collateral to the liability of the assignee of the lease, to pay if he does not, but is a covenant that the lessee or his assignee shall pay: *per* Fry L.J. 22 Q.B.D. at 81. In truth the liability of the lessee is not undertaken in contemplation of a principal liability to be contracted by an assignee of the lease towards the lessor. The liability of the assignee to the lessor upon the privity of the estate, is, as regards the lessee, an accident. And the position of a mortgagor who has assigned his equity remaining liable upon his covenant, is in this respect very like that of a lessee who has assigned. See also Chap. 14.

[40] The mortgagor has an implied right of indemnity against his assignee; *Waring v. Ward* (1802) 7 Ves. 332 at 337; *Bridgman v. Daw* (1891) 40 W.R. 253. There is no privity of contract between the assignee and the mortgagee: see *Re Errington* [1894] 1 QB 11 at 14. The mortgagee cannot sue the mortgagor upon his covenant, if by reason of anything that has passed between him and the transferee of the equity, he is precluded from reconveying. See *Palmer v. Hendrie* (1859) 27 Beav. 349; 28 Beav. 341; *Walker v. Jones* (1866) L.R. 1 P.C. 50; *Rudge v. Richens* (1873) L.R. 8 C.P. 358; *Kinnaird v. Trollope* (1888) 39 Ch D 636. But this does not depend upon the law of suretyship. See also *Ellis v. Dixon-Johnson* [1925] A.C. 489.

[41] For the distinction between a right of reimbursement and a right to indemnity or protection against being called upon to pay see *Johnston v. Salvage Association* (1887) 19 Q.B.D. 458 at 460.

[42] See below, Chap. 7.

[43] *Keith Murphy Pty Ltd v. Custom Credit Corp. Ltd* (1992) 6 W.A.R. 332 at 343, where the passage in the previous edition of this work was approved.

[44] *Bolton v. Salmon* [1891] 2 Ch. 48; *Smith v. Wood* [1929] 1 Ch. 14; *Re Conley* [1938] 2 All E.R. 127 *per* Luxmoore J. at 137 *et seq.*

[45] *Re Keily* (1856) 6 Ir.Ch.R. 394; *McNeale v. Reed* (1857) 7 Ir.Ch. R. 251; *Hodgson v. Hodgson* (1837) 2 Keen 704; *Ex p. Ford* (1885) 16 Q.B.D. 305; *Bolton v. Salmon*, above; *Rouse v. Bradford Banking Co.* [1894] A.C. 586. He has, moreover, what a surety by covenant has not—a charge from the date of his mortgage on property of the principal mortgaged by the same instrument for the same debt; *Gee v. Liddell* [1913] 2 Ch. 62; *Re Marley* [1976] 1 W.L.R. 952. But see *Kennedy v. Campbell* [1899] 1 I.R. 59.

for her husband's benefit is regarded as having the right to have her property exonerated out of her husband's estate.[46]

Surety and insurance

The subject-matter of a contract by way of suretyship is always **1–10** a debt either incurred or intended to be incurred by the principal to the person taking the guarantee, or which, though not incurred or intended to be incurred, may result in the future from some default or miscarriage of the principal in a relation already existing or intended to be entered into between himself and that person. The province of guarantee is therefore narrower than that of insurance by which indemnity may be secured against losses by the acts or omissions of strangers, considered as perils analogous to the risk of accident, and without regard to any legal responsibility of the persons guilty of them. The domain of insurance, however, is not restricted to the class of losses which cannot be provided against by taking sureties. The risk of default by a debtor can be insured against as effectually[47] as the debt can be guaranteed.

But the two securities are not identical either in the form of the obligation imposed or in respect of the basis upon which the parties are taken to contract. A surety becomes bound, it may be, unconditionally and without previous notice or demand, to pay the debt or make good the default which the principal is or shall be liable to pay or make good, and the surety must see he does it.[48] An insurer only engages to pay the loss, measured in a certain way, upon the happening of a defined contingency,[49] against the happening of which, however, he is not considered capable of exercising an influence. An insurer is entitled to a disclosure of all facts material to the risk within the knowledge of the assured. But a surety can only complain of positive deception, by representations expressed or implied.[50] When a principal debtor procures a third party to become bound for his, the principal's debt by an instrument in form

---

[46] *Hudson v. Carmichael* (1854) Kay. 613; *Dixon v. Steel* [1901] 2 Ch. 602; *Paget v. Paget* [1898] 1 Ch. 471; *Hall v. Hall* [1911] 1 Ch. 487. In the last edition of this work the question was raised as to how far such old cases would apply in modern social conditions where property is put into the joint names of a husband and wife, referring to *Re Berry* [1978] 2 N.Z.L.R. 373 and *Re Woodstock* (1980) C.L.Y. 148. *Re Pittortou* [1985] 1 W.L.R. 58 confirms that the old principles apply save where the wife's security is given for the joint benefit of the household.
[47] *Dane v. Mortgage Insurance Corporation* [1894] 1 QB 54; *Finlay v. Mexican Investment Corporation* [1897] 1 QB 517.
[48] See below, Chap. 4.
[49] See *Dane v. Mortgage Insurance Corporation*, above, *cf. Mortgage Insurance Corporation v. Pound* (1894) 64 L.J. QB 394.
[50] See *Seaton v. Heath* [1899] 1 QB 782 reversed without reference to this point *sub. nom. Seaton v. Bernard* [1900] A.C. 135; *Workington Harbour, etc. v. Trade Indemnity Co.* (1933) 47 Ll.L.R. 305; 49 Ll.L.Rep. 430, CA, where this passage was cited with approval by Greer L.J. at 443. The decision was reversed on another point, [1937] A.C. 1, the House of Lords expressly not deciding the question whether in contracts of guarantee there is a duty to disclose similar to that in contracts of insurance. See also *Westcott v. J. H. Jenner Ltd* [1962] 1 Lloyd's Rep. 307 where a contract by sub-contractors to indemnify the contractors against all employers and third party risks was held to cover claims resulting from the contractor's own negligence; the substance and not the form of the transaction was held to be decisive.

a policy of insurance, the result appears to be similar to that in the parallel case where the third party is bound by a promissory note or a bond.[51] With regard to such matters as concealment[52] and equitable rights generally,[53] the third person is in the position of a surety, but the document remains a policy of insurance as far as concerns the form and extent of the obligation undertaken.[54]

Letters of comfort

1–11   So-called "letters of comfort" or "letters of respectability" are often given by a parent company to reassure a lender or supplier to its subsidiary of the parent's commitment to maintain and support in the subsidiary. They are usually worded as statements of present intention, are not guarantees in a legally binding sense[55] and are not dealt with further in this work. There is no magic in the label "letter of comfort" and it can sometimes be a difficult question of construction whether or not a binding guarantee has been created.[56]

Subjects not dealt with

1–12   Usage of the term "guarantee" has broadened considerably dependent upon the context. It has come to mean a warranty as employed in the Sale of Goods Act 1979, or a retailer's obligation to undertake repairs, whether free or not,[57] or even a contract conferring rights upon a buyer against a manufacturer in return for giving up some or all of his rights against a seller. None of these meanings are considered in this work. Nor is any mention made of the law of bail in which the concept of suretyship is also employed, and as to which reference should be made to the various textbooks on criminal law.

---

[51] See above.

[52] See *Seaton v. Heath*, below. The result of this case seems to be that the test for this purpose is whether the instrument was obtained by the principal or the creditor.

[53] *Re Denton* [1904] 2 Ch. 178. *Cf. Parr's Bank v. Albert Mines Syndicate* (1900) 5 Com. Cas. 116.

[54] This appears to be the explanation of the dicta in *Shaw v. Rogers* [1911] 1 Ch. 138, see also *Re Law Guarantee, Liverpool Mortgage Insurance Co.'s Case* [1914] 2 Ch. 617; *American Surety Co. v. Wrightson* (1910) 103 L.T. 663.

[55] *Kleinwort Benson Ltd v. Malaysian Mining Corp.* [1989] 1 W.L.R. 379; an attempt to make a letter of comfort "binding" by using it as a basis for fraudulent trading allegations against the parent company failed in *Re Augustus Barnett & Son Ltd* [1986] B.C.L.C. 170.

[56] See *Kleinwort Benson Ltd v. Malaysian Mining Corp.* [1989] 1 W.L.R. 379. Contrast the result reached on similar wording in New South Wales in *Banque Brussels Lambert SA v. Australian National Industries Ltd* [1989] 21 N.S.W.L.R. 502. See also *Chemco Leasing v. Rediffusion* [1987] 1 F.T.L.R. 201; *Commonwealth Bank of Australia v. TLI Management Pty Ltd* [1990] V.R. 510.

[57] See, *e.g. Adams v. Richardson and Starling Ltd.* [1969] 1 W.L.R. 1645.

CHAPTER 2

CONSIDERATION

Consideration necessary

Like every other contract, a guarantee if not under seal must have **2–01** a consideration to support it. It need hardly be added that the fact of its being in writing according to the Statute of Frauds does not dispense with the necessity[1]; nor that if the consideration totally fails a guarantee cannot be enforced.[2]

It is not necessary that the consideration directly benefits the surety, although it may often do so.[3] The consideration will often be in the form of a creditor incurring some detriment in reliance on the promise to guarantee,[4] rather than conferring a benefit on the guarantor.[5] It may equally consist wholly of some advantage given to or conferred on the principal debtor by the creditor at the guarantor's request.[6]

---

[1] *Barrell v. Trussell* (1811) 4 Taunt. 117; *Sheffield v. Lord Castleton* (1700) 2 Vern. 399; *Pillans v. Van Mierop* (1765) 3 Burr. 1664; *Saunders v. Wakefield* (1821) 4 B. & Ald. 395; *Ex p. Gardom* (1808) 15 Ves. 286; *Boyd v. Moyle* (1846) 2 C.B. 644; *French v. French* (1841) 2 Man. & G. 644. And see *Rann v. Hughes* (1778) 7 Term Rep. 350, note. See also *Performance Systems v. Pazim* [1971] 5 N.W.R. 433. Note that the Law of Property (Miscellaneous Provisions) Act 1989, s.1(1)(b) which came into force on July 31, 1990 abolished the requirement for a deed executed by an individual to be sealed up. On the same date the requirement for a company in England and Wales to have a common seal was abolished. See also *Decouvreur v. Jordan, The Times*, May 25, 1987, CA (CAT No. 525 of 1987).
[2] See *Cooper v. Joel* (1859) 27 Beav. 313; *Latter v. White* (1870) L.R. 5 Q.R. 622; 5 HL 578; *Walton v. Cook* (1888) 40 Ch.D 325; *Re Barber, ex p. Agra Bank* (1870) L.R. 9 Eq. 725; *Rolt v. Cozens* (1856) 18 C.B. 673. See also *Chan v. Cresdon Proprietary* [1989] 168 C.L.R. 242; *Averbrian v. Willmalight* (unreported) March 9, 1994 (Recorder Dedman, Willesden County Court) where there was no demise of property as far as the sureties were concerned and therefore no consideration.
[3] *Morley v. Boothby* (1825) 10 Moore C.P. 395; 3 Bing 107; *Ex p. Minet* (1807) 14 Ves. 189 at 190, *per* Lord Eldon L.C.; *Seaton v. Heath* [1899] 1 QB 782 at 793, CA (reversed on a different point *sub nom. Seaton v. Burnand* [1900] A.C. 135); *Raikes v. Todd* (1838) 3 Ad. & E. 846; 112 E.R. 1058; *Royal Bank v. Kisha* [1967] 2 O.R. 379, CA For an example of a case where the surety did benefit directly see *Re Willis, ex p. Brook* (1850) 6 De G.M. & G. 771. Note also that even in the absence of consideration, if the parties assume the guarantee is valid and binding, it may be possible to establish the existence of a guarantee by means of the doctrine of estoppel by convention. See Goff J. in *Amalgamated Investment & Property Co. Ltd (in liq.) v. Texas Commerce International Bank Ltd* [1982] QB 84 at 108. See also *Lee Aitken*, "The Compensated Surety" [1992] L.M.C.L.Q. 177 for consideration of two Australian authorities where the surety was rewarded: *Tricontinental Corp. Ltd v. HDFI Ltd* (1990) 21 N.S.W.L.R. 689, CA; *Corumo Holdings Pty Ltd v. C. Itoh* (1991) 24 N.S.W.L.R. 370.
[4] *Pillans and Rose v. Van Mierop and Hopkins* (1765) 3 Burr. 1663; 97 E.R. 1035; *Jones v. Ashburnham* (1804) 4 East. 455; 102 E.R. 905; *Bailey v. Croft* (1812) 4 Taunt. 611; 128 E.R. 470.
[5] *Erskine-Smith Co. v. Bordeleau* [1929] 2 D.L.R. 877. See also *Fitzgerald v. Dressler* (1859) 7 C.B.N.S. 374; 141 E.R. 861; *Davys v. Buswell* [1913] 2 K.B. 47; *Fred T Brooks Ltd v. Claude Neon Gen Advertising Ltd* [1932] 2 D.L.R. 45, Ont. CA. See also *Seaton v. Heath* [1899] 1 QB 782 at 793, *per* Romer L.J. reversed on other grounds *Seaton v. Burnand* [1900] A.C. 135, HL; *Royal Bank v. Kiska* [1967] 2 O.R. 379, CA.
[6] *Coghlan v. SH Lock (Australia) Ltd* (1987) 3 B.C.C. 183, PC. See also *Morely v. Boothby* (1825) 10 Moore C.P. 395.

The consideration for the guarantee must move from the person to whom the guarantee is given,[7] although the whole consideration need not move from him.[8]

Where debt has been already incurred

2–02   In accordance with the well-known principal that an executed consideration will not support a promise,[9] a guarantee not under seal for a debt already incurred will not be valid unless there be some further consideration moving from the creditor.[10]

Where debt to be guaranteed has not yet been incurred

2–03   Where the guarantee is to secure a further debt or sums which may be due by virtue of a relation not yet entered into between a creditor and the debtor, the granting of the creditor or entering into the relation will always be sufficient consideration. Such a consideration is either (i) entire, as where a lease is granted[11] or an employment conferred, in consideration of which a third person guarantees the performance of the duties of the lessee or employee[12]; or (ii) fragmentary, supplied from time to time, and therefore divisible, as where a guarantee is given for a running account in respect of money to be advanced or goods to be supplied.[13] The distinction is important upon the question of the right of a guarantor to bring his guarantee to an end.[14]

---

[7] *Dutchman v. Tooth* (1839) 5 Bing. N.C. 577; 132 E.R. 1222, CP; *Fleming v. Bank of New Zealand* [1900] A.C. 577, PC; *Rattenbury v. Fenton* (1834) 3 My & K. 505; 40 E.R. 192; *Bank of Montreal v. Sperling Hotel Co.* (1973) 36 D.L.R. (3d) 130 (Man).

[8] *Hodson v. Lee* (1847) 9 L.T.O.S. 312 at 313, *per* Patterson J.

[9] For an example see *Astley Ind. Trust v. Grimston Electric Tools* (1965) 109 S.J. 149. See also *Bailey v. Manos* [1992] A.C.L. Rep. 220.

[10] *French v. French* (1841) 2 Man. & G. 644; *Forth v. Stanton* (1669) Saund. 210; *Jones v. Ashburnham* (1804) 3 East 455 at 463, and see *Wigan v. English and Scottish Law Life Assurance Association* [1909] 1 Ch. 291 at 297 holding that the mere existence of an antecedent debt cannot be valuable consideration for the giving of a security by a debtor; *Currie v. Misa* (1875) L.R. 10 Ex. 153 affirmed on other grounds *sub nom. Misa v. Currie* (1876) 1 App. Cas. 554, H.L; *Crofts v. Beale* (1851) 11 C.B. 172; *Astley Industrial Trust Ltd v. Grimston Electric Tools* (1965) 109 S.J. 149 (where a surety guaranteed payments under a hire-purchase agreement entered into four days previously, it was held that the guarantee was given for past consideration only and was void).

[11] *Chan v. Cresdon Pty Ltd* (1989) 168 C.L.R. 242.

[12] *Newbury v. Armstrong* (1829) 6 Bing. 201; 130 1257; *Kennaway v. Treleavan* (1839) 5 M. & W. 498; 151 E.R. 211; *Lysaght v. Walker* (1831) 2 Dow. & Cl. 211; 6 E.R. 707; *Montefiore v. Lloyd* (1863) 15 C.B.N.S. 203; *Leathley v. Spyer* (1870) L.R. 5 C.P. 595.

[13] *Lloyds v. Harper* (1880) 16 Ch D 290 at 319. See also *Raikes v. Todd* (1838) 8 Ad. & E. 846 at 857; 112 E.R. 1058 at 1062, *per* Patterson J.; *Robertson v. Healy* (1866) 5 S.C.R. (N.S.W.) 290; *Chapman v. Sutton* (1846) 2 C.B. 634; 135 E.R. 1095; *Bank of Montreal v. Germain* [1976] W.W.D. 75; *Horsman Bros. Hldgs Ltd v. Dolphin Elec. Contrs Ltd* (1984) 52 B.C.L.R. 334 (Co. Ct.) (granting of credit); *Morrell v. Cowan* (1877) 7 Ch D 151, CA; *Wood v. Benson* (1831) 2 Cr. & J. 94 (supply of particular goods); *Jenkins v. Ruttan* (1852) 8 U.C.Q.B. 625 8 U.C.Q.B. 625, CA (supply of services) and also *Smith v. Passmore* (1883) 4 L.R. (N.S.W.) 274; *SH Lock Discounts & Credits Pty Ltd v. Miles* [1963] V.R. 656; *Westhead v. Sproson* (1861) 6 H. & N. 728; 158 E.R. 301; *Mockett v. Ames* (1871) 23 L.T. 729; *Edwards v. Jevons* (1849) 8 C.B. 436; *Boom v. Batchelor* (1856) 1 H. & N. 255; *Grahame v. Grahame* (1887) 19 L.R. Ir. 249. Note that each advance made under a continuing guarantee is severable consideration. See *Offord v. Davies* (1862) 12 C.B.N.S. 748; *Coulthart v. Clementson* (1879) 5 Q.B.D. 42 at 46; *Lloyds v. Harper* (1880) 16 Ch D 270 at 314, 319–320; see also *Hartland v. Jukes* (1863) 1 H. & C. 667 (making of advances to the principal).

[14] *ibid.*

If the stipulated act does not take place the consideration for the guarantee will totally fail.[15]

Consideration must be sufficient and it has been held that a creditor's "promise to consider a request" to enter into the principal transaction is good consideration.[16]

Merely keeping a customer's overdrawn account open on the other hand does not amount to sufficient consideration.[17]

Consideration for guaranteeing existing debt

The consideration for a guarantee of an existing debt is com- **2–04** monly either a forbearance on the part of the creditor to press for the debt, or the allowance of a further credit[18] or advance. But it may also be a payment by or on behalf of the creditor to the guarantor,[19] or any other legal consideration moving from the creditor to the principal or the guarantor. A consideration moving merely from the principal to the surety will not suffice.[20]

In certain circumstances consideration provided by the creditor's agent may suffice. However, a guarantee given for purely past consideration is unenforceable although *Simmons v. Keating*[21] appears to be an exception to this rule. In that case the creditor had agreed to supply goods to the principal before the guarantee was made, but did not actually supply them until afterwards. The guarantee was held to be enforceable. The case can be explained, however, as an illustration of the rule in *Pao On v. Lau Yiu Lang*,[22] namely that an act done before the giving of a promise can be good consideration if it was done at the promisor's request, and the parties had understood that the act was to be renumerated either by payment or the conferment of a benefit and the payment or conferment of a benefit would have been enforceable had it been promised in advance.

---

[15] *Cornell v. Bradford* [1929] Q.W.N. 45; *Cooper v. Joel* (1859) 1 De G.F. & J. 240; 45 E.R. 350. See however *Chan v. Cresdon Pty Ltd* (1989) 168 C.L.R. 242 where the consideration was expressed to be "entering into this lease". The execution of an instrument equivalent to an equitable lease satisfied this description, even though other wording in the guarantee indicated that the guarantor would only be liable for obligations arising pursuant to a registered lease.

[16] *Coghlan v. SH Lock (Aust.) Ltd* (1987) 61 A.L.J.R. 289 at 292; affirmed (1987) 3 B.C.C. 183, PC disagreeing with McHugh J.C. in the New South Wales Court of Appeal (1985) 4 N.S.W.L.R. 158.

[17] *Royal Bank of Canada v. Salvatori* [1928] 3 W.W.R. 501.

[18] See *Nap Dummond Lee v. Nelco Ltd* (1981) 33 N.B.R. (2d) 661, CA.

[19] See, *e.g. Hartland v. Ukes* (1863) 1 H. & C. 667; *Grahame v. Grahame* (1887) 19 L.R. Ir. 249; *Edwards v. Jeavons* (1848) 8 C.B. 436; *Broom v. Batchelor* (1856) 1 H. & N. 255; *Mockett v. Ames* (1871) 23 L.T. 729.

[20] *White v. Cuyler* (1795) 6 Term. Rep. 1176; *Dutchman v. Tooth* (1839) 5 Bing. N.C. 577; *Fleming v. Bank of New Zealand* [1900] A.C. 577, PC; *French v. French* (1841) 2 M. & G. 644; *Astley Industrial Trust Ltd v. Grimston Electric Tools Ltd* (1965) 109 S.J. 149; *Power v. Ahern* [1935] Q.W.N. 22 (Aus).

[21] (1818) 2 Stark 426.

[22] [1980] A.C. 614, PC.

Guarantee in the form of a promissory note

2–05   It has been suggested by some commentators that where the guarantee is given in the form of a promissory note or bill of exchange that the creditor need not prove that fresh consideration for the note was given, because section 27 of the Bills of Exchange Act 1882 provides that an antecedent debt or liability is sufficient consideration for a promissory note or bill of exchange.[23] However, the Court of Appeal in *Oliver v. Davis*[24] held that there must be some relationship between the giving of the bill and the antecedent debt or liability.

Forbearance

2–06   Where the consideration for a guarantee is forbearance, it was a long debated question as to whether the time of forbearance should be defined, or whether any forbearance or forbearance for a reasonable time would be sufficient. The modern decisions in reversing the previous rule[25] seem now to have made it clear in the first place that it is not necessary that there should have been a binding contract by the creditor with the guarantor to forbear, inasmuch as if the promise of the guarantor is to pay if the creditor at his request will forbear, and the creditor does forbear and so accepts the offer, the guarantor is bound.[26] Upon the question how far the time of forbearance must be specified the cases fall into two classes. The first is where, though the time of forbearance is not directly specified, the promise of the guarantor names a time at or before which he will pay, and the creditor has forborne until that time.[27] In these cases it is settled that the promise is enforceable upon the ground that the transaction amounts at least to an offer by the guarantor that if the creditor forbears until that time he will pay then; and the forbearance is an acceptance of that offer. Here the question whether a reasonable time for the forbearance is to be implied does not arise, the construction of such a contract being that the forbearance is to be until the date when the surety is to pay.[28] The second class is where the time for payment is also undefined.[29]

---

[23] McGuinness, *The Law of Guarantee* (Carswell/Sweet & Maxwell, 1986), para. 4.77.
[24] [1949] 2 K.B. 727.
[25] See 3rd edition of this work for fuller historical discussion. The old rule was laid down in *Phillips v. Sackford* (1595) Cro. Eliz. 455.
[26] *Oldershaw v. King* (1853) 2 H. & N. 517; *Wynne v. Hughes* (1873) 21 W.R. 628; *Miles v. New Zealand Alford Estate Co.* (1886) 32 Ch D 266; *Crears v. Hunter* (1887) 19 Q.B.D. 341.
[27] *Payne v. Wilson* (1827) 7 B. & C. 423; *Rolt v. Cozens* (1856) 18 C.B. 673; *Wynne v. Hughes*, above. And see *Coe v. Duffield* (1822) 7 Moore 252. See also *Isbell Dean (Bean) Co. v. Avery* [1923] 1 D.L.R. 708, CA; *Willatts v. Kennedy* (1831) 8 Bing 5; 131 E.R. 301.
[28] *Rolt v. Cozens* (1856) 18 C.B. 673. Cf. *Harris v. Venables* (1872) L.R. 7 Exch. 235.
[29] *Semple v. Pink* (1847) 1 Exch. 74; *Oldershaw v. King* (1853) 2 H. & N. 517; *Miles v. New Zealand Alford Estates Co.* (1886) 32 Ch D 266; *Crears v. Hunter* (1887) 19 Q.B.D. 341. For a modern illustration of undertaking to forbear see *Board v. Hoey* 65 T.L.R. 43, applying *Rolt v. Cozens*. Similarly continuing with an overdraft facility is good consideration: *Catley Farms Ltd v. ANZ Banking Group (NZ) Ltd* [1982] 1 N.Z.L.R. 430 at 439.

Notwithstanding a decision to the contrary never formerly over-ruled,[30] it is submitted that in this case also the promise is enforceable, if the creditor has forborne for such a time as judging from the circumstances and presumable intentions of the parties at the date of the promise a court may find to have been a reasonable time.[31] There need not be any obligation to forbear nor any express request.[32] In *Payne v. Wilson*[33] the declaration alleged that in consideration that the plaintiff would consent to stay proceedings upon a cognovit,[34] the defendant promised to pay "on the first April then next", and there was an averment that the plaintiff "did suspend all further proceedings." This was held good after verdict upon the ground that it must be taken that proceedings had been suspended either for a time required by law or for a definite or reasonable time. Following some uncertainty[35] it was finally decided that the mere fact of forbearance *per se* will not constitute consideration for a surety becoming liable for payment of the debt by the debtor: there must be in addition either an undertaking to forbear or an actual forbearance at the surety's express or implied request.[36]

The creditor must forbear from the assertion of an actual right. If there is nobody he can sue for payment of the debt, a promise to forbear from suing is no consideration.[37]

Forbearance by agreeing to accept a composition

The measure of forbearance contemplated by the guarantee, whatever it is, must of course be accorded. In *Latter v. White*,[38] creditors of a debtor agreed to accept a composition secured by a

2-07

---

[30] *Semple v. Pink* (1847) 1 Exch. 74, above.

[31] See *Mapes v. Sidney* (1624) Cr. Jac. 683; 79 E.R. 592; *Emmott v. Kearns* (1839) 5 Bing. (N.C.) 559; 132 E.R. 1214; *Johnson v. Whitchcott* (1639) 1 All Ebr. 24 at 33; *Beven v. Cowling* (1626) Poph. 183; 79 E.R. 1277; *Barber v. Mackrell* (1892) 41 W.R. 618; 41 W.R. 341; *Nikaldi Sportswear Inc. v. Mear* (1977) 5 B.C.L.R. 79 (Can.).

[32] *Crears v. Hunter*, above; see also *Alliance Bank v. Broom* (1864) 2 Dr. and Sm. 289; *Fullerton v. Prov. Bank of Ireland* [1903] A.C. 309 at 313, 315. See also *Glegg v. Bromley* [1912] 3 K.B. 474 per Parker J. at 491; *Provincial Bank of Ireland v. Donnell* [1934] N.I. 33; *Murphy v. Timms* [1987] 2 Qd.R. 550; *Colonial Bank of A/asia v. Kerr* (1889) 15 V.L.R. 314; *Harris v. Venables* (1872) L.R. 7 Exch. 235; *Payne v. Wilson* (1827) 7 B. & C. 423; 108 E.R. 781; *Paulger v. Butland Industries Ltd* [1989] 3 N.Z.L.R. 549; *Re Pacific Projects Ltd* [1990] 2 Qd.R. 541. *Cf. Commodity Broking Company Ltd v. Meehan* [1985] I.R. 12 where there was no request express or implied to forbear.

[33] (1827) 7 B. & C. 423.

[34] A formal written admission. Repealed by the Administration of Justice Act 1956. Mrs Bardell gave Dodson and Fogg a cognovit in respect of their costs in the action of *Bardell v. Pickwick* and ended up being taken in execution for those costs to Fleet Prison.

[35] For a detailed study of the older cases see the 3rd edition of this work, pp. 15–17.

[36] It would now appear that an agreement to forbear for an indefinite period will provide consideration, at least where a reasonable time can be inferred or where the surety has benefited from the forbearance. In *Barber v. Mackrell* (1892) 40 W.R. 618; 41 W.R. 341, the renewal of bills was held sufficient consideration, though the period for which the bills were to run had not been specified.

[37] *Jones v. Ashburnham* (1804) 4 East 455; *White v. Bluett* (1853) 23 L.J. Ex. 36; *Papworth v. Johnson* (1614) 2 Bulst 91; 80 E.R. 984. See also *Pyers v. Turner* (1592) Cro. Eliz. 283; 78 E.R. 537 where the giving of time did not support the guarantee where the principal was not indebted to the creditor. *Cf. Dunton v. Dunton* (1892) 18 V.L.R. 114; *Ward v. Byham* [1956] 1 W.L.R. 496, CA.

[38] (1870) L.R. 8 QB 622; (1871) L.R. 6 QB 474; 5 HL 572.

surety to whom the estate was to be made over. One of the creditors afterwards refused to execute the deed, alleging that he was not bound by it, and upon that issue recovered judgment for his debt against the principal. It was held in the Exchequer Chamber, reversing the decision of the Queen's Bench, that the surety was released, on the ground of failure of the consideration, from the demand of that creditor, even though the judgment was useless to the creditor by reason of the subsequent bankruptcy of the debtor, and even though the surety had under the deed received all the property of the debtor. Where, in consideration that the creditor would take effectively a composition of 50 per cent on a certain debt, a surety guaranteed the payment of that amount, it was held that the consideration was not performed by the creditor agreeing to take such a composition in instalments, with a proviso that on default of paying any instalment or the commission of an act of bankruptcy the whole original debt should become due.[39] But a guarantee for a composition is held to contemplate that the creditor, if the composition as guaranteed is not paid, shall be remitted to his former rights, and in such case the surety is not released from his liability to pay the composition.[40] Where a composition deed contained a clause to the effect that it should be void if the debtor were adjudicated bankrupt, this was construed as against the sureties for the composition to mean voidable at the election of the creditors.[41] In *Ex p. Powell*,[42] a creditor, with the assent of a surety by whom the debt was guaranteed, agreed to accept in satisfaction a reduced amount payable by instalments, for which notes were given, the surety becoming liable for the instalments; default being made in one of the instalments, it was held that the surety remained liable (upon the construction of that particular arrangement) only for the composition, and that the original guarantee did not revive. Under the former section 126 of the Bankruptcy Act 1869, it was held that a surety for a composition was not released by the debtor being made bankrupt at the suit of the creditors outside the composition, as the composition was not thereby put an end to; although upon default in payment of the composition the compounding creditors might prove in the bankruptcy for the whole of their original debts.[43] Under section 16(16) of the Bankruptcy Act 1914 re-enacting section 18(11) of the Bankruptcy Act 1883, if default was made in payment of any instalment due in pursuance of a composition or scheme under the Act, the court could annul the scheme and adjudge the debtor bankrupt: this effected the total discharge of the

---

[39] *Clarke v. Green* (1849) 3 Exch. 619.
[40] *Glegg v. Gilbey* (1876) 2 Q.B.D. 6, 209; *Ex p. Gilbey* (1878) 8 Ch D 248.
[41] *Hughes v. Palmer* (1865) 19 C.B. (N.S.) 393.
[42] (1836) 2 M. & A. 533.
[43] *Glegg v. Gilbey* (1876) 2 Q.B.D. 6; *Ex p. Gilbey* (1878) 8 Ch D 248.

surety from any liability in respect of the scheme.[44] A surety for a composition to which a number of creditors are parties would not, it seems, be released if one creditor proceeded against the debtor contrary to the agreement. But in such a case he would probably be entitled to have the action stayed, at any rate if upon paying the composition he was to have the right to recover the debts for himself.[45] Similarly a surety for a composition has a right to have given up securities taken by one creditor for a preferential payment by the debtor.[46] Where there was no composition, but the creditors agreed to take payment by instalments, and one creditor carried in his debt at half its real value and took a security for the rest, a surety for the instalments obtained a decree for cancelling the security so taken.[47]

Total forbearance

If the consideration is the total forbearance by the creditor, he can **2–08** recover from the guarantor upon showing that he has forborne to the date of the writ; for he is not bound, it is said, to wait all his life.[48] Whether in such a case, he could be required to wait a reasonable time before suing the guarantor will turn upon the terms of the particular bargain.[49] There would seem to be nothing to prevent a man undertaking to pay immediately himself in con-sideration of the creditor forbearing for good to sue the debtor. So forbearance until after a certain day will support a promise to pay on or before that day.[50]

Withdrawal of a legal process

When the consideration is a definite act, such as the withdrawal **2–09** of a legal process, this will be sufficient of itself, even though a new process may be launched immediately.[51] In such a case the guaran-tee may be enforced even though such new process is launched, at any rate if such new process has not the effect of disabling the

---

[44] *Walton v. Cook* (1888) 40 Ch D 325. For a general discussion see Williams and Muir Hunter, *Law of Bankruptcy* (19th ed., 1979), pp. 95, 837. In *Cole v. Lynn* [1942] 1 K.B. 142 there was a deed of arrangement whereby creditors covenanted not to sue the debtor without prejudice to their remedies against the surety who was held entitled to an indemnity against the debtor in respect of payment made.
[45] See *Anstey v. Marden* (1804) 1 B. & P.N.R. 124.
[46] *Middleton v. Lord Onslow* (1721) 1 P.W. 768; *cf. Walton v. Cook*, above. See also *Re Stock* (1896) 3 Mans. 324.
[47] *Cecil v. Plaistow* (1793) 2 Anstr. 202.
[48] *Mapes v. Sidney* (1624) Cr. Jac. 683. See also *Therne v. Fuller*, *ibid.* 306; *Edwards v. Roberts* (1675) 2 Mod. 24.
[49] *Mapes v. Sidney*, above; *Clarke v. Green* (1849) 3 Exch. 619.
[50] *Waters v. Glassop* (1704) 1 Ld. Raym. 357.
[51] *Harris v. Venables* (1872) L.R. 7 Ex. 325 questioning *Ross v. Moss* (1597) Cr. Eliz. 560, *contra*. In *Harris v. Venables*, it was held that the withdrawal of a winding up petition constituted sufficient consideration to support a promise to pay costs of and relating to the petition. *Cf. Clarke and Walker v. Thew* (1967) 116 C.L.R. 465 (service of notice under Australian equivalent of s.123(1)(a) of the Insolvency Act 1986 held not to be consideration where there was an undertaking not to "take proceedings").

principal debtor. And though the promise of the guarantor is only to pay at some future date, it will not be implied that the creditor was to wait until that date. Such a term is, however, implied where the consideration is not a definite act, but forbearance merely.[52] As to what constitutes a withdrawal of a legal process, it is sufficient if leave is obtained not to proceed with it,[53] or even if notice is given to the person against whom it is issued that he need not attend, and it will not be proceeded with.[54]

If the withdrawn claim was "a serious claim honestly made" it does not matter whether it would have succeeded or not.[55]

Surrender of invalid guarantee

2–10 In *Haigh v. Brooks*[56] the opinion was expressed by the Exchequer Chamber that the delivery up of a guarantee which does not comply with the Statute of Frauds, of the mere paper in fact, may be a good consideration for a new guarantee; but the decision itself was that the surrendered guarantee did comply with the Statute.

Further credit

2–11 Further advances or credit, or supply of goods or services on the part of the creditor, if and when granted, will support a guarantee covering not only the further advances, etc., but also the liability existing at the date of the guarantee, even though there might be no obligation to grant any such further advances.[57] But unless there is, or is to be,[58] a binding agreement to supply certain further goods or make certain further advances, a guarantee for the existing liability will not attach unless the further supply or advance is granted within the meaning of the parties—that is to say, if no amount is named,[59] a real and bona fide further supply or advance.[60] And the

---

[52] *Rolt v. Cozens* (1856) 18 C.B. 673.
[53] *Harris v. Venables* (1872) L.R. 7 Ex. 235.
[54] *Alhusen v. Prest* (1851) 6 Exch. 720.
[55] See *Miles v. New Zealand Alford Estate Co* (1886) 32 Ch D 266; *Callisher v. Bischoffschein* (1870) L.R. 5 QB 449.
[56] (1839) 10 A. & E. 309.
[57] *Russell v. Moseley* (1822) 3 B. & B. 211; *Kennaway v. Treleavan* (1839) 5 M.W. 498; *Mayhew v. Crickett* (1818) 2 Swanst. 185; *Johnston v. Nicholls* (1845) 1 C.B. 251; *White v. Woodward* (1848) 5 C.B. 810; *Oldershaw v. King* (1857) 2 H. & N. 399, 517; *Harris v. Venables* (1872) L.R. 7 Ex. 235. For the difficulties arising in such cases prior to the 1856 Act, see the 3rd edition of the work at p. 21, footnote (c). Forbearance or the granting of extended time for payment at the request of the surety may be implied from the taking of security: *Glegg v. Bromley* [1912] 3 K.B. 491. See also *Leask v. Scott Bros.* (1877) 2 Q.B.D. 376. This will usually be avoided by such phrases as "opening or continuing an account" or "continuing advance". Note also *Provincial Bank of Ireland v. Donnell* [1934] N.I. 33. Similar principles apply in the case of equitable mortgages of debts to secure existing loans. See, *e.g. Gorringe v. Irwell India* (1886) 34 Ch D 128. For a case where the creditor knew of surety's belief that future advances would be made, but no advances were made, see *Bank of Montreal v. Sperling Hotel Co. Ltd* (1973) 36 D.L.R. (3d) 130.
[58] See *King v. Cole* (1848) 2 Exch. 628; *Bell v. Welch* (1850) 9 C.B. 154.
[59] See *White v. Woodward* (1848) 5 C.B. 810 at 818; *Broom v. Batchelor* (1856) 1 H. & N. 255 at 264; *Morrell v. Cowan* (1877) 6 Ch D 166 at 170; 7 Ch D 151.
[60] *Westhead v. Sproson* (1861) 6 H. & N. 728; *Morrell v. Cowan*, above; *Provincial Bank of Ireland v. Donnell* [1934] N.I. 33.

mere use of a phrase such as "in consideration of your agreeing to supply," etc., when the amount to be supplied is not specified, but is left to the discretion of the creditor, does not imply either that the creditor has contemporaneously undertaken any liability to supply or that he is to undertake such liability. Such a guarantee will therefore only attach if and when a further supply is granted, as if it had run "in consideration of your supplying," etc.[61] If a guarantee is in consideration of an advance or supply "to the extent" of a sum named, it is a question of construction whether the guarantee is not to attach until that amount has been supplied or advanced, or whether that amount is merely the maximum for which the surety will be liable.[62]

Guarantees in consideration of present agreement

It may be, however, that the meaning is that the guarantee is to attach when some definite binding agreement for the advance or the like is made by the creditor; as where it ran "in consideration of your having by indenture agreed."[63] Similarly where, in consideration of the creditor "agreeing" to take a composition from his debtor, a surety undertook to guarantee the composition.[64] In such cases the specified agreement must be made; but the guarantee attaches without waiting for it to be performed.[65] Where an agreement recited the delivery of certain securities and proceeded "in consideration of the money so secured to be paid to us aforesaid, we hereby indemnify you" against certain other liabilities, it was held that the deposit of the securities was the consideration, and not the payment of the money secured.[66]   **2–12**

When consideration may be proved by parol evidence

Consideration should not be a matter of conjecture.[67] The court will examine the guarantee itself in the light of the surrounding circumstances, for example, the state of the accounts between the parties. In line with contractual principles the court will attempt to give business sense and efficacy to the agreement and parol evidence is admissible to explain and interpret the consideration, where it is ambiguously expressed.   **2–13**

[61] *Westhead v. Sproson*, above; *Morrell v. Cowan*, above. But see *White v. Woodward* (1848) 5 C.B. 810 where however the goods had been supplied; see *per* Martin B. in *Broom v. Batchelor* (1856) 1 H. & N. 255 at 265. *Cf.* also *Payne v. Wilson* (1827) 7 B. & C. 423; *Thornton v. Jenyns* (1840) I M. & Gr. 166; *Dally v. Poolly* (1844) 6 QB 494. As to promissory notes given for existing debts and further advances, see *Mayhew v. Crickett* (1818) 2 Swanst. 185; *Re Boys, ex p. Hop Planters Co.* (1870) L.R. 10 Eq. 467. See also *Greenham Ready Mixed Concrete v. CAS (Industrial Developments) Ltd* (1965) 109 S.J. 209.
[62] *Dimmock v. Sturla* (1845) 14 M. & W. 758. *Cf. Hill v. Nuttall* (1864) 17 C.B. (N.S.) 262.
[63] *King v. Cole* (1848) 2 Exch. 628.
[64] *Clarke v. Green* (1849) 3 Exch. 619.
[65] If afterwards repudiated, the surety will be released, see above.
[66] *Ikin v. Brook* (1830) 1 B. & Ad. 124.
[67] See *Raikes v. Todd* (1838) 8 Ad. & E. 846; 112 E.R. 1058.

In guarantees given before the Mercantile Law Amendment Act 1856,[68] the consideration had to appear in or by necessary implication from the note or memorandum required by section 4 of the Statute of Frauds, which otherwise was not sufficient.[69] The Act of 1856 removed this necessity and made it possible to have an enforceable guarantee in which there was no statement of the consideration in any note or memorandum in writing.[70] Where, however, the contract itself is reduced to writing, and a consideration stated, the admission of parol evidence is governed by the ordinary law as to the construction of documents; and the 1856 Act has no bearing. Where therefore a consideration is stated in the contract which is in law no consideration, and the terms of the contract do not show that there was in fact some other good consideration,[71] or where the contract states or shows that there was no consideration, oral evidence cannot be admitted to prove, in contradiction of the contract, that in fact there was a good consideration. Anything referred to in a contract may be identified by parol evidence within the limits of the description in the contract, though not so as to contradict that description. The evidence, however, must not be that of conversations tending to show what the intention of the parties was apart from the words used in the contract,[72] but must be directed to show what state of circumstances the parties either knew then to exist or contemplated as about to come into existence, so as to establish in what sense the words were used by showing what the situation of the parties was at the time.[73]

Words capable of denoting either a past or a future consideration

2–14   In accordance with these principles, where words are used which may denote either a past or a future consideration, parol evidence of the circumstances may be admitted in order to show that a future consideration must have been referred to.[74] Therefore in *Butcher v. Steuart*,[75] where the phrase was "in consideration of your having

---

[68] 19 & 20 Vict. c.97, s.3. See Appendix 2.
[69] *Wain v. Warlters* (1804) 5 East 10; *Saunders v. Wakefield* (1821) 4 B. & Ald. 595.
[70] *Vetro Glass Pty Ltd v. Fitzpatrick* [1963] S.R. (N.S.W.) 697; *Elanco Pty Ltd v. Wyman* (unreported), Qld Sup. Ct, Connolly J., No. 1985 of 1978. This is even so in those jurisdictions where contracts which cannot be performed within one year must be in writing: *Barron v. Geddes* (1897) 19 A.L.T. 27; 3 A.L.R. 159. But where one guarantee is substituted for another the consideration supporting the original may be relied upon to support its substitute: *Northern Crown Bank v. Elford* (1916) 34 D.L.R. 280.
[71] See, *e.g. Oldershaw v. King* (1857) 2 H. & N. 517.
[72] See *Laurie v. Scholefield* (1869) L.R. 4 C.P. 622 at 626. But note general inadmissibility of extrinsic evidence of parties' intentions and negotiations. See *Prenn v. Simmonds* [1971] 1 W.L.R. 1381 at 1385, 1390 and *Moschi v. Lep Air Services Ltd* [1973] A.C. 331 at 354.
[73] See Lord Campbell C.J. in *Bainbridge v. Wade* (1850) 16 QB 89 at 98. And see *Macdonald v. Longbottom* (1860) I.E. & E. 977 at 983; *Heffield v. Meadows* (1869) L.R. 4 C.P. 595 at 600; *Grahame v. Grahame* (1887) 19 L.R. Ir. 249.
[74] See *Hamilton v. Watson* (1845) 12 Cl. & Fin. 109; 8 E.R. 1339; *Haigh v. Brooks* (1839) 10 Ad. & El. 309; 113 E.R. 119.
[75] (1843) 11 M. & W. 857.

released," etc., and in *Goldshede v. Swan*,[76] where it was "in consideration of your having advanced," etc., it being proved that the only release and advance respectively were not before but in pursuance of the guarantees, the plaintiffs recovered.[77]

The same rule was followed in *Steele v. Hoe*.[78] There the promise was "in consideration of your having resigned the office of Deacon," etc. "The expression," said Patteson, J., delivering the judgment of the court,[79] "that a promise is founded upon a consideration conveys the notion that the consideration precedes the promise in the mind of the party making the promise; he promises because the consideration exists, and this form of expression is shown by the authorities to have been frequently used when the consideration and the promise are concurrent. Each side of a contract is consideration or promise according to the party speaking, and, if each party were to put into writing his own promise, each side of the contract would in turn appear to have preceded the other, though both have formed one agreement: the plaintiff might write 'you having guaranteed, I resign'; the defendant 'you having resigned, I guarantee'."[80]

If it is evident that the guarantee was intended to be limited to past transactions alone, for example, because the surety knew that the principal debtor was already indebted to the creditor in an amount exceeding the limit of the surety's guarantee, the guarantee will be void as being given without consideration.[81]

On the other hand, a guarantee to a bank in consideration of the bank's agreeing to advance £750 to the principal debtor was held to be good although in fact the debtor already owed the bank more than £750 and the new advance was merely used to pay off the existing debt without any money actually passing.[82]

Construction ut res magis valeat quam pereat

In some of the older cases it did not appear that there was any **2–15** past advance, supply, or other dealing which could answer the description of the consideration. But even if there is an existing liability to which the description could apply, it seems established that, at any rate where the circumstances show that a future liability was also in contemplation, reference may be taken to be to the latter, an illustration of the operation of the maxim *ut res magis*

---

[76] (1847) 1 Exch. 154. And see *King v. Cole* (1848) 2 Exch. 628.
[77] See also *Haigh v. Brooks* (1839) 10 Ad. & El. 309.
[78] (1849) 14 QB 431.
[79] *ibid* at 445.
[80] See for further examples, *Bainbridge v. Wade*, above; *Hoard v. Grace* (1861) 7 H. & N. 494. And see also *Bastow v. Bennett* (1812) 3 Camp. 220.
[81] *Bell v. Welch* (1850) 9 C.B. 154.
[82] *Hamilton v. Watson* (1845) 12 Cl. & F. 109; *cf. Glyn v. Hertel* (1818) 8 Taunt 208, and as to the making of an "advance" *Burnes v. Trade Credits Ltd* [1981] 1 W.L.R. 805.

valeat quam pereat.[83] Where the consideration for a guarantee is
expressed to be that the person to whom it is given "has agreed" or
"has consented" to do something, the meaning has usually been
taken to be that the future act, and not any past or contemporaneous
binding agreement, is the consideration.[84]

Where the principal transaction is executed simultaneously with
the guarantee this will be sufficient consideration and it has been
held that where two transactions are executed at the same meeting
it does not matter which instrument was signed first: the court will
treat them as if they were signed concurrently.[85]

Consideration executed on the faith of a guarantee to be given

2–16   Where the only circumstance to which the words expressing the
consideration can refer was past at the date of the guarantee, it
would still be open to the plaintiff to prove that the guarantee was
agreed to be given before the consideration was executed, and was
only reduced into writing afterwards.[86]

Where advances were made to one of the makers of a promissory
note upon the representation that the defendant would also sign it,
and afterwards the defendant did sign it, he was held liable as
having adopted the promise.[87]

Illusory consideration

2–17   The guarantee will not be binding if the consideration expressed
in the instrument is illusory or a sham.[88]

---

[83] See *Steele v. Hoe* (1849) 14 QB 431; *Broom v. Batchelor* (1856) 1 H. & N. 255; *Hoad v. Grace*, above; *Wood v. Priestner* (1866) L.R. 2 Ex. 66, 282. Bramwell B. protested in the three last-named cases against the application of this principle where the language was in its primary sense past and there existed facts to which it could refer. Illustrations of the principle can be found in *Allnutt v. Ashenden* (1843) 5 M. & Gr. 392; *Edwards v. Jevons* (1849) 8 C.B. 436; *Colbourn v. Dawson* (1851) 10 C.B. 765; *Broom v. Batchelor* (1856) 1 H. & N. 255; *Grahame v. Grahame* (1887) 19 L.R. Ir. 249; *Wood v. Priestner* (1866) L.R. 2 Ex. 66, 282; *Mocket v. Ames* (1871) 23 L.T. 729. See also *Chalmers v. Victors* (1868) 18 L.T. 481. *Cf. Brunning v. Oldham Bros.* (1896) 75 L.T. 602. See also *King v. Cole* (1848) 2 Exch. 628; 154 E.R. 642; *Tanner v. Moore* (1846) 9 QB 1; 115 E.R. 1176; *Johnston v. Nicholls* (1845) 1 C.B. 251; 135 E.R. 535.

[84] *Payne v. Wilson* (1827) 7 B. & C. 423; *Thornton v. Jenyns* (1840) 1 M. & Gr. 166; *Dally v. Poolly* (1844) 6 QB 494; *Tanner v. Moore* (1846) 9 QB 1; *Westhead v. Sproson* (1861) 6 H. & N. 728; *Morrell v. Cowan* (1877) 6 Ch D 166; 7 Ch D 151. But see *White v. Woodward* (1848) 5 C.B. 810, explained by Martin B. in *Broom v. Batchelor* (1856) 1 H. & N. 255 at 264. In cases where the statement of consideration in the guarantee may itself give the appearance of being past consideration note that McHugh J.A. in *Breusch v. Watts Development Division Pty Ltd* (1987) 10 N.S.W.L.R. 311 at 317 specifically left open the question whether the court could look beyond the document to ascertain whether good consideration in fact existed.

[85] *M'Ewan v. Newman* (1874) 5 A.J.R. 167.

[86] *Mumford v. Gething* (1859) 7 C.B. (N.S.) 305. See also *Dodge v. Pringle* (1860) 29 L.J. Ex. 115. This argument was raised in *Power v. Ahern* [1935] Q.W.N. 222 but rejected because there was no evidence that the defendant had the necessary *animus contrahendi* at the time he gave his promise.

[87] *Dodge v. Pringle* (1860) 29 L.J. Ex. 115.

[88] See *Reid Murray Holdings Ltd (in liq.) v. David Murray Holdings Pty Ltd* (1972) 5 S.A.S.R. 386; *Hodson v. Lee* (1847) 9 L.T.O.S. 312 at 313; *White v. Woodward* (1848) 5 C.B. 810; 136 E.R. 1097.

Illegal consideration

A guarantee cannot be supported by an illegal consideration. It **2–18** may also constitute a voidable preference where one creditor is preferred, by dint of the transaction, to the general body of creditors at the stance of an insolvent individual or company.[89]

It may be good consideration to refrain from enforcing an irregular court order which has resulted in the unlawful detention of a party in custody, particularly if no objection has been taken to the order at the time when the guarantee is given.

Where a guarantee has been given in order to stifle a criminal prosecution it will not be enforced, whether or not the promise to refrain from prosecution is made expressly or implicitly. Similarly a guarantee to assist one of the parties to break the law is void.[90]

A forged alteration to a document does not render an instrument void unless it goes to the whole or the essence of the instrument.[91]

---

[89] *Coles v. Strick* (1850) 15 QB 2; *Wood v. Barker* (1865) L.R. 1 Eq. 139; for an example of where the guaranteed debt itself was illegal and thus irrecoverable even from the surety, see *Lougher v. Molyneux* [1916] 1 K.B. 718. For a discussion of *ultra vires* loans and loans to minors see Chaps 4 and 6. *Cf. Re O'Shea, ex p. Lancaster* [1911] 2 K.B. 981 (guarantee of overdraft by principal debtor used to pay back debts held enforceable). A guarantee for an illegal consideration cannot be enforced and may be ordered to be delivered up and cancelled. *Jackman v. Mitchell* (1807) 13 Ves. 581. See also *Coleman v. Waller* (1829) 31 Y. & J. 212; *McKewan v. Sanderson* (1875) L.R. 20 Eq. 65. See also *Nerot v. Wallace* (1789) 3 Term Rep. 17; *Herman v. Jeuchner* (1885) 15 Q.B.D. 561; *Cannon v. Rands* (1870) 23 L.T. 817; *Jones v. Merionethshire Permanent Benefit Building Society* [1891] 2 Ch. 587; affirmed [1892] 1 Ch. 173, CA; *cf. Coutts & Co. v. Browne-Lecky* [1947] K.B. 104 at 109; [1946] 2 All E.R. 207 at 209; *Heald v. O'Connor* [1971] 2 All E.R. 1105; [1971] 1 W.L.R. 497.

[90] See *Jones v. Merionethshire Permanent Benefit Building Society* [1891] 2 Ch. 587, affirmed [1892] 1 Ch. 173; *Cannon v. Rands* (1870) 23 L.T. 817; *Sear v. Cohen* (1881) 45 L.T. 589; *Ritchie v. Smith* (1848) 6 C.B. 462; 136 E.R. 1329.

[91] *Lombard Finance v. Brookplain Trading* [1991] 1 W.L.R. 271, CA.

CHAPTER 3

STATUTE OF FRAUDS

1. *To What Contracts it Applies*

3–01 By Section 4 of the Statute of Frauds 1677[1]

> "No action shall be brought whereby to charge the defendant
> upon any special promise to answer for the debt, default, or
> miscarriage of another person . . . unless the agreement upon
> which such action shall be brought, or some memorandum or
> note thereof, shall be in writing and signed by the party to be
> charged therewith or some other person thereunto by him
> lawfully authorised."

This enactment does not, except by requiring a writing as evidence of the promises to which it applies, in any way affect the common rules governing the validity of such promises. It does not dispense with the necessity for a consideration to support a promise not under seal, or make valid any contract not valid at common law.[2] Its only effect is to make unenforceable contracts, coming within its terms, which would have been valid at common law. If the contract is within its terms, it does not matter what the consideration was.[3] Further, the doctrine of part performance is not applicable to contracts of guarantee.[4] A guarantee, though given abroad, cannot be sued upon in England unless it fulfils the requirements of the Statute.[5]

The Statute only says that no action shall be brought whereby to charge, etc. Therefore, if a solicitor in an action gave an undertaking to pay the claim, the old Common Law Courts enforced it against him summarily notwithstanding the Statute.[6] And each division of the High Court would no doubt do the same by virtue of its summary jurisdiction over its officers. Similarly money paid

---

[1] For fuller treatment of the Statute of Frauds see Williams, *Section 4 of the Statute of Frauds* (Cambridge, 1932) and generally *Chitty on Contracts* (27th ed.), Vol. I, para. 4–004 and Vol. II, para. 42–024. For questions relating to effect of the Statute of Frauds on the question of bills of exchange, see Chap. 13.

[2] *Barrell v. Trussell* (1811) 4 Taunt. 117; *Rann v. Hughes* (1778) 7 Term.Rep. 350, note.

[3] See the notes to *Forth v. Stanton* (1669) 1 Williams' Saund. 211 e(1); *Fitzgerald v. Dressler* (1859) 7 C.B. (N.S.) 374 at 392; *Sutton v. Grey* [1894] 1 QB 285 at 288. For an illustration of how a contract within the Statute can only be raised as a defence when recovery is sought of money or property passing under that contract, see *Brady v. Lewis* [1951] 3 D.L.R. 845.

[4] *Maddison v. Alderson* (1883) 8 App.Cas. 467 at 490.

[5] *Leroux v. Brown* (1852) 12 C.B. 801. For questions of conflict of laws see Chap. 19.

[6] *Evans v. Duncombe* (1831) 1 C. & J. 372; *Re Greaves, ibid.* 374, note; *Re A Solicitor* (1990) 45 S.J. 104.

under a promise unenforceable by reason of the Statute cannot be recovered back.[7]

It has been held in a number of cases that the Statute will be an **3–02** answer to any action which has the effect of charging the defendant upon a promise which by the Statute is unenforceable, even though the action is not on the promise.[8] None of such cases, however, affect the only clause of the Statute material to the subject of this work; nor is it easy to see how a defendant could be charged on a promise to answer for the debt of another, unless directly by an action on the promise. The cases referred to are therefore not discussed here.

Since before the Mercantile Law Amendment Act 1856,[9] it was necessary that the consideration for the promise should appear by the writing,[10] many of the older cases, in which now the writing should be sufficient, had to be discussed on the footing that there was no sufficient writing, and that the plaintiff could only succeed by showing that the Statute did not apply. In appreciating these cases, this change in the law must be borne in mind.

The Statute has no application to a liability under a bill of exchange, as opposed to liability under the underlying contract.[11]

It seems that a plaintiff can make use of the Statute to prevent a set-off against his claim by a defendant relying on an oral guarantee.[12]

Forms of liability, in the nature of suretyship, without express guarantee

The effect of the clause now under consideration upon the law of **3–03** principal and surety is, speaking generally, to require that every guarantee shall be evidenced by a writing fulfilling the conditions prescribed by the Statute. It must be remembered, however, that liabilities can exist to which some, at any rate, of the incidents of suretyship attach, which nevertheless do not come within this clause; as, for instance, the liability of a retired partner[13] or of a *del credere* agent.[14]

Where a sum of money is due from one person to another upon a judgment no writing under the Statute is necessary to show that it was agreed that it should stand as security for the debt of another,

---

[7] *Sweet v. Lee* (1841) 3 Mr. & Gr. 452. And see *Shaw v. Woodcock* (1827) 7 B. & C. 73. For the case of executors or administrators retaining debts in respect of oral guarantees and the commission thereby of a devastavit, see *Re Rownson* (1885) 29 Ch D 358; *Re Midgley* [1893] 3 Ch. 222.
[8] *Carrington v. Roots* (1837) 2 M. & W. 248; *Sykes v. Dixon* (1839) 9 A. & E. 693; *Felthouse v. Bindley* (1862) 11 C.B. (N.S.) 869.
[9] 19 & 20 Vict. c.97, s.3. See Appendix 2.
[10] *Wain v. Warlters* (1804) 5 East. 10; *Saunders v. Wakefield* (1821) 4 B. 7 Ald. 595.
[11] *Montage v. Irvani* [1990] 1 W.L.R. 667, CA. See also Chap. 13.
[12] *Coady v. J. Lewis & Sons Ltd* [1951] 3 D.L.R. 845.
[13] See *Rouse v. Bradford Banking Co.* [1894] A.C. 586.
[14] See generally Bowstead & Reynolds, *Agency* (16th. ed., 1996), para. 1–036.

notwithstanding that facts have occurred which without such agreement would have put an end to the liability upon it.[15]

Former restriction of Statute to promises to pay existing debts, etc.

3–04   It was said at one time to have been laid down that the Statute did not apply to promises to answer future debts of another,[16] but this distinction is now clearly not law.[17] The rule has long been settled that the question is whether the promise is original or collateral, it being within the Statute only if it is collateral. It cannot, however, be collateral unless another is, or is to be, also liable.[18]

Promise must be collateral

3–05   When the promise is to be answerable for demands which may thereafter accrue to the promisee by reason of dealings with another, the question is whether the promisor intervenes to procure credit for the third person who is himself also to be liable to the promisee, or whether his own credit only is pledged to secure the consideration of the third person, to whom credit is not given.[19] In *Birkmyr v. Darnell*,[20] according to some reporters,[21] the phrases "I will be your paymaster," "I will see you paid," are instanced as creating an original and not a collateral undertaking. But whatever the form of words used, it is a question of fact to be ascertained from the transaction as a whole[22] and all its circumstances, as to whom credit was given.[23] And the words, "I will see you paid," have been held, under the circumstances of individual cases, to effect a collateral liability only.[24]

---

[15] *Macrory v. Scott* (1880) 5 Exch. 907.
[16] See *Mowbray v. Cunningham* cited (1774) 2 Term.Rep. 81; 1 Cowper 228; *Peckham v. Faria* (1781) 3 Doug. K.B. 13.
[17] *Peckham v. Faria*, above; *Matson v. Wharam* (1787) 2 Term.Rep. 80; *Anderson v. Hayman* (1789) 1 H.B. 120.
[18] *Birkmyr v. Darnell* (1704) 2 Lord Raym. 1085; 6 Mod. 248; 1 Salk. 27; 1 Sm. L.C. (12th ed.) 335; *Read v. Nash* (1751) 1 Wils. 305; *Hargreaves v. Parsons* (1844) 13 M. & W. 561. And see the notes to *Forth v. Stanton* (1669) 1 Williams' Saund. 211 e(1).
[19] *Watkins v. Perkins* (1697) 1 Lord Raym. 224; *Birkmyr v. Darnell*, above.
[20] Above.
[21] Note in 2 Lord Raym. 1085.
[22] *Simpson v. Penton* (1834) 2 C. & M. 430.
[23] *Keate v. Temple* (1797) 1 B. & P. 158; *Croft v. Smallwood* (1793) 1 Esp. 121; *Simpson v. Penton*, above; *Beard v. Hardy* (1901) 17 T.L.R. 633. In *Tomlinson v. Gill* (1756) Ambl. 330, Lord Hardwicke called the distinction in *Birkmyr v. Darnell* "a slight and cobweb distinction." See also *Guild v. Conrad* [1894] 2 QB 885 at 895 *per* Lopes L.J.
[24] *Matson v. Wharam* (1787) 2 Term.Rep. 80; *Anderson v. Hayman* (1789) 1 H.B1. 121; *Barber v. Fox* (1816) 1 Stark 270; *Keate v. Temple*, above; *Bateman v. Phillips* (1812) 15 East. 272; *Thompson v. Bond* (1807) 1 Camp. 4; *Rains v. Storry* (1827) 3 C. & P. 130; *Walker v. Taylor* (1834) 6 C. & P. 752; *Clancy v. Piggott* (1835) 2 A. & E. 473; contra, *Austen v. Baker* (1698) 12 Mod. 250; *Mountstephen v. Lakeman* (1871) L.R. 5 QB 613. These cases also show that in order to bring a case within the Statute there is no requirement that the principal debtor's liability precede the surety's undertaking to be answerable. See also *Jones v. Cooper* (1774) 1 Cowp. 227.

In *Birkmyr v. Darnell*[25] the promise was to answer for the safe return of a horse lent to another and it was held within the Statute, the bailment having been to that other. If the bailment had been to the defendant it would not have been within the Statute even though in tort a direct liability to the owner might have been afterwards incurred by a third person in whose hands the horse had been placed by the bailee.[26] Similarly, in cases where the promise is to pay for goods to be supplied or services to be rendered to another, the question is who is to be the purchaser or employer. If it is the promisor, the promise is not within the Statute, though the consideration is exclusively for the use of the other,[27] and whether or not there is any further consideration for the promise.[28] Even where two promised jointly to pay for goods which it was known to the seller were for the use of one only, the Statute was held not to apply, though the seller knew that there was no partnership nor community of interest between the two, and that the second joined only to procure credit for the first.[29]

Prima facie rule as to whom primarily liable

Prima facie, it is taken that the person for whom the goods or services are ordered is intended to be liable, although another may give the order. Thus where a creditor of a landlord promised to pay a man who went into possession upon a distress by the landlord, the Statute was considered applicable.[30] Similarly where a friend of a debtor who had been arrested promised a solicitor to pay his charges if he would continue to act for the debtor, it was held that the debtor must have been intended to be liable, though the object was that through the solicitor he should take the benefit of the bankruptcy laws.[31] But where an execution creditor employed a solicitor to move for a new trial in an action against a sheriff arising out of the execution, the execution creditor, and not the sheriff, was treated as primarily liable.[32] In *Austen v. Baker*[33] Holt C.J. said that when such questions arose on the supply of goods, he always required the tradesman to produce his books to show he had not debited the person for whom they were ordered. Where it cannot be said that the goods were for any individual, as where the order was

3–06

---

[25] (1704) 2 Lord Raym. 1085. See Williams, *op. cit.* at p. 5, who points out that the principle of *Birkmy v. Darnell* is repeatedly accepted in the later cases, *i.e.* that the only contracts included under the present head of the Statute are those of a guarantor.
[26] See the report in 2 Lord Raym. 1085.
[27] See *Edge v. Frost* (1824) 4 D. & R. 243.
[28] See the notes to *Forth v. Stanton* (1669) 1 Williams' Saund. 211 e(1); *Fitzgerald v. Dressler* (1859) 7 C.B. (N.S.) 374 at 379, 392; *Sutton v. Grey* [1894] 1 QB 285 at 288.
[29] *Hampson v. Merriott Lancaster Spring Assizes* (1806) *per* Chambre J., reported in *Fell on Mercantile Guarantees* (2nd ed., 1820), pp. 27, 28, where some doubt is expressed as to the correctness of the decision.
[30] *Colman v. Eyles* (1817) 2 Stark 62.
[31] *Barber v. Fox* (1816) 1 Stark 270.
[32] *Noel v. Hart* (1837) 8 C. & P. 230.
[33] (1698) 12 Mod. 250.

for a cup intended to be presented to the winner of a race, if one
person is debited it requires very clear evidence to show that any
other persons who may have promised to pay is primarily and not
merely collaterally liable.[34]

A person requesting a consideration for himself may have actual
or ostensible authority to make another exclusively liable for it.[35]
Conversely, a person requesting a consideration for another may,
though he pledges his own credit, also purport to pledge primarily
the credit of the other. If in such cases the meaning is that the first-
named is to make good the payment for which the other is assumed
to be liable, this is a collateral promise. It will not become an
original promise if it turns out that the other is not liable, but will
become void.[36]

Promise to pay whether another is liable or not

3–07   When the purport of a promise is to secure the promisee, not
against the failure of the person named to meet what is assumed to
be a liability upon him, but against the possibility that the intended
transaction may not impose any valid liability upon that person at
all, the promise is an original promise and not within the Statute.
Thus, in *Mountstephen v. Lakeman*,[37] where a contractor was asked
by the chairman of a local board to do certain work to sewers vested
in the board, and hesitated for want of a formal order, whereupon
the chairman said, "You do the work, and I will see you paid," the
promise was held original and not within the Statute. It was pointed
out by Lord Selborne in the House of Lords that to construe it as a
promise to pay, if the board became liable, would defeat the very
intention of the parties, which was that the contractor should be
protected against the chance of the board not becoming liable.[38]

It is clear from this decision that the Statute does not apply
where, though it is contemplated that the person who is to enjoy the
consideration may become liable, the promise is intended to hold
good whether he becomes liable or not.[39] On this principle a
promise for something to be supplied to one who is known to be an
infant is not within the Statute, unless perhaps where the things
supplied are assumed on both sides to be necessaries.[40]

In such cases as *Mountstephen v. Lakeman*, if the person enjoying the consideration should afterwards ratify the transaction and
become liable, it is submitted that the promise would not be brought

---

[34] See *Storr v. Scott* (1833) 6 C. &. P. 241.
[35] *Darnell v. Tratt* (1825) 2 C. & P. 82; *Smith v. Rudhall* (1862) 3 F. & F. 143.
[36] *Mountstephen v. Lakeman* (1871) L.R. 5 QB 613; 7 QB 196; 7 HL 17. See *per* Willes J. (1871)
L.R. 7 QB at 202.
[37] Above. The House of Lords affirmed the judgment of the Court of Exchequer Chamber which
had reversed the Court of Queen's Bench.
[38] (1874) L.R. 7 HL at 25.
[39] (1871) L.R. 7 QB at 203 *per* Willes J.
[40] *Harris v. Huntbach* (1757) 1 Burr. 373. And see *Duncomb v. Tickridge* (1648) Aleyn 94. Note
the discussion at Chap. 4, part. 7, *i.e.* guarantees of infants' contracts.

ex post facto within the Statute. This seems justified by the language of Willes J.,[41] in the Exchequer Chamber, and by that of Lord Cairns in the House of Lords. "Against that primary liability," said Lord Cairns, "the defendant might afterwards have sheltered himself by obtaining from the board the consent to make a formal order and acting upon and paying under that formal order."[42]

On a similar principle, where the object of a promise is to prevent **3–08** the prosecution of a disputed claim against another, the promise being absolute to pay a certain amount without regard to the validity of the claim, the Statute does not apply. It was apparently so held very early in the history of the Statute in *Stephens v. Squire.*[43] In that case the promise which was held not within the Statute was to pay the promisee £10 and his costs, if he would not further prosecute an action against a solicitor and two others for appearing for him without warrant. But the promisor himself appears to have been the solicitor. The point arose clearly, however, in *Read v. Nash*,[44] where the record in an action for assault was withdrawn in consideration of a promise by a third person to pay a lump sum, and the Statute was held not to apply. This decision is questioned in the notes to *Forth v. Stanton*[45] as indistinguishable from the cases where the promise is in consideration of forbearing to sue, which cases are within the Statute.[46] But in *Bird v. Gammon*,[47] *Read v. Nash* was treated as proceeding on the ground that the intention was that the claim (which was not admitted) should not be prosecuted. In *Kirkham v. Marter*,[48] which is said in the notes to *Forth v. Stanton* to overrule *Read v. Nash*, the promise was in consideration of forbearance to sue one who had killed the plaintiff's horse; and the Statute was held to apply. There seems to have been no dispute as to the liability. The promise was simply to pay the value of the horse, which was to be ascertained. There was nothing to suggest that the wrongdoer was to be discharged, and *Read v. Nash* was distinguished as proceeding on the compromise of a doubtful claim.[49]

If a claim is preferred against several, and one promises to pay a sum by way of compromise of the whole matter, the Statute does

[41] (1871) L.R. 7 QB at 203. And see the reasoning on *Birkmyr v. Darnell* as reported in 2 Lord Raym. 1085.
[42] (1874) L.R. 7 HL at 23. It might be a question on any given transaction whether the original promisor was to remain liable after the other had accepted the liability.
[43] (1696) 3 Mod. 205.
[44] (1751) 1 Wils. 305. *Cf. Roe v. Haugh* (1703) 1 Salk. 29; 3 Salk. 14.
[45] (1669) Williams Saund. 211 e(1), *i.e.* notes to Saunders' Reports 1871 edition, p. 232.
[46] *Fish v. Hutchinson* (1759) 2 Wils. 94; *Kirkham v. Marter* (1819) 2 B. & Ald. 613: *Cole v. Dyer* (1831) 1 C. & J. 461.
[47] (1837) 3 Bing. N.C. 883. And see *Williams v. Leper* (1766) 3 Burr. 1886; *Tomlinson v. Gill* (1756) Ambl. 330; *Fish v. Hutchinson* (1759) 2 Wils. 94.
[48] (1819) 2 B. & Ald. 613. This case also established that the Statute applied to guarantees of liability arising *ex delicto* as well as to those arising *ex contractu, i.e.* liability for tort was to be included in the term "miscarriage". For the meaning of "default," apparently referable to any future liability whether contractual or not, see *Re Young and Harston's Contract* (1885) 31 Ch.D 168.
[49] This distinction is discussed and criticised by Williams, *op. cit.*, on the ground that such an objection would apply to any guarantee where the third party's liability had not first been ascertained by the judgment of a court of law.

not apply, though it could have been shown that the others were liable.[50]

The principal must remain liable notwithstanding the promise

3–09		Where the promise has relation to a claim already incurred by the third person, it is not collateral, so as to be within the Statute, unless the third person is also to remain liable after the promise becomes binding. If it is agreed between all parties that a sale be transferred to the account of a third party and the original buyer released, the Statute will not apply.[51] But a promise to pay a debt transferred from another's account to that of the promisor may be shown to be a guarantee from circumstances indicating that the original debtor was not treated as released.[52] And a promise by an original debtor, if the creditor will transfer the debt to the account of another, to pay it if that other does not, is within the Statute.[53] But no writing is required to make a new partner in a firm liable to an existing creditor, the joint liability of the partners being substituted for that of the original debtor.[54]

No writing is required where the promise is to pay if the creditor will release the debtor by deed.[55] And this is so even where the promise is that, after his release, the debtor shall pay, if this only means that the promisor will get him to pay by his hand, and not that the debtor is to renew his liability to the promisee.[56] If the promise is that, if the creditor will release his present claim and take from the debtor a new liability (*e.g.* take a bill or note) the promisor will see he fulfils that liability, this would clearly be within the Statute.[57]

Novation

3–10	If A is owed money by B, and B is owed money by C, and all three agree that C shall owe the money to A and B be released, the promise of C is not within the Statute.[58] In such a case A could at common law recover from C.[59] But unless B was discharged by the new arrangement, such an action would not lie.[60] However, upon a promise by C to pay A out of money then being or thereafter to be

[50] *Orrell v. Coppock* (1856) 26 L.J. Ch. 269.
[51] *Browning v. Stallard* (1814) 5 Taunt. 480. And see *Taylor v. Hilary* (1835) 1 C.M. & R. 741; *Goodman v. Chase* (1818) 1 B. & Ald. 297; *Butcher v. Steuart* (1843) 11 M. & W. 857; *Scarf v. Jardine* (1882) 7 App.Cas. 345.
[52] *French v. French* (1841) 2 M. & Gr. 644.
[53] *Brunton v. Dullens* (1859) 1 F. & F. 450.
[54] *Re Lendon, ex p. Lane* (1846) De Gex 300.
[55] See *Emmett v. Dewhurst* (1851) 3 Mac. & G. 587.
[56] *Lane v. Burghart* (1841) 1 QB 933.
[57] *Maggs v. Ames* (1828) 4 Bing. 470; *Emmett v. Dewhurst* (1851) 3 Mac. & G. 587.
[58] *Lucy v. McNeile* (1824) 4 D. & R. 7: *Hodgson v. Anderson* (1825) 3 B. & C. 842.
[59] *Israel v. Douglas* (1789) 1 H.Bl. 239; *Tatlock v. Harris* (1789) 3 Term.Rep. 174; *Hodgson v. Anderson*, above; *Wilson v. Coupland* (1821) 5 B. & Ald. 228; *Lucy v. McNeile*, above.
[60] *Wharton v. Walker* (1825) 4 B. & C. 163; *Fairlie v. Denton* (1828) 8 B. & C. 395.

in C's hands for B, an action would lie and would not be within the Statute, even though B is not discharged.[61] Apart from such cases are those where a debtor assigns equitably to his creditor a debt owing to him. In this case the assignee could recover at law only in the name of an upon the promise of the assignor, and no question upon the Statute could arise. And though now since the Judicature Acts the assignee can (if the statutory criteria are met) sue the debtor directly, the Statute of Frauds has clearly no application. It is the defendant's own debt, not that of another, that is sued for.[62]

A promise to pay the debt of another is within the Statute though the promisee undertakes with the promisor not to sue the debtor. For this affords no defence to the debtor, who thus remains liable after the promise.[63] Thus a promise to pay a sum in satisfaction of a debt is within the Statute if the debtor remains liable till the payment.[64] If there is a general arrangement by which a third person takes over the property of a debtor and promises the creditors to pay in his stead, the promise of such third person is not within the Statute, inasmuch as such an arrangement itself, without a formal release of the debtor, prevents an action being brought by any creditor being party to the arrangement.[65]

Consent to material variation and estoppels

If a surety consents to a material variation of the principal **3–11** indebtedness which, without such consent, would have led to the discharge of the guarantee, no new guarantee is created and no fresh compliance with the Statute is required, since the creditor sues on the original guarantee.[66] Nor does the Statute preclude reliance upon an estoppel (where no consent has been given) which would prevent the surety from relying upon such material variation.[67] Conversely, the Statute does not prevent a surety relying upon an oral variation of the principal indebtedness in seeking to defend himself against the creditor's claim.[68]

---

[61] *Dixon v. Hatfield* (1825) 2 Bing. 439; *Andrews v. Smith* (1835) 2 C.M. & R. 627; *Sweeting v. Asplin* (1840) 7 M. & W. 165; *Walker v. Rostron* (1842) 9 M. & W. 411. But *cf. Parkins v. Moravia* (1824) 1 C. & P. 376.

[62] *Hodgson v. Anderson* (1825) 3 B. & C. 842; *Commercial Bank of Tasmania v. Jones* [1893] A.C. 313; *Re Lendon, ex p. Lane* (1846) De G. 300. See also *Wilson v. Coupland* (1821) 5 B. & Ald. 228.

[63] *Rothery v. Curry* (T. 21 Geo. 2) cited in Buller's N.P. 281; *Lee v. Bashpole* (M.1 W. & M.), *ibid. King v. Wilson, ibid.*; 2 Stra. 873.

[64] *Case v. Barber* (1681) T. Raym. 450; *Chater v. Beckett* (1797) 7 Term Rep. 201; *Tomlinson v. Gell* (1837) 6 A. & E. 564 at 569.

[65] *Bird v. Gammon* (1837) 3 Bing. N.C. 883; and *cf. Anstey v. Marden* (1804) 1 B. & P.N.R. 124.

[66] *Credit Suisse v. Borough Council of Allerdale* [1995] 1 Lloyd's Rep. 315 at 370–371.

[67] *ibid.* at 371–372; *Bank of Scotland v. Wright* [1991] B.C.L.C. 244 at 263–266.

[68] *Re A Debtor (No. 517 of 1991), The Times*, November 25, 1991 (Ferris J.).

Agreement to purchase debt

3–12   An executory agreement to purchase a debt seems not to be within the Statute. This at least seems to have been the opinion of the Court of Common Pleas in *Anstey v. Marden*,[69] where, however, the transaction was not so much an executory agreement for the sale of the debt as a present transfer of the debt in consideration of a promise to pay the price, the arrangement being a general one among creditors, which *ipso facto* puts an end to the right of every creditor party to it to sue on his own behalf.[70] In *Mallet v. Bateman*,[71] it was held in the Common Pleas and in the Exchequer Chamber, that a promise, in consideration that the promisee would supply goods to a third party and draw bills upon the buyer for the price, to take over the bills from the seller, indorsed without recourse to him, or indorsed with a collateral indemnity to him against his liability as indorser, was within the Statute, the transaction being in substance a guarantee of the intended debt. Some of the judges seem to have suggested that a promise to purchase a debt is always within the Statute.[72] But these dicta ought perhaps to be confined to cases like that then before the court, where the substantial object in view is to secure that the money owing should be paid from one source or another to the creditor. They do not seem to apply where the object is not that the debt should be paid to the creditor, but, on the contrary, that the purchaser should collect it for himself, the creditor receiving from him a price for parting with his right.

When a promise is to pay a sum which is not shown to be the debt of another, the Statute does not apply. Thus, where it was in consideration of forbearance to sell under a bill of sale which appeared to be absolute and was not shown to be security for any debt, the Statute did not apply.[73] However, a promise to pay the debt of a deceased person is within the Statute, apparently even though no personal legal representative has been constituted.[74]

Promises to pay debt not owed to the promisee

3–13   It follows from the principle that the Statute only applies where the other person is or is to be also liable that it does not apply to a promise to make good the debt of another not owed to the promisee. This may have been the reasoning of Lord Hardwicke in *Tomlinson v. Gill*[75] where he decided that the Statute did not apply to a promise to an intending administratrix that if she would admit the promisor

---

[69] Above.
[70] See *per* Sir J. Mansfield C.J., 1 B. & P.N.R. at 131.
[71] (1865) 16 C.B. (N.S.) 530; L.R. 1 C.P. 163 (Exch. Ch.).
[72] See *per* Blackburn J., L.R. 1 C.P. at 169, and *per* Pollock C.B. at 170.
[73] *Barrell v. Trussel* (1811) 4 Taunt. 117.
[74] *Lexington v. Clarke* (1689) 2 Vent. 223. But *cf. Tomlinson v. Gill* (1756) Ambl. 330.
[75] Above and see also *Lexington v. Clarke*, above.

to join in the administration he would pay the creditors in full. And in *Howes v. Martin*,[76] it was held that a promise to indemnify against the demand of another was not within the Statute. The rule was, however, finally settled in *Eastwood v. Kenyon*,[77] where the promise was made to the debtor; and it had been adhered to ever since.[78]

On the same principle, a guarantee given by one person party to a contract to another person to whom he transferred the benefit of the contract, that the contractor would carry it out, was held enforceable though not in writing, on the ground that there was no privity between the contractor and the transferee, and that the so-called guarantee operated only as a contract to procure another to do such and such a thing.[79] Such contracts, if the person who is to be procured to do or to abstain from doing the thing in question, neither is, nor is to be, under any obligation in that behalf to the promisee, are not within the Statute. Thus, a promise that a debtor should not leave the country,[80] and even a promise that another should pay, provided that credit was not stipulated to be given to that other[81] are not within the Statute. So too a promise to procure another to give a guarantee.[82] Similarly a promise by a third person to a county court bailiff, about to arrest a debtor for contempt in not paying under an order, that he will pay himself or surrender the debtor by a given date, is not within the Statute.[83] And even a promise by one partner to make good to the firm the debt of a debtor of the firm has been held not within the Statute on the ground that the true effect of the transaction was not a promise to his partners and himself to pay the debt, but a promise to his partners (who could not alone sue the debtor) to indemnify them against individual loss if the firm debt should turn out bad.[84]

Indemnities

A promise is not the less within the Statute because it is called an **3–14** indemnity, if the effect of it is to indemnify at the expense of a stranger a creditor against the default of his debtor.[85] The word "indemnity" is, however, often employed in cases such as those just examined where the Statute does not apply, namely where one

---

[76] (1764) 1 Esp. 162.
[77] (1840) 11 A. & E. 438. And see *Harburg India Rubber Co. v. Martin* [1902] 1 K.B. 778 at 784.
[78] See *Hargreaves v. Parsons* (1844) 13 M. & W. 881; *Reader v. Kingham* (1862) 13 C.B. (N.S.) 344; *Re Hoyle* [1893] 1 Ch. 84.
[79] *Hargreaves v. Parsons* (1844) 13 M. & W. 561.
[80] *Elkins v. Heart* (1731) Fitz. 202.
[81] *Gordon v. Martin* (1731) Fitz. 302; *Lane v. Burghart* (1841) 1 QB 933. And see *Mountstephen v. Lakeman* (1871) L.R. 5 QB 613; 7 QB 196; 7 HL 17.
[82] *Bushell v. Beavan* (1834) 1 Bing. N.C. 103.
[83] *Reader v. Kingham* (1862) 13 C.B. (N.S.) 34. See also *Love's Case* (1706) 1 Salk. 28.
[84] *Re Hoyle* [1893] 1 Ch. 84.
[85] *Mallet v. Bateman* (1865) 16 C.B. (N.S.) 530.

co-adventurer undertakes to relieve another from all loss,[86] or where a person engages to protect another from demands by a third person.[87]

There has been some conflict of authority upon the question whether a promise to indemnify against loss by becoming a surety is within the Statute.[88] In *Thomas v. Cook*,[89] it was held that a promise by one surety to indemnify another was not within the Statute: and in Ireland it has been held that a surety could successfully rely upon such a verbal promise, at any rate for the purpose of resisting contribution.[90] In *Green v. Cresswell*[91] it was held, apparently questioning *Thomas v. Cook*, that a promise to indemnify against becoming bail in civil proceedings was within the Statute, because there was an obligation on the debtor towards his bail to keep him harmless. In *Batson v. King*[92] a drawer of a bill who had received a verbal indemnity from the acceptor and a subsequent indorser, who were both found to be the principals in the transaction, recovered against that indorser the money he had been compelled to pay without any writing to show the promise to indemnify. In this case the defendant was himself principal, and Martin B., with whom the court concurred, expressly reserved the case of a surety who was promised by a stranger indemnity against default by the principal. In *Cripps v. Hartnoll*[93] it was held in the Exchequer Chamber, reversing the decision of the Queen's Bench, that a promise by a stranger to indemnify bail in a criminal proceeding need not be in writing, there being no obligation on the prisoner towards the bail.[94] And *Green v. Cresswell* was distinguished as relating to bail in a civil proceeding.

3–15   In *Wildes v. Dudlow*,[95] however, Malins V.-C. treated *Green v. Cresswell* as overruled, and decided that a promise by a stranger to indemnify a person who joined as surety in a promissory note given by a third person was not within the Statute, this being the point left open in *Batson v. King*. *Wildes v. Dudlow* was followed by Chitty J., in *Re Bolton*,[96] and was approved with *Thomas v. Cook* and *Re Bolton* by the Court of Appeal in *Guild v. Conrad*.[97] In that case the plaintiffs had accepted without assets bills drawn on them by a firm abroad, upon the verbal undertaking of the defendant to find the money to enable the plaintiffs to meet these acceptances, there

---

[86] See *Re Hoyle* [1893] 1 Ch. 84; *Sutton v. Grey* [1984] 1 QB 295.

[87] *Adams v. Dansey* (1830) 6 Bing. 506; *Guild v. Conrad* [1894] 2 QB 885. But see *Winckworth v. Mills* (1796) 2 Esp. 484.

[88] The history of the principle that the guaranteed obligation need not be owed to the person to whom the guarantee is given as is reflected in this paragraph is treated in detail in Williams, *op. cit.*

[89] (1828) 8 B. & C. 728.

[90] *Rae v. Rae* (1857) 6 Ir. Ch. R. 490.

[91] (1837) 10 A. & E. 453.

[92] (1859) 4 H. & N. 739.

[93] (1863) 4 B. & S. 414.

[94] cf. *Herman v. Jeuchner* (1885) 15 QBD. 561.

[95] (1874) L.R. 19 Eq. 198.

[96] [1892] W.N. 163; 8 T.L.R. 668.

[97] [1894] 2 QB 885.

being no expectation that the drawers would be able to pay. It was held that the Statute did not apply.

Contract to give a guarantee

A contract to give a guarantee is as much within the Statute as a **3–16** guarantee.[98] But a contract to procure another to give a guarantee is not. If, however, the guarantee contracted for would be unenforceable by reason of the Statute, the damages would be nominal.[99]

Where promisor is also liable independently of the promise

The Statute does not apply where the person promising is, inde- **3–17** pendently of the promise, under a liability personally or by his property for the debt to which the promise relates.[1] So a promise by a member of a firm to be separately liable for a debt of the firm need not apparently be in writing.[2] On the same principle, where a sub-purchaser, in consideration of the original vendor delivering to him the property, on which he had a lien for the purchase-money payable by his immediate purchaser, promised to pay that money, the Statute did not apply, inasmuch as the promisor was, subject to that lien, entitled to that property.[3]

Promise in consideration of the relinquishment of a lien

It has been held, moreover, in a number of cases, that if a creditor **3–18** gives up to a third person, though not a purchaser, property upon which he has a lien for debt, in consideration of a promise by a third person to pay the debt, that promise is not within the Statute.[4] If the promise by the third person is merely to realise the property and pay the debt out of the proceeds, its only effect is to secure the due administration of a fund.[5] Similarly, a promise to pay merely out of the moneys of the debtor which shall come to the hands of the promisor is not in any case within the Statute. Thus, where an employer[6] of a contractor, or an agent of such employer,[7] promises

---

[98] *Compagnie Generale v. Myson Group Ltd* (1984) 134 N.L.J. 788 (Hirst J.); *Mallet v. Bateman* (1865) 16 C.B. (N.S.) 530; L.R. 1 C.P. 163. But see *Jarmain v. Algar* (1862) 2 C. & P. 249.
[99] *Bushell v. Beavan* (1834) 1 Bing. N.C. 103.
[1] See notes to *Forth v. Stanton* (1669) 1 Williams Saund. 211 e(1).
[2] *Ex p. Harding* (1879) 12 Ch D 557 at 566.
[3] *Fitzgerald v. Dressler* (1859) 7 C.B. (N.S.) 274. And compare *Williams v. Leper* (1766) 3 Burr. 1886; *Castling v. Aubert* (1802) 2 East. 325; *Huggard v. Representative Church Body* [1916] 1 I.R. 1.
[4] *Williams v. Leper*, above; *Castling v. Aubert*, above; *Houlditch v. Milne* (1800) 3 Esp. 86; *Edwards v. Kelly* (1817) 6 M. & S. 204; *Thomas v. Williams* (1830(10 B. & C. 604; *Bampton v. Paulin* (1827) 4 Bing. 264; *Walker v. Taylor* (1834) 6 C.& P. 752; *Gregory v. Williams* (1817) 3 Mer. 582. Williams, *op. cit.* at p. 19 in discussing these cases, states it is clear they do not require evidence that the fund or property which is disencumbered, produced more or was more valuable than the debt constituting the encumbrance.
[5] *Macrory v. Scott* (1850) 5 Exch. 907.
[6] *Dixon v. Hatfield* (1825) 2 Bing. 439; *cf. Griffith v. Young* (1810) 12 East 513 at 514.
[7] *Andrews v. Smith* (1835) 2 C.M. & R. 627; *Sweeting v. Asplin* (1840) 7 M. & W. 165 (see the distinction *per* Parke B., at 170, 171); *Walker v. Rostron* (1842) 9 M. & W. 411. *cf. Morley v. Boothby* (1825) 3 Bing. 107, but see *Parkins v. Moravia* (1824) I.C. & P. 376.

to a sub-contractor to pay him out of moneys, not his own, but which he shall have in his hands for the contractor, the Statute does not apply. So a promise by the drawee of a cheque to the payee to pay the amount out of a balance to the credit of the drawer, if the payee would discount it for the drawer, was held good to the extent of such balance without writing.[8] Some of the cases where the Statute has been held inapplicable to a promise by a person to whom property subject to a lien is surrendered, and where the claim does not extend beyond money actually realised, may be supported on this principle.[9] It is established, however, that the exemption goes further than this, and takes the promise out of the Statute, though the goods have not produced, or cannot produce, the amount to which the lien extended.

The principle is that the object of the transaction was not merely to secure the debt by the interposition of the promise of a stranger but to secure an arrangement in which the promisor was independently interested.[10] A person who is or who intends to become interested in property upon which there is a charge, and on obtaining possession promises to pay the same, intervenes not as a stranger guaranteeing a debt, but as a person interested bargaining for the disencumbrance of his own interest.[11]

3–19   The explanation is consistent with two limitations to which the rule is undoubtedly subject. These (i) that the promisor cannot without writing go beyond the amount charged upon the goods; (ii) that the goods must be surrendered to the promisor and not to the debtor. The first was laid down in *Thomas v. Williams*,[12] where, upon goods under distress being surrendered to a broker for sale, the broker promised to pay not only the rent then in arrear, but also that which would fall due next quarter day; and it was held that the Statute applied. But in such cases, to the extent of the amount charged on the goods, the promise can be enforced and the excess rejected.[13] The second limitation mentioned above seems involved in *Rounce v. Woodyard*[14] and the Irish case of *Fennell v. Mulcahy*.[15] In both those cases it was held that a promise by a third party to pay

---

[8] *Ardern v. Rowney* (1805) 5 Esp. 254.
[9] *Williams v. Leper* (1766) 3 Burr. 1886; 2 Wils 308 (see *per* Aston J.); *Castling v. Aubert* (1802) 2 East 325.
[10] A money payment merely to induce one who is otherwise a stranger to guarantee a debt does not make him independently interested within the meaning of this rule; see *Couturier v. Hastie* (1856) 8 Exch. 40 at 55; *Tomlinson v. Gell* (1837) 6 A. & E. 564 at 571.
[11] *Sutton v. Grey* [1894] 1 QB 285. See also *Harburg India Rubber Comb. Co. v. Martin* [1902] 1 K.B. 778; *Davys v. Buswell* [1913] 2 K.B. 47 (no distinction appears to exist between legal as distinct from equitable rights *per* Joyce J. at 58; *Fitzgeraled v. Dressler* (1859) 7 C.B. (N.S.) 374; *Huggard v. Representative Church Body* [1916] 1 I.R. 1. For a more detailed discussion of the earlier cases, see the first edition of this book.
[12] (1830) 10 B. & C. 664.
[13] *Wood v. Benson* (1813) 2 C. & J. 94, where *Lexington v. Clarke* (1689) 2 Vent. 223, *Chater v. Beckett* (1797) 7 Term Rep. 201 and *Thomas v. Williams* (1870) 10 B. & C. 667 (where the contrary appeared to be decided), were explained on the ground that in those cases there was no count applicable to a severed portion of the claim. See too *Head v. Baldrey* (1837) 6 A. & E. 459; *Lord Falmouth v. Thomas* (1832) 1 C. & M. 89 at 101 *per* Bayley J.
[14] (1846) 8 L.T. (O.S.) 186.
[15] (1845) 8 Ir. L.R. 434.

rent distrained for, if the landlord withdrew and allowed the tenant to resume the goods, was within the Statute, notwithstanding a dictum attributed to Lord Eldon in *Houlditch v. Milne*,[16] to the effect that the Statute never applied where the plaintiff gave up a lien. That dictum as reported was questioned in the notes to *Forth v. Stanton*.[17] It is not clear to whom the property was given, or whether the owner, who was apparently abroad, had ever been looked to by the plaintiff, whose claim and lien was for work done to the property.

Promises in consideration of a lien not being asserted

Further, the case is not taken out of the Statute, where the **3–20** promise is not in consideration of the surrender of a lien, but in consideration of a lien not being asserted, without regard to the question whether it existed or not.[18]

Promises by a person independently interested in the transaction

It is on the same principle that a *del credere* agent is not within **3–21** the Statute.[19] That was decided in *Couturier v. Hastie*,[20] where it was held, following an American decision, that the responsibility of the agent was regarded, not as a collateral undertaking, but as an incident of the agency. In *Wickham v. Wickham*,[21] Wood V.-C. seems to have treated the decision as proceeding on the ground that the agent was primarily liable.[22] But in *Fleet v. Murton*,[23] Blackburn J. applies the decision in *Couturier v. Hastie* to an agent liable by custom to make good the engagements of those with whom he deals, and excludes his engagement from the operation of the Statute, as "merely regulating the terms of the employment." And in *Sutton v. Grey*,[24] where a person who was to receive from a stockbroker half of the commission payable by clients whom he should introduce, undertook also to pay half the loss which might be incurred by their default, the Court of Appeal, in deciding that the Statute did not apply, laid down the doctrine, as deducible from *Couturier v. Hastie*,[25] and *Fitzgerald v. Dressler*,[26] that the Statute

[16] (1800) 3 Esp. 86.
[17] (1669) 1 Williams Saund. 211 e(1).
[18] *Gull v. Lindsay* (1849) 4 Exch. 45.
[19] *Harburg India Rubber Comb. Co. v. Marten* [1902] 1 K.B. 778.
[20] (1852) 8 Exch. 40. The decision appears to be based to a large extent on the American case of *Wolff v. Koppel*, 5 Hill N.Y. Rep. 458 (1843).
[21] (1855) 2 K. & J. 478.
[22] *ibid.* at 486. The agent is certainly not primarily liable: *Gabriel v. Churchill and Sim* [1914] 3 K.B. 1272.
[23] (1871) L.R. 7 QB 126 at 133.
[24] [1894] 1 QB 285.
[25] (1852) 8 Exch. 40.
[26] (1859) 7 C.B. (N.S.) 374. But the mere fact that the promisor is financially interested in the principal's business, and even that he is the holder of a floating charge on the principal's assets, does not make him interested in the transaction for the purposes of this rule: *Harburg India Rubber Comb. Co. v. Martin* [1902] 1 K.B. 778; *Davys v. Bushell* [1913] 2 K.B. 47.

only applies where a promisor is, but for his promise, totally unconnected with the transaction. And this distinction was treated as the dividing line between a guarantee and an indemnity.

3–22   Where the defendant became agent to the plaintiff on the terms that his first six months' salary should be applied to the liquidation of the former agent's account, it was held, in an action by the employer for money in the hands of the agent on the balance of accounts, that the latter could not claim such six months' salary.[27] There was no promise to answer for the debt, but only in effect to serve the six months for nothing.[27]

A promise to pay a sum in compromise of the liability of another is not within the Statute, if the promisor is also alleged to be liable to the same claim, even though in truth he could have resisted the claim successfully.[28] And a promise to honour a bill to be drawn upon the promisor for the account of a third person is not within the Statute, at any rate if the facts are consistent with the supposition that the party undertaking undertakes because he has, or expects to have, goods of the third person in his hands.[29]

Guarantee amounting to a representation

3–23   In *Pasley v. Freeman*[30] it was established that an action would lie for a fraudulent misrepresentation by word of mouth only of the credit or solvency of another. This opened the door to evasion of section 4 of the Statute of Frauds; for many transactions, intended to operate as verbal guarantees, might also support a claim of this kind. By the Statute of Frauds Amendment Act 1828,[31] s.6, this was put to an end, it being there enacted that no representations of that kind should be actionable unless in writing. This branch of the law is, however, not properly within the scope of this work.[32]

2. *What Note or Memorandum is Sufficient*

3–24   If a defendant by his pleading admits an enforceable contract, he cannot take the objection that there is no sufficient memorandum to satisfy the Statute of Frauds.[33]

---

[27] *Walker v. Hill* (1860) 5 H. & N. 419.
[28] *Orrell v. Coppock* (1856) L.J. ch. 269.
[29] *Pillans v. Van Mierop* (1765) 3 Burr. 1664 at 1666, 1667.
[30] (1789) 3 Term.Rep. 51.
[31] Lord Tenterden's Act, (9 Geo. 4, c.14). See Appendix 2.
[32] s.6 has been held applicable to fraudulent representations only. *Banbury v. Bank of Montreal* [1918] A.C. 626; *Anderson and Sons Ltd v. Rhodes* [1967] 2 All E.R. 850. See generally Clerk and Lindsell, *Torts* (17th ed., 1995), para. 14–46.
[33] *Lucas v. Dixon* (1889) 22 QBD. 357 *per* Bowen L.J. at 361. The written memorandum need not be contemporaneous with the actual contract and will usually be a memorandum of an already completed contract. See *Parker v. Clark* [1960] 1 W.L.R. 286 at 295 *per* Devlin J., where reliance was placed on a written offer subsequently accepted.

Memorandum made after action

The memorandum must, moreover, be in existence when the **3–25** action is commenced. Therefore an affidavit in the cause admitting the facts will not do.[34] It has been said, however, that it could be made available by discontinuing the action and commencing another.[35] This dictum was followed in *Farr, Smith v. Messers*,[36] where a paragraph in a defence put in before the plaintiffs, who ultimately succeeded, had been joined, was held to be a good memorandum under section 4 of the Sale of Goods Act 1893. In *Rondeau v. Wyatt*,[37] however, the Court of Common Pleas held that an answer in Chancery admitting the facts, but taking the objection there was no memorandum, was not available in an action subsequently commenced.

Statement of consideration

Section 4 of the Statute requires that the agreement, or some note **3–26** or memorandum thereof should be in writing. This was held to require that not only the promise but the consideration should be in writing.[38] But now by section 3 of the Mercantile Law Amendment Act 1856,[39]

"no special promise made by any person after the passing of this Act to answer for the debt, default or miscarriage of another person, being in writing and signed by the party to be charged therewith or some other person by him thereunto lawfully authorised, shall be deemed invalid to support an action, suit or other proceeding to charge the person by whom such promise shall have been made, by reason only that the consideration of such promise does not appear in writing or by necessary inference from a written document."[40]

In *Wynne v. Hughes*,[41] the question was raised but not decided, whether, where an executor personally guarantees the debt of his

---

[34] *Middleton v. Brewer* (1790) 1 Peake 20; *Spurrier v. Fitzgerald* (1801) 6 Ves. 548. Semble where the original written evidence of a guarantee is lost, oral evidence of its having existed is admissible. *Barass v. Reed, The Times*, March 28, 1898; *Grays Gas Co. v. Bromley Gas Co., The Times*, March 23, 1901, CA.

[35] *Lucas v. Dixon* (1889) 22 QBD. 357 *per* Fry L.J. at 363.

[36] [1928] 1 K.B. 397. See above, *Grindell v. Bass* [1920] 2 Ch. 48. Section 4 of the 1893 Act was later repealed.

[37] (1792) 2 H.Bl. 63.

[38] *Wain v. Warlters* (1804) 5 East 10; *Saunders v. Wakefield* (1821) 4 B. & Ald. 595. It was otherwise under s.17 *Egerton v. Mathews* (1805) 6 East 807.

[39] 19 & 20 Vict. c.97.

[40] This statute only applies to "special promises being in writing," whereas the Statute of Frauds allows not only agreements in writing, but agreements of which there is a note or memorandum in writing. It has never been suggested, however, that the Mercantile Law Amendment Act 1856, does not cover the whole ground covered by the Statute of Frauds, or that where there is not a promise in writing, but only a memorandum of an oral promise (*e.g.* in a letter to a third person), the consideration must still appear. The words "promise being in writing" seem to have included promises evidenced by a note or memorandum.

[41] (1873) 21 W.R. 628.

testator, in order to get delay, the Mercantile Law Amendment Act applies: the terms of that section follow the very words of clause 2 of section 4 of the Statute, whereas there is a separate clause requiring any special promise by an executor to be in writing. Bramwell B. appeared to favour the doubt.

Limits of the ambit of the 1856 Act

3–27   It has always been held, even before the Mercantile Law Amendment Act 1856, that where it sufficiently appeared on the writing that the liability to be guaranteed was a prospective one, a consideration—namely, the permitting of that liability to be incurred—was sufficiently stated.[42] Where, however, the liability, though itself sufficiently defined (as where it was described as such and such a bill or account), appeared to be already existent, and the writing did not state any consideration, such as forbearance, the plaintiff failed.[43] It is this difficulty that the Mercantile Law Amendment Act removed; so that if a good consideration exists in fact for a guarantee of an existing debt, it may be proved by parol according to the ordinary law applicable to a contract partly oral.

Parol evidence not admissible to explain the promise

3–28   There must in every guarantee be sufficient statement in writing of the liability which a guarantee is to cover. Before the 1856 Act the question whether there was such a sufficient statement was generally involved in the discussion whether there was such sufficient statement of the consideration.[44] The explanation is obvious. In nearly every case the consideration for a guarantee is either the forbearing a present liability or the permitting a new one to be incurred, and the promise is to make good the liability so to be forborne or incurred. A statement of the consideration, therefore, reveals the liability guaranteed, and so serves also to measure the promise. Accordingly decisions upon the sufficiency, as disclosing the consideration, of a statement of the liability guaranteed, are also decisions upon its sufficiency, as disclosing the scope of the promise, and cover the whole question of the sufficiency of the writing.

---

[42] *Stadt (or Stapp) v. Lill* (1808) 1 Camp. 242; 9 East 348; *Morris v. Stacey* (1816) Holt N.P. 153; *Ex p. Gardom* (1808) 15 Ves. 286; *Boehm v. Campbell* (1820) 3 Moore 15; *Russell v. Moseley* (1822) 3 B. & B. 211; *Lysaght v. Walker* (1831) 5 Bligh (N.S.) 1; *Pace v. Marsh* (1823) 1 Bing. 216; *Newbury v. Armstrong* (1829) 6 Bing. 201; *Combe v. Woolf* (1832) 8 Bing. 156; *Kennaway v. Treleavan* (1839) 5 M. & W. 498; *Jarvis v. Wilkins* (1814) 7 M. & W. 410; *Emmott v. Kearns* (1839) 5 Bing. N.C. 599; *Johnston v. Nicholls* (1845) 1 C.B. 251; *Chapman v. Sutton* (1846) 2 C.B. 634.
[43] *Wain v. Warlters* (1804) 5 East 10; *Saunders v. Wakefield* (1821) 4 B. & Ald. 595; *Jenkins v. Reynolds* (1821) 8 B. & B. 14; *Morley v. Boothby* (1825) 3 Bing. 107; *Cole v. Dyer* (1831) 1 C. & J. 461; *Wood v. Benson* (1831) 2 C. & J. 94; *James v. Williams* (1834) 5 B. & Ad. 1109; *Bentham v. Cooper* (1839) 5 M. & W. 621; *Price v. Richardson* (1846) 15 M. & W. 539; *Clancy v. Piggott* (1835) 2 A. & E. 473; *Hawes v. Armstrong* (1835) 1 Bing. N.C. 761; *Raikes v. Todd* (1838) 8 A. & E. 846; *Allnutt v. Ashenden* (1843) 5 M. & Gr. 392.
[44] *Bateman v. Phillips* (1812) 15 East. 272; *Shortrede v. Cheek* (1834) 1 A. & E. 57. And see *Holmes v. Mitchell* (1859) 7 C.B. (N.S.) 361.

Such decisions still contain the law. Although since the 1856 Act the consideration need not be in writing, the promise must still be so. And parol evidence of the consideration cannot be used to bring in what is wanted in the written statement of the promise.[45]

Parol evidence to identify matters referred to in memorandum

Anything referred to in the guarantee can and must be identified **3–29** by parol evidence.[46] Therefore where payment is to be made out of a particular fund, the fund may be identified by parol evidence, provided it answers to the description.[47] Where the guarantee refers to a liability existing at the date of the guarantee, it may be identified by parol evidence; as where the promise was to pay "the promissory note," it was identified by parol.[48] Where the only description of the debt was that involved in the phrase in a letter, "I trust you will give D. W. indulgence till next week when I will see you paid," it was held that the plaintiff might show what debt D. W. was owing him at that date, and also that the person to whom the letter was addressed was the plaintiff's agent, and that the debt referred to was a debt owing to the plaintiff and not to the addressee of the letter.[49]

Parol evidence of principal liability not yet existing

The following passage appeared in the fourth edition of this **3–30** work—

> "Where, however, the liability guaranteed is a future liability, it must appear in the writing what the liability is to be which the guarantee is to cover. Otherwise there might arise a conflict of parol testimony as to the limit of a guarantee—in other words, as to the extent of the promise. Thus where the guarantee was to cover 'the mortgage,' no mortgage then being in existence, it was held that the action could not succeed."[50]

In *Perrylease v. Imecar A. G.*,[51] Scott J. distinguished the authority relied on in the passage, *Holmes v. Mitchell*, and stated that he could not accept the passage without qualification—

---

[45] *Holmes v. Mitchell*, above.
[46] *Perrylease Ltd v. Imecar A. G.* [1988] 1 W.L.R. 463; *Holmes v. Mitchell*, above; *Heffield v. Meadows* (1869) L.R. 4 C.P. 595; *Shears v. Thimbleby & Son* (1897) 76 L.T. 709.
[47] See *Brown v. Fletcher* (1876) 35 L.T. 165.
[48] *Shortrede v. Cheek* (1834) 1 A. & E. 57.
[49] *Bateman v. Phillips* (1812) 15 East. 272.
[50] *Holmes v. Mitchell* (1859) 7 C.B. (N.S.) 361 *per* Cockburn C.J. at 368. See also *Sheers v. Thimbleby* (1897) 76 L.T. 709. In *Fleetwood Corp v. Imperial Investments Corp Ltd* [1965] 51 D.L.R. (2d) 654, it was held to be a sufficient memorandum when a guarantor signed a sales order at the bottom having written "to be paid Jan. 19, 1960" at the top.
[51] [1988] 1 W.L.R. 463.

"For the purpose of the rules governing the admission of extrinsic evidence, and for the purpose of the Statute of Frauds, I can see no reason why there should be any difference between a present liability and a future liability of the principal debtor."[52]

In that case, the guarantee was in respect of liability for "the proposed leasing" and extrinsic evidence of facts known to both parties was admitted to identify the liabilities guaranteed.

Writing to identify person to whom guarantee given

3–31　　The word "guarantee" need not appear in the memorandum, and indeed no particular form of words is necessary.[53] The person to whom the guarantee is given must appear from the written document or documents evidencing the guarantee,[54] or from a written answer accepting a guarantee offered.[55] But this does not prevent it being shown that the addressee of the guarantee was an agent only; in which case the principal can sue upon it.[56]

Alteration of document

3–32　　Where the agreement has been altered, parol evidence is admissible to show what the state of the document was when it became an agreement and the parties meant their signatures to apply to it. Thus in *Stewart v. Eddowes*,[57] where the document was altered after one party had signed, but before the other had done so, and then as so altered was signed by the latter, and agreed to by the former, becoming then for the first time a binding contract, there was held to be a sufficient memorandum. The reasoning in that case seems to indicate that, if an alteration were interpolated by consent after the document became an agreement, a recognition of the previous signature would not suffice. However, in *Bluck v. Gompertz*,[58] where an error in a guarantee was corrected, after it had been delivered to the plaintiff and after he had performed the consideration, by an endorsement, written on the face of it by the guarantor,

---

[52] at 472.

[53] *Welford v. Beazeley* (1747) 3 Atk. 503. See also *Seaton v. Heath* [1899] 1 QB 782 at 792; *Re Denton's Estate* [1904] 2 Ch. 178 at 188; *Reynolds v. Wheeler* (1861) 10 C.B. (N.S.) 561. As to the evidence of intention see, *e.g. Dane v. Mortgage Insurance Corp.* [1894] 1 QB 54.

[54] *Williams v. Lake* (1863) 2 E. & E. 349; *Williams v. Byrnes* (1863) 1 Moo. P.C. (N.S) 154. *cf. Glover v. Halkett* (1857) 2 H. & N. 487; *Brettel v. Williams* (1849) 4 Exch. 623; *Vanderbergh v. Spooner* (1866) L.R. 1 Exch. 316; *Gibson v. Holland* (1865) L.R. 1 C.P. 1. But see *Walton v. Dodson* (1827) 3 C. & P. 162.

[55] *Williams v. Byrnes*, above at 198. *Re Agra and Masterman's Bank* (1867) L.R. 2 Ch. App. 391.

[56] *Bateman v. Phillips* (1812) 15 East 272; *Gibson v. Holland* (1865) L.R. 1 C.P. 1. *cf. Walton v. Dodson*, above; *Garrett v. Handley* (1825) 4 B. & C. 664.

[57] (1874) L.R. 9 C.P. 311.

[58] (1852) 7 Exch. 862.

but not signed by him, the Court of Exchequer held that the Statute
had been complied with.

Memorandum may consist of several documents

The note or memorandum may consist of several documents[59] **3–33**
provided that the document signed by the guarantor refers to the
other document or documents requisite to complete the memorandum, as the connection cannot be supplied by oral evidence.[60] If,
however, the document contains the reference, the paper referred to
can be identified by parol,[61] and the covering envelope may be
looked at to supply the name and addressee of a letter of guarantee.[62] It is immaterial whether the guarantor ever saw the other
document to which the paper signed by him refers.[63]

Memorandum need not be of contract itself

The memorandum need not contain or form part of the contract **3–34**
itself, nor need it be addressed to the person to whom the guarantee
is given. All that is required is that there should be evidence of the
guarantee under the hand of the guarantor. Therefore even a recital
of a guarantee in the will of the guarantor is sufficient.[64] A letter to
a third party and an affidavit made in a different matter have been
held to suffice and it has been said that an entry in a man's own
diary, if signed by him and if the contents were sufficient, could be
sufficient.[65]

Signature

The signature may be by a printing of the name,[66] if done with **3–35**
authority,[67] or by initials,[68] or, in the case of an illiterate (who, if he
so executes, must be taken to be such), by a mark.[69] It need not be

[59] *Coe v. Duffield* (1822) 7 Moo. 252; *Macrory v. Scott* (1850) 5 Exch. 907; *Brettel v. Williams* (1849) 4 Exch. 623; *Williams v. Byrnes* (1863) 1 Moo. P.C. (N.S.) at 198; *Sheers v. Thimbleby* (1899) 76 L.T. 709. *cf. Timmins v. Moreland Street Property Co. Ltd* [1958] 1 Ch. 110.
[60] *Boydell v. Drummond* (1809) 11 East 142.
[61] *Oliver v. Hunting* (1890) 44 Ch D 205; *Macrory v. Scott*, above.
[62] *Freeman v. Freeman* (1891) 7 T.L.R. 431. It is permissible to identify by parol evidence a document actually referred to in another document so as to connect them, or to show that a reference in the document which may be to another is so in fact. *Long v. Millar* (1879) 4 C.P.D. 450; *Ridgway v. Wharton* (1857) 6 HLC. 238. For examples of where the written evidence consists of correspon-
dence see *Bristol, Cardiff and Swansea Aerated Bread Co. v. Maggs* (1890) 44 Ch D 616; *Hussey v. Horne Payne* (1879) 4 App.Cas. 311.
[63] *Macrory v. Scott* (1850) 5 Exch. 907.
[64] *Re Hoyle* [1893] 1 Ch. 84.
[65] *per* A. L. Smith L.J. in *Re Hoyle* [1893] 1 Ch. 84 at 100, cited with approval by the House of Lords in *Elpis Maritime Co. Ltd v. Marti Chartering Co. Inc.* [1992] 1 A.C. 21 at 32–33.
[66] *Saunderson v. Jackson* (1800) 2 B. & P. 238; *Casey v. Irish Intercontinental Bank* [1979] I.R. 364 SC.
[67] *Schneider v. Norris* (1814) 2 M. & S. 286. See also *Leeman v. Stocks* [1951] Ch. 94.
[68] *Re Blewitt* (1879) L.R. 5 P.D. 116. The signatures may be printed or pencilled: *Geary v. Physic* (1826) 5 B. & C. 234.
[69] *Baker v. Dening* (1838) 8 A. & E. 94. Or even semble by signed instructions for a telephone or telegraphic message: *Godwin v. Francis* (1870) L.R. 5 C.P. 295.

at the foot or end of the memorandum, provided it governs and authenticates the whole.[70] It need not be witnessed.[71]

A memorandum may be signed by an agent, and it is well settled that such agent need not be authorised in writing; verbal authority,[72] or subsequent verbal ratification,[73] is sufficient. Two parties may be represented by a common agent who signs for both, as, in the case of sales within the Statute, an auctioneer.[74] But one party cannot be agent to sign for the other.[75] The agent of one party may also be agent of the other to sign the memorandum, if in fact authorised by him to put his name to it as a binding memorandum.[76] But a mere note, by way of record of the promise, written by the clerk of the promisee in the presence of the guarantor, is not sufficient.[77]

The intention with which or the capacity in which the guarantor signs the memorandum is irrelevant. Thus in *Elpis Maritime v. Marti Chartering*[78] the House of Lords held that even if the guarantor had signed the memorandum in his capacity as agent of the principal debtor rather than as guarantor, it would be sufficient.

Guarantee by a partner

3–36   A partner has no implied authority to bind his firm by guarantee, unless the giving of guarantees is necessary to the conduct of the business.[79] It is not enough that the guarantee was given incidentally to further objects within the scope of the partnership, as that it was given by merchants for merchants,[80] by contractors for subcontractors,[81] or by solicitors for a client.[82] It is necessary to show that it has been usual, to the knowledge of the partners, to give such guarantees.[83] And the same rule holds with regard to the manager of a company.[84] If authority to give guarantees, express or implied,

---

[70] See *Caton v. Caton* (1865–7) L.R. 2 HL 127; *Durrell v. Evans* (1862) 1 H. & C. 174. On the question of the intention with which the memorandum is signed as not being decisive, see *Wallace v. Roe* [1903] 1 I.R. 32; *Welford v. Beazley* (1747) 3 Atk. 503. *cf. Gobbell v. Archer* (1855) 2 A. & E. 800. One surety signing where several are the subject of the guarantee is bound *per Norton v. Powell* (1842) 4 M. & G. 42.
[71] *Canadian Imperial Bank v. Hardy Bay Inn Ltd* [1985] 1 W.W.R. 405.
[72] *Emmerson v. Heelis* (1809) 2 Taunt. 38.
[73] *Maclean v. Dunn* (1828) 4 Bing. 722.
[74] Where though the agent expressly signs as principal he remains liable as such, no doubt in an action on the guarantee oral evidence would establish the existence of an undisclosed principal. See *Higgins v. Senior* (1841) 8 M. & W. 834; *Basma v. Weekes* [1950] A.C. 441.
[75] *Wright v. Dannah* (1809) 2 Camp. 203; *Farebrother v. Simmons* (1822) 5 B. & Ald. 333; *Sharman v. Brandt* (1871) L.R. 6 QB 720.
[76] See *Durrell v. Evans* (1862) 1 H. & C. 174 at 187, 191; *Peirce v. Corf* (1874) L.R. 9 QB 210 at 215; *Caton v. Caton* (1867) L.R. 2 HL 127.
[77] *Dixon v. Broomfield* (1814) 2 Chit 205.
[78] [1992] 1 A.C. 21.
[79] *Brettel v. Williams* (1849) 4 Exch. 623. But *cf. ex p. Gardom* (1808) 15 Ves. 286; *Hope v. Cust* (1774) cited 1 East at 53. See also the Partnership Act 1890, s.5. The giving of guarantees will be outside the normal business of an average partnership, in which case all partners should be required to sign a guarantee by a firm.
[80] *Duncan v. Lowndes* (1813) 3 Camp. 478.
[81] *Brettel v. Williams* (1849) 4 Exch. 623.
[82] *Hasleham v. Young* (1844) 5 QB 833. See *Mayfield v. Sankey* (1890) 6 T.L.R. 185.
[83] *Duncan v. Lowndes* (1813) 3 Camp. 478; *Crawford v. Stirling* (1802) 4 Esp. 207.
[84] *Simpson's Claim* (1887) 36 Ch D 532.

exists, or if the giving of it has been ratified, sufficient signature by one partner is sufficient within the Statute of Frauds.[85]

Guarantees by company

Provided they have authority so to do, the directors of a company **3–37** can bind it by signing a guarantee thereby satisfying the requirements of the Statute of Frauds.[86] The extent of a director's authority to bind his company is outside the scope of this work and reference should be made to specialist works on company law.

---

[85] *Duncan v. Lowndes*, above; *Sandilands v. Marsh* (1819) 2 B. & Ald. 673.
[86] *Re Eva Life Ass. Soc.* [1866] W.N. 309. See also *Colman v. Eastern Counties Ry Co.* (1846) 10 Beav. 1; *Reading v. Plymouth Grinding Co.* (1843) 2 Exch. 711; *Simpson's Claim* (1887) 36 Ch D 532. Note *Jay v. Gainsford* (October 4, 1977, CA, Transcript No. 362B of 1977) illustrating how a note or memorandum satisfying the Statute of Frauds can be effected by a company in respect of the liabilities as guarantors of its individual directors.

CHAPTER 4

CONSTRUCTION AND EFFECT OF GUARANTEES

1. *General Rules*

4–01   It was said by Bayley B. in *Nicholson v. Paget*[1] that guarantees were to be construed favourably to the guarantor. This dictum which was contrary to the ruling in earlier cases,[2] has since been disapproved, and it is now settled that guarantees are not to be construed more strictly than other contracts.[3]

The ordinary rules of construction do, however, include the *contra proferentem* rule, to the effect that in the case of ambiguity a document is construed against the party putting it forward. This principle has on occasions been applied to guarantees.[4,5] Ordinary contractual provisions also require any terms imposed as conditions of the suretyship to be strictly complied with.[6] However, modern standard form guarantees are usually very widely drawn and the courts give effect to extensive liabilities imposed on sureties in such documents.[7] English courts have not, at least overtly, favoured paid as opposed to unpaid sureties in the way in which they interpret guarantees.[8]

Intention to assume liability

4–02   In a series of cases concerned with the collapse of the Bank of Credit and Commerce ("BCCI"), sureties who had charged deposits at the bank to secure lending to their companies argued, with varying degrees of success, that the charge documentation also

---

[1] (1832) 1 C. & M. at 52.

[2] *Merle v. Wells* (1840) 2 Camp. 413; *Mason v. Pritchard* (1810) 2 Camp. 436; *Bastow v. Bennett* (1812) 3 Camp. 220.

[3] *Mayer v. Isaac* (1840) 6 M. & W. 605; *Hargreave v. Smee* (1829) 6 Bing. 244; *Edwards v. Jevons* (1849) 8 C.B. 436 at 440; *Wood v. Priestner* (1866) L.R. 2 Ex. 66, 282, *Heffield v. Meadows* (1869) L.R. 4 C.P. 595; *Nottingham Hide, Skin, etc., Co. v. Bottrill* (1873) L.R. 8 C.P. 694. See also *Eshelby v. Federated European Bank* [1932] 1 K.B. at 266.

[4] *Eastern Counties Building Society v. Russell* [1947] 2 All E.R. 734 at 736, 739; *Coghlan v. Lock* (1987) 3 B.C.C. 183, PC; See also *Ankar Pty Ltd v. National Westminster Finance* (1987) 162 C.L.R. 549 at 561; *Chan v. Cresdon Pty Ltd* (1989) 168 C.L.R. 242; *Tam Wing Chuen v. Bank of Credit and Commerce Hong Kong Ltd* [1996] 2 B.C.L.C. 69, PC.

[5] In the *Tam* case, the Privy Council stated of the principle, described as an "argument", that " . . . the cases show that it can have some weight, even today . . . ".

[6] See, *e.g. Wheatley v. Bastow* (1855) 7 De G.M. & G. 261 at 279 *per* Turner L.J. and cases cited at n.2, above.

[7] See, *e.g. Coghlan v. Lock* (1987) 3 B.C.C. 183, PC; *Bank of Scotland v. Wright* [1991] B.C.L.C. 244.

[8] Compare the U.S. and Australian approaches noted in O'Donovan and Phillips (3rd ed., 1996), p. 218.

created immediate personal liability.[9] This was in order to take advantage of automatic insolvency set-off and in order to treat the loan to the company as having been repaid by such set-off.[10] In construing such collateral charge documents, there is no presumption against personal liability, but if the surety argues for such liability he

> " . . . must give a convincing account of why he did not write down what he intended."[11]

A letter requesting a person to deliver goods to a third party, and stating that payment will be promptly made, does not necessarily amount to a guarantee. It may appear from the terms of the document and the surrounding circumstances that a mere favour was requested and no liability intended to be undertaken.[12] But where an actual order is given, the person ordering must be liable either as principal or as guarantor.[13] Where a person guaranteed the "performance" of a contract which provided for the supply of goods, the terms of settlement being expressed by the clause "month's account and bill at 5 months," it was held that the guarantee was that the bills should be paid, not merely that they should be given.[14]

Construction with reference to surrounding circumstances and recitals

Guarantees are to be construed with reference to the surrounding **4–03** circumstances and the relative positions of the parties at the time.[15] However, evidence of surrounding circumstances must be restricted to " . . . evidence of the factual background known to the parties at or before the date of the contract, including evidence of the 'genesis' and objectively the 'aim' of the transaction."[16]

---

[9] *MS Fashions v. BCCI* [1993] Ch. 425; *Tam Wing Chuen v. Bank of Credit and Commerce Hong Kong Ltd* [1996] 2 B.C.L.C. 69, PC; *BCCI (No. 8)* [1997] 3 W.L.R. 909, HL.
[10] *ibid.*
[11] *Tam Wing Chuen v. Bank of Credit and Commerce Hong Kong Ltd* [1996] 2 B.C.L.C. 69, PC; See also *Re Conley* [1938] 2 All E.R. 127 at 128 *per* Lord Greene M.R. and 133–134 *per* Luxmoore J.
[12] *Bank of Montreal v. Munster Bank* (1876) 11 Ir. C.L. 47. See also *Faber v. Earl of Lathom* (1897) 77 L.T. 162 at 169.
[13] *Langdale v. Parry* (1823) 2 D. & R. 337.
[14] *Haymen v. Gover* (1872) 25 L.T. 903.
[15] *Horlor v. Carpenter* (1857) 3 C.B. (N.S.) 172 at 180; *Montefiore v. Lloyd* (1863) 15 C.B. (N.S.) 203; *Wood v. Priestner* (1866) L.R. 2 Ex. 66, 282; *Heffield v. Meadows* (1869) L.R. 4 C.P. 595; *Laurie v. Scholefield* (1869) L.R. 4 C.P. 622; *Burgess v. Eve* (1872) L.R. 13 Eq. 450; *Coles v. Pack* (1869) L.R. 5 C.P. 65; *Leathley v. Spyer* (1870) L.R. 5 C.P. 595; *Nottingham Hide, Skin, etc. Co. v. Bottrill* (1873) L.R. 8 C.P. 694; *Morrell v. Cowan* (1877) 6 Ch D 166; 7 Ch D 151. And see *Carr v. Montefiore* (1864) 5 B. & S. 408; *Grahame v. Grahame* (1887) 19 L.R.Ir. 249. In *Hyundai Shipbuilding & Heavy Industries Co. Ltd v. Pournaras* [1978] 2 Lloyd's Rep. 502 at 506; Roskill L.J. said that the guarantee should be construed as a whole against "the factual matrix of the background." See also the approach of the Privy Council in *Coghlan v. Lock* (1987) 3 B.C.C. 183, PC and of Brooke J. in *Bank of Scotland v. Wright* [1991] B.C.L.C. 244.
[16] *per* Lord Wilberforce in *Prenn v. Simmonds* [1971] 1 W.L.R. 1381 at 1385, applied to guarantees by Scott J. in *Perrylease Ltd v. Imecar AG* [1988] 1 W.L.R. 463 at 470.

The condition, expressed in general terms, of a bond given by a surety will be restricted in construction by a recital qualifying the nature or duration of the principal engagement.[17] Upon a similar principle a promise in general terms contained in a letter or other inartificial document may be cut down by the words in which the request or the consideration is expressed.[18] A guarantee for the price of work "done and to be done" was held to be limited to the work included in an estimate shown to the guarantor before he became liable, and not to include extra work ordered afterwards.[19]

Guarantee by estoppel

4–04   A contract of guarantee cannot be created by estoppel.[20] However, a similar result was achieved in *Amalgamated Investment & Property Co. Ltd (in liq.) v. Texas Commerce International Bank Ltd.*[21] In that case a guarantee was signed by a parent company in respect of a loan expected to be made to its subsidiary by a bank. For exchange control reasons, the loan was actually made via a subsidiary of the bank. The expectation of all parties was that this loan would be covered by the guarantee and the bank acted on that basis. The guarantor made representations to the bank as to this perceived effect of the guarantee and this had confirmed the bank's own mistaken belief. The bank later realised security belonging to the guarantor and applied part of the proceeds to the liability under the relevant loan. This was challenged by the liquidator of the guarantor. The Court of Appeal were unanimous in upholding the bank's right to apply the monies. The minority would not have allowed the bank to sue under the guarantee, but the majority would. One ground for the decision of the majority was estoppel by convention, based on the fact that the parties had proceeded on the common basis that the guarantee covered the loan made by the subsidiary of the bank. This width of this principle was disapproved of in a subsequent Court of Appeal case.[22]

[17] *Lord Arlington v. Merricke* (1672) 2 Williams' Saund. 411a; *Horton v. Day* cited *ibid.* at 414; *African Co. v. Mason* cited in *Stibbs v. Clough* (1733) 1 Str. 227; *Barker v. Parker* (1786) 1 T.R. 287; *Pearsall v. Summersett* (1812) 4 Taunt. 593; *Liverpool W.W. Co. v. Atkinson* (1805) 6 East. 507; *Webb v. James* (1840) 7 M. & W. 279; *Napier v. Bruce* (1842) 8 C. & F. 470; *Chapman v. Beckinton* (1842) 3 QB 703; *Re Medewe's Trusts* (1859) 26 Beav. 588. The conditions of fidelity bonds are often explained in the recital. See the above cases and also *London Assurance Co. v. Bold* (1844) 6 QB 514; *Danby v. Coutts & Co.* (1885) 29 Ch D 500.
[18] See *Smith v. Brandram* (1841) 2 M. & Gr. 244; *Morrell v. Cowan* (1877) 6 Ch D 166; 7 Ch D 151. In *National Bank of New Zealand Ltd v. West* [1978] 2 N.Z.L.R. 451 a standard form bank guarantee was restrictively interpreted on the basis of a recital referring to consideration.
[19] *Plastic Decoration Co. v. Massey-Mainwaring* (1895) 11 T.L.R. 205. *Cf. Mann, Taylor & Co. v. Royal Bank of Canada* (1935) 40 Com. Cas. 267.
[20] *Amalgamated Investment & Property Co. Ltd (in liq.) v. Texas Commerce International Bank Ltd* [1982] QB 84, CA.
[21] [1982] QB 84, CA.
[22] *Keen v. Holland* [1984] 1 W.L.R. 251 at 261–262.

It now seems that estoppel "by convention" of this type requires not only (a) that the parties should have established by their construction of a guarantee, or their apprehension as to its legal effect, a conventional basis upon which they have regulated their subsequent dealings,[23] but also (b) one party should have made a representation across the line between the parties which produced some belief or expectation in the mind of the other party in circumstances which would make it wrong to allow the representor to challenge the belief or expectation he has engendered.[24]

Estoppel by recital

A surety is not estopped by a recital in a guarantee if it was **4-05** included as the statement of the creditor and not of the surety.[25]

If the obligation is expressly carried beyond the recital, it must have effect.[26] The question is in every case whether it can be collected from the recital that the intention of the parties requires that the condition should be qualified.[27] Where a bond recited that the obligees, bankers, had agreed to make advances not exceeding a certain amount, it was held that the condition, which was for the repayment of such advances, could not be read as making the security conditional on the amount not being exceeded, though, of course, it was limited to that amount.[27] And where the recital is only explanatory of the motive of the principal in requesting credit, the condition must not be read as applying only to the transactions referred to as part of such explanation,[28] as where it was recited that advances were required by C to continue the business of a late firm, but the operative words of guarantee included all C's debts to the obligee in respect of his trade and commerce.[29] But if the bond recites duties to be performed by the principal under a certain agreement referred to, and then is conditioned for his discharge of all his duties under that agreement, the engagement of the surety is nevertheless restricted to the duties recited, at any rate where the surety has no notice of the whole terms of the agreement.[30]

---

[23] *Amalgamated Investment & Property Co. Ltd (in liq.) v. Texas Commerce International Bank Ltd* [1982] QB 84, CA; *Keen v. Holland* [1984] 1 W.L.R. 251 at 261F–G; *Coghlan v. Lock* (1985) 4 N.S.W.L.R. 458 (affirmed on other grounds, (1987) 3 B.C.C. 183, PC; *Eslea Holdings Ltd v. Butts* (1986) 6 N.S.W.L.R. 175.

[24] *The Augustus Leonhardt* [1985] 2 Lloyd's Rep. 29, CA; *Eslea Holdings Ltd v. Butts* (1986) 6 N.S.W.L.R. 175; *Bank of Scotland v. Wright* [1990] B.C.C. 663.

[25] See *Greer v. Kettle* [1938] A.C. 156, HL; *Bank of Scotland v. Wright* [1990] B.C.C. 663 at 678; *Anglo-Canadia Bank Ltd v. London & Provincial Marine Co. Ltd* (1904) 20 T.L.R. 665.

[26] *Sansom v. Bell* (1809) 2 Camp. 39; *Bank of British N. America v. Cuvillier* (1861) 4 L.T. 159; *Saunders v. Taylor* (1829) 9 B. & C. 35; *Dumbell v. Isle of Man Ry* (1880) 42 L.T. 945.

[27] *Parker v. Wise* (1817) 6 M. & S. 239 at 247; *Australian Joint Stock Bank v. Bailey* [1899] A.C. 396.

[28] *Bank of British N. American v. Cuvillier* (1861) 4 L.T. 159.

[29] *ibid.* And see *Dumbell v. Isle of Man Ry* (1880) 42 L.T. 745.

[30] *Napier v. Bruce* (1842) 8 C. & F. 470. And see *Pemberton v. Oakes* (1827) 4 Russ. 154; *Chapman v. Beckinton* (1842) 3 QB 703.

Guarantees for officers

4–06   A guarantee for the performance of the duties of an office created by law, or owed to an officer or body created by law, must be construed with reference to the duration, incidents and character of the office according to the then law.[31] So a bond for the payment over of moneys collected for commissioners of sewers was held applicable to moneys collected under a commission which had expired before the date of the bond, the court taking notice of the fact that the commissioners to whom the bond was given were entitled to receive the moneys outstanding when they took office.[32] On the other hand, the duration of the guarantee will prima facie be confined to the period for which the office is by law held, and will not cover the officer if re-elected[33]; nor, speaking generally, will it cover the officer when his duties or position have been changed by law, even in respect of matters not specially mentioned in the guarantee.[34]

Guarantees for performance of contractual duties

4–07   A guarantee for the performance of duties resting merely on contract must be construed in favour of the creditor with reference to the actual terms of that contract, being one which comes within the general scope of the guarantee, although not specifically agreed to by the surety.[35] Also in favour of the surety it must be taken to embody all the essential terms of that contract, material to his risk, though not specifically contracted for by the surety[36]—that is to say, all the terms that may affect, not merely that do affect, his position.[37]

The canons of construction applicable to guarantees and the rules governing the reference to surrounding circumstances and the admission of parol evidence for that purpose, deal, of course, only with those documents which on the face of them are guarantees.[38] Where a promissory note or common money bond has been given to secure the existing or future debt of another, the terms on which it was given, and the debt it was to cover, are matters entirely for

---

[31] See *McGahey v. Alston* (1836) 1 M. & W. 386. Fidelity bonds, not having principal debtors, are not within the Statute of Frauds.

[32] *Saunders v. Taylor* (1829) 9 B. & C. 35.

[33] See below.

[34] See part 8 of this Chapter.

[35] *Simpson v. Manley* (1831) 2 C. & J. 12; *Coombe v. Woolf* (1832) 8 Bing. 156; *Howell v. Jones* (1834) 1 C.M. & R. 97 at 107; *Grahame v. Grahame* (1887) 19 L.R.Ir. 249.

[36] *Holme v. Brunskill* (1878) 3 Q.B.D. 499 at 505; *Croydon Gas Co. v. Dickinson* (1876) 2 C.P.D. 46; *Sanderson v. Aston* (1873) L.R. 8 Ex. 73.

[37] *Holme v. Brunskill*, above. See below.

[38] For an interesting example of the evidence required to convert an indemnity ("deficiency agreement" by a vendor of commercial premises to make up underpayment of rent by tenants) into a guarantee, see *Royal Trust Co. v. Pacific Petroleum Ltd* (1967) 63 D.L.R. (2d) 255, citing the last edition of this work.

parol evidence.[39] It is not here a question of the construction of a written promise, but merely of the debt to which it refers.

Surety liable on joint contract

The legal incidents of a joint contract are not modified by the **4–08** circumstance that one of the joint debtors is a surety.[40] If therefore either dies, the remedy of the creditor survives against the other only, whether principal[41] or surety.[42] It formerly followed that if judgment was recovered against either upon the joint contract the creditor could not afterwards sue the other.[43] But in England this rule has been abolished and under section 3 of the Civil Liability (Contribution) Act 1978 judgment recovered against any person liable in respect of any debt shall not be a bar to an action against any other person jointly liable with him in the same debt. Where surety and principal are not bound by a joint contract, recovery of judgment against one party is no bar to an action against the other.[44]

2. *Retrospective or Prospective*

The first question upon the promise in a guarantee is whether it **4–09** covers a past or future debt. If an existing debt is recited, mere general words will not extend the obligation to future debts,[45] but express mention of them will, of course, do so.[46] If future debts only are recited, mere general words will not make the guarantee also retrospective.[47]

When words used are ambiguous

The principles of construction applicable, where the difficulty **4–10** arises from the use of words of doubtful tense, have already been

---

[39] *Ex p. Brook* (1815) 2 Rose 334; *Henniker v. Wigg* (1843) 4 QB 792; *Hartland v. Jukes* (1863) 1 H. & C. 667; *Macrory v. Scott* (1850) 5 Exch. 907; *Re Boys* (1870) L.R. 10 Eq. 467.
[40] But the principal debtor will not necessarily be a party to the surety's contract to be answerable to the creditor. See *Bain v. Cooper* (1841) 1 Dowl. (N.S.) 11 at 14 *per* Parke B.
[41] *Rawstone v. Parr* (1827) 3 Russ 424, 539; *Jones v. Beach* (1851) 2 De G.M. & C. 886; *Other v. Iveson* (1855) 3 Drew. 177; *Strong v. Foster* (1855) 17 C.B. 201. See also *General Produce Co. v. United Bank Ltd* [1979] 2 Lloyd's Rep. 255 for an illustration of a plaintiff's liability starting as that of a guarantor and continuing, after release of the principal debtor's liability, as that of a principal debtor. *Cf.* approach in *Khan v. United Bank Ltd* (May 22, 1982, CA Transcript No. 237 of 1981). Both these cases dealt with so-called letters of lien, construed as ordinary guarantees and held binding on the guarantor, even though on the facts the principal debtor had been deprived of its title to the principal debt and was therefore no longer indebted to the creditor. In the latter case, the Court of Appeal emphasised the commercial reality of the transaction.
[42] *Richardson v. Horton* (1843) 6 Beav. 185.
[43] See *King v. Hoare* (1844) 13 M. & W. 494. But *cf. Wegg-Prosser v. Evans* [1894] 2 QB 101; [1895] 1 QB 108.
[44] *Bermondsey v. Ramsey* (1871) L.R. 6 C.P. 247 at 252.
[45] *Pearsall v. Summersett* (1812) 4 Taunt 593.
[46] *Sansom v. Bell* (1809) 2 Camp. 39.
[47] *Morrell v. Cowan* (1877) 6 Ch D 166; 7 Ch D 151. But see *Wilson v. Craven* (1841) 8 M. & W. 584. and *cf. Napier v. Bruce* (1842) 8 C. & F. 470.

discussed, and all the cases dealt with in the chapter on consideration, and it is sufficient here to refer to that chapter.[48] Of course a future credit may be the consideration for a guarantee exclusively for a past debt and not including the future debt.[49] But where continuing credit, resulting in a fresh debt, is the consideration, the guarantee prima facie covers the future debt.[50] If in such a case it is intended that a past debt should also be included, that must be clearly expressed.[51]

Where a bond was given, conditioned for payment over to commissioners of sewers of moneys already received, or to be thereafter received, by a collector on their account, reciting the appointment by the then commissioners, under which the collector would be entrusted to receive various moneys, it was held that this security was applicable to moneys received under a commission which had expired before the date of the bond, the court observing that the commissioners were entitled to the balances due to their predecessors.[52]

In *Morrell v. Cowan*,[53] the guarantee was: "in consideration of you having at my request agreed to supply and furnish goods to M. M. Cowan, I hereby guarantee to you the sum of £500. This guarantee is to continue in force for a period of six years and no longer." At the date of the guarantee there was money owing to the principal for goods already supplied in consequence of which further supply had been refused. The Court of Appeal, reversing Fry J., held that the guarantee was prospective only. In *Glyn v. Hertel*[54] the guarantee was "I will be answerable to the extent of £5,000 for the use of the House of S. & Co." It was treated throughout the case as being prospective only.[55]

A guarantee under seal, given by a father to a banking company in consideration of their discounting a note for £2,000 given by him to his son, and of the sum of 5s., by which the father undertook liability for all money due or to become due from the son to the company on any account whatsoever, was held to cover not only the £2,000 but also a large sum then already due to the bank, as well as further advances beyond the £2,000.[56]

4–11   In *Chalmers v. Victors*[57] a promise "to be responsible for liabilities incurred by AB to the extent of £50," the fact being that AB was then indebted to the extent of £41 was construed as a guarantee

[48] See also *Woolley v. Jennings* (1826) 5 B. & C. 165.
[49] See above, Chapter 2.
[50] *Mayer v. Isaac* (1840) 6 M. & W. 605; *Wood v. Priestner* (1866) L.R. 2 Ex. 66, 282.
[51] *Morrell v. Cowan* (1877) 6 Ch D 166; 7 Ch D 151. Cf. *Brunning v. Odhams Bros* (1896) 13 T.L.R. 65. But see *Wilson v. Craven* (1841) 8 M. & W. 584 and cf. *Napier v. Bruce* (1842) 8 C. & F. 470.
[52] *Saunders v. Taylor* (1829) 9 B. & C. 35.
[53] (1877) 6 Ch D 166; 7 Ch D 151.
[54] (1818) 2 Moore 134.
[55] See *ibid.* at 151, *per* Dallas C.J.
[56] *Burgess v. Eve* (1872) L.R. 13 Eq. 450.
[57] (1868) 18 L.T. 481.

of a future indebtedness which, with the existing debt, should make up £50.[58]

In *Re Medewe's Trust*,[59] a deed recited that there was a considerable balance due on three banking accounts, and that "the bank having required security for the balance due on the said several banking accounts," M had agreed to charge his estate with the payment of the balance of all the said several accounts limited to £3,000. The deed then charged M's estate with the three several sums of money which should or might be found due on the balance of the said several accounts, not exceeding £3,000. It was held to apply to the existing balances only, and the charge was extinguished by the satisfaction under the rules in *Clayton's Case*[60] of the existing debit items.

Where a bond conditioned for the payment of money with interest from the date of the bond is executed by a surety, this prima facie applies only to a present debt. It might be given as security for a future advance or for an ultimate balance, but if so it must be proved that the surety has so agreed.[61] It is not enough in the case of such a bond to prove that the principal delivered it to the creditor as such.[62]

A guarantee for the price of goods to be supplied covers goods contracted for before the guarantee if not delivered till after.[62] It has been held in Ireland that sureties for a Clerk to an Urban District council were liable for sums embezzled before the date of their bond, although the bond was only for the future good behaviour of the clerk, inasmuch as his failure to account for moneys so embezzled took place after the date of the bond.[63]

The Hyundai Shipbuilding cases

In *Hyundai Shipbuilding & Heavy Industries Co. Ltd v. Pournaras*[64] and *Hyundai Heavy Industries Co. Ltd v. Papadopoulos*,[65] the Court of Appeal and House of Lords respectively had to consider identical guarantees of instalments due from shipbuilders who had entered into shipbuilding contracts. On the wording employed, the guarantors guaranteed "the payment in accordance with the terms of the contract of all sums due or to become due by the buyer to you under the contract". In the first case there were instalments accrued due when there was a repudiation which was accepted by the builder and the contract was terminated. The Court of Appeal, construing the guarantee as a whole against "the factual matrix of

4–12

[58] (1864) 33 L.J. Q.B. 209.
[59] (1859) 26 Beav. 588.
[60] (1816) 1 Mer. 572.
[61] *Walker v. Hardman* (1837) 4 C. & F. 258.
[62] *Simmons v. Keating* (1818) 2 Stark 426.
[63] *Tullamore Urban District Council v. Robins* (1913) 48 I.L.T. 160.
[64] [1978] 2 Lloyd's Rep. 502.
[65] [1979] 1 Lloyd's Rep. 130, CA and [1980] 1 W.L.R. 1129, HL.

the background"[66] held that the true meaning of the guarantee was that if the buyer did not pay the instalments accrued due, the guarantor would.[67] This liability resulted on the true construction of the guarantee[68] despite the termination of the main contract.[69]

In *Hyundai Heavy Industries Co. Ltd v. Papadopoulos*,[70] there were two factual differences from the *Pournaras* case: first, in this case, the builder had invoked a contractual provision entitling him to retain any instalments paid, but which provision did not in terms deal with any rights to any instalments accrued due prior to cancellation under the provision and, secondly, the action against the guarantor in the *Papadopoulos* case was instituted before repudiation, whereas in the *Pournaras* decision, proceedings had apparently been issued after termination. The House of Lords followed the decision in the *Pournaras* case holding that the cancellation of the contract had not deprived the builders of their accrued rights to payments as against the guarantors.[71]

3. *Specific or Continuing*

General rule

4–13   A guarantee for a future debt may either be restricted to a debt of that amount to be incurred once and for all, or it may be continuing.[72] The construction will turn upon the wording of the individual contract, the principle being that the guarantee is continuing, unless either it appears that only dealings to the extent of the limit, which are then to cease, are contemplated, or the guarantor distinctly limits his undertaking to a definite transaction or to the first items of the credit amounting to the total named.[73]

---

[66] At 504. The commercial background was that there were "too many ships chasing too few cargoes so that those who had in more optimistic days entered into shipbuilding contracts were trying to escape from them, as were their guarantors." The purchasers were "one-ship Liberian companies" not thought to have substantial assets.

[67] Relying on passages from the speeches of Lords Reid and Diplock in *Moschi v. Lep Air Services Ltd* [1973] A.C. 331 at 344, 380. In that case the liability of the guarantor was to ensure that the principal debtor made certain instalment payments at a weekly rate.

[68] Another ground of the decision involving the guarantor's right to enjoy a right of set-off otherwise enuring to the benefit of the principal debtor is dealt with below.

[69] This decision is probably to be limited to the special background involved. *Cf.* the result in *Moschi v. Lep Air Services Ltd*, above, where it was held that after the main contract had been terminated as a result of a repudiatory breach, the guarantor's obligation continued, but was transmuted by operation of law into an obligation to compensate the creditor by way of damages for his loss.

[70] [1980] 1 W.L.R. 1129.

[71] *ibid.* at 1137F–1137H, 1142H–1143A, 1144B, 1144C, 1153A and 1153B.

[72] The term "revolving credit" is sometimes used of bankers' commercial credits. Such credits are not contracts of guarantee. But it would seem that the term "revolving" as applied to such credits has the same meaning as "continuing" applied to a guarantee.

[73] See *per* Alderson B. in *Mayer v. Isaac* (1840) 6 M. & W. 605 at 612 questioning the dictum of Bayley B. in *Nicholson v. Paget* (1832) 1 C. & M. at 52. See also *Merle v. Wells* (1910) 2 Camp. 413; *Mason v. Pritchard* (1810) 2 Camp. 436; *Bastow v. Bennett* (1812) 3 Camp. 220; *Woolley v. Jennings* (1826) 5 C.B. 165; *Edwards v. Jevons* (1849) 8 C.B. 436 at 440.

Continuing guarantees: examples

The following have been held to be continuing guarantees, but of **4–14** course in each case the circumstances under which the document was given influenced the construction put upon it:

> "I consider myself bound to you for any debt my brother may contract for his business as a jeweller, not exceeding £100, after this date."[74]

> "I hereby promise to be responsible to T.M. for any goods he hath or may supply my brother W.P. to the amount of £100."[75]

> "I undertake to be answerable to the extent of £300 for any tallow or soap supplied by B to F and B, provided they shall neglect to pay in due time."[76]

> "My son, G.C.D., is desirous of commencing business in your line and wants the usual credit for four or six months. If you think well to supply him I will be answerable for the amount of £100."[77]

> "I agree to guarantee the payment of goods to be delivered to S according to the custom of their trading with you in the sum of £200."[78]

> "Whereas W.C. is indebted to you in a sum of money and may have occasion to make further purchases from you, as an inducement to you to sell him such goods and continue your dealings with him I hereby undertake to guarantee you in the sum of £100, payable to you on default on the part of W.C. for two months."[79]

> "In consideration of your supplying A.L.V. with china and earthenware, I hereby guarantee the payment of any bills you may draw upon him on account thereof to the amount of £200."[80]

> "In consideration of your extending the credit already given to T.H., and agreeing to draw upon him at 3 months from first of

---

[74] *Merle v. Wells* (1910) 2 Camp. 413.
[75] *Mason v. Pritchard* (1810) 2 Camp. 436, *cf. Weston v. Empire Assurance Corporation* (1868) 19 L.T. 305.
[76] *Bastow v. Bennett* (1812) 3 Camp. 220. See also *Grahame v. Grahame* (1887) 19 L.R. Ir. 249.
[77] *Dry v. Davy* (1839) 10 A. & E. 30.
[78] *Hargreave v. Smee* (1829) 6 Bing. 244.
[79] *Allan v. Kenning* (1833) 9 Bing. 618.
[80] *Mayer v. Isaac* (1840) 6 M. & W. 605.

the following month for all goods purchased up to the 20th of the preceding month, I hereby at your request guarantee the payment and agree to pay you any sum that shall be due and owing to you upon his account for goods supplied."[81]

"In consideration of your agreeing to supply goods to F.K. at 2 months' credit, we agree to guarantee his present or any future debt with you to the amount of £60."[82]

"In consideration of the credit given by the H.G. Co. to J.P. for coal supplied by them to him, I hereby hold myself responsible as a guarantee to them for the sum of £100, and in default of his payment of any accounts due I bind myself by this note to pay to the H.G. Co. whatever may be owing to an amount not exceeding the sum of £100."[83]

"I, T.M. will be answerable for £50 sterling that W.Y., butcher, may buy of J.H." [It appeared from the surrounding circumstances that a continued supply of stock by the plaintiff, a dealer, to the principal, a butcher, was contemplated.][84]

"In consideration of the Union Bank agreeing to advance and advancing to R. & Co. any sum or sums of money they may require during the next 18 months, not exceeding in the whole £1,000, we guarantee the payment of any such sum as may be owing to the said bank at the expiration of the said period of 18 months and hereby undertake to pay the same on demand in the event of R. & Co. making default in the payment of the same."[85]

In reply to a request for a guarantee for the price of particular goods to be supplied by the plaintiffs to D, the defendants wrote giving such guarantee and adding:

" . . . having every confidence in him, he has but to call upon us for a cheque and have it with pleasure for any account he may have with you." The plaintiffs afterwards supplied still further goods to D. It was held that they were also covered by the guarantee.[86]

"We request you to accept the drafts of W.P.L in your London House at 60 days' sight to the extent of £1,000 and we

[81] *Hitchcock v. Humfry* (1843) 5 M. & Gr. 559.
[82] *Makin v. Wright* (1845) 6 QB 917.
[83] *Wood v. Priestner* (1866) L.R. 2 Ex. 66, 282.
[84] *Heffield v. Matthews* (1869) L.R. 4 C.P. 595.
[85] *Laurie v. Scholefield* (1869) L.R. 4 C.P. 622.
[86] *Nottingham Hide, Skin, etc. Co. v. Bottrill* (1873) L.R. 8 C.P. 694. See also *Burgess v. Eve* (1872) L.R. 13 Eq. 450.

undertake to provide you with funds to meet such acceptances before maturity."[87]

Non-continuing guarantees: examples

The following have been held not to be continuing guarantees: **4–15**

"You may let L. have coals to £50 for which I will be answerable at any time."[88]

"I.V., hereby engages to be responsible for liabilities incurred by M. & V. to the extent of £50 to A. & Co."[89]

"I engage to guarantee payment of A.M. to the extent of £60 at quarterly account, bill two months, for goods to be purchased by him of W. & D. M."[90]

"I hereby agree to be answerable to K. for the amount of five sacks of flour to be delivered to W.T. payable in one month."[91]

"I hereby agree to be answerable for the payment of £50 from T.L., in case T.L. does not pay for the gin, etc., which he receives from you and I will pay the amount."[92]

"You having agreed to advance to Messrs. H. S. & Co. a sum not exceeding £,000 on deposit of their lease ... and policies ... we hereby undertake and agree to guarantee, and indemnify you to the extent of £800 each, or to the extent of a sixth part of any deficiency of the said advance that may remain due to you after the sale of the said lease; this undertaking being given on the understanding that the said lease shall be sold and the purchase money realised before we are severally called upon for the deficiency (if any) and that this guarantee shall last for a period not exceeding two years from this date."[93]

Where amount is limited

A limitation of the amount risked by the surety, whatever its **4–16**
form, does not prevent a guarantee being continuing so as to cover

---

[87] *Browning v. Baldwin* (1879) 40 L.T. 248. See also *Simpson v. Manley* (1831) 2 C. & J. 12; *Australian Joint Stock Bank v. Bailey* [1899] A.C. 396.
[88] *Bovill v. Turner* (1815) 2 Chit. 205.
[89] *Chalmers v. Victors* (1868) 18 L.T. 481.
[90] *Melville v. Hayden* (1820) 3 B. & Ald. 593.
[91] *Kay v. Groves* (1829) 6 Bing. 276.
[92] *Nicholson v. Paget* (1832) 1 C. & M. 48. But see *Mayer v. Isaac* (1840) 6 M. & W. 605.
[93] *City Discount Co. v. McLean* (1874) L.R. 9 C.P. 692.

to the extent named the balance ultimately due from the debtor. Where, however, the limiting words are meant to define a particular transaction contemplated, a guarantee is not continuing. For instance, a bond reciting a general agreement by the obligees, as bankers, to discount bills and pay and advance money for the principal, and conditioned for the payment of the sums for the time being due, with a limit in amount, is a continuing guarantee.[94] But where, though the condition was general, the recital referred only to an agreement to advance a definite amount, the security was held not to be continuing.[95]

Promissory notes and bonds

4–17   Where a promissory note is given by a surety the presumption is that it is given to secure a definite advance or an existing debt, and it lies upon the creditor to show that it was intended by the surety to stand as security for the ultimate balance on a running account.[96] Where the document itself suggests the contrary, the material thing to show is not that the principal delivered it to the creditor as such security, but that the surety gave it as such.[97] The same applies where the document itself indicates that an existing debt is contemplated, as where a bond was conditioned for payment of a sum with interest from the date of the bond,[98] or that a definite advance is intended, as where a note was payable, not on demand, but on a future day.[99] The case of *Pease v. Hirst*,[1] where a promissory note payable on demand with interest was treated as a continuing security, is not inconsistent with this principle. It was taken there that the intention in fact was that it should be so. Moreover, in that case, even had it not been a continuing security, the result would have been the same, as the advance covered by the note was kept outstanding on the accounts notwithstanding subsequent credits.[2] Where the sureties in a bond after the date at which, if not a continuing security, the bond would have been satisfied by payments in account, wrote letters treating the bond as still available to cover the creditor, the court treated this as showing that it was always intended as a continuing security.[3] In any case, a collateral

---

[94] *Batson v. Spearman* (1838) 9 A. & E. 298. And see *Williams v. Rawlinson* (1825) 3 Bing. 71; *Parker v. Wise* (1817) 6 M. & S. 239; *Seller v. Jones* (1846) 16 M. & W. 112; *Gee v. Pack* (1863) 33 L.J. Q.B. 49; *Gordon v. Rae* (1858) 8 E. & B. 1065; *Henniker v. Wigg* (1843) 4 QB 792; *Laurie v. Scholefield* (1869) L.R. 4 C.P. 622.
[95] *Kirby v. Duke of Marlborough* (1813) 2 M. & S. 18.
[96] *Re Boys* (1870) L.R. 10 Eq. 467. See *Ex p. Brook* (1815) 2 Rose 334; *Walker v. Hardman* (1837) 4 C. & F. 258. Cf. *Ex p. Whitworth* (1841) 2 M.D. & De G. 164.
[97] *Walker v. Hardman* (1837) 4 C. & F. 258.
[98] *ibid.*
[99] *Re Boys* (1870) L.R. 10 Eq. 467.
[1] (1829) 10 B & C. 122.
[2] See too *Ex p. Whitworth* (1841) 2 M.D. & De G. 164.
[3] *Henniker v. Wegg* (1843) 4 QB 792.

memorandum between the parties defining the object of a promissory note, and what it was given to cover, will have effect given to it.[4]

In *Woolley v. Jennings*,[5] a warrant of attorney given by the debtors themselves, with the following defeasance[6]: "The within warrant of attorney is given to secure the payment of the sum of £4,000 with lawful interest thereon," was held a continuing security on the ground that there was nothing expressed to the contrary. This, however, was not the case of a surety at all, and the debtors who gave the warrant of attorney were, when they gave it, dealing upon a current account with the persons to whom it was given and to this account it was obviously applicable.

4. Limitations in Time

A continuing guarantee may either be subject to a limit of time **4–18** within which the liabilities which are to be covered by it must be contracted, and at the end of which it will expire *ipso facto* without any express revocation[7]; or it may be unlimited in that respect, in which case it will cover all liabilities falling within its scope, until put an end to, where that is possible, by revocation.[8]

Limitation introduced by recital

The condition of a bond given by a surety in general terms will **4–19** be restricted in construction by a recital qualifying the duration of the engagement of the principal. Thus in *Lord Arlington v. Mer-ricke*,[9] a surety bond reciting an employment of the principal for six months was conditioned for his due accounting during all the time he should be employed. The surety was held not liable for default after the six months. Similarly, where a bond was given to one of two partners to secure him against default by the other, the partnership, as was recited, being for five years, it was conceded that the bond only covered defaults in respect of matters occurring during those five years, though the partnership was afterwards to continue.[10] But a provision that on the death of a surety another is to be found will generally be read to be merely for the protection of the

---

[4] *Hartland v. Jukes* (1863) 1 H. & C. 667.

[5] (1826) 5 B. & C. 165.

[6] A collateral and contemporaneous deed containing certain conditions on the performance of which the appropriate bond, etc., is undone.

[7] What is here referred to is a maximum limit of time, which may not prevent the security being revoked before that limit is reached. There may also be a limit of time named as a maximum within which it shall not be revoked. This subject is discussed below, para. 4–33. For a case dealing with the construction of a guarantee of present and future performance see *Newman Industries Ltd v. Indo-British Securities Ltd* [1956] 2 Lloyd's Rep. 279, *per* Sellers J. and [1957] Lloyd's Rep. 219, CA.

[8] See below, paras 4–27 *et seq.*

[9] (1672) 2 Williams' Saund. 411a. See also *Horton v. Day*, cited *ibid.* at 414; *African Co. v. Mason*, cited (1733) 1 Str. 227; *Liverpool W.W. Co. v. Atkinson* (1805) 6 East. 507; *Sansom v. Bell* (1809) 2 Camp. 39; *Webb v. James* (1840) 7 M. & W. 279; *Bamford v. Iles* (1849) 3 Exch. 380; *N.W. Ry v. Whinray* (1854) 10 Exch. 77, *cf.* above, in part 1 of this Chapter.

[10] *Small v. Currie* (1854) 2 Drew. 102.

creditor, and the estate of the deceased surety (if otherwise liable) will not be discharged by a new surety becoming bound in pursuance of such a provision.[11]

In *Coles v. Pack*,[12] the guarantee was worded as follows:

> "I do hereby, in consideration of your forbearing to take immediate steps for recovery of the said sum (outstanding debts to the amount of £2,205.3s.9d., covered by a guarantee of the defendant), guarantee the payment of and agree to become responsible for any sum of money for the time being due from D.F. to you whether in addition to the said sum of £2,205.3s.9d. or not."

This was held unlimited as to time as well as in amount, and not confined to the time during which the sum involved was outstanding on the former guarantee.

Guarantees for officers appointed for fixed periods

4–20   A guarantee in general terms for the faithful discharge of duties of an office which by law is annual, or under an appointment made in fact for a year only, does not extend beyond the year,[13] although the legal period of the office[14] or the time for which the appointment has actually been made[15] is not recited; and the mere assent of a surety to a reappointment does not renew his liability.[16]

If, though the appointment is annual only, there are words in the bond expressly extending the surety's engagement to future years, they must, naturally, have effect,[17] as where the guarantee was for money to be received upon any reappointment to the office.[18] But mere general words such as, "at all times hereafter during the continuation of such his employment",[19] or a reference to the "successors" of the obligees,[20] or to "rates or taxes which might thereafter be imposed" which the officer would have to collect,[21] or to future statutes which might govern his duties,[22] being all capable

---

[11] *Re Ennis* [1893] 3 Ch. 238.
[12] (1869) L.R. 5 C.P. 65.
[13] *Wardens of St Saviour's, Southwark v. Bostock* (1806) 2 B. & P.N.R. 175; *Hassell v. Long* (1814) 2 M. & S. 353; *Curling v. Chalklen* (1815) 3 M. & S. 502; *Peppin v. Cooper* (1819) 2 B. & Ald. 431; *Leadley v. Evans* (1824) 2 Bing. 32; *Bamford v. Iles* (1849) 3 Exch. 380; *Kitson v. Julian* (1854) 4 E. & B. 854.
[14] *Wardens of St Saviour's Southwark v. Bostock*, above; *Hassell v. Long*, above.
[15] *Kitson v. Julian* (1854) 4 E. & B. 854; *Bamford v. Iles* (1849) 3 Exch. 380; *Mayor of Birmingham v. Wright* (1851) 16 QB 623.
[16] *Kitson v. Julian*, above.
[17] *Augero v. Keen* (1836) 1 M. & W. 390: *Mayor of Berwick on Tweed v. Oswald* (1856) 1 E. & B. 295; *Mayor of Dartmouth v. Silly* (1857) 7 E. & B. 9.
[18] *ibid.*
[19] *Liverpool W.W. Co. v. Atkinson* (1805) 6 East 507; *Peppin v. Cooper* (1879) 2 B. & Ald. 431; *Bamford v. Iles* (1849) 3 Exch. 380; *Kitson v. Julian* (1854) 4 E.& B. 854.
[20] *Leadley v. Evans* (1824) 2 Bing. 32.
[21] *Warden of St Saviour's Southwark v. Bostock* (1806) 2 B. & P.N.R. 175; *Hassell v. Long* (1814) 2 M. & S. 363; *Peppin v. Cooper* (1819) 2 B. & Ald. 431.
[22] *Mayor of Cambridge v. Dennis* (1858) E.B. & E. 660.

of being read as provisions for contingencies which might happen within the year, do not, if the office is annual, continue the liability of a surety beyond the year.

Guarantees for officers in other cases

If the office is not annual, but is held from year to year until **4–21** determined, the guarantee covers it until that event happens[23]; and this notwithstanding the fact that the superior officer who is secured by the bond is an annual officer.[24] The same applies with sureties for a tenant from year to year.[25] A mere reduction of salary corresponding to a reduction of duties, or a reduction of rent in consideration of the surrender of a small portion of the premises, do not of themselves constitute a determination of the office or tenancy and a reappointment or reletting, so as to prevent, on that ground, the guarantee continuing applicable.[26] But such a change might discharge the surety, as being a variation of the principal obligation capable of prejudicing him.[27]

Guarantees of tenancy

Where there is a surety for a tenant, and the tenancy is deter- **4–22** mined by a notice to quit, which is afterwards withdrawn, the surety is not liable in respect of the obligations of the tenant after the date for which the notice to quit was given, it being, after that date, a new tenancy.[28] But if the tenancy is brought to a close at the date on which the notice to quit would in fact have brought it to a close, if that had not been withdrawn, though it purported to be given for an earlier date, the surety is bound to the end of the tenancy.[29]

Guarantees of building work

Where directors of a construction company guaranteed losses **4–23** incurred by the creditor arising from defective work of the company in respect of houses sold over the next three years and defective work and sales took place within the three years, the directors were liable on the guarantee even though the losses from the defects were only established and quantified after the end of the three years.[30]

---

[23] *Frank v. Edwards* (1852) 8 Exch. 214.
[24] *McGahey v. Alston* (1836) 1 M. & W. 386; *Frank v. Edwards*, above.
[25] *Holme v. Brunskill* (1878) 3 Q.B.D. 495 at 504.
[26] *Frank v. Edwards* (1852) 8 Exch. 214; *Holme v. Brunskill*, above.
[27] This happened in *Holme v. Brunskill*, above. In *Frank v. Edwards*, above, the condition of the bond could alone be looked at; so this point could not arise.
[28] *Giddens v. Dodd* (1856) 3 Drew 485; *Tayleur v. Wildin* (1868) L.R. 3 Ex. 303. So where the guarantee was for the fidelity of the holder of an office who resigned and was reappointed at a larger salary: *Toames v. Foley* [1910] 2 I.R. 277. The effect of waiving a notice to quit served on a yearly tenant is to create a fresh tenancy: *Freeman v. Evans* [1922] 1 Ch. 36. The surety of rent of a business tenancy is not liable for rent accruing due for the period in which the tenancy is statutorily extended: *Junction Estates Ltd v. Cope* (1974) 27 P. & C.R. 482. See also Chap. 14.
[29] *Holme v. Brunskill* (1878) 3 Q.B.D. 495.
[30] *NHBC v. Fraser* [1983] 1 All E.R. 1090.

Guarantees to cover bills

4–24   Where a guarantee "to continue in force for a year" is given to secure repayment of moneys which may become payable by the acceptor of bills, or to cover other similar future contingent liabilities, the question will arise whether the limit of time applies to the maturity of the liability or to the transaction out of which it grows. It was decided in *Hollond v. Teed*,[31] upon such a guarantee that bills accepted payable before the date when it would have in the ordinary course expired were covered, although the guarantee was subsequently determined by the death of the guarantor before the maturity of the bills. It was expressly pointed out, however, that this did not decide what the effect would be if bills payable at a future date were accepted on the day preceding the contemplated expiry of the guarantee.

Termination of guarantee of bank facility

4–25   In *Westminster Bank Ltd v. Sassoon*,[32] Rowlatt J. and the Court of Appeal dealt with the case of continuing guarantee of a bank overdraft where the guarantee was expressed to expire on June 10, 1925, and where demand was made in October 1925. The guarantor argued that since she had heard nothing from the bank by June 10, 1925, she was free of liability. It was held by Rowlatt J. in forceful terms that the liability under the guarantee continued but was limited to the sum due as at the date on which the guarantee expired. This was upheld by a strong Court of Appeal, including Scrutton L.J., without even calling on the bank to argue.

In *Thomas v. Nottingham F.C.*,[33] a guarantor was held to have a right after giving notice determining his guarantee, even in the absence of a demand having been made on him, to require the principal debtor to exonerate him. The right of exoneration depended upon liability continuing after notice of termination had expired, despite the absence of any demand. It was held that the termination did not relieve the guarantor of liability for the position as it stood at the time of termination, but only meant that the guarantee would cease to operate for the future.

In *National Westminster Bank v. French*,[34] a continuing guarantee was terminable by three months' notice by the guarantor. The guarantee provided that the " . . . determination shall not affect the liability of the Guarantor for the amount recoverable at the date of the expiration of the notice". It was held that in this context

---

[31] (1848) 7 Hare. 50. See also *NHBC v. Fraser* [1983] 1 All E.R. 1090.
[32] *The Times*, November 27, 1936, CA, and Vol. V, *Legal Decisions Affecting Bankers* (1955 ed.), p. 19, upholding the decision of Rowlatt J. reported in *The Times*, June 8, 1925. Note *Wright v. New Zealand Farmers Co-operative Association of Canterbury* [1939] A.C. 439 where a guarantee for goods supplied was held to constitute a liability by the surety for the balance due from time to time up to the termination of the guarantee.
[33] [1972] 1 Ch. 596.
[34] unreported, October, 20, 1977, Robert Goff J.

"recoverable" meant "capable of being recovered" so that what was recoverable at the expiry of the guarantee was "any sum which falls within the scope of the guarantee which is outstanding from the principal debtor at the date of the expiration of the notice." It was held that a sum was "recoverable" even though demand had not been made as a matter of the natural and ordinary meaning of the expression.

In *National Westminster Bank v. Hardman*,[35] a similar situation **4–26** arose but the word "due" was used in the Scottish form of guarantee rather than "recoverable". It was held by the Court of Appeal that since no demand was made prior to termination, no sum was "due". This result seems not only unjust and impracticable, but appears to ignore a whole line of cases which point in the opposite direction.[36]

In *Royal Bank of Scotland v. Slinn*,[37] the guarantor was entitled to give one month's notice of termination. The notice was not to affect the liability of the guarantor in respect of the principal debtor's obligations at the date of the expiry of the notice. The Court of Appeal held that it was arguable that this left the guarantor liable in respect of a contingent liability of the principal debtor.

In *BCCI v. Simjee*[38] the result in *Hardman* was avoided by the Court of Appeal despite the wording of the guarantee being in many ways similar, by focusing on wording which was not present in *Hardman*, to the effect that the liability, save in respect of contingent, etc. liabilities, "crystallised", at the end of the notice period. The guarantor was liable for both crystallised actual liabilities of the principal debtor and for contingent liabilities existing at the time of termination.

Revocation of guarantees not under seal

A continuing guarantee not under seal for future advances or **4–27** supplies, in consideration of the granting of such advances or supplies, as it does not become binding until the person to whom it

---

[35] [1988] F.L.R. 302, CA. See the analysis and criticism of the decision in Marks, "Guarantees: The Rights and Wrongs of Determination" [1994] J.B.L. 124.

[36] *Westminster Bank Ltd v. Sassoon*, *The Times*, November 27, 1926, CA and Vol. V, *Legal Decisions Affecting Bankers* (1955 ed.), p. 19, upholding the decision of Rowlatt J. reported in *The Times*, June 8, 1925; *Wright v. New Zealand Farmers Co-operative Association of Canterbury* [1939] A.C. 439; *Thomas v. Nottingham F.C.* [1972] 1 Ch. 596; *National Westminster Bank v. French*, unreported, October 20, 1977, Robert Goff J.; *National House-Building Council v. Fraser* [1983] 1 AER 1090. But note the comment of Hobhouse L.J. in *BCCI v. Simjee*, [1997] C.L.C. 135, CA that it was the bank's own fault in the *Hardman* case if its standard form wording was not clear. It is suggested that the wording was clear in the light of the case law and indeed common sense—the construction put on the words in *Hardman* meant that the bank never had a sensible point at which to make a demand: a demand just a day prior to the date of expiry might miss an increase in indebtedness on the last day, whereas a demand even a day after expiry was too late.

[37] Unreported, Court of Appeal Transcript No. 259 of 1989 (March, 10, 1989).

[38] [1997] C.L.C. 135.

is given acts upon it, may be revoked before it is acted upon.[39] And even if it has been acted upon it may, if it contain no stipulation to the contrary, be revoked as to further transactions.[40] The reason for this as given by the Court of Common Pleas in *Offord v. Davies*,[41] is that each advance is a separate transaction, the view apparently being that the guarantee is divisible as to each advance, and ripens as to each advance into an irrevocable promise or guarantee only when the advance is made.[42] It has been held, too, that the acceptor of bills for the accommodation of another, who endorses them over, may reclaim the bills in the hands of the indorsee, if at the time they fall due there is nothing owing to him from the party accommodated.[43] But if not so reclaimed they will stand, if originally intended as a continuing security, as cover for subsequent advances.[43]

Where, however, a continuing guarantee for the price of future advances or supplies is under seal, this reasoning cannot apply. And it seems that at common law no right to determine a future operation of security exists in such cases.[44] In *Hough v. Warr*[45] it was suggested before Abbott C.J., that after receipt of notice of revocation the advances could not be considered as in fact made upon the guarantee. It was intimated, however, that the only relief was in equity, though the decision proceeded on the ground that at any rate the point ought to have been specially pleaded. It ought to be noted that in that case, as in other cases referred to above,[46] the guarantee was not for divisible advances or the like, but for the performance of the duties of an employment, to which special considerations apply[47]: but, apart from this, it is hard to see on principle how any bond or specialty guarantee could at common law be got rid of by a mere notice from the obligor.[48]

Principle in equity

4–28   But whatever may have been the common law rule, there seems no reason to doubt that in equity a guarantor in a continuing

---

[39] *Offord v. Davies* (1862) 12 C.B. (N.S.) 748.
[40] *ibid.* And see *Coulthart v. Clementson* (1879) 5 Q.B.D. 42 at 46; *Becket v. Addyman* (1882) 9 Q.B.D. 783 at 791; *Lloyds v. Harper* (1880) 16 Ch D 290 at 314, 318 and 320.
[41] (1862) 12 C.B. (N.S.) 748.
[42] See *per* Bowen J. in *Coulthart v. Clementson* (1879) 5 Q.B.D. at 46; *Lloyd's v. Harper* (1880) 16 Ch D 290 at 314, 318 and 320.
[43] *Atwood v. Crowdie* (1816) 1 Stark 483. See *Sturtevant v. Ford* (1842) 4 M. & Gr. at 106, note.
[44] *Hassell v. Long* (1814) 2 M. & S. 363 at 370; *Calvert v. Gordon* (1828) 7 B. & C. 809; 3 M. & Ry 124; *cf.* the report of this case in 7 L.J. (O.S.) K.B. at 77; *Hough v. Warr* (1824) 1 C. & P. 151.
[45] above.
[46] See note 44, above.
[47] See below, para. 4–30.
[48] See, too, *Burgess v. Eve* (1872) L.R. 13 Eq. 450 at 460.

guarantee under seal for future indebtedness can, where the consideration is "fragmentary, supplied from time to time, and therefore divisible,"[49] prohibit by notice the further use of the guarantee.

In *Burgess v. Eve*,[50] Malins V.-C., speaking of a guarantee under seal to a bank for future advances, said that he had no doubt that, if the guarantor found the customer untrustworthy, he was entitled, on payment of what had been advanced up to date, to get the guarantee back, and that advances made after notice not to advance more would in equity, upon the principle of *Hopkinson v. Rolt*,[51] not be chargeable upon the security. In *Beckett v. Addyman*,[52] where the guarantee was by bond, the court clearly thought that its continuance as a future security might be interrupted by notice to the creditor. In *Coulthart v. Clementson*,[53] and *Lloyd's v. Harper*,[54] though the instruments before the court in those cases were not under seal, the right to determine a guarantee is affirmed in general terms without anything to suggest that guarantees under seal were excluded. "It may be considered equitable and right," said James L.J., in the latter case,

> "that where a man is not under any obligation to make further advances or to sell further goods, a person who has guaranteed repayment of such advances, or payment of the price of the goods, may say, 'Do not sell any further goods or make any further advances. I give you warning that you are not to rely on my guarantee for any further advances which you make, or any further goods you sell.' That might be in many cases a very equitable view. It might perhaps be hardly equitable for a banker or merchant to go on making advances after receiving a distinct notice from a guarantor that he would not further be liable."

It is submitted that this reasoning applies to all guarantees, whether under seal or not, where the dealings between the principals, which may give rise to the liability guaranteed, can be at once put an end to; and that the right to determine is not subject to the rather vague limitation suggested in *Burgess v. Eve* that the principal must have been "found untrustworthy." Such limitation is only necessary in cases where, unless the principal has been "found untrustworthy," the creditor is bound to continue to trust him, and a continuing relation, created on the strength of the guarantee,

---

[49] *per* Lush L.J. in *Lloyd's v. Harper* (1880) 16 Ch D at 319; *Re Crace* [1902] 1 Ch. 733 at 738.
[50] (1872) L.R. 13 Eq. 450 at 460.
[51] (1861) 9 H.L.C. 514.
[52] (1882) 9 Q.B.D. at 791.
[53] (1879) 5 Q.B.D. at 46.
[54] (1880) 16 Ch D 290.

would be left uncovered by the determination, as a continuing security, of the guarantee.[55]

No revocation where consideration moves once for all

4–29   The right to revoke a guarantee by notice forthwith does not, however, exist where the consideration moves to the principal once for all; as where he was elected to a member of Lloyd's, which membership he was entitled to retain until he did some act which under the rules deprived him of his right to retain it,[56] or where he obtains a lease[57] or an office or employment which cannot be arbitrarily determined.[58]

A guarantee of the rent of a cottage held on a weekly tenancy has, however, been held to be revocable.[59]

Where principal has committed default

4–30   Where the principal has committed any defaults or breaches of duty, whether amounting to dishonesty or not, under such circumstances that the employer might have dismissed him, the surety is regarded in equity as entitled to call on the employer to dismiss him, even though the guarantee be under seal.[60] Upon the discovery of misconduct, the whole foundation for the continuation of the contract as regards the surety fails,[61] and the master, who knows that the surety anticipated good conduct, has no just claim to continue the employment at the risk of the surety in the altered circumstances against his will.

Whether surety can require principal liability to be determined by notice

4–31   It is an open question whether, if there is no misconduct, the guarantee must go on for an indefinite period or whether the

---

[55] See *Lloyd's v. Harper* (1880) 16 Ch D at 305, 306. The third edition of this work commented that the phrase "revocation of the guarantee' is apt to cause some confusion. The right of the surety is not so much to revoke the security (which, if it is a deed, is hardly intelligible) as to call upon the creditor not to give, and upon the principal not to take, further advances upon it. The principle depends, perhaps, upon the relation between the principal and the surety. The surety has the right to call upon the principal to pay off debts that have been incurred upon the guarantee and it seems only just, seeing that there is no consideration (in such cases as those above considered) between the principal and the surety, that the surety should be able to call upon the principal not to incur further debts. The creditor, being notified of this, and having no right on his part to insist on further advances being accepted by the principal suffers no wrong in not being allowed to collude with the principal further to charge the surety.
[56] *Lloyd's v. Harper* (1880) 16 Ch D 290.
[57] *ibid.* at 319.
[58] *Burgess v. Eve* (1872) L.R. 13 Eq. 450. As to offices held during pleasure see *Reilly v. Dodge*, 131 N.Y. 153; 29 N.E. 1011 (1892) discussed in Simpson, *Suretyship* (West. 1950), p. 56.
[59] *Wingfield v. de St Croix* (1919) 35 T.L.R. 432.
[60] *Shepherd v. Beecher* (1725) 2 P.W. 288; *Burgess v. Eve* (1872) L.R. 13 Eq. 450; *Phillips v. Foxall* (1872) L.R. 7 QB 666; *Sanderson v. Aston* (1873) L.R. 8 Ex. 73.
[61] *Philips v. Foxall*, above.

guarantor may not, to obtain his release, take advantage of provisions in the contract itself, performance of which is guaranteed, for its determination by the parties to it. It seems extraordinary that a surety for rent upon a tenancy from year to year should continue bound, and perhaps his estate after death,[62] during the joint lives of the landlord and tenant (which, if they are both corporations, might be for ever), because neither party will give notice to determine the tenancy; or that a surety for a servant must wait for and take the risk of alleging actual misconduct, and cannot take the more moderate course of asking that notice be given to determine the service.

This, however, seems to have been the view of Joyce J., in *Re Crace*, though the judgment on this point was *obiter*.[63]

What is sufficient notice of revocation

Notice determining the continuance of a guarantee need not by **4–32** law be in writing, but it is frequently stipulated in guarantees that it must be so; and so it may be specified that the writing shall fulfil certain conditions, as that it must be addressed to such and such person (especially if the creditor is a firm or company), or be signed by the surety, etc.[64] Further, it is often stipulated that the guarantee shall continue until a given period after notice of revocation shall have been given.[65] In such cases the right of revocation, at any rate where the guarantee has been once acted upon, must be limited in accordance with the stipulation.[66] A guarantee not under seal, which has not been acted upon can be revoked independently of any stipulation to that effect. This is because the transaction has never progressed beyond the stage of a proposal and there is no consideration binding upon the proposed guarantor.[67]

Right of revocation may be limited by express stipulation

It may, again, be stipulated that a guarantee shall continue for a **4–33** fixed period; or for a fixed period and, in default of a stipulated notice to determine it, a further fixed period; or for a series of fixed periods until determination by such notice or by such event as may be stipulated.[68] And such stipulation, where the guarantee is given

---

[62] See *Lloyd's v. Harper* (1880) 13 Ch D 290. *Cf.* below, para. 4–35.
[63] [1902] 1 Ch. 733, following *Gordon v. Calvert* (1828) 2 Sim. 253. See also *Burgess v. Eve* (1872) L.R. 13 Eq. 450, 459, 460; *Hassell v. Long* (1814) 2 M. & S. 363 at 370; *Calvert v. Gordon* (1828) 7 B. & C. 809 and 3 M. & Ry 124. But *cf.* report in 7 L.J. (O.S.) K.B. 77; *Hough v. Warr* (1824) 1 C.& P. 151.
[64] *Harris v. Fawcett* (1872) L.R. 15 Eq. 311; *Coulthart v. Clementson* (1879) 5 Q.B.D. 42.
[65] *ibid.*
[66] *ibid.* and see *Bradbury v. Morgan* (1862) 1 H. & C. 249.
[67] See *Offord v. Davies* (1862) 12 C.B. (N.S.) 748. *Cf.* above, para. 4–27.
[68] See *Solvency Mutual Guarantee Co. v. Froane* (1861) 7 H. & N. 5; *Solvency Mutual Guarantee Co. v. Freeman, ibid.* at 17. In *Egbert v. National Crown Bank* [1918] A.C. 903 the Privy Council held on the construction of the guarantee in that case that it was irrevocable except by notice given by all the guarantors, and that a notice given by one of them was inoperative. This decision is of importance in the context of revocation in the case of a guarantee by several guarantors. See the following section in the text.

in consideration of a reward payable to the guarantor, may be relied upon by the guarantor to enable him, if the guarantee has not been determined as stipulated, to recover his fee from the party liable to pay it.[68] But if it is intended that the guarantee should, in default of this agreed notice, run on indefinitely, from period to period, that intention should be clearly expressed. Where it was a condition that, from the expiration of the original term, the guarantee should "be treated as a renewed contract of the like nature and conditions," unless either party should give two months' notice of an intention not to renew, it was held that only one renewal, and not renewal from time to time, was meant.[69]

The ordinary phrase in a continuing guarantee to the effect that the guarantor guarantees for such and such a period repayment of advances, etc., made to the principal, does not import that the guarantee is necessarily to continue for that period, but only that it will *ipso facto* cease to be available for advances after that date. Consequently, in such a case the right to revoke before that period is not excluded by such language.[70]

Revocation in case of guarantee by several guarantors

4–34   Where a guarantee was entered into by several guarantors and provided that it should be continuing "until the undersigned or the executor of the undersigned shall have given the bank notice in writing to make no further advances," it was held that notice by only one executor was ineffective.[71]

Death of guarantor

4–35   As to the effect of the death of the guarantor by way of revocation of a guarantee, several difficult questions have arisen. In the case of a guarantee not under seal (whether continuing or limited to an isolated transaction) for further advances or supplies, where the making of such advances is the only consideration for the guarantee, and when there is no obligation to make them, the question will arise as to what is the result of the death of the guarantor before any advances are made. The guarantee at the moment of the death would seem to amount to an offer only, there being as yet no consideration to make it binding.[72] If, as has been assumed to follow from the decisions on questions of agency, an offer is revoked by the death of the maker *ipso facto*, though no notice of it reached the person to whom it was made before he accepts it by

---

[69] *Solvency Mutual Guarantee Co. v. Froane*, above.
[70] *Offord v. Davies* (1862) 12 C.B. (N.S.) 748.
[71] See note 68, above.
[72] See *Offord v. Davies*, above; *Coulthart v. Clementson* (1879) 5 Q.B.D. 42 at 46; *Beckett v. Addyman* (1882) 9 Q.B.D. 783 at 791; *Lloyd's v. Harper* (1880) 16 Ch D 290. It seems that the offer should be taken as intended to remain open notwithstanding the death, if unknown to the recipient of the offer.

performance, it might be said that in the case of such a guarantee the creditor would not be covered if he made the advances after, though without notice of, the death of the guarantor. However, in *Bradbury v. Morgan*,[73] there is a dictum directly to the contrary. "If the guarantee", said Bramwell B., "had been in these terms, 'I request you to deliver to A tomorrow morning goods to the value of £50, and in consideration of your doing so I will repay you', and before the morning the guarantor died, but the goods were duly delivered, I can see no reason why the personal representative of the guarantor should not be liable." In that case the guarantee had been acted upon, and the question was only as to the effect of the death of the guarantor as to further advances made subsequently. In such circumstances, at any rate, it is now settled that the death of the guarantor does not put an end to the continuance of the security, unless it comes to the knowledge of the creditor.[74]

Where, however, it does come to his knowledge, it was held by Bowen J., in *Coulthart v. Clementson*,[75] that the right to continue advances upon the security ceases unless the guarantee contains a provision for special notice not confined to the case where the guarantor is still alive. The principle followed by Bowen J., was that notice of the death of a surety, and that he left a will, is notice of the creation of new interests in the property liable to be applied in satisfaction of the guarantee, which cannot be assumed to be compatible with the continuance of the security, and the guarantee must, therefore, be taken to have been determined, unless the will has provided for its continuance. This reasoning, however, as pointed out in the Irish case of *Re Whelan*,[76] must apply *a fortiori* to an intestacy. The question of the effect of notice of the death of a surety in a continuing guarantee was treated as an open one in by the Court of Appeal in *Beckett v. Addyman*[77] and *Re Sherry*.[78] The reasoning of Bowen J. in *Coulthart v. Clementson*[79] has been disapproved by Romer J. and Joyce J.[80] but was acted upon by the Vice-Chancellor in Ireland in *Re Whelan*.[81]

Where the guarantee contains a stipulation that it shall be withdrawn only upon a certain notice from the guarantor, but the terms of such stipulations show that it can refer only to a notice given by the guarantor during his life, as where it has to be under his hand, the effect of notice of death of the guarantor is held not to be subject

---

[73] (1862) 1 H. & C. 249 at 255, 256.
[74] *Bradbury v. Morgan*, above; *Harris v. Fawcett* (1873) L.R. 15 Eq. 311; *Coulthart v. Clementson* (1879) 5 Q.B.D. 42.
[75] See n. 74, above.
[76] [1879] 1 I.R. 575.
[77] (1882) 9 Q.B.D. at 792.
[78] (1884) 25 Ch.D at 703, 705.
[79] (1879) 5 Q.B.D. 42.
[80] *Re Silvester* [1895] 1 Ch. 573 at 577 (where, however, there was a special provision for notice applicable after the death of the surety); *Re Crace* [1902] 1 Ch. 733 (where there was no such special provision).
[81] See n. 76, above.

in its operation to revoke the guarantee to the terms of the stipulation as to the length of the notice which the guarantor himself would have been required to give; and the revocation may therefore be immediate.[82] This is so even in cases where the stipulation as to the length of notice might be read as binding the executor, and the notice is to be taken as given at once if the principal is to the knowledge of the creditor the executor, and under a duty to the estate to terminate the guarantee.[83] But where there is merely notice of the death and of the existence of a will, it is not to be assumed that it would be a breach of trust to omit to give the special notice required, without which the guarantee by the terms of it runs on.[84]

Revocation by notice of the death of the guarantor, however, can only take place where the guarantee is such as, apart from special stipulation, might have been revoked by the guarantor himself at any moment.[85]

Death of surety only jointly bound

4–36   Where the surety is bound jointly with his principal, or with another surety,[86] and not severally also, his whole liability both for existing and future debts of the principal comes to an end with his death, and the survivor or survivors become alone liable both at law and in equity unless it can be shown that the security was made joint by mistake, and was intended to be joint and several.[87] But the death of one joint and several surety in a continuing guarantee for advances to be made does not, even when notified to the creditor, prevent the surviving surety remaining liable for further advances.[88] Nor does the death of one guarantor have such effect even if the guarantee was joint only, and not joint and several.[89]

The death of the principal debtor before he has committed default, discharges the surety, at least in circumstances where the obligation to the principal ceases upon death.[90]

Lunacy of guarantor

4–37   Lunacy of a guarantor operates as a revocation from the date of notice to the creditor.[91]

[82] *Coulthart v. Clementson* (1879) 5 Q.B.D. 42.
[83] See *Harris v. Fawcett* (1873) L.R. 8 Ch. App. 866.
[84] *Re Silvester* [1895] 1 Ch. 573.
[85] This appears to follow from *Re Crace* [1902] 1 Ch. 733.
[86] See *Pratt's Trustees v. Pratt* [1936] 3 All E.R. 901 on whether an equitable charge can be created between co-sureties.
[87] *Rawstone v. Parr* (1827) 3 Russ. 424, 539; *Jones v. Beach* (1852) 2 De G.M. & G. 886; *Other v. Iveson* (1855) 3 Drewr. 177.
[88] *Beckett v. Addyman* (1882) 9 Q.B.D. 783.
[89] *Ashby v. Day* (1885) 33 W.R. 631. This point was not dealt with in the Court of Appeal (1886) 34 W.R. 32 but see 54 L.T. 410.
[90] *Sparrow v. Sowgate* (1621) W.Jo. 29.
[91] *Bradford Old Bank v. Sutcliffe* [1918] 2 K.B. 833.

Bankruptcy of guarantor

It seems that the bankruptcy of a surety would not operate as the **4–38** revocation of a guarantee.[92] The discharge of a bankrupt principal debtor does not release any person other than the bankrupt from any liability, and such other person includes a surety or person in the nature of a surety.[93]

5. *Limitation in Amount*

Two forms of limitation

Besides a possible limit as to time, a guarantee may be subject to **4–39** a limit upon the amount for which the surety may be liable.

A distinction is drawn in the case law between cases where the surety guarantees part of an ascertained debt and cases where he guarantees the whole debt but subject to a limit on his liability.[94] In the former case, the payment of the amount guaranteed entitles the surety to be subrogated to the creditor's position to the extent of the payment, since he has discharged the whole of his liability to the creditor.[95] In the latter case, as long as any part of the whole debt remains unpaid, the surety, even if he has paid up to the limit of his liability is treated as not having paid the whole debt and is therefore not entitled to subrogation.[96] The rule is subject to the qualification that if the guarantee is of the whole of a fluctuating balance, a limited guarantee is construed as a guarantee of part only of the whole indebtedness.[97] Accordingly, a surety paying his limit can be subrogated even if part of the whole debt remains unpaid.[98] The rationale for this is that it would be inequitable to construe the guarantee so as to enable the creditor to permit the balance on the fluctuating account to go up in a way which causes prejudice to the surety.[99]

A common example of a limited guarantee of a fluctuating balance occurs where there is a guarantee of a bank current account. In such cases, bank standard forms of guarantee often exclude a surety's right to be subrogated upon paying merely the limit of his

---

[92] *Boyd v. Robins* (1859) 5 C.B. (N.S.) 59.

[93] s.281(7) of the Insolvency Act 1986. See formerly the Bankruptcy Act 1914, s.28(4).

[94] *Barclays Bank v. TOSG* [1984] A.C. 626 *per* Oliver L.J. at 643–644, where he stated that the distinction " . . . is not altogether easy to understand" and is one which " . . . may seem over-subtle" but which is " . . . clearly established by authority". See also *Ellis v. Emmanuel* (1876) 1 Ex. D. 157, where the previous authorities are reviewed and see also *Forster Dry Cleaning Co. Ltd v. Davidson* (1963) 187 E.G. 519; *Ulster Bank v. Lambe* [1966] N.I. 161; *Re An Arranging Debtor* [1971] N.I. 96.

[95] *Barclays Bank v. TOSG* [1984] A.C. 626 *per* Oliver L.J. at 643–644; *Re Butlers Wharf Ltd* [1995] B.C.C. 717. Subrogation is dealt with in Chap. 7, below.

[96] *Barclays Bank v. TOSG* [1984] A.C. 626 *per* Oliver L.J. at 643–644.

[97] *ibid.*

[98] *ibid. Ex parte Rushworth* (1804) 10 Ves. Jun. 409; *Gray v. Seckham* (1872) L.R. 7 Ch. App. 680.

[99] *Barclays Bank v. TOSG* [1984] A.C. 626 *per* Oliver L.J. at 644 G–H; *Ellis v. Emmanuel* (1876) 1 Ex. D. 157 at 163–164.

liability. There usually has to be an express exclusion,[1] since an exclusion will not readily be inferred from the form of the transaction.[2]

4–40 There is a dispute in the authorities as to whether the common provision in bank guarantees to the effect that the guarantee is to be in addition to and without prejudice to any other securities held from or on account of the debtor and that it is to be a continuing security notwithstanding any settlement of account is sufficient to exclude subrogation by the surety upon paying his limit.[3]

The distinction between guarantees of part of an indebtedness and guarantees of the whole debt but limited as to amount payable is not only important to questions of when rights of subrogation arise[4] but can be critical to the question of how far a surety can compete with the creditor and have rights to the creditor's security in the insolvency of the principal debtor.[5] Standard form bank guarantees often exclude the right of the surety to compete in this type of situation.[6]

Where a bond was given to a banker conditioned for the repayment of advances with interest and charges, with a proviso that the principal moneys to be recovered on the bond should not exceed £250, it was held by a majority of the Court of Queen's Bench that not more than £250 and interest on that amount should be recovered, and that the obligor was not liable for interest on the balance of the advances.[7] Where two persons by one instrument guaranteed "the sum of £400, in the proportion of £200 each," it was held that each was liable for a separate £200, but neither liable for more.[8]

Limitation introduced by recital

4–41 A limitation of the amount guaranteed may be introduced by the recital,[9] or, in a more informal document, by the terms of the request by the surety for the credit or advance to the principal, in consideration of which he promises,[10] even though the subsequent promise itself may be in general words. So where a surety wrote, "I beg that you will continue to advance the sum of £2 per week to Mr

---

[1] *Barclays Bank v. TOSG* [1984] A.C. 626 *per* Oliver L.J. at 644; *Hobson v. Bass* (1871) L.R. 6 Ch. App. 792; *Midland Banking Co. v. Chambers* (1869) L.R. 4 Ch. App. 398.
[2] *Barclays Bank v. TOSG* [1984] A.C. 626 *per* Oliver L.J. at 644; *Gray v. Seckham* (1872) L.R. 7 Ch. App. 680.
[3] *Barclays Bank v. TOSG* [1984] A.C. 626 *per* Oliver L.J. at 644 B–C suggested that such a provision is "probably sufficient", citing *Re Sass* [1896] 2 QB 12. However, this view was refuted in detail in *Re Butlers Wharf Ltd* [1995] B.C.C. 717 at 724–727. The latter case itself however may well have been in error in failing to find that on the very special facts of that case any entitlement to subrogation in competition with the bank creditor was impliedly excluded.
[4] Creditors' rights subrogation are dealt with in Chap. 7, below.
[5] These rights are dealt with in Chap. 11, below.
[6] *Re Butlers Wharf Ltd* [1995] B.C.C. 717 illustrates the dangers to banks of not excluding a surety's rights to share in the creditor's security upon payment of part of a debt.
[7] *Meek v. Wallis* (1872) 27 L.T. 650.
[8] *Fell v. Goslin* (1852) 7 Exch. 185.
[9] *ibid.*
[10] *Smith v. Brandram* (1841) 2 M & Gr. 244.

B, and I hereby engage to repay you all moneys you may advance to him in addition to the £24 which you have already let him have at my request to this date" he was liable only for the £2 per week and the £24 and not for other advances which had been made since the letter.[10]

6. *When the Liability of the Surety Attaches*

Guarantees for future advances or credit

A guarantee for which the consideration is a future advance, supply, or other credit, the forbearance of any existing liability, or the withdrawal of any existing process, is not binding until the creditor acts upon it,[11] and performs the consideration. The surety will become liable as soon as the consideration is performed without notice from the creditor of its performance.[11] Notice of the performance of an act upon which a liability is to arise need only be given where such act is unknown to anyone save the creditor, as where liability is to arise on his election to do or refrain from doing something.[12] Where the act is to give credit, discontinue proceedings, or even intimate that proceedings will be discontinued, no notice of performance need be given to the guarantor.

4–42

Acceptance of offer of guarantee

This is, however, true only of concluded guarantees. Where a letter is addressed by one person to another the true effect of which is only to offer a guarantee, the offer must be accepted, or notice given that the document is about to be treated as a concluded guarantee.[13] Where a guarantee is offered, and references named for approval, the person to whom it is addressed must give notice that he has approved,[14] or, or if he waives the references, must give notice that he waives them.[15]

4–43

7. *Parties*

Guarantees enforceable by trustees on behalf of others

A bond or guarantee, whether under seal,[16] or not, may be given to a trustee on behalf of third persons to secure the performance of obligations to those persons, as, for instance, obligations to be

4–44

---

[11] *Offord v. Davies* (1862) 12 C.B. (N.S.) 748; *Westhead v. Sproson* (1861) 6 M. & N. 728; *Morrell v. Cowan* (1877) 6 Ch D 166; 7 Ch D 151.

[12] *Alhusen v. Prest* (1851) 6 Exch. 720.

[13] *Melver v. Richardson* (1813) 1 M. & S. 557; *Symmons v. Want* (1818) 2 Stark. 371; *Mozley v. Tinkler* (1835) 1 C.M. & R. 692; *Morten v. Marshall* (1863) 2 M. & C. 309; *Bank of Montreal v. Munster Bank* (1876) 11 Ir. R.C.L.47; *cf. Sorby v. Gordon* (1874) 30 L.T. 528; *Gaunt v. Hill* (1815) 1 Stark 10; *Pope v. Andrews* (1840) 9 C. & P. 564; *Nash v. Spencer* (1896) 13 T.L.R. 78.

[14] *Mozley v. Tinkler*, above; *Morten v. Marshall*, above.

[15] *Morten v. Marshall* (1863) 2 H. & C. 305.

[16] See *Lloyds v. Harper* (1880) 16 Ch D 290.

incurred towards a shifting body like an unincorporated associa-tion,[17] or towards unknown persons,[18] or intending shareholders in a company,[19] or the persons to whom, whether members or not, the person guaranteed should be under liability in respect of business done at Lloyd's.[20] In such cases the obligee is bound to enforce the security for the protection of those concerned, and can recover for them the full damages which they have incurred.[20] So the holders of a guarantee given to them jointly can recover the amount of the default by the principal for the benefit of those among them whom it may concern, although no joint damage can be shown[21]; and one partner can sue alone on behalf of his firm upon a guarantee for a debt owing to the firm given to him alone.[22] This principle applies even when the obligee is not, strictly speaking, in a position of a trustee, provided that it appears from the instrument creating or evidencing the obligation that it was the intention of the parties to that instrument to protect the persons who have actually suffered the damage. It need not appear that the person so intended to be protected had any right to the protection or even was informed of it at the time. Thus, in the Irish case of *Kenney v. Employers' Liability Insurance Corporation*[23] the mortgagees of an estate appointed a receiver under their statutory power and took a bond from the defendants for the due discharge by the receiver of his duties as such. The receiver made default, but the mortgagees by selling the estate were paid their demand in full. It was held by the Irish Court of Appeal that the mortgagees could recover under the bond the amount of the default for the benefit of the mortgagor, notwith-standing that they were under no duty to the mortgagor to take the bond at all, or having taken it, to put it in suit on his behalf. With this case may usefully be contrasted *Re British Power, etc., Co.*[24] There a receiver and manager in a debenture holders' action prop-erly incurred and was held to be entitled to be indemnified by the estate against trade liabilities for £900, but was deficient in his cash account by £400 which he could not pay, and it was held that trade creditors had no rights against the receiver's sureties, inasmuch as their bond was given to secure the estate and the estate had suffered no loss.[25]

[17] *Metcalf v. Bruin* (1810) 12 East 400. *Cf. McGahey v. Alston* (1836) 1 M. & W. 386; *Worth v. Newton* (1854) 10 Exch. 247.
[18] *Lamb v. Vice* (1840) 6 M. & W. 467; *Stansfield v. Hellawell* (1852) 7 Ex. 373.
[19] *Hallet v. Taylor* (1921) 6 Ll.L.R. 416.
[20] *Lloyd's v. Harper* (1880) 16 Ch D 290. *Cf. Leathley v. Spyer* (1870) L.R. 5 C.P. 595. But see *Cosford v. Poor Law, etc., Association* (1910) 103 L.T. 463 at 465 *per* Phllimore J.
[21] *Pugh v. Stringfield* (1858) 4 C.B. (N.S.) 364.
[22] *Agacio v. Forbes* (1861) 14 Moo. P.C. 160.
[23] [1901] 1 I.R. 301; *cf. Robertson v. Wait* (1853) 8 Exch. 299.
[24] [1910] 2 Ch. 470; *cf. Re Barned's Banking Co., ex p. Stephens* (1868) L.R. 3 Ch. 753; *Sheers v. Thimbleby* (1897) 76 L.T. 709.
[25] The judgment is directed to the point that the trade creditors had only the rights of the receiver against the estate, but his was only material on the basis that the sureties were not liable except for loss to the estate, and as going to show that there had been no such loss.

Guarantees of minors' debts

In the case of guarantees of minors' debts it has been decided in **4-45** *Coutts & Co. v. Browne-Lecky*[26] that once a guarantee, as distinct from an indemnity is found to exist, no liability will attach to the guarantor for what is in essence no debt at all.[27] *Stadium Finance Co. Ltd v. Helm*[28] although in the result endorsing this view, appears to have involved a concession that the particular guarantee of a minor's void debt was unenforceable.[29] One resolution of this problem may be to treat such a guarantee as enforceable if the guarantor knew the debtor was a minor,[30] in which case his promise is in effect the assumption of primary liability, *i.e.* an indemnity.

Persons who may sue although not named in guarantee

Generally speaking, the person to sue on a guarantee must be the **4-46** person named therein as party[31] but a guarantee given to an agent, as representing his principal, for a debt due to his principal,[32] or given to a partner for his firm[33] may be issued upon by the principal or the firm, as the case may be. The benefit of a guarantee is usually assignable.[34]

Moreover, a letter of credit, written in order to be shown, promising to honour bills to be drawn upon the writer, particulars of which were to be endorsed upon the letter, constitutes an offer which will make the writer liable to persons who act upon it.[35] Where the defendant, upon the occasion of a run upon a bank, undertook, by a notice addressed to the inhabitants of the neighbourhood, to be accountable for the payment of the notes of the bank "so far as £30,000 would extend," it was held he could not be sued by an individual holder who had taken some of the notes after notice of the undertaking.[36] The discounters of bills accepted for the accommodation of the drawers cannot enforce a guarantee or indemnity,

---

[26] [1947] K.B. 104.
[27] See E.J. Cohn (1947) 10 M.L.R. 40. But note the suggestion in *Heald v. O'Connor* [1971] 1 W.L.R. 497 at 506 that the real question is whether on the true construction of the guarantee the guarantor undertakes to pay only those sums which the principal debtor could lawfully be called upon to pay or whether he undertakes to pay regardless of whether the principal debtor could lawfully be called upon to pay. See also Chap. 6, below.
[28] (1965) 109 S.J. 44.
[29] *per* Steyn, "The Co-Extensiveness Principle" (1974) 90 L.Q.R. 246 at 253.
[30] Steyn, *op. cit.* p. 253. See also Furmston (1961) 24 M.L.R. 644 who points out that the problem is now less important in practice than formerly and that in any event the appropriate documents ought to be drafted as indemnities to invoke the rule applied in *Yeoman Credit Ltd v. Latter* [1961] 1 W.L.R. 828 whereby the indemnifier of an infant's contract will be bound.
[31] But see *Alcoy, etc. v. Greenhill* (1897) 76 L.T. 542. *Cf. Brandt v. Dunlop* [1905] A.C. 454 at 462.
[32] *Bateman v. Phillips* (1812) 15 East 272.
[33] *Walton v. Dodson* (1827) 3 C. & P. 162; *Garrett v. Handley* (1825) 4 B. & C. 664.
[34] See *Wheatley v. Bastow* (1855) 7 De G.M. & G. at 279; *Re Barrington* (1804) 2 Sch. & L. 112; *Re Hallett & Co.* [1894] 2 QB 256; *British Union v. Rawson* [1916] 2 Ch. 476; *Bradford Old Bank v. Sutcliffe* [1918] 2 K.B. 837. *Cf. Sheers v. Thimbleby* (1897) 76 L.T. 709 *per* Chitty L.J.
[35] *Re Agra and Masterman's Bank* (1870) L.R. 2 Ch. App. 391. *Cf. Autocar, etc., Insurance v. London J.C. and M. Bank* (1924) 19 Ll.L.R. 292.
[36] *Phillips v. Bateman* (1872) 16 East. 356.

of which they had notice, given by third parties to the acceptors to protect them against liability.[37]

*Limited to transactions between the principals named:
Partnership Act 1890, s. 18*

4–47   Unless a contrary intention appears, a guarantee to or for a given person or number of persons will prima facie not cover debts incurred to or by such person or persons and others, or to or by some only of those persons,[38] nor to the executors of the original obligee,[39] even if a time was named for the continuance of the guarantee, and the debt was incurred within that time.[40] This rule in the case of guarantees given to or for firms, (with regard to which the question has mainly arisen) is now declared by section 18 of the Partnership Act 1890[41] which is as follows:

> "A continuing guaranty . . . given either by a firm or to a third person in respect of the transactions of a firm is, in the absence of agreement to the contrary, revoked as to future transactions by any change in the constitution of the firm to which, or of a firm in respect of the transactions of which, the guaranty . . . was given."[42]

Examples

4–48   The difficulty, both before the statute and since, has been to determine whether an intention that the guarantee shall continue sufficiently appears. Where a bond was given to trustees for an unincorporated association the changes in the membership of which were proved to number from 50 to 100 in a year, conditioned for the due accounting of a clerk "during his continuance in the service of the said company, to the said company or to such persons as the court of directors thereof for the time being should appoint . . . and for the indemnity of the said company and the directors and all the members thereof," it was held that the security continued notwithstanding changes in the members of the company.[43] There is no difficulty in providing by proper words that the security should

---

[37] *Re Barned's Banking Co., ex p. Stephens* (1868) L.R. 3 Ch. App. 753.
[38] *Wright v. Russell* (1774) 3 Wils. 530; *Myers v. Edge* (1797) 7 T.R. 254; *Bellairs v. Ebsworth* (1811) 3 Camp. 53; *Strange v. Lee* (1803) 3 East 484; *Dance v. Girdler* (1804) 1 B. & P.N.R. 34; *Weston v. Barton* (1812) 4 Taunt. 673; *Simson v. Cooke* (1824) 1 Bing. 452; *Dry v. Davy* (1839) 10 A. & E. 30; *Bank of Scotland v. Christie* (1841) 8 C. & F. 214; *Spiers v. Houston* (1829) 4 Bligh (N.S.) 515; *Chapman v. Beckinton* (1842) 3 QB 703; *Hollond v. Teed* (1848) 7 Hare 50; *Montefiore v. Lloyd* (1863) 15 C.B. (N.S.) 203; *London Assurance Co. v. Bold* (1844) 6 QB 614; *Mills v. Alderbury Union* (1849) 3 Exch. 50; *Backhouse v. Hall* (1865) 6 B. & S. 50.
[39] *Barker v. Parker* (1786) 1 T.R. 287.
[40] *Pemberton v. Oakes* (1827) 4 Russ. 154; *Chapman v. Beckinton* (1842) 3 QB 703; *Hollond v. Teed* (1848) 7 Hare 50.
[41] Replacing s.4 of the Mercantile Law Amendment Act 1856.
[42] The operation of this provision would be very inconvenient in practice and standard form bank guarantees often do contain an "agreement to the contrary".
[43] *Metcalf v. Bruin* (1810) 12 East 400.

continue notwithstanding a change in the persons intended to be secured.[44] The point is that the surety may rely on the discretion of a particular obligee or principal to prevent any loss occurring.[45]

Knowledge of intended changes in firms

The mere fact that a surety for an intended agent knows that the **4–49** agent is about to take a partner does not make him responsible for the default of the firm, unless the circumstances show that the surety contemplated that the firm was to have the agency[46] and where the surety is bound for an agent who has an existing partner, knowledge of that fact by the surety only makes clearer his intention to limit his liability to the acts of the agent personally.[47] So where a surety became bound for money to be received by a treasurer to guardians, and the guardians paid their money into an account of their own with a bank in which the treasurer was a partner, drawing cheques on that account for their payments, it was held that the surety was not responsible; and he recovered back a payment which he had made to the guardians in ignorance of the facts.[48]

But surrounding circumstances may show that the guarantee was intended to cover debts incurred by the principal named and his partner. Thus, in *Leathley v. Spyer*,[49] a guarantee given to the committee of Lloyd's to secure the debts which a proposed member might incur, had been revoked, and then afterwards renewed after the sureties had learned that the principal had taken a partner. By the rules of Lloyd's only one partner in a firm could be a member; but by means of a "substitute's ticket" another partner could deal for him. It was held that the guarantee as renewed covered the debts of the firm, whether resulting from dealings of the partner named in the guarantee or those of the other partner acting for him.[50]

Intention to cover credit to be given after change in firm to be clearly expressed

Similar to the principle declared by the Partnership Act 1890, it **4–50** has often been held that a guarantee is not extended to transactions entered into after a change in the creditors merely by the use of words which can be read as providing for the case of debts being incurred towards some of the obligees on behalf of all, or of

---

[44] See *Strange v. Lee* (1807) 3 East. 484.
[45] See *Myers v. Edge* (1797) 7 T.R. 254 at 255; *per* Mansfield C.J., in *Weston v. Barton* (1812) 4 Taunt. at 681, 682; *Backhouse v. Hall* (1865) 6 B. & S. 507 at 519; *Strange v. Lee* (1807) 3 East. 484 at 490.
[46] *Bellairs v. Ebsworth* (1811) 3 Camp. 53; *London Assurance Co. v. Bold* (1844) 6 QB 514; *Montefiore v. Lloyd* (1863) 15 C.B. (N.S.) 203.
[47] *Mills v. Alderbury Union* (1849) 3 Exch. 590; *London Assurance Co. v. Bold*, above.
[48] *Mills v. Alderbury Union*, above. And see *Lacey v. Hill* (1872) L.R. 8 Ch. App. 441.
[49] (1870) L.R. 5 C.P. 595.
[50] See also *Bank of British North America v. Cuvillier* (1861) 4 L.R. 159.

defaults being committed towards the new body arising out of transactions with the old.

A bond given to five persons, bankers, to secure repayment to the five, their executors or administrators, of certain advances to be made by them "or any of them," was held not to cover advances made by four of them after the death of one, the words "or any of them" being read as merely providing for the case of an advance made by some on behalf of the five.[51] The same applied where the condition was for repayment to the obligees, or "either of them," of all moneys advanced "at their banking house."[52] And where the bond was for advances to meet bills drawn by SC and TC (who were described in the bond as partners), "or either of them, or any other person authorised by them or either of them," it was held not to cover advances to meet bills drawn after the death of one of them.[53] Similarly, where the bond, reciting that ET had taken JH into his employment as "clerk to the said EP," was conditioned for due accounting by JH to "the said EP, his executors or administrators," it was held that these words did not extend the obligation to moneys received by the clerk after the death of the obligee and as the servant of the executors, but only to money in his hands at the date of the death.[54]

When the bond recited a co-partnership for a term of years between three persons, of whom one was to be acting partner, and was conditioned for the honesty of the acting partner "during such time as he shall continue the acting partner in the said trade or business of the said co-partnership," it was held that defaults after the death of one partner were not covered, although the time from which the partnership had been entered into had not expired, and the partnership deed contained provisions for the transmission of the share of a deceased partner and a continuance of the business.[55] Where a guarantee to a firm was expressly framed to cover debts which might be incurred to the survivors of the surviving partners, it was held that it did not apply after the death of one partner, where under his will and pursuant to the articles his representative assumed his share in the business and intervened in every way as partners.[56]

Where a bond, given for a firm of three, was expressed to cover also the defaults of the survivors or survivor of them, and of any future partners of them or either of them, it was held that defaults after the retirement of one of the original partners were not covered.[57]

---

[51] *Weston v. Barton* (1812) 4 Taunt. 673.
[52] *Strange v. Lee* (1803) 3 East 484.
[53] *Simson v. Cooke* (1824) 1 Bing. 452.
[54] *Barker v. Parker* (1786) 1 Term Rep. 287.
[55] *Chapman v. Beckinton* (1842) 3 QB 703.
[56] *Pemberton v. Oakes* (1827) 4 Russ. 154.
[57] *University of Cambridge v. Baldwin* (1839) 5 M. & W. 580.

In *Blackhouse v. Hall*,[58] decided after the Mercantile Law Amendment Act 1856, but before the Partnership Act, the guarantee was for advances to be made to "the firm of G.W. & W.J. Hall, shipbuilders." The business so described was really, as both plaintiff and defendant knew, carried on by S. Hall, E. Hall, and G. E. Moore. It was held that the mere use of the firm name in the guarantee did not show an intention that it should continue after a change in the then partners. But where a bond was conditioned for indemnifying certain plaintiffs against costs awarded to "the defendants," it was held that costs awarded to one defendant, the other having died, were covered by the words of the condition.[59] Where a guarantee was to extend to all the engagements of C to the obligee "in trade and commerce," it was held in the Privy Council that it covered debts incurred after C had taken in a partner.[60] Where a bond was given to the governors of an unincorporated society for due accounting by the collector of the society, to the governors or their successors, it was held that defaults after the society had been incorporated were not covered.[61]

Form of instrument intended to operate notwithstanding changes in firm

Where it is intended that a bond or guarantee should continue to enure for the benefit of a firm, notwithstanding changes in its composition, this should not perhaps, as a point of form, be specified in that part of the instrument which describes the obligees or addressees of the guarantee, for these cannot be a shifting body.[62] There is no objection to the persons to whom the debts secured shall be payable being a shifting body, and being so described in the condition of a bond or in the body of a guarantee; and the original obligees, or the survivor or his representatives, will be trustees to enforce the bond or guarantee for the creditors for the time being.[63] A promissory note payable to order and deposited with a firm to secure a debt may, of course, as a negotiable instrument, be enforced directly by the indorsees for the time being,[64] but, if not **4–51**

---

[58] (1865) 6 B. & S. 507.

[59] *Kipling v. Turner* (1821) 5 B. & Ald. 261.

[60] *Bank of British North America v. Cuvillier* (1861) 4 L.T. 159. The principal, who had previously carried on business with two others of whom one had died and the other was absent, apparently obtained the guarantee in order to carry on the business. It seems to have been contemplated that he would or might have partners. Their Lordships considered that the decisions upon changes in the construction of a firm had no bearing on the question in that case.

[61] *Dance v. Girdler* (1804) 1 B. & P.N.R. 34.

[62] *ibid*. A bond given to a firm by a firm name could be sued upon by those who were the members at the date of the bond; *Moller v. Lambert* (1810) 2 Camp. 548.

[63] See above, para. 4–44. The object of the parties is commonly attained by inserting a clause to the effect that the guarantee shall subsist notwithstanding changes in the parties secured. This in point of law operates on the theory explained in the text.

[64] *Pease v. Hirst* (1829) 10 B. & C. 122.

endorsed, it should be sued upon by the original payees or the survivors of them.[64] And it will be inferred that such a note given to a firm, upon the face of which the maker does not appear to be merely a surety, is intended to continue as security notwithstanding any changes in the firm.[64]

Amalgamation of companies

4–52   Where a bond was given to a railway company to secure the payment over of moneys to be received by a booking clerk at a station jointly used by that and two other railway companies for the three railways, the surety was held bound for defaults after the company to which the bond had been given had been by statute amalgamated with one of the others under the name of the latter, the statute likewise transferring the rights of action.[65] So, where two railway companies were amalgamated by statute, which enacted that the new company should be entitled to enforce all the bonds, etc., belonging to the old, and should take over its staff, it was held that a surety for a clerk to one of the old companies was bound for defaults after the amalgamation, notwithstanding the increase of business.[66]

Where a guarantee defined the creditor "Bank" as including "its successors and assigns and any company with which it may amalgamate", the guarantor was held liable in respect of advances made to the principal debtor by the bank with which the original creditor amalgamated.[67]

Principal's appointment to new office

4–53   Where a bond was given to overseers to secure the faithful execution of his office by an assistant overseer, who was bound to accept for all moneys received by him, not to the overseers, but to the person or persons duly authorised to receive the same when required by the overseers or vestry, and the assistant overseer was appointed an overseer by the justices, it was held that such appointment did not affect the liability of the surety, first, because the possibility that he might use his position to prevent the accounts being called for by the overseers was too remote; and, secondly, because the change was made not by the obligees but by the justices.[68]

---

[65] *L.B. & S.C. Ry v. Goodwin* (1849) 3 Exch. 320.
[66] *Eastern Union Ry v. Cochrane* (1853) 9 Exch. 197. *Cf. Wilson v. Craven* (1841) 8 M. & W. 584.
[67] *First National Finance Corp. v. Goodman* [1983] B.C.L.C. 203, CA, distinguishing on this point a dictum of Pickford L.J. in *Bradford Old Bank v. Sutcliffe* [1918] 2 K.B. 833, CA.
[68] *Worth v. Newton* (1854) 10 Exch. 247.

8. *What Principal Liability is Covered*

General rule

A guarantee will only extend to a liability precisely answering **4–54** the description contained in the guarantee.[69] The onus is upon the creditor to show that the surety consented to any alteration.[70] But the surety can afterwards ratify his liability, though the principal contract has been varied or only partly performed.[71] "It must always be recollected," said Lord Westbury in *Blest v. Brown*,[72]

> "in what manner a surety becomes bound. You bind him to the letter of his engagement. Beyond the proper interpretation of that engagement you have no hold upon him. He receives no benefit and no consideration. He is bound therefore, merely according to the proper meaning and effect of the written engagement that he entered into. If that written engagement be altered in a single line, no matter whether it be altered for his benefit, no matter whether the alteration be innocently made, he has a right to say, 'the contract is no longer that for which I engaged to be surety: you have put an end to the contract that I guaranteed, and my obligation, therefore, is at an end.'"

Immaterial variations

With regard to any alterations "for the benefit" of the surety, a **4–55** surety is not discharged by a change which is not contrary to any express stipulation and could only operate for his benefit.[73] If the creditor releases a portion of the principal debt, the surety remains liable for the remainder.[74] This applies where the change is in respect to a matter not reasonably capable of being considered by the surety, either from its bearing on the risk or in any other way, as of any importance whatever; as where a bond was given for the good conduct of an engineer to be employed in India "at a salary to commence from his embarkation at Southampton," and his

---

[69] Often referred to as the principle of co-extensiveness. See Else Mitchell, "Is a Surety's Liability Co-extensive with that of the Principal?" (1941) 63 L.Q.R. 355, and Steyn, "Guarantees, the Co-Extensiveness Principle" (1974) 90 L.Q.R. 246; see generally Chap. 8 of this work; *Compania Sudamericana de Fletes S.A. v. African Continental Bank* [1973] 1 Lloyd's Rep. 21 (guarantee whereby party's obligation under charterparty containing arbitration clause fulfilled); British Columbia Law Reform Commission, Report on Suretyship (1979) Ch. IX. A rather extreme example of this principle occurred in *Chan v. Cresdon Pty Ltd* (1989) 168 C.L.R. 242, where a 3–2 majority of the High Court of Australia held that a guarantee of an obligation "under this lease" was restricted to a registered lease and did not extend to either a common law or equitable lease arising from the unregistered agreement, the entry into possession and the payment of rent by the lessee.
[70] *General Steam Navigation Co. v. Holt* (1858) 6 C.B. (N.S.) 530.
[71] *Ex p. Ashwell* (1832) 2 Deac. & Ch. 281; *Mayhew v. Crickett* (1818) 2 Swanst. 185.
[72] (1862) 4 De G.F. & J. 367 at 376. And see *Straton v. Rastall* (1788) 2 T.R. 366 at 370; *Bacon v. Chesney* (1816) 1 Stark. 192.
[73] *General Steam Navigation Co. v. Rolt* (1858) 6 C.B. (N.S.) 550 at 575; *Holme v. Brunskill* (1878) 8 Q.B.D. 495 at 507.
[74] See *Hollier v. Eyre* (1840) 9 C. & F. 1 at 57. *Holme v. Brunskill* (1878) 3 Q.B.D. 495 at 507. *Cf. Egbert v. National Crown Bank* [1918] A.C. 903.

employers sent him overland, it was held that the surety was bound.[75] But any change, either contrary to express stipulation or such as cannot plainly be seen without enquiry to be insubstantial or necessarily beneficial to the surety,[76] will discharge him whether in fact prejudiced or not.[77] Where a surety gave a bond to secure an obligee being indemnified according to a deed providing for a partnership for five years between the obligee and the principal, and the partnership was not wound up at the end of the five years, but was continued, the surety was held to have been discharged.[78]

Change in office, duties of which are guaranteed

4–56   A guarantee given for the due performance of the duties of an office created by the law applies only so long as it remains the same office, though its tenure or duties are not recited in the guarantee,[79] unless the guarantee is so expressed as to cover the office after the alteration.[80] It was held in *Bartlett v. Att.-Gen.*,[81] that a guarantee for a collector of customs did not extend to a new duty, afterwards imposed by statute, which the collector was by a new deputation appointed to collect. A surety for a county court bailiff was held not liable after the duties of the office had been largely extended by legislation, even for defaults in the performance of duties which existed at the date of the bond.[82]

A mere reduction in the salary of an officer whose office is created by law, accompanied by a reduction of the duties performance of which is guaranteed, the office itself remaining the same, will not put an end to a guarantee in which the salary is not referred to.[83] Where a bond was given for a collector of rates for a parish generally, the surety was not liberated because the class of rates assigned to that collector to collect had been changed.[84]

---

[75] *Evans v. Earle* (1854) 10 Exch. 1.
[76] *Holme v. Brunskill* (1878) 3 Q.B.D. 495 (where it was held that this was a question to be decided by the court, as distinct from being left to the jury); *Whitcher v. Hall* (1826) 5 B. & C. 269. The rule has often been applied. See *e.g. Adelaide Motors Ltd v. Byrne* (1963) 49 M.P.R. 197; *Bell v. National Forest Products Ltd* (1964) 45 D.L.R. (2d) 249; *Nelson Fisheries Ltd v. Boese* [1975] 2 N.Z.L.R. 233. Note however that the acceptance by the creditor of wrongful repudiation by the debtor is not such a change or variation. *Moschi v. Lep Air Services Ltd* [1973] A.C. 331.
[77] See *Blest v. Brown* (1862) 4 De G.F. & J. at 376; *General Steam Navigation Co. v. Rolt* (1858) 6 C.B. (N.S.) at 575; *Holme v. Brunskill* (1878) 3 Q.B.D. at 507. In *Burnes v. Trade Credits Ltd* [1981] 2 All E.R. 122, the Privy Council held that an increase in the rate of interest from 9% to 16% was not a liability which was contemplated by the guarantee. It was also held that it could not be said to constitute the granting to the principal debtor of "any other indulgence or consideration" such as to dispense with the guarantors' consent.
[78] *Small v. Currie* (1854) 5 De G.m. M. & G. 741.
[79] *Oswald v. Mayor of Berwick-upon-Tweed* (1856) H.L.C. 856 at 866; *Pybus v. Gibb* (1866) 6 E. & B. 902. And see *Wardens of St Saviour's, Southwark v. Bostock* (1806) B. & P. (N.S.) 175; *Hassell v. Long* (1814) 2 M & S. 363; *Wembley U.D.C. v. Local Government, etc., Association* (1901) 17 T.L.R. 516.
[80] *Oswald v. Mayor of Berwick-Upon-Tweed*, above; but *cf. R. v. Herron* [1903] 2 I.R. 474.
[81] (1709) Parker 277. *Cf. Skillett v. Fletcher* (1867) L.R. 1 C.P. 217, below, para. 4–61.
[82] *Pybus v. Gibb* (1866) 6 E. & B. 902. See also *Malling Union v. Graham* (1870) L.R. 5 C.P. 201; *Holland v. Lea* (1854) 9 Exch. 430; *N.W. Ry v. Whinray* (1854) 10 Exch. 77.
[83] *Frank v. Edwards* (1852) 8 Exch. 214. But see *Holme v. Brunskill* (1878) 3 Q.B.D. 495.
[84] *Portsea Island Union v. Whillier* (1860) 2 E. & E. 755.

Defaults must be in the performance of the duties guaranteed

Sureties for an officer will only be responsible for defaults in the **4–57** duties of the office.[85] Sureties for the due accounting by a collector of rates or taxes are not liable for moneys which have been collected illegally as such rates or taxes.[86] It will always be a question upon the construction of the contract, whether the money in the hands of the collector has been collected, even though not quite regularly, in such a way as was contemplated by the surety[87]; and if so, unless perhaps where the collection has been quite illegal, and the employers of the collector could not enforce payment over by him to them,[88] the sureties would be liable. Where a banker's clerk was sent eleven miles in the country to fetch money from a customer and lost the money, it was held that the guarantor for the clerk was responsible, though it was not customary for bankers to send a clerk to fetch money as mentioned.[89]

Principal liabilities unconnected with offices

Where the guarantee is for the performance of duties other than **4–58** those of an office, the principal liability must answer to the guarantee in character, in extent, and in respect of the circumstances out of which it arises. Thus a guarantee for the price of goods to be sold will not cover the amount of bills on third persons, transferred without endorsement in exchange for goods supplied, there being a distinction between payment for goods by bill and transferring bills by way of discounting.[90] A surety on a replevin bond (the condition of which is that the tenant shall prosecute his action for the taking of the distress, and, if unsuccessful, return the things distrained) cannot be made liable for the amount of rent found due to the landlord by an arbitrator to whom the action had been referred by a judge's order expressing that the bond should stand as security for the award.[91] Where a surety gave a bond conditioned for payment of bills of exchange, if returned from abroad protested for non-payment, he was held not liable where they had been returned protested for non-acceptance, under circumstances where they might have been protested for non-payment.[92]

---

[85] Even where the holder of the office by statute holds another office besides that guaranteed: *Cosford v. Poor Law, etc., Association* (1892) 103 L.T. 463.

[86] *Nares v. Rowles* (181) 14 East 510; *Weiss v. James* (1840) 7 M. & W. 279 at 287; *Kepp v. Wiggett* (1850) 10 C.B. 35; *Re Walker* [1907] 2 Ch. 120 (moneys received by a receiver in lunacy after the death of the lunatic).

[87] *Mayor of Durham v. Fowler* (1889) 22 Q.B.D. 394 at 415.

[88] See *Nares v. Rowles* (1811) 14 East 510.

[89] *Melville v. Doidge* (1848) 6 C.B. 450.

[90] *Evans v. Whyle* (1829) 5 Bing. 485.

[91] *Archer v. Hall* (1828) 4 Bing. 464, following *Bowmaker v. Moore* (1816) 3 Price 214; (1819) 7 Price 223.

[92] *Campbell v. French* (1795) 6 Term Rep. 200; reversing the decision in C.P. 2 H. Bl. 163.

Extent of the principal liability

4–59   With regard to the extent of the principal contract, in *Whitcher v. Hall*,[93] a leading case on this point, where the surety guaranteed rent payable for the milking of 30 cows, and the lessor by agreement with the lessee let him have 32 for a short time and 28 for another short time, which was found to make no difference to the profits, the surety was held not liable, it being a contract for 30, neither more nor less. Where an Act of Parliament authorised the abandonment of part of a railway undertaking, deviations in the route, and an increase of capital, it was held, in a question between the vendor and purchaser of lands which had belonged to a surety in a bond given to the Crown, conditioned for the completion of the undertaking as originally authorised, that the surety (and consequently the land) was discharged.[94] Similarly, a surety for the payment of instalments under a hire purchase agreement was held not liable after the lessor had seized the goods for default in paying such instalments, since by such seizure the agreement and the principal's liability to pay the instalments thereunder were determined.[95]

A guarantee for payment of a bill of £500 will apparently only cover a bill for that amount exactly.[96] But where the contract was, "I hereby guarantee the payment by F of two bills you intend to renew for him, one for £1,048. 10s. 5d. and the other for £462. 6s. 6d., due respectively on the 28th instant and 4th proximo," it was held by the Court of Appeal, reversing North J., that the guarantee was substantially for the debt and covered two bills drawn in place of the old bills for £1,025. 6s. 11d. and £485. 10s. 0d. respectively though they also differed from the former bills in parties and in length of currency.[97]

Guarantees for limited amounts

4–60   A guarantee for a debt of a certain amount will cover that amount though more is incurred, unless this is contrary to express stipulation. If there is a guarantee for "£500, say a bill," and a bill for more is given, it seems it would be a question of degree whether the excess would prevent the accommodation given up to £500 answering the description.[98]

A guarantee for advances "not exceeding" a certain sum is construed as merely limiting the liability of the surety to that

---

[93] (1826) 5 B. & C. 269. But *cf. Hoole Urban Council v. Fidelity and Deposit Corporation* [1916] 2 K.B. 568.
[94] *Finch v. Jukes* [1877] W.N. at 211.
[95] *Hewison v. Ricketts* (1894) 63 L.J.Q.B. 711. *Cf. Astley Ind. Trust v. Grimston Electric Tools Ltd* (1965) 109 S.J. 149.
[96] *Philips v. Astling* (1809) 2 Taunt. 206.
[97] *Barber v. Mackrell* (1892) 67 L.T. 108.
[98] See *Philips v. Astling* (1809) 2 Taunt. 206. *Cf.* the point argued but not decided in *Pickles v. Thornton* (1874) 33 L.T. 658.

amount, and not, unless it clearly appears to be the intention, as making the liability conditional upon the debtor's liability being limited to that sum.[99] And this construction has been adopted, even where grammatically the limit seems imposed, not upon the liability, but upon the advance.[1] A bond to brewers conditioned to be void if the principal, a publican, from time to time should pay the obligees for all ale, etc., which he should from time to time have had from them, to an amount not exceeding £50, before he should have a fresh supply, was held to cover the debt of the publican, although a fresh supply was granted in spite of there being already an outstanding indebtedness of £50.[2]

Permitting principal to incur other liabilities

Permitting the principal to incur other liabilities to the creditor **4–61** beyond and separable from the liability guaranteed does not affect the guarantee as to the last-named liability. Thus an office does not cease to be within a guarantee merely because the officer is allowed to contract other liabilities towards his employers, unless this is contrary to stipulation or amounts to the substitution of a new office for that which the surety had in view.[3] In *Bonar v. Macdonald*,[4] where a bond was given for the good conduct of a bank official, who joined in the bond and undertook not to become connected with any trade, and afterwards without communication with the surety the official received a rise of salary and became liable for one-quarter of losses on discounts, it was held in the House of Lords, that the bond could not be enforced, even to make good defaults in the course of the original duties of the official, on the ground that there had been an essential change in the principal obligation. Following this decision, it was held in *Pybus v. Gibb*[5] that a surety for a county court high bailiff was not liable after the

---

[99] See *Ex p. Rushforth* (1805) 10 Ves. 409; *Paley v. Field* (1806) 12 Ves. 435; *Parker v. Wise* (1817) 6 M. & S. 239; *Seller v. Jones* (1846) 16 M. & W. 112; *Gee v. Pack* (1863) 33 L.J.Q.B. 49; *Backhouse v. Hall* (1865) 6 B. & S. 507; *Gordon v. Rae* (1858) 8 E. & B. 1065; *Laurie v. Scholefield* (1869) L.R. 4 C.P. 622.
[1] *Laurie v. Scholefield*, above. As pointed out by the South Australian Law Reform Committee Report on Suretyship (39th Report, 1976), para. 3, as the law now stands, a surety may restrict his liability under the contract of suretyship to a certain fixed amount but the creditor can still lend up to any amount and thereby bring into existence other debts which will compete with that of the surety forcing the principal debtor into bankruptcy to produce a liability on the surety quite unintended by him: see, *e.g. Total Oil Products (Aust.) Pty Ltd v. Robinson* (1970) 1 N.S.W.L.R. 701. The typical bank guarantee therefore will not make the guarantor's liability conditional upon the principal debtor's liability remaining beneath that sum. See *Queensland National Bank Ltd v. Queensland Trustees Ltd* (1899) 9 Q.L.J. 282. The Report therefore suggests that when a creditor advances money to the debtor beyond the limit of liability so imposed and accepted by the creditor without first obtaining the consent of the surety, the latter's liability should be diminished to the extent of those further advances.
[2] *Seller v. Jones* (1846) 16 M. & W. 112.
[3] *cf.* in addition to the cases cited on this point, *Eyre v. Everett* (1826) 2 Russ. 381.
[4] (1850) 3 H.L.C. 226.
[5] (1856) 6 E. & B. 902.

duties had been largely extended by legislation, even for defaults in the performance of duties which existed at the date of the bond. The ground of the decision was that the office was no longer the office mentioned in the bond. Coleridge J., however, seems to suggest that the mere fact that the person to whom a guarantee is given putting collateral liabilities upon the person for whom the guarantee is given operates as a discharge of the surety, because his risks are thereby increased.[6] The dictum, if it means this, was however disapproved in *Skillett v. Fletcher*[7] where *Bonar v. Macdonald*,[8] is explained as turning on the stipulation that there should be no collateral liabilities,[9] and where *Pybus v. Gibb* is supported on the ground that the office which the parties had in view had been changed.

In *Skillet v. Fletcher*[10] the bond was for the due performance of his duties by a collector of poor rates and of sewers rates, and was to remain valid if either office was held separately, the breach assigned being default in both capacities. It was held no defence that by Act of Parliament a main drainage rate had been created, of which he had also been appointed collector, and that the sewers rate, though not changed in nature, had been increased by further charges upon it.[11] Similarly, a guarantee for the faithful service of a clerk will not be put an end to by a mere extension of the business of his employer.[12]

The transaction out of which the liability guaranteed is to spring

4–62   The question whether a given liability is covered by a given guarantee must not be considered merely with reference to the extent and incidents of the liability itself, which is imposed upon the principal. It is also necessary that the transaction as a whole out of which it springs should be such as was contemplated by the surety. A very strong instance of this is *Blest v. Brown*.[13] In that case the defendant had given a bond, reciting that M had entered into a contract with the Government for the supply of a certain quantity of bread, and had applied to the obligees to supply him with flour "to enable him to carry out such contract," which the obligees had

---

[6] *ibid.* at 914.
[7] (1867) L.R. 1 C.P. 217.
[8] (1850) 3 H.L.C. 226.
[9] From Lord Cottenham's speech, which was adopted by the House, this stipulation appears to have been in wider terms than appears from the statement at the commencement of the report.
[10] (1867) L.R. 1 C.P. 217.
[11] See also *Worth v. Newton* (1854) 10 Exch. 247. *Cf. Bartlett v. Att.-Gen.* (1709) Parker 277, above, para. 4–56.
[12] See *L.B. & S.C. Ry v. Goodwin* (1849) 3 Exch. 320 at 321. And *cf. Eastern Union Ry v. Cochrane* (1853) 9 Exch. 197.
[13] (1862) 4 De G.F. & J. 367. See also *Vavaseur Trust Co. Ltd v. Ashmore*, unreported, April 2, 1976, CA, discussed below, n. 19.

agreed to do, and conditioned for the payment of the price of "the flour so supplied as aforesaid." It turned out that the flour, which was supplied in good faith to the order of the contractor, did not comply with the requirements of the Government contract. The surety was held not liable, because the vendor was by the terms of the bond bound to know (whether in fact he did or did not know) what those requirements were.[14] But where the defendant guaranteed to the plaintiffs, a firm in New York, acceptance and payment of any bills, to be drawn on him on his account by his agent in Charlestown, which the plaintiffs should discount, it was held that the plaintiffs were justified in discounting any bill drawn by the agent on the defendant, and represented by the agent to be on the defendant's account, and could recover against the defendant in respect of every such bill, whether in fact drawn on his account or not.[15]

In *Squire v. Whitton*,[16] a lady executed a bond (in blank and therefore invalid as a bond) conditioned to secure a 'loan." The real transaction, however, was that the obligee permitted the so-called borrower to realise for his own use funds of a trust under which the obligee and his wife (who concurred in the arrangement) were beneficiaries. The Court of Chancery and the House of Lords refused to give effect to the imperfect bond in order to cover such a transaction. And where a promissory note was given by a lady to secure the floating balance on a bank account, and the bank, after so treating it for three years, upon the eve of the marriage of the lady, in order to make the note "a tangible security" and without apparently consulting the principal, placed £500 to his credit so as to "have it on the passbook before the marriage," Lord Langdale said he would, had it been necessary, have held the surety discharged upon the ground that this was not carrying out the transaction agreed upon.[17]

Where a surety joined in a deed, whereby the principal covenanted to repay to A all that A might pay to B, the deed reciting that A was under a liability to B, the surety was held not to be bound upon it turning out that A was not in fact liable to B.[18]

The principal must enjoy the full benefit stipulated for

It is essential that the principal should get the full benefit to **4–63** procure which the surety intervened; otherwise the surety will not

[14] If the Government had waived the inferiority, the surety might have been liable. See *Oastler v. Pound* (1863) 7 L.T. 852, below, para. 4–63.
[15] *Ogden v. Aspinall* (1826) 7 D. & R. 637.
[16] (1848) 1 H.L.C. 333.
[17] *Archer v. Hudson* (1844) 7 Beav. 551, affirmed (1846) 15 L.J. Ch. App. 211.
[18] *Lake v. Brutton* (1856) 18 Beav. 34.

be bound.[19] Thus where the debt guaranteed was to be incurred in consideration of the conveyance of property subject to specified incumbrances, and there was another incumbrance unknown to the surety and forgotten by the creditor, the surety was relieved.[20]

Where in consideration that the plaintiffs would give up to WY certain goods upon which they had a lien, and would take his acceptance for £140, the defendant guaranteed due payment of such acceptance, it was held that the plaintiffs could not recover anything, if they only gave up the goods on receiving acceptances for £145.[21] Where a surety guaranteed payment by a building owner of £1,500 in four equal instalments for repairs and decorations to be executed by a builder "subject to the said works being duly executed in accordance with this agreement" and the owner did not pay the first instalment, but it was found that at the date of the writ it was necessary to spend £80 in order to complete the work in accordance with the agreement, the surety was held not liable.[22]

Where the guarantee was in consideration of a bank "lending" the principal the sum of £1,000 for seven days from the date of the guarantee, and the bank, without placing £1,000 to his credit, merely honoured cheques upon his current account, which did not create an overdraft of £1,000 within the seven days, it was held that the surety was not liable.[23] Where again a surety joined in a promissory note "for value received by a draft at three months' date," and the creditor advanced cash, the surety was held not liable, though no demand was made upon him until after the three months.[24] On the other hand, a guarantee for "advances" to be made by a bank has been held to include sums placed to the credit of the principal in respect of notes and bills discounted.[25]

4–64   Where the defendant gave a continuing guarantee for the price of goods to be supplied, and after goods had been supplied the purchasers being in difficulties called their creditors together, who agreed to continue to supply goods against cash which was to be applied to the existing debts until they were satisfied, it was held that the guarantee did not cover the price of the goods supplied by

[19] This passage and some cases cited below, *e.g. Bacon v. Chesney* (1816) 1 Stark. 192 and *Blest v. Brown* (1862) 4 De C.F. & J. 367 were referred to and discussed in *Vavaseur Trust Co. Ltd v. Ashmore*, unreported, April 2, 1976, CA, Transcript No. 157 of 1976. *Blest v. Brown* was described as a case of "embodied terms" since the guarantee referred to the Government contract but without setting out its terms. In *Vavaseur* the Court of Appeal found, for the purposes of upsetting an order for summary judgment, that it was reasonably arguable that there was an implied term in a guarantee that certain principal fixed term contracts of loan would be adhered to, where there had been a breach of such contracts by the creditor with the principal debtor. See also *Royal Bank of Canada v. Salvatori* (1928) 3 W.W.R. 501, PC, and *National Westminster Bank v. Riley* [1986] B.C.L.C. 268, CA.
[20] *Willis v. Willis* (1850) 17 Sim. 218. See also *Vavaseur Trust Co. Ltd v. Ashmore*, above.
[21] *Pickles v. Thornton* (1875) 33 L.T. 658.
[22] *Eshelby v. Federated European Bank* [1932] 1 K.B. 254, 423.
[23] *Burton v. Gray* (1873) L.R. 8 Ch. App. 932.
[24] *Bacon v. Chesney* (1816) 1 Stark. 192; *Bosner v. Cox* (1841) 6 Beav. 110.
[25] *Grahame v. Grahame* (1887) 19 L.R. Ir. 249. In *Burnes v. Trade Credits Ltd* [1981] 2 All E.R. 122, PC, it was held that the word "advance" normally implies the furnishing of money for a specified purpose. Therefore the term "further advances" did not cover an extension of the period for repayment of the original principal sum.

the plaintiffs, on these terms.[26] So in *Pidcock v. Bishop*,[27] where a surety guaranteed payment for iron to be supplied to the principal, but it had been secretly arranged that 10s. per ton was to be added to the price of each consignment, and was to go in liquidation of an old debt, a verdict for the plaintiff creditor was set aside and a nonsuit entered.

Where a guarantee was given for the price of goods to be supplied to a Government contractor, and the goods were not supplied in time, but the Government waived the consequent delay and the contractor accepted the goods, the surety was held bound for the full price of the goods, though it was alleged that a specially high price had been given by the contractor, owing to the short time allowed for the supply.[28]

Where, in compliance with an order giving conditional leave to defend, two sureties became bound for the amount which should be recovered from the defendants in the action, and upon the bankruptcy of one of the sureties an order was made, without notice to the other surety, that further security should be found, or in default the judgment should be entered for the plaintiff, and no further security being found judgment was entered without a trial, it was held that the other surety was discharged.[29] Similarly, where judgment was entered by consent for an amount to be paid by instalments.[30]

Breach of terms of principal contract by creditor

Difficult questions arise where the surety alleges that the creditor **4-65** is in breach of the creditor's contract with the principal debtor. The first question is whether the term breached is one that was "embodied" in the contract,[31] in which case a "departure" from the embodied terms will discharge the surety.[32] In other cases, a second question arises, as to whether the breach by the creditor is repudiatory.[33] If the breach is non-repudiatory, it will not without more discharge the surety.[34] A repudiatory breach by the creditor, if accepted, will discharge the surety.[35]

Variation of terms of principal liability not set forth in guarantee

Where the terms of the principal contract are not set forth in the **4-66** bond or guarantee of the surety, the rule is laid down in *Holme v.*

---

[26] *Bastow v. Bennett* (1812) 3 Camp. 220.
[27] (1825) 3 B. & C. 605.
[28] *Oastler v. Pound* (1863) 7 L.T. 852.
[29] *Luning v. Milton* (1890) 7 T.L.R. 12.
[30] *Tatum v. Evans* (1885) 54 L.T. 336.
[31] As in the case of *Blest v. Brown* (1862) 4 De C.F. & J. 367, discussed above at para. 4–62.
[32] *National Westminster Bank v. Riley* [1986] B.C.L.C. 268, CA; *Holme v. Brunskill* (1878) 3 Q.B.D. 495, discussed below.
[33] *National Westminster Bank v. Riley* [1986] B.C.L.C. 268, CA.
[34] *ibid.*
[35] *ibid.*

Brunskill[36] that a material variation in the contract will discharge the surety—a material variation meaning for this purpose any variation which cannot be seen to be insubstantial, or one that cannot be otherwise than beneficial to the surety.[36] If this is not self-evident, no enquiry as to the materiality of the variation will be entered on.[37] It is not necessary that the variation should result from an agreement between the creditor and the principal: it is enough if the principal's liability is altered by the exercise of a right by the creditor, such as the forfeiture of shares for non-payment of calls.[37]

In *Calvert v. London Dock Co.*,[38] a bond had been given for the performance of the "promises and agreements" in a contract for works "which on the part of the contractor were or ought to be performed, according to the true intent and meaning of the contract." The contractee advanced to the principal the retention money provided for by the contract, and the obligor was held discharged in equity, though at law it had been held that he was liable for nominal damages, the condition of the bond not having been performed.[39]

In *Sanderson v. Aston*,[40] the guarantee was for the good conduct of a servant, and the plea material for the present purpose alleged that the engagement of the latter had been altered by being made terminable on three months' instead of one month's notice. The term as to notice had not been made part of the surety's contract. The court held that the surety was not discharged, the change being neither a breach of any condition in the guarantee nor material.[41] The latter finding seems to have meant that the engagement of the surety would remain, notwithstanding the alteration, terminable by one month's notice to the servant, so that the alteration could produce no effect on the surety's position.[42] If, however, it was

---

[36] (1878) 3 Q.B.D. at 505. And see *per* Cockburn L.J. in *General Steam Navigation Co. v. Rolt* (1858) 6 C.B. (N.S.) at 575; and see *Re Darwen and Peace* [1927] 1 Ch. 176 at 183, 184 noted in (1927) 163 L.T. 424 and said by Megaw L.J. in *Lep Air Services Ltd v. Rolloswin* [1971] 3 All E.R. 45 to depend on the special terms of the guarantee there involved. See also *Vavaseur Trust Co. Ltd v. Ashmore* above. Most guarantees will make provision for variation of the terms of the principal contract without effecting a discharge of the surety. But for a recent illustration of such a clause proving to be ineffective in a particular case, see *Dowling v. Ditanda* (1975) 236 E.G. 485. *Holme v. Brunskill* was applied in *National Bank of Nigeria Ltd v. Awolesi* [1965] 2 Lloyd's Rep. 389 where a bank guaranteed an "existing" bank account which the Privy Council found on its true construction to contemplate the account as it existed at the date of the guarantee. Consequently by permitting the opening of a second account, the bank allowed a substantial variation of the terms of the principal contract to occur without the guarantor's consent, thereby discharging him. In *National Bank of New Zealand Ltd v. West* [1977] 1 N.Z.L.R. 31 at 33, Casey J. held that a guarantee of all moneys which a bank was "at liberty to charge or debit to the account" of the principal debtor was not wide enough to impose liability for the debtor's own further guarantee of a third party's indebtedness. The learned judge applied Lord Hodson's dictum at p. 315 in *Awolesi* that the way in which the consideration for a guarantee is expressed is not conclusive but may be relevant in construing the terms of the contract itself.

[37] *Re Darwen and Pearce Ltd*, above; *Stiff v. Eastbourne Local Board* (1868) 19 L.T. 408; (1869) 20 L.T. 339. See also *per* Cockburn L.J. in *General Steam Navigation Co. v. Rolt* (1858) 6 C.B. (N.S.) at 575.

[38] (1838) 2 Keen 638.

[39] *Warne v. Calvert* (1837) 7 A. & E. 143.

[40] (1873) L.R. 8 Ex. 73.

[41] *cf.*, however, *Nicholson v. Burt* (1882) 10 R. 121, SC.

[42] See *per* Pigot B. (1873) L.R. 8 Ex. at 78. This is not the only point, however. The surety might think a servant with a less secure tenure would be more scrupulous in performing his duty.

meant (as the language held by Pollock B. seems to imply) that the surety is not discharged if, though the change was capable of operating disadvantageously on the surety's position, the court are of opinion that he is not injured in fact, such a doctrine was disapproved in *Holme v. Brunskill*,[43] and is not to be regarded as law.

In *Holme v. Brunskill*[43] the guarantee was to secure the redelivery **4–67** of a flock of sheep, let with a farm called Riggindale. The landlord afterwards accepted a surrender of one field and made a small reduction in rent. The jury found that the variation was not material. In the Court of Appeal it was held that, though the tenancy was not a new one, but still the tenancy which had subsisted when the bond was given, nevertheless the surety was discharged on the ground that the alteration was not one which could be said, without inquiry, to be incapable of prejudicing the surety, and that the question of its materiality could not in effect be litigated. Brett L.J., however, dissented from this judgment, holding that the change, when not violating a specific condition of the surety's contract must be proved to be material.

Application of rule where guarantee is for liability under future transactions not precisely specified

The application of the rule in *Holme v. Brunskill*,[43] presents no **4–68** difficulty, where, as in that case, in *Calvert v. London Dock Co.*,[44] and in *Sanderson v. Aston*,[45] the guarantee, though in general terms, was given with reference to a principal contract then already negotiated, of the existence of which (though not perhaps of its exact terms), the surety was aware.[46] It would also apply, it is submitted, to cases where the creditor alters in any material particular liabilities already incurred by the principal debtor, and covered by an antecedent general guarantee, even though the alteration would leave the liability such as, if incurred in that form in the first instance, would have been covered by the guarantee.[47]

---

[43] (1878) 3 Q.B.D. 495.
[44] (1838) 2 Keen 638.
[45] (1873) L.R. 8 Ex. 73.
[46] But see *Nicholson v. Burt* (1882) 10 R. 121, SC.
[47] The authorities are indistinct on this point. It is established that the surety is discharged if the creditor interferes with the "principal obligation, performance of which is guaranteed." See *Ward v. National Bank of New Zealand* (1883) 8 A.C. 755 at 763; *Taylor v. Bank of New South Wales* (1886) 11 A.C. 596 at 603. But this might be taken to refer only to a principal obligation existing or provisionally arranged before the guarantee is entered into, which might be said to be specifically guaranteed, and the terms of which, so far as they can affect the surety, might be considered as incorporated in the guarantee. See *Vavaseur Trust Co. Ltd v. Ashmore*, above. Guarantees to cover transactions entirely in the future, and which permit to the creditor some latitude as to the exact terms on which those transactions shall be arranged, might be treated as standing on a somewhat different footing: it is submitted, however, that the moment the principal comes under any liability to the creditor to which the guarantee attaches, the surety acquires an interest in every term of that liability and that the creditor has no authority to modify it even though he would in the first instance have been within his rights if he had taken it in another form. So much, at any rate, seems warranted by the principle upon which a surety has a vested interest in all collateral securities which the creditor may have taken for the debt, even though he was under no obligation to obtain them, and even though the surety is ignorant of their having been taken, and has not intervened to pay the debt and claim the benefit of them (see below, Chapter 7). In such cases the surety is entitled to relief by way of compensation for the actual loss suffered by him, if such securities are interfered with by the creditor;

However, where a guarantee is given in general terms to cover the liabilities which are to result from a future course of dealing generically specified in the guarantee, the creditor can vary the course of dealing under which successive liabilities arise, so long as the course of dealing continues to be of the character coming within the scope of the guarantee, and no change is made in the terms of any liability after it is actually incurred and the guarantee is attached to it.[48] If a course of dealing other than that subsequently adopted had been arranged between the principals at the date of the guarantee, this will not cause the surety to be discharged by the alteration, unless at the time of the giving of the guarantee the surety knew that some arrangement existed, so that the liabilities to arise out of such arrangement, whatever it might be (and no other), were really the subject matter of the guarantee.[48]

4–69　　In *Stewart v. McKean*,[49] a guarantee was given simply for W.M.'s "intromissions as agent," intromission being a Scottish term signifying dealings by an agent with stock and cash, for which he is accountable. At the time when the guarantee was given a course of dealing had been arranged by which the agent was to account monthly; but the surety was unaware that any arrangement had been made at the date of the guarantee, and knew nothing and never asked about the manner in which the principal was to account, nor the nature of his employment. At first the agent accounted monthly, then every six months, but afterwards it was arranged that he should give promissory notes at four months, which often largely exceeded the amount for which he had to account, and the employers discounted the notes, and when they became due, furnished the agent with cash to the extent by which the amount for which he was then accountable fell short of the amount of the note. The result that the agent accounted monthly instead of every six months; and, on the other hand, the employers obtained accommodation from him, for which they paid him commission. It was held by the majority of the Court of Exchequer that, the mode of accounting being left open by the surety, he was liable. Pollock C.B. dissented, on the ground that the position of the principal was not such as could have been contemplated by the surety when he guaranteed his intromissions "as agent."

In *Egbert v. National Crown Bank*,[50] the guarantee was for further advances, and the creditor and the principal agreed on a

and the question raised in the text seems to be reduced to this, whether the surety under the circumstances there stated is entitled to any relief beyond such damage as can show himself to have suffered by the alteration. It is submitted that he cannot be compensated in that way when it is the principal obligation itself, and not a mere collateral advantage, that has been interfered with.
[48] *Stewart v. McKean* (1855) 16 Exch. 675. And see the following Scottish cases, *Ellice v. Finlayson* (1832) 10 S. 345; *Stewart v. Brown* (1871) 9 R. 763; *Nicolson v. Burt* (1882) 10 R. 121.
[49] above. See *per* Parke B. at 690.
[50] [1918] A.C. 903. See also *Nelson Fisheries Ltd v. Boese* [1975] 2 N.Z.L.R. 233 where it was stated that there must be a variation to effect a discharge, not simply a "waiver" or "default" under the terms of the guarantee.

higher rate of interest than the creditor could legally charge. It was held by the Privy Council that the agreement as to interest was merely invalid and that therefore the surety was liable for interest at the rate properly chargeable by the creditor against the principal.

Variation of one of several distinct obligations guaranteed

Where the guarantee extends to several distinct debts, duties or **4–70** obligations, a variation in the nature of one of them not capable of affecting the position of the surety with respect to the other or others will not discharge him as to that other or others.[51] However, a binding agreement to give time to pay instalments in arrears under a hire purchase agreement will discharge a surety not only in respect of those instalments, but from any other further liability in respect of the whole contract.[52]

Assent of surety to variation

A surety will not be discharged by a variation to which the **4–71** creditor (on whom the onus lies) can show he assented,[53] or which is provided for in the guarantee.[54] This, however, must be an assent to a transaction between the creditor and the principal which the surety knows to be a variation of the contract; he is not put upon inquiry as to every transaction he hears of so as to ascertain whether it is a variation of the contract.[55] Thus a surety for a contractor was released by the advance of the retention money, notwithstanding that he knew of payments which had been made (though he did not know they represented advances in variation of the contract), and notwithstanding that some of the money had come into his own pocket, to be paid over to him by the contractor in respect of independent accounts pending between them.[56] Where the surety takes any active part in the transaction constituting the variation, he is clearly not discharged; as where solicitors, who were sureties, prepared documents referable to the variation.[57] Similarly, if the

---

[51] *Bingham v. Corbitt* (1864) 34 L.J.Q.B. 37; *Skillett v. Fletcher* (1867) L.R. 1 C.P. 217; 2 C.P. 469; *Harrison v. Seymour* (1866) L.R. 1 C.P. 518; *Croydon Gas Co. v. Dickinson* (1876) 1 C.P.D. 707, 2 C.P.D. 46, where the surety had joined in a bond for £1,000 and the creditor subsequently agreed with the debtor that the debt should only be £500 which was held not to discharge the surety from liability for the greater amount. As pointed out by the South Australian Law Reform Committee Report on Suretyship (39th Report, 1976) at para. 6, since the surety was guaranteeing whatever the debtor's liability was, it should have been limited to the lesser amount. In *W. R. Simmons Ltd v. Meek* [1939] 2 All E.R. 645 Oliver J., in applying *Croydon Gas Co. v. Dickinson*, discusses the concept of a "severable" guarantee, *i.e.* whenever a surety is liable for two separate liabilities, a subsequent variation as to one will not affect his liability for the other. See also *Davies v. Stainbank* (1855) 6 De G.M. & G. 679 at 689. *Cf. Eyre v. Bartrop* (1818) 3 Madd. 221; *Polak v. Everett* (1876) 1 Q.B.D. 669; *Midland Motor Showrooms v. Newman* [1929] 2 K.B. 256.
[52] *Midland Motor Showrooms v. Newman* above; *cf. W. R. Simmons Ltd v. Meek*, above.
[53] *General Steam Navigation Co. v. Rolt* (1858) 6 C.B. (N.S.) 550.
[54] *British Motor Trust Co. v. Hyams* (1934) 50 T.L.R. 230.
[55] *General Steam Navigation Co. v. Rolt* (1858) 6 C.B. (N.S.) 550.
[56] *ibid. Cf. Enright v. Falvey* (1879) 4 L.R. Ir. 397.
[57] *Woodcock v. Oxford and Worcester Ry* (1853) 1 Drew 521.

surety permits the creditor to think he has assented.[58] However, mere knowledge by the surety of an intended variation, against which he does not protest, is not the equivalent of assent, nor is the surety bound to warn the creditor against carrying it out.[59] And guarantors of instalments to be paid on shares will be discharged if the company, on non-payment of a call, exercises its right under the original contract for the shares to forfeit them[60]

Assent by surety without fresh consideration

4–72   A surety is not discharged by a variation to which he assents afterwards, even though there may be no fresh consideration for the assent.[61] However, it is apprehended that assent, whether previous or subsequent to a variation, only renders the surety liable for the contract as varied, where it remains a contract within the general purview of the original guarantee,[62] and the assent can operate as the waiver of something in the nature of a condition, or of an equitable claim to the cancellation of a security whose express terms cover the contract as varied.[63] If a new contract is to be secured, there must be a new guarantee.[64]

Breach of principal contract by principal debtor

4–73   The decision of the House of Lords in *Moschi v. Lep Air Services Ltd*[65] makes it clear that a guarantor's position is not affected by a breach of the principal contract which leads to the termination of that contract by reason of an acceptance of the breach by the creditor. The House of Lords held that the nature of a guarantor's contractual promise was to ensure that the debtor performed his obligations under his contract with the creditor.[66] Consequently when the debtor failed to perform his obligations *vis-à-vis* the creditor the latter could recover damages from the guarantor by dint of such failure, the measure of damages being in theory the same. The obligation of both guarantor and debtor upon default by the latter was a secondary obligation to pay damages as distinct from the primary obligation under the main contract itself.[67] Much of the decision turns upon the actual wording of the guarantee involved,

---

[58] See *Hollier v. Eyre* (1840) 9 C. & F. at 52.
[59] *Polak v. Everett* (1876) 1 Q.B.D. 669 at 673.
[60] *Re Darwen and Pearce* [1927] 1 Ch. 176 at 187.
[61] *Mayhew v. Crickett* (1818) 2 Swanst. 185; *Smith v. Winter* (1838) 4 M. & W. 454.
[62] *Trade Indemnity Co. v. Workington Harbour, etc.* [1937] A.C. 1 especially, *per* Lord Atkin.
[63] All releases come under one or other of these heads: *e.g. General Steam Navigation Co. v. Rolt* (1858) 6 C.B. (N.S.) 550 under the former; and *Hollier v. Eyre* (1840) 9 C. & F. 1, *Mayhew v. Crickett* (1818) 2 Swanst. 185 and *Smith v. Winter* (1838) 4 M. & W. 454 under the latter.
[64] See *Pybus v. Gibb* (1856) 6 E. & B. 902 at 911. *Cf. Kitson v. Julian* (1855) 4 F. & B. 854; *Leathley v. Spyer* (1870) L.R. 5 C.P. 595. The effect of the Statute of Frauds must also be borne in mind. See Chapter 3.
[65] [1973] A.C. 331.
[66] See below at para. 4–97.
[67] See, *e.g. per* Lord Reid at 345, *per* Lord Diplock at 350, and *per* Lord Simon at 352. *Cf.* the approach of Megaw L.J. in the Court of Appeal [1971] 3 All E.R. 45.

but some reliance was placed on *Chatterton v. Maclean*,[68] where it was assumed by Parker J.[69] that on a creditor's acceptance of the principal debtor's repudiation of the contract between them, the surety will not be released in respect of the indebtedness accrued due or future liabilities for damages.[70]

9. With What Amount the Surety is Chargeable

Amount owing by principal

The surety can only be made liable for the amount which the **4–74** principal owes in respect of the debt secured.[71] Thus, if a promissory note is given to secure advances, it cannot be relied on to sue either party to it, whether principal or surety, for more than the amount actually advanced.[72] Similarly, if one person accepts or endorses a bill to secure the debt of another to the drawer or indorsee, the latter can only sue him for the amount of the debt.[73] Where a promissory note is given to secure a proportion of an advance to be made, and only part of that advance is given, his note will in equity be available to the creditor only to secure a similar proportion of the credit actually given, even though the amount owing be more than the ex facie amount of the note.[74]

Payment by the principal

The surety is, of course, not liable if the principal has paid the **4–75** guaranteed debt, nor, if part has been paid, for more than the amount unpaid.[75] It would be beyond the scope of this work to examine the law as to what constitutes a valid payment, the question in each case being in no way affected by the circumstance that there is a surety for the debt.[76]

Where the condition of a surety's bond was that the treasurer of a union (a banker) should "honestly, diligently and faithfully perform and discharge the duties of his office," one such duty being to pay out of any money of the guardians in his hands all orders drawn upon him, and the treasurer paid an order with his own notes, which the plaintiffs accepted, and at the time of the banker stopping payment still held, the surety was held not liable on the ground that the case came within the principle whereby a bank note, taken for

[68] [1951] 1 All E.R. 761. See *Moschi v. Lep Air Services Ltd*, above at 357.
[69] above at 764, 765.
[70] *cf. Hyundai Shipbuilding and Heavy Industries Ltd v. Pournaras* [1978] 2 Lloyd's Rep. 502 and *Hyundai Heavy Industries Co. Ltd v. Papadopoulos* [1980] 1 W.L.R. 1129, HL, both discussed above at para. 4–12.
[71] The so-called "principle of co-extensiveness" which reflects this rule is discussed above at para. 4–54.
[72] *Hartland v. Jukes* (1863) 1 H. & C. 667.
[73] *Ex p. Reader* (1819) Buck 381.
[74] *Mayhew v. Crickett* (1918) 2 Swanst. 185.
[75] *Perry v. National Provincial Bank* [1910] 1 Ch. 464.
[76] See *City Discount Bank v. McLean* (1874) L.R. 9 C.P. at 698; *Guardians of Lichfield Union v. Greene* (1857) 1 H. & N. 884.

a debt at the time of the transaction which gives rise to it, is taken at the peril of the taker[77]; and that the circumstance that the person paying was also the maker made no difference.[78] Even if a creditor takes a bank note for a pre-existing guaranteed debt, so that it would not, prima facie, according to the above rule be taken at his peril, still, if he neglects to present it, he makes it his own, and the liability of the surety is extinguished, even though the debtor be himself the maker of the note.[78] Similarly, if in the place of cash the creditor takes for his own convenience a draft payable at another place.[78] If a creditor takes a bill or note for the debt, not being by express understanding but by the operation of the rules just mentioned a satisfaction of the debt, a surety (apart from any effect which the transaction may have as a giving of time),[79] remains liable in the event of the bill being dishonoured, the giving of the bill being conditional payment only.[80] Where a bond was given to secure payment for goods to be supplied at the expiration of the usual period of credit, and the purchaser gave a bill which was dishonoured, whereupon the creditor gave him the money to take up the bill, calling it a "loan," it was held that in substance it was not a loan, but that the goods had never been paid for, and that the surety was liable.[81]

Payment by co-sureties

4–76   With regard to payments by co-sureties, a deposit of money by some of a number of sureties to a suspense account with a creditor, as security for payment by those sureties of the amount deposited, beyond which they are not to be liable, the remedies against other sureties being reserved, is not a payment in relief of another surety not a party to the arrangement.[82]

Payment by third parties

4–77   A payment by a third party not in the position of a co-surety under circumstances such that there is no discharge of the principal does not discharge the surety.[83]

Repayment voidable as a preference

4–78   If a payment received by the creditor from the principal is afterwards, upon the bankruptcy of the principal, adjudged a voidable preference, and has to be restored to the estate by the creditor,

---

[77] *Camidge v. Allenby* (1827) 6 B. & C. 373.
[78] *Guardians of Lichfield Union v. Greene* (1857) 1 H. & N. 884.
[79] See below.
[80] See *Belshaw v. Bush* (1851) 11 C.B. 191; *Bottomley v. Nuttall* (1858) 5 C.B. (N.S.) 122; *Keay v. Fenwick* (1870) 1 C.P.D. 745.
[81] *Davey v. Phelps* (1841) 2 M. & Gr. 300.
[82] *Commercial Bank of Australia v. Official Assignee* [1893] A.C. 181.
[83] cf. *Kenney v. Employers' Liability Assurance Corporation* [1901] 1 I.R. 3.

the surety is liable for the amount[84] where the creditor was not a party to the voidable preference.[85] There has been no valid payment, and the creditor has not done anything to discharge the surety upon equitable grounds.[86] In such a case the decision as between a creditor and the trustee of the bankrupt's estate, though admissible in evidence as between the creditor and the surety, is not binding upon the surety, but the creditor must prove in the action against the latter that the payment was a voidable preference.[87]

Appropriation of payments

The question whether payments made by the principal debtor, not being dividends in his bankruptcy, are to be appropriated in discharge or reduction of the guaranteed or some other indebtedness, is one which, in the absence of special agreement between the creditor and the surety, must be determined as if it arose merely between the creditor and the principal debtor,[88] a surety having no right of his own to dictate either to the creditor or the debtor how payments made by the latter are to be appropriated.[89] The surety's ignorance of the other debt is immaterial.[89] Similarly, a surety for a collector or other accountable agent is liable, although the collector or agent has paid over the full amount that he received during the period covered by the guarantee, if the payment was appropriated to pre-existing arrears either by the act of the collector or agent or of the person who received it from him.[90]   **4–79**

Separate accounts

The creditor may close the account guaranteed when the guarantee expires (as at the death of the guarantor), and open a new account without transferring to it the old debit; and the payments into the new account will not wipe off the old debt.[91] However, the creditor cannot, by dividing the account guaranteed during the   **4–80**

---

[84] *Pritchard v. Hitchcock* (1843) 6 M. & Gr. 151; *Petty v. Cooke* (1871) L.R. 6 QB 790. Sections 241(1)(e) (corporate insolvency) and s.342(1)(e) (individual insolvency) of the Insolvency Act 1986 now expressly give the court power to create new or revived surety obligations in order to reverse a voidable preference.

[85] *cf. Re Seymour* [1937] Ch. 668.

[86] *Petty v. Cooke* (1871) L.R. 6 QB 790.

[87] *Pritchard v. Hitchcock* (1843) Man. & G. 151. When a creditor is sued for the return of a voidable preference he can join the surety as a third party so that the latter will become bound by the decision.

[88] See *City Discount Co. v. McLean* (1874) L.R. 9 C.P. at 698; *Ex p. Whitworth* (1841) 2 M.D. & De G. 164 at 169.

[89] *Kirby v. Duke of Marlborough* (1813) 2 M. & S. 18; *Williams v. Rawlinson* (1813) 3 Bing. at 76; *Lysaght v. Walker* (1831) 5 Bligh (N.S.) 1; *Re Sherry* (1884) 25 Ch D 692.

[90] *Att.-Gen. for Jamaica v. Manderson* (1848) 6 Moo. P.C. 239; *Gwynne v. Burrell* (1835) 6 Bing. N.C. 453; *L.B. & S.C. Ry v. Goodwin* (1849) 3 Exch. 736. This passage in the third edition was approved by the Privy Council in *Fahey v. M. S. D. Spiers Ltd* [1975] 1 N.Z.L.R. 240, where on the facts it was held not necessary in order to give business efficacy to a guarantee to imply a term that the guarantor would be entitled to the benefit of any payment which might be made by the principal debtor.

[91] *Re Sherry* (1884) 25 Ch D 692.

currency of the guarantee, charge the surety with the debits and withhold from him the benefits of the credits; the two accounts should be looked at as one.[92]

A surety for a loan by a money club to a member cannot claim credit, as extinguishing the loan, for the monthly subscriptions paid by the principal, the loan and the subscriptions being distinct matters.[93]

Where a guarantee is given to a banker for a loan account, or advances by way of the acceptance of bills, the surety has no right to have any credit balance that may exist from time to time on a current account kept by the principal with the same banker applied in reduction of the account guaranteed.[94] A balance on current account existing at the moment when the guarantee terminates may be afterwards paid over by the banker to the principal without affecting his rights against the surety.[95] Similarly, even if separate accounts are not kept, where it is the intention of the parties that the advance shall remain at the disposal of the customer, so that he shall be at liberty to draw against the items credited to him.[96] Thus where £5,000 had been advanced by a discount company to a customer on a guarantee to last for two years, and in the same account there appeared as credits the amounts of accommodation bills given by him to the company, as well as trade bills discounted, the proceeds of which were handed to him, and debited in the account, it was held that the advance guaranteed was not wiped out though the guarantee was not a continuing one.[97] However where in consideration of an advance to the principal, for which the principal gave a series of promissory notes, a surety agreed, if the notes were not paid at the due dates, to give a mortgage to secure the amount, it was held that the mortgage was only to be given if there was not money in hand to meet the notes, and that, sufficient money coming in, the creditor could not appropriate it to other purposes.[98]

By whom payments are to be appropriated

4–81   The well-settled rule as to the appropriation of payments is that the debtor may at the time of the payment appropriate it to any subsisting debt he chooses. If he makes no appropriation, the creditor can either then or at any time afterwards,[99] appropriate the

---

[92] *ibid.* And see *Bechervaise v. Lewis* (1872) L.R. 7 C.P. 372; *Ex p. Hanson* (1806) 18 Ves. 232.

[93] *Wright v. Hickling* (1866) L.R. 2 C.P. 199.

[94] *Hollond v. Teed* (1848) 7 Hare 50; *York City and County Banking Co. v. Bainbridge* (1880) 43 L.T. 732; *Bradford Old Bank v. Sutcliffe* [1918] 2 K.B. 833.

[95] *Hollond v. Teed*, above.

[96] *City Discount Co. v. McLean* (1874) L.R. 9 C.P. 692; *Browning v. Baldwin* (1879) 40 L.T. 248.

[97] *City Discount Co. v. McLean*, above.

[98] *Kinnaird v. Webster* (1878) 10 Ch D 139, explained in *Browning v. Baldwin* (1879) 40 L.T. 248.

[99] *Simson v. Ingham* (1823) 2 B. & C. 65; *Mills v. Fowkes* (1839) 5 Bing. N.C. 455; *City Discount Co. v. McLean* (1874) L.R. 9 C.P. 692 at 700.

money as he pleases,[1] even to a debt statute-barred,[2] though not to a debt incurred during infancy[3] and the payment will not be presumed to have been appropriated by the debtor to the more burdensome debt.[4] An appropriation by the creditor is not complete, and is therefore irrevocable until it is communicated to the debtor.[4] Appropriation by the debtor need not be expressed, if it is sufficiently shown by the circumstances. Thus where the debtor paid sums exactly tallying in amount with certain items, and obtained discount for prompt payment, which he was only entitled to if those items were discharged by those payments, it was held that he had appropriated the payment to those items.[5] Where new bills were given in exchange for dishonoured bills, it was held that they must be applied to the debt for which the old bills had been given, and could not be appropriated by the creditor to debts incurred since the old bills had been given.[6] Similarly, where an interview was held between an attorney employed by the agents of the creditor, the principal debtor, and the surety, at which the attorney pressed the principal debtor to make a payment and the surety also remonstrated with him for not paying, and the principal said he would pay something that afternoon, and on the following day did pay a large sum, it was held that it must be taken as appropriate to the debt guaranteed, and could not be applied to other debts which he owed the agents personally.[7]

The right of the creditor to appropriate payments made without appropriation by the debtor does not extend to sums which he has received from third persons for the debtor, without the knowledge of the debtor, and which the latter had therefore had no opportunity of appropriating.[8]

The rule in Clayton's Case

If, there being no appropriation by the debtor, the payments are credited by the creditor to a current account, and nothing points to a contrary intention, they will be taken, from the moment when that   **4–82**

---

[1] See *Goddard v. Cox* (1743) 2 Str. 1194; *Newmarch v. Clay* (1811) 14 East 229; *Plomer v. Long* (1816) 1 Stark. 153.
[2] *Mills v. Fowkes* (1839) 5 Bing. N.C. 455.
[3] *Keeping v. Broom* (1895) 11 T.L.R. 595.
[4] *Simson v. Ingham* (1827) 2 B. & C. 65. As pointed out by the South Australian Law Reform Committee Report on Suretyship (39th Report, 1976) at para. 4, where this passage is cited, it seems wrong that a creditor, with or without the principal debtor, should be able to appropriate payments without informing the surety. The Report suggests that legislation should impose an option on the creditor either to retain his power to appropriate payments as he pleases or to secure himself by obtaining a surety but not allow both. See further herein at para. 4–89, below, where *Blackstone Bank v. Hill* (1830) 10 Pick. 129 is discussed. The recommended solution is therefore to cause all payments by the debtor to operate to relieve the surety *pro tanto* of his obligation to the creditor in the absence of agreement to the contrary by the surety of the time of appropriation.
[5] *Marryatts v. White* (1817) 2 Stark. 101.
[6] *Newmarch v. Clay* (1811) 14 East 239.
[7] *Shaw v. Picton* (1825) 4 B. & C. 715. And see *Att.-Gen. for Jamaica v. Manderson* (1848) 6 Moo. P.C. 239.
[8] *Walker v. Lacy* 1 M. & Gr. 34.

fact is communicated to the debtor,[9] to have been applied to the earliest items in the account then unpaid.[10] Interest is presumed to be paid before principal, unless by a course of dealing binding upon the parties it has been added to and become part of the principal.[11]

The general rule as to the presumed appropriation of payments is known as the rule in *Clayton's Case.*[12] It cannot operate where the question is which of two debts in different accounts is to be taken as paid, nor where there having been a current account, that account is closed, and a new account not covered by the guarantee is opened, to which payment is credited.[13] It applies only where a person who has the right to appropriate money received as he pleases appropriates it in the manner shown in his books.[14] In a word, it is no more than a rule for the interpretation prima facie of the creditor's conduct in carrying the payment to the credit of the same account as is debited with the sum guaranteed. It may be excluded by circumstances showing that no appropriation was intended by the manner of keeping the account; as where the amounts credited were intended to be at the disposal of the debtor to draw out again, or merely represented bills discounted, of which he took the proceeds in cash.[15] Of course as regards a surety the rule in *Clayton's Case,* even if applicable, does not help the surety where the guarantee is a continuing one covering the ultimate balance on the account.[16] It helps the surety, if applicable, where the guarantee is only for a specific debt, which is carried by the creditor into a running account, or where a continuing guarantee has ceased to cover the further items in an account by reason of effluxion of time, revocation, death of parties or otherwise.[17] Furthermore, inasmuch as the creditor's right of appropriation does not arise, and

[9] *Simson v. Ingham* (1823) 2 B. & C. 65.
[10] *Devaynes v. Noble,* known as *Clayton's Case* (1816) 1 Mer. 572; *Brooke v. Enderby* (1820) 2 B. & B. 70; *Bodenham v. Purchas* (1816) 2 B. & Ald. 39; *Pemberton v. Oakes* (1827) 4 Russ. at 168; *Bank of Scotland v. Christie* (1841) 8 C. & F. 214; *Cory Brothers v. Owners of Turkish SS. Mecca* [1897] A.C. 286; *Deeley v. Lloyds Bank* [1912] A.C. 788; *Albermarle Supply Co. v. Hird* [1928] 1 K.B. 307. See also *Bank of Nova Scotia v. Neil* (1968) 69 D.L.R. (2d) 357. This last decision is criticised by the South Australian Law Reform Committee in its report on Suretyship (39th Report, 1976) on the broad ground that it allows the creditor to circumvent any limitation imposed under the guarantee simply by entering into a new agreement with the debtor leaving the surety's contract intact and without notifying the surety of what he is doing. In that case the guarantee was for $2,000. The creditor bank later entered into fresh agreements with the debtor unknown to the surety, amounting to $8,000. The bank in recovering the greater sum were held to remain entitled to recover the $2,000 from the surety. See also *Royal Bank of Canada v. Slack* (1958) 11 D.L.R. (2d) 737; *Dickson v. Royal Bank of Canada* (1976) 66 D.L.R. (3d) 242; *Hopkinson v. C.I.B.C.* [1977] 6 W.W.R. 490. The law in some American States appears to allow a more equitable allocation. See Stearns and Elder, *The Law of Suretyship* (5th ed., 1951, Section 7.23). See also the British Columbia Law Reform Commission Report on Consumer Guarantees (1979).
[11] *Parr's Banking Co. v. Yates* [1898] 2 QB 460.
[12] (1816) 1 Mer. 572.
[13] *Simson v. Ingham* (1823) 2 B. & C. 65; *Re Sherry* (1884) 25 Ch D 692.
[14] per Lord Selborne in *Blackburn Building Society v. Cunliffe Brooks & Co.* (1882) 22 Ch D at 71.
[15] *City Discount Co. v. McLean* (1874) L.R. 9 C.P. 692; *Browning v. Baldwin* (1879) 40 L.T. 248. And see *Ex p. Whitworth* (1841) 2 M.D. & De G. 164.
[16] *Henniker v. Wigg* (1843) 4 QB 792.
[17] See *Eyton v. Knight* (1838) 2 Jur. 8.

consequently no rule interpreting his conduct comes into play, unless the debtor pays without himself making any appropriation, it does not signify how the payments are dealt with by the creditor, if there is evidence of appropriation by the debtor.[18]

Dividends in bankruptcy[19]

With regard to dividends obtained by the creditor in the bank-   **4–83**
ruptcy of the principal, these are considered as made rateably in respect of every part of the debt, and operate, if not otherwise agreed by the surety, in relief of the guarantor or guarantors rateably. The creditor, therefore, in suing the surety, must give credit for all dividends received from the bankrupt upon the amount for which he is suing the surety, unless the proper construction of the guarantee is that it covered the amount remaining due after payment of any such dividends.[20] Where a surety was bound for the payment of the principal debt by instalments, and, the principal debtor becoming bankrupt, the creditor received a dividend on the whole debt, it was held that this must be distributed over all the instalments, and that the surety could not have it applied in discharge of the next instalment that fell due.[21] However, dividends which are declared upon the amount of the debt and interest owing at the date of the bankruptcy may be applied as against the surety to interest accrued since the bankruptcy, though such is not the subject of proof against the bankrupt.[22]

Guarantees for running accounts[23]

If the amount for which the surety is liable is less than the total   **4–84**
debt owing to the creditor by the principal, it becomes material to consider whether the surety is bound for the whole of that debt with a limitation of his liability, or whether he is bound only for a part of it equal to the amount for which he is liable. If the former is the case, he has no right to a dividend until the creditor has received 100 pence in the pound on the whole. If the latter, he is relieved to the extent of the proportion of the dividend attributable to that part of the debt which he has guaranteed, just as if the amount he had guaranteed were a separate distinct debt from the rest of the creditor's claim. The rule is that where the surety gives a continuing guarantee of limited amount to secure an indefinite liability, as, for instance, the amount of advances which may be made to the

---

[18] *Marryatts v. White* (1817) 2 Stark. 101; *Lysaght v. Walker* (1831) 5 Bligh (N.S.) 1.
[19] See also Chap. 11, below.
[20] *Ex p. Rushforth* (1805) 10 Ves. 409; *Paley v. Field* (1806) 12 Ves. 435; *Martin v. Brecknell* (1813) 2 M. & S. 39; *Raikes v. Todd* (1838) 8 A. & E. 846; *London Assurance Co. v. Buckle* (1820) 4 Moore 153; *Ellis v. Emmanuel* (1876) 1 Ex. D. 157. And see the cases cited below, notes 24 and 25.
[21] *Martin v. Brecknell*, above.
[22] *Bower v. Morris* (1841) Cr. & Ph. 351.
[23] See also part 5 of this Chapter, above.

principal, the guarantee is prima facie[24] to be taken as extending only to a part of the ultimate amount of the debt equal to the amount of the guarantee, and the surety will be entitled to that proportion of the dividends, the principle being that the surety is a stranger to the excess, and that the creditor swells his demand beyond the sum guaranteed at his own risk. The principle is exemplified in a line of cases referred to and distinguished in *Ellis v. Emmanuel*.[25]

Such a principle does not apparently apply where the surety is not a stranger to the excess, but expressly guarantees (subject to the limit as to the amount he is actually to pay) the whole amount to become due from the principal,[26] even though that may be the ultimate balance on a running account.[26] And in such cases the creditor would, perhaps, be entitled to retain the dividends even without an express proviso to that effect.[26]

Guarantees for ascertained debt of larger amount

4–85   Where the guarantee is given in respect of a floating balance, it is clear from *Ellis v. Emmanuel*,[27] that, where it is given in respect of an ascertained debt, the full amount of which is named as the subject of the guarantee, a limitation of the liability cast upon the surety will not be construed as preventing the guarantee applying to the whole debt, so that in such a case the surety has no right to dividends until 100 pence in the pound is paid on the whole debt. In that case, a number of sureties gave a joint and several bond for £14,000 conditioned to be void if the obligors or any or either of them should pay £7,000 and interest by certain instalments, with the proviso that the individual sureties should not be liable, whether by reason of a joint or several demand, for more than certain amounts in each case, making in all £7,000. Accordingly, the creditor was held entitled to recover from one of the sureties the full amount of his liability although a dividend of almost 50 pence in the pound had been received out of the estate of the principal. If, however, the sureties had engaged not jointly for the whole but severally for the amounts, together equalling the whole, for which they respectively became liable, it is probable that the true construction would have been that the engagement of each was confined to his proportionate part, and that each would have shared rateably in the dividends received by the creditor.[28]

---

[24] It is therefore usual in bank guarantees to insert a clause providing that the bank may prove for its own benefit and that the guarantee is to stand security for the ultimate balance. See, *e.g. Midland Banking Co. v. Chambers* (1869) L.R. 7 Eq. 149; *Re Sass* [1896] 2 QB 12.

[25] (1876) 1 Ex. D. 157.

[26] *Re Rees* (1881) 17 Ch D 98; *Re Sass* [1896] 2 QB 12.

[27] (1876) 1 Ex. D. 157.

[28] (1876) 1 Ex. D. 157 at 162. And see *Pendlebury v. Walker* (1841) 4 Y. & C. Ex. 424; *Collins v. Prosser* (1823) 1 B. & C. 682. See also *Ex p. Brook* (1815) 2 Rose 334; *Mayhew v. Crickett* (1818) 2 Swanst. 185.

Undertaking to pay a fixed proportion of unascertained loss

Where the plaintiffs were entitled to certain bills of lading to **4–86** enable them to recoup themselves an amount which they had paid for the consignee, and the defendants, who were interested in one-half of the goods, promised in consideration of the sale of the goods being left in their hands "to bear one-half of whatever loss might appear on the transaction," it was held, the consignee having become bankrupt, that the defendants were liable to pay half the loss upon the sale, without any deduction in respect of dividends which had been received by the plaintiffs out of the estate of the consignee of the whole of such loss.[29]

Special proviso dealing with dividends

It is open to the surety, in a case where prima facie he would be **4–87** entitled to a proportion of any dividend received out of the estate of the principal, expressly to make over this right to the creditor and permit him to receive all dividends until he has received 100 pence in the pound,[30] and a clause to this effect is commonly found. It is no objection to the creditor's right to prove for the full amount, after receiving payment from the surety, that the surety had a security upon the debtor's estate by means of which he has paid the creditor the amount of the guarantee at the expense of the debtor.[31]

Proceeds of execution

In 1830 it was held by the Supreme Court of Massachusetts that **4–88** when a creditor obtained one judgment in respect of several debts, some of which were and some were not covered by guarantee, the proceeds of an execution issued upon the judgment could not be appropriated by the creditor to the unguaranteed debts, but must be apportioned rateably to all the debts included in the judgment.[32]

Appropriation of payments as between several sureties

With regard to payments made by a debtor owing several debts **4–89** and not appropriated by him, it has been seen that the general rule is that the creditor can appropriate them at his pleasure. But where a number of sureties guarantee the same debt, but in distinct portions, splitting it up amongst themselves for that purpose, the point arises whether payments by the principal reducing the debt

---

[29] *Liverpool Borough Bank v. Logan* (1860) 5 H. & N. 464.
[30] See, *e.g. Midland Banking Co. v. Chambers* (1869) L.R. 7 Eq. 179; *Re Rees* (1881) 17 Ch D 98; *Re Sass* [1876] 2 QB 12.
[31] *Midland Banking Co. v. Chambers*, above. *Cf. Re Melton* [1918] 1 Ch. 37; *Re Lennard* [1934] 1 Ch. 235.
[32] *Blackstone Bank v. Hill*, 10 Pick. 129 (1830). See above at para. 4–81.

below the total of all the guarantees put together must not be rateably applied in reducing the liability of each. In *Pendlebury v. Walker*,[33] the liability for the principal debt was by contract with each surety (each being bound in a separate instrument) to be distributed by means of the rateable apportionment of any payments by the principal among a specified number of named co-sureties; and in *Ellis v. Emmanuel*,[34] it seems to have been thought by Blackburn J., that even without such a stipulation the creditor would probably have been bound impliedly to apportion any payments by the principal among a number of sureties guaranteeing by the same instrument the same debt in distinct portions.[35]

In cases like *Pendlebury v. Walker*,[36] and the case put by Blackburn J. in *Ellis v. Emmanuel*,[37] one result of the compulsory rateable appropriation of payments by the principal would be that no case would arise for contribution. It does not appear, however, to follow that conversely where there is no contribution, payments by the principal must be apportioned. In *Coope v. Twynam*,[38] the principal was to give three separate bonds, in each of which a separate surety was to join, each bond being for a third of the debt. Lord Eldon held there would be no contribution, but there is nothing to show that he thought payments by the principal would be apportionable. He considered each bond "a separate transaction," and upon this footing it would seem that the principal could pay off any bond he chose. The surety in another bond, if he paid the whole of the sum secured by that bond would have no claim for contribution upon the surety in the bond paid off by the principal. If each bond had been security for every part of the principal debt, though involving the liability of only one-third of the amount of that debt, there would be no apportionment; but any surety paying more than his proportion of the deficiency would have had contribution.[39]

Payment by other sureties

4–90   Where a number of sureties engage severally by one instrument for a limited sum (or jointly or severally if there is a proviso limiting the effective liability of each by reason of either a joint or several demand),[40] the question arises whether they are liable for that sum each, so that the full amount can be recovered from each and all of them one after another, or whether, though severally liable, they all engage for the same sum, so that when once that sum

---

[33] (1841) 4 Y. & C. Ex. 424.
[34] (1876) 1 Ex. D. 157.
[35] *ibid.* at 162. *Cf.* the form of guarantee in *Fell v. Goslin* (1852) 7 Exch. 185.
[36] See n. 33, above.
[37] See n. 34, above.
[38] (1823) T. & R. 426.
[39] *Coope v. Twynam*, above; *Ellis v. Emmanuel* (1876) 1 Ex. D. 157; *Ellesmere Bravery Co. v. Cooper* [1896] 1 QB 75.
[40] See the bond in *Ellis v. Emmanuel*, above, set out below.

is paid by any one of them all are relieved.[41] In *Collins v. Prosser*,[42] a bond for a number of sureties ran, so far as concerned three of them, as follows: "We are held firmly bound for £1,000 each, for which we bind ourselves and each of us for himself, for the whole and entire sum of £1,000 each." It was held that each surety was severally liable, and that a separate £1,000 was recoverable from each, that is to say £3,000 in all. In that case there was a total debt secured of £12,000, which amount, as appeared from the recital in the condition, was to be secured by the bond, each obligor being liable for the sum set against his name, and the construction adopted effected this object. In *Ellis v. Emmanuel*,[43] seven sureties were bound, and every two or more and each of them jointly and severally, in the penal sum of £14,000, conditioned for avoidance if the obligors or any or either of them should pay £7,000; and there was a proviso that four of the sureties "shall not, nor shall either of them, be liable (whether by reason of a joint or several action or demand) for a sum or sums exceeding altogether in debt or damages £1,300." It was held that each of the four was liable for a separate £1,300 and that nothing paid by one of them reduced the liability of the others. This construction made the seven sureties between them responsible for the whole principal debt of £7,000; the other construction would have left some of the principal debt uncovered.

Similarly, where two persons by one instrument guaranteed "the sum of £400, in the proportion of £200 each," it was held that each was liable for a separate £200, but that neither was liable for more.[44]

In *Armstrong v. Cahill*,[45] a fidelity bond for four sureties ran, "we, A, B, C and D are hereby held and firmly bound in the sum of £50 each to E, his executors, administrators, and assigns, to which payment we hereby bind us and each of us, our and each of our heirs, executors and administrators, and every of them." There was nothing to show whether the total amount intended to be secured was £50 or £200. It was held by the Common Pleas Division in Ireland that each surety was liable for a separate sum of £50, and that the others were not discharged when one had paid £50.[46]

Where principal entitled to set-off

Where the principal is entitled to a set-off against the creditor's **4–91** demand arising out of the same transaction as the debt guaranteed, and in fact reducing that debt, the surety is entitled to plead it in an

---

[41] See *Collins v. Prosser* (1823) 1 B. & C. 682 *per* Holroyd J. at 687, 688. See generally, Chap. 8, Part 3.
[42] above.
[43] (1876) 1 Ex. D. 157.
[44] *Fell v. Goslin* (1852) 7 Exch. 185.
[45] (1880) 6 L.R. Ir. 440.
[46] See also *R. v. O'Callaghan* (1838) 1 Ir. Eq. R. 439.

action by the creditor against the surety alone.[47] This rule has been doubted as a general proposition in Australia,[48] but has been approved by the Court of Appeal in England.[49]

If the creditor is merely a trustee for other persons and is suing for their benefit and not his own, a set-off against the persons beneficially interested will be available to the surety, even though they are not before the court.[50]

In *Murphy v. Glass*,[51] it was held that a surety for the price of lands bought in a colony under a contract by which any dispute as to the matters connected with the sale was not to annul the sale, but be referred to arbitration, might plead in reduction of his liability an award of compensation to the purchaser in respect of a deficiency in the acreage of the lands on the grounds that such compensation was an abatement of the price. In *Bechervaise v. Lewis*,[52] a surety who had joined with the principal in a joint and several promissory note given for the price of the interest of the payee in certain debts to be transferred by him to the principal, but which the payee was to collect, was allowed to set off against the demand upon the note the amount of certain of those debts which had been collected by the payee and not paid over to the principal.[53]

But where the principal is not before the court, the mere existence of an independent cross-debt from the creditor to the principal is no defence to the surety.[54] In *Bowyear v. Pawson*,[55] where the

---

[47] See *Murphy v. Glass* (1869) L.R. 2 P.C. 408; *Bechervaise v. Lewis* (1872) L.R. 7 C.P. 372; See also *Gillespie v. Torrance*, 25 N.Y. 30 (1862); *Newton v. Lee*, 139 N.Y. 332 (1893). Cf. *Wilson v. Mitchell* [1939] 2 K.B. 869, where Finlay L.J. was of the view that a guarantor could not pray in aid a counterclaim for damages for breach of warranty against the creditor, and held that even if he was wrong in that view, it would not be available as a defence in an action between co-sureties without bringing in the debtor whose claim it was.

[48] *Cellulose Products Pty Ltd v. Truda* (1970) 92 W.N. (N.S.W.) 561; *Covino v. Bandag Mfg Pty Ltd* [1983] 1 N.S.W.L.R. 237; *Indrisie v. General Credits Ltd* [1985] V.R. 251.

[49] In *Hyundai Shipbuilding & Heavy Industries Co. Ltd v. Pournaras* [1978] 2 Lloyd's Rep. 502 the court accepted the correctness of the rule as set out in the third edition of this work but on the special facts of that case and in the light of the commercial policy reasons involved, the Court of Appeal refused to allow the guarantors to avail themselves of any right of set-off enuring to the benefit of the principal debtor. On the question of excluding set-off, the House of Lords in the related case of *Hyundai v. Papadopoulos* [1980] 1 W.L.R. 1129 followed *Pournaras*. In *National Westminster Bank v. Skelton* [1993] 1 W.L.R. 72, a case of guarantee by mortgage, the divergence of authority was noted and the point left open by the Court of Appeal, although they were prepared to assume for the purposes of their reasoning that the approach in *Hyundai Shipbuilding & Heavy Industries Co. Ltd v. Pournaras* [1978] 2 Lloyd's Rep. 502 was correct, since reliance on the principle debtor's set-off was held to be excluded in any event by a clause allowing the creditor to treat the surety as a principal debtor. In *Ashley Guarantee v. Zacaria* [1993] 1 W.L.R. 62, CA, also a case of guarantee by mortgage, there was no such exclusion and the ability to set off was assumed, but there was insufficient evidence that the guarantor's cross-claims exceeded the mortgagee's claim, so that the mortgagee was entitled to possession. This topic is discussed by Steyn, "The Co-Extensiveness Principle" (1974) 90 L.Q.R. 246 at 261 *et seq*. See also a note on the *Cellulose* decision in (1970) 44 A.L.J. 562. *Semble* a surety cannot rely on a possible claim for rescission by the principal debtor: see *First National Bank of Chicago Ltd v. Moorgate Properties Ltd*, *The Times*, October 20, 1975, CA. See also *Barclays Bank Plc v. Gruffydd*, October 30, 1992, CA, doubting correctness of *Wilson v. Mitchell* and *Cellulose*, *supra*.

[50] *Alcoy, etc. v. Greenhill* (1897) 76 L.T. 542. See also preceding note.

[51] (1869) L.R. 2 P.C. 408.

[52] (1872) L.R. 7 C.P. 372.

[53] See (1952) 96 S.J. 659 on the possible application of these two cases to the question of whether a tenant's surety can claim relief if the landlord has failed to discharge some obligation, *e.g.* to repair, as a result of which the tenant's ability to perform his own obligations becomes impossible.

[54] See *Wilson v. Mitchell* [1939] 2 K.B. 869 discussed above at n. 47.

[55] (1881) 6 Q.B.D. 540.

defendant and one Wilson were co-sureties in a joint and several covenant, and the defendant, being sued for the whole amount due, pleaded an indebtedness of the plaintiff to Wilson in an amount exceeding the amount sued for, and claimed the benefit of the moiety of that indebtedness on the ground that as to a moiety he was entitled to be exonerated by his co-surety Wilson, it was held by Watkin, Williams and Mathew JJ., that no defence was disclosed, as it was not shown that "the defendant had any right to call upon Wilson to appropriate the debt due to him from the plaintiff to the exoneration of the defendant nor any contract with the plaintiff to accept a set-off of Wilson's debt as a discharge of the defendant." It has been held in America that a surety for the price of goods sold cannot set up a breach of warranty to the principal, even though the principal might have set it up in reduction of damages.[56]

Any other view than that adopted in *Bowyear v. Pawson* would lead to great difficulties. For example the principal might owe other debts than the debt guaranteed, for which, moreover, other sureties might be bound, and complete justice would not be done to all parties. Therefore in any case where a surety claims the benefit of a set-off or cross-claim available to the principal, and not operating directly to reduce the debt guaranteed, the principal ought at least to be made a party in order that the surety's right to the benefit of the set-off may be established against him, and that he may be bound by the set-off and precluded from afterwards requiring payment from the creditor.[57]

Set-off in foreign law

If a guarantee, though securing an English debt, falls to be **4–92** construed by the law of a country where a debt is extinguished by set-off according to its law, and a surety is not liable for an amount to which the principal has a set-off, a set-off available in England available to the principal against the creditor which would have

---

[56] *Gillespie v. Torrance* 25 N.Y. 306 (1862); *Newton v. Lee* N.Y. 332 (1893), both discussed at length by Isaacs J. in *Cellulose Products Pty Ltd v. Truda* (1970) 92 W.N. (N.S.W.) 561 at 571 *et seq.*, as to which see above at n. 48. But see next note.
[57] See *Murphy v. Glass* (1869) L.R. 2 P.C. 408; *Bowyear v. Pawson* (1881) 6 Q.B.D. 540. And *cf. Ex p. Hippins* (1826) 2 Gl. & J. 93; *Cheetham v. Crook* (1825) McCl. & Y. 307; *Gillespie v. Torrance*, above. Isaacs J. in *Cellulose Products Pty Ltd*, above, at 587 approves the passage in the text. At 588 Isaacs J. concludes that when sued, the surety has the right to join the debtor as third party who can in turn join the plaintiff as fourth party, etc., all of which claims can then be determined at once. In the United States, despite the rules reflected in the cases discussed in the text, a guarantor may be allowed to assert his principal's cross-claim, in certain circumstances, *e.g.* if the latter is insolvent. See. *e.g. U.S. ex. rel. Johnson v. Morley Construction Co..* 98 F (2d) 781 (2nd Circuit, 1938) at 789. See also *Restatement, Security*, s. 133 (1941). A leading Canadian authority is *Diebel v. Stratford Improvement Co.* (1917) 33 D.L.R. 29, where the Ontario Court of Appeal allowed the guarantor to set up a claim for breach of warranty available to the debtor. See the British Columbia Law Reform Commission Report on Consumer Guarantees (1979), Chap. IV, Section F in generally recommending such a right, but stopping short of requiring the guarantor to join his principal as a party to the proceedings.

extinguished the debt by the foreign law affords a defence to the surety by virtue of that law.[58]

Set-off by principal

4–93   The principal debtor may of course set-off whatever a creditor owes him against the demand of the creditor against him upon the debt guaranteed,[59] and this even though the principal and surety are jointly liable, the debt being really that of the principal alone, and the joint liability being a security only.[60] If the principal has done this the liability of the surety ought to be extinguished to the amount of the set-off,[61] otherwise the principal would not be protected, as the surety if called upon to pay would come to him for indemnity.[62] On this ground, if the creditor sues the surety alone, and so gives the principal no opportunity of establishing his set-off, the principal may, it seems, in order to protect himself from the liability which judgment against the surety would indirectly bring upon him, go to the court himself and have the set-off declared, and, if the set-off is equal to the debt, have the guarantee or accommodation bill given up.[63]

Set-off by surety

4–94   If a surety, being severally liable, has money in the hands of the creditor, who becomes bankrupt, he is entitled to assent that there has been an automatic mandatory insolvency set-off.[64] The existence of the set-off does not depend on any fraudulent concealment of the presence of the money by the creditor.[65] A surety jointly liable with the principal can at any time on learning the facts insist on the application to the extinction of the joint debt of the proceeds of securities belonging to himself severally, but pledged for the joint debt and wrongfully sold by the creditor before the debt became due, without the knowledge of the pledgor.[66]

A bank which has made advances to a customer abroad on the security of a guarantee given in England, is entitled, when recovering against the surety, to compare the sum owing abroad at the rate

---

[58] *Allen v. Kemble* (1848) 6 Moo. P.C. 314, explained in *Rouquette v. Overman* (1875) L.R. 10 QB 540. See also Chap. 19, below.
[59] *Ex p. Hanson* (1806) 12 Ves. 346; 18 Ves. 232; *Ex p. Hippins* (1826) 2 Gl. & J. 93; *Vulliamy v. Noble* (1817) 3 Mer. 593.
[60] *Ex p. Hanson*, above; *Vulliamy v. Noble*, above.
[61] *per* Willes J. in *Owen v. Wilkinson* (1858) 5 C.B. (N.S.) 526.
[62] *Ex p. Hippins* (1896) 2 Gl. & J. 93.
[63] *Ex p. Hanson* (1806) 12 Ves. 346; *Ex p. Hippins*, above.
[64] *Ex p. Stephens* (1805) 11 Ves. 24, as explained by Jessel M.R. in *Middleton v. Pollock* (1875) L.R. 20 Eq. 515 at 519 and re-explained by Hoffmann L.J. in *MS Fashions v. BCCI* [1993] Ch. 425. See also the explanations in *Vulliamy v. Noble* (1817) 3 Mer. at 621; *Ex p. Hanson* (1806) 12 Ves. at 348; *Jones v. Mossop* (1844) 3 Hare at 573; *BCCI (No. 8)* [1996] Ch. 245, CA (affirmed on other grounds, [1997] 3 W.L.R. 909, HL).
[65] *ibid.*
[66] *Vulliamy v. Noble*, above, as explained by Jessel M.R. in *Middleton v. Pollock*, above, at 521.

of exchange prevailing when the liability accrued and not that at the date of judgment.[67]

Where a surety deposited monies with a bank which subsequently went into insolvent liquidation and the surety agreed to be not merely a guarantor but to have principal liability in respect of the bank's lending to the principal debtor, the automatic mandatory insolvency set-off of the deposit against the surety's obligation to the bank operated so as to repay the principal debtor's indebtedness to the bank.[68]

Interest

Whether sureties can be made liable for interest or costs recoverable from the principal is of course a question upon the construction of their engagement.[69] Where sureties had given a bond conditioned to be void if a receiver should "duly account for and pay what he should receive, as the Court had directed or should direct," Lord Eldon thought the penalty should in an ordinary case only be delivered against upon the terms of the money being accounted for with interest; but, under the special circumstances of that particular case, he did not act on that view.[70] A surety for the payment of a bill of exchange by the acceptor is liable for interest from the date it becomes due.[71] If the creditor obtains judgment against the principal for the debt, a surety for the payment of interest under the original contract is not liable for the interest carried by the judgment debt.[72] A surety for the payment of principal and interest is liable for interest though his liability for the principal may be barred by the statute of limitations.[73]

4–95

A guarantor of an advance by a banker to his customer was held not to be entitled to the repayment of tax on payments under his guarantee in respect of interest made without deduction of tax under section 36(1) of the Income Tax Act 1918.[74] In *Re Hawkins, deceased*[75] it was held that any sum that a guarantor paid in respect of interest due from the principal debtor ranked as payment of interest and not payment of a sum in lieu of interest, particularly

---

[67] *Mann, Taylor & Co. v. Royal Bank of Canada* (1935) 40 Com. Cas. 267 at 280. Note generally effect of *Miliangos v. George Frank (Textiles) Ltd* [1976] A.C. 443.

[68] *M.S. Fashions v. BCCI* [1993] Ch. 425 (Hoffmann L.J. and CA).

[69] As to penal interest payable by a defaulting trustee in bankruptcy see *Board of Trade v. Employers' Liability Association* [1910] 2 K.B. 649.

[70] *Dawson v. Raynes* (1826) 2 Russ. 466. A bond is here regarded as a security carrying interest beyond the date on which payment is due. See *Re Dixon* [1900] 2 Ch. 561.

[71] *Ackerman v. Ehrenspeger* (1846) 16 M. & W. 99.

[72] *Faber v. Earl of Lathom* (1897) L.T. 168.

[73] *Parr's Banking Co. v. Yates* [1898] 2 QB 460; *cf. Wright v. New Zealand Farmers' Co-operative Assn of Canterbury Ltd* [1939] A.C. 439, PC. See further Chap. 10, below.

[74] *Holder v. Commissioners of Inland Revenue* [1932] A.C. 624.

[75] [1972] Ch. 714 applying dicta of Lord Atkin in *Holder v. Commissioners of Inland Revenue*, above. See also *Westminster Bank Executor and Trustee Co. (Channel Islands) Ltd v. National Bank of Greece S.A.* [1970] 1 QB 236. Interest will not, at least as between guarantor and creditor, forego its character simply because it is paid pursuant to an obligation imposed by a guarantee. *Re Hawkins* was followed in *Re-Amalgamated Investment & Property Co. Ltd* [1984] B.C.L.C. 341.

where the guarantor had in terms guaranteed "the payment of interest."

Costs

4–96   Standard form bank guarantees often provide for the guarantor to pay all the costs of the enforcement of the guarantee. Such a provision will be interpreted as providing for the payment of indemnity costs, and although it cannot oust the jurisdiction of the court to decide on the correct order for costs in its discretion, it will provide a convenient contractual starting point for the exercise of the court's discretion.[76]

Where a committee of a lunatic was ordered to pay over a balance in his hands and certain costs of proceedings against him, the sureties in a bond of which the condition was that the committee should obey the Lord Chancellor's orders attaching or concerning the lunatic's estate, were ordered to pay the costs.[77] In Ireland it was held that a surety by recognisance for a tenant under the Court was liable for the costs of an attachment against the tenant, provided he was not made liable for more than the amount of the recognisance.[78] A surety for a receiver is chargeable (subject to the same limitation) with the costs of an attachment against the receiver being in default, and also of removing him and appointing another.[79] The principle is that the surety is answerable, to the extent of the penalty, for whatever sum of money, whether principal, interest or costs, the receiver has become liable for.[80] So a surety in a recognisance conditioned that a receiver should duly account for all money which he should receive "on account of the rents and the profits of the real estate" of a testator, and duly pay the balance which should from time to time be certified to be due from him, was held liable for insurance moneys received by the receiver upon a fire insurance effected by him, also for income paid to him under orders of the court of funds in court designed to be reinvested in real estate, and also for money paid to him under order of the court to be spent on repairs.[80]

10. *When the Liability of the Surety becomes Enforceable*

General rule

4–97   The common expressions (accurate enough in their true sense) that a surety "is only liable on default of the principal," or "only

---

[76] *Bank of Baroda v. Panessar* [1987] Ch. 335.
[77] *Re Lockey* (1845) 1 Ph. 509. But *cf. Hoole v. Fidelity and Deposit Co.* [1916] 1 K.B. 25 affirmed on different grounds [1916] 2 K.B. 568, distinguished in *The Rosarino* [1973] 1 Lloyd's Rep. 21.
[78] *Keily v. Murphy* (1837) 1 Sau. & Sc. 479 approved in *Maunsell v. Egan* (1846) 9 Ir. Eq. R. 283.
[79] *Maunsell v. Egan*, above; *Re Graham* [1895] 1 Ch. 66.
[80] *Re Graham*, above.

promises to pay if he does not," must not be construed to convey that there must, before the surety becomes liable, be any demand and refusal between the parties of the principal contract, or any final failure to pay on the part of the principal debtor. When the subject-matter of the guarantee is conduct, some breach of duty by the principal causing damage to the holder of the guarantee must, of course, arise before there is anything which the surety can be called upon to make good. But as soon as a breach is committed of the duty performance of which is guaranteed, or in the case of a debt that day of payment arrives, the default of the principal is complete, and every surety is, apart from any term to the contrary, immediately liable to the full extent of his obligation, without being entitled to require notice of the default.[81]

It is the surety's duty to see that the principal pays or performs his duty, as the case may be.[82] This was the reason given in the third edition of this work for the rule that as soon as "the default of the principal is complete . . . every surety is, apart from special stipulation, immediately liable to the full extent of his obligation, without being entitled to require either notice of the default, or previous recourse against the principal, or simultaneous recourse against co-sureties."[83]

Surety contracting jointly with principal

A surety who contracts only jointly with the principal or with another surety is entitled by the general law of contract to have his co-contractor sued with him, a right formally enforced by a plea in abatement.[84] A promissory note beginning "I promise to pay," and signed by two persons, is the several note of each.[85] Where a number of sureties (say three) join in a guarantee each for a separate limited sum, this involves that the instrument imposes a several liability only on each; otherwise all might be sued three times over; and if only one was solvent, he might be compelled to pay three times the amount which *ex hypothesi* he has engaged for.[86] But the engagement might be joint in such a case if it provided that no

4–98

---

[81] A surety for the performance of a contract of indemnity could probably be sued *quia timet* as soon as it was shown that damage was imminent but he could not be sued before: *Antrobus v. Davidson* (1817) 3 Mer. 569. The third edition of this work took the view that the surety could not require previous recourse against the principal or simultaneous recourse against co-securities. See now discussion in Chap. 7.

[82] *Re Lockey* (1845) 1 Ph. 809; *Wright v. Simpson* (1802) 6 Ves. at 734. This passage in the text was cited and approved in *Moschi v. Lep Air Services Ltd* [1973] A.C. 337 *per* Lord Simon at 356.

[83] See *Ewart v. Latta* (1865) 4 Macq. 983. For a discussion of the rule and possible exceptions see below, Chapter 7.

[84] Now see R.S.C., Ord. 15, r. 4. Note effect of Civil Liability (Contribution) Act 1978 as to which see paras A–31 *et seq.* in the Appendix.

[85] *March v. Ward* (1790) 1 Peake 177; *Clerk v. Blackstock* (1816) Holt 474.

[86] See *Collins v. Prosser* (1823) 1 B. & C. 682 *per* Bayley J. at 686.

surety shall be liable (whether by reason of a joint or several demand) for more than the amount limited in his case.[87]

Default by the principal

4–99   In the sense above[88] explained there must be a default by the principal before the surety can be made liable. Thus where the guarantee is that the principal will duly account for moneys coming into his hands it must be shown that money has been received by him.[89] In *Guardians of Belford Union v. Pattison*,[90] a surety for a treasurer was held liable for moneys due to his employers from their debtor with which the treasurer had debited himself in account with the debtor (who had supplied him with goods) in pursuance of a course of dealing between them the effect of which was that as between the two money had in substance passed, the employer having also treated the treasurer as paid by the debtor. In that case the treasurer had in effect been paid in goods which was owing to the employer. But it is suggested that it would not be open to an employer, generally speaking, to authorise his servant, instead of collecting the moneys due to the employer, to set them off against debts due by the servant, and then charge the surety for the servant, if the latter, perhaps having no money of his own, did not account to the employer for the amount of the sums set off. That would, in effect, be supplying the servant at the expense of the surety with money to pay his own debts to the debtors of his employer.[91]

Where a bond was conditioned that a collector should duly demand certain taxes, and duly enforce the law against those who should make default, the obligees were held entitled to recover on proof merely that less had been received than the proper amount, and that the collector had not returned a list of any defaulters, as was by law his duty, if there were any.[92] Similarly, a surety for an administrator is liable if the administrator has misapplied funds of the deceased, even though the time has not yet arrived for their distribution.[93]

Where the guarantee was that a poor law officer "should duly and faithfully discharge all and every the duties of his said office," it was held that the sureties were liable whether the breach of duty complained of was committed fraudulently or not.[94]

---

[87] See, *e.g.* the bond in *Ellis v. Emmanuel* (1876) 1 Ex. D. 157, *i.e.* in previous sections of this part.

[88] See also *Rickaby v. Lewis* (1905) 22 T.L.R. 130; *Eshelby v. Federated European Bank* [1932] 1 K.B. 254; 423, CA.

[89] *Guardians of Belford Union v. Pattison* (1856) 11 Exch. 623; *Jephson v. Howkins* (1841) 2 M. & Gr. 366. *Cf. Harvell v. Foster* [1954] 2 QB 367.

[90] above.

[91] *cf.* the cases as to payments to agents, *e.g. Stewart v. Aberdeen* (1838) 4 M. & W. 211; *Sweeting v. Pearce* (1861) 9 C.B. (N.S.) 534.

[92] *Loveland v. Knight* (1828) 3 C. & P. 106.

[93] *Archbishop of Canterbury v. Robertson* (1833) 1 C. & M. 690; *Dobbs v. Brain* (1898) 8 T.L.R. 630; *Harvell v. Foster* [1954] 2 QB 367.

[94] *Bramley v. Guarantee Society* (1900) 64 J.P. 308.

Where it is necessary to show that a loss has been sustained, it is not enough for the creditor merely to give evidence that the debtor has signed the deed of assignment for the benefit of his creditors.[95]

Surety for bill never presented

A surety for payment of a bill or note by the acceptor, is liable, **4–100** though it is never presented, as it is his duty to see it is paid.[96] But where payment by the drawer or an indorser is guaranteed, the surety is discharged if the bill is not presented, or the drawer or indorser does not receive notice of dishonour, because then the drawer or indorser is discharged.[97] But where the principal is liable without demand so is the surety.[98] The surety becomes liable to be sued when all the facts have occurred which show a default within the meaning of the guarantee, not when the fact of the default has been ascertained by litigation.[99]

Default involves a liability by the principal

There is no default by the principal, and the surety is, therefore, **4–101** not liable, where the principal has a lawful excuse (not founded on the personal disability[1] or the statutes of limitation[2]) for the omission of which the creditor complains. Therefore where there was a guarantee for due accounting by a treasurer for moneys in his hands, and the treasurer was robbed by irresistible violence of such moneys specifically, the sureties were not liable.[3] Similarly, a mere mistake in book-keeping is not necessarily a breach of a bond for the good conduct of a clerk.[4] But where money was alleged by an employee to have been lost as he was travelling in his employer's service his surety was held liable.[5]

Refusal by creditor to accept performance

A surety is not liable when the creditor has refused to accept the **4–102** performance of the duty guaranteed, as where a bond is given conditioned for service by an apprentice, and the master bids him go about his business.[6] The same applies if the apprentice leaves the

---

[95] *Montague Stanley & Co. v. Solomons Ltd* [1932] 2 K.B. 287.
[96] *Warrington v. Furbor* (1807) 8 East. 242; *Hitchcock v. Humfrey* (1843) 5 M. & Gr. 559; *Walton v. Mascoll* (1844) 13 M. & W. 452. It is said in these cases that the surety might be discharged if damnified.
[97] *Philips v. Astling* (1809) 2 Taunt. 206. And see *Hitchcock v. Humfrey,* above at 564.
[98] See *Rede v. Farr* (1817) 6 M. & S. 121.
[99] See *Colvin v. Buckle* (1844) 8 M. & W. 680.
[1] See above.
[2] See Chap. 10, below.
[3] *Walker v. British Guarantee Association* (1852) 18 QB 277.
[4] *Jephson v. Howkins* (1841) 2 M. & Gr. 366.
[5] *Melville v. Dridge* (1848) 6 C.B. 450.
[6] See *MacTaggart v. Watson* (1836) 3 C. & F. 525 at 543.

service under a reasonable fear of ill-treatment.[7] However, where a banking company gave a letter of credit authorising a company to draw upon the bank, and it was stipulated that the company should forward goods the proceeds of which were to be applicable to the bills accepted by the bank, and the agents of the company guaranteed repayment to the bank of the amount to be due under the credit, it was held that they were not discharged although, owing to the bank stopping payment after it had accepted the bills, the principals declined to forward the goods. This was on the ground that the stoppage of the bank did not justify the principals in not forwarding the goods.[8]

Liability independent of default

4–103   The necessity of proof that the principal has failed to meet a valid claim does not, however, always exist. It is, of course, open to a party to agree to pay a sum in any event in order to put an end to a disputed claim against another. It is not necessary to show in such a case that the claim was valid.[9] But such agreements are not in reality guarantees, as the liability assumed is not collateral, but original.

Negligence of creditor

4–104   As it is the surety's duty to see the principal makes no default, he is liable notwithstanding any mere neglect by the creditor to safeguard his own interests.[10] Thus where the principal is a servant or agent, if the employer has omitted for long period to check and examine his accounts, the surety is not discharged.[11] Nor will neglect in the superintendence of a contract during the execution of works discharge a surety for the contractor.[12]

The surety guarantees the honesty of the person employed, and is not to be relieved because the employer fails to use all the means in his power to guard against the consequences of dishonesty.[13] And even where a bond is given under statute for securing the performance of the duties of an officer appointed under the statute, it is the duty of the surety to see that he does perform those duties and if any directions for securing that end are given by the statute to the superiors of the officer, those directions are for the additional security of the public only and neglect of them does not discharge

---

[7] *Halliwell v. Counsell* (1878) 38 L.T. 176.
[8] *Ex p. Agra Bank* (1870) L.R. 9 Eq. 725.
[9] *Tempson v. Knowles* (1849) 7 C.B. 651. And see *Gull v. Lindsay* (1849) 4 Exch. 45.
[10] In *Bank of India v. Transcontinental Commodity Merchants Ltd*, [1982] 1 Lloyd's Rep. 506, Bingham J. held there was no duty on a credit or to avoid irregular dealings by the principal debtor which could prejudice both the creditor and the surety.
[11] *Trent Navigation Co. v. Harley* (1808) I.O. East. 34; *Black v. Ottoman Bank* (1862) 15 Moo. P.C. 472; *Wilks v. Heeley* (1832) I.C. & M. 249.
[12] *Mayor, etc., of Kingston-upon-Hull v. Harding* (1892) 2 QB 494.
[13] *Black v. Ottoman Bank* (1862) 15 Moo. P.C. at 484.

the surety,[14] and this even though the persons guilty of that neglect are the obligees in the bond and plaintiffs in the action.[15] In Ireland it has been held that the neglect or laches of a court officer will not discharge the surety.[16] Upon this ground not calling an officer to account according to a statute[17] and the omission to require him to bank moneys in his hands which the guarantors undertook he should bank[18] have been held not to discharge the sureties. However, actual connivance at the retention of moneys might discharge the surety,[19] as amounting to a receipt and a fresh credit to the principal.[20] And it might be that a statute directing a surety to be taken and that the principal be promptly called to account, should be so framed as to secure to the surety the benefit of that provision, and operate to discharge him if it was disobeyed.[21]

Express stipulations for diligence against the principal

A surety may, of course, by stipulation make it a condition **4–105** precedent that active steps be taken by the creditor. Therefore, where the surety was not to be liable "but on failure of the creditor's utmost efforts and legal proceedings" to obtain the money from the principal, it was held that the meaning was that the surety was not liable unless these measures were taken promptly, and not, that the surety was liable whenever they had been taken.[22] If the creditor, in taking a promissory note from principal and surety, agrees with the surety to call it in within three years, and does not, the surety is released.[23] However, a mere memorandum, "This note to be paid off within three years," does not bind the creditor to enforce it within that time. And where it was stipulated by a surety that the creditor should "see the principal make up his cash every month," the surety was not discharged in respect of the first month's embezzlements by neglect to carry this out, though he was discharged as to subsequent defalcations on the ground (it does

[14] *Wilks v. Heeley* (1832) 1 C. & M. 249; *Collins v. Gwynne* (1833) 9 Bing. 544; SC in error 2 Bing. N.C. 7; 6 Bing. N.C. 453, HL; *MacTaggart v. Watson* (1836) 3 C. & F. 525; *Madden v. McMullen* (1860) 13 Ir. C.L.R. 305; *Guardians of Mansfield Union v. Wright* (1872) 9 Q.B.D. 683. See further *Donegal C.C. v. Life and Health Assurance Association* (1909) 2 I.R. 700; *Wicklow C.C. v. Hibernian Fire & General Ins. Co.* (1932) I.R. 58.
[15] See previous note. This proposition was doubted by Sir J. Hannen in *Guardians of Mansfield Union v. Wright* (1882) 9 Q.B.D. 683 where, however, *Collins v. Gwynne* was not cited. Jessel M.R. in that case expressed a view in accordance with the principle stated in the text.
[16] *Jephson v. Maunsell* (1847) 10 Ir. Eq. R. 38, 132.
[17] *ibid.*
[18] *Creighton v. Rankin* (1840) 7 C. & F. 325.
[19] See *per* Lord Brougham in *MacTaggart v. Watson* (1836) 3 C. & F. at 543; *Dawson v. Lawes* (1854) Kay 280. See further *Dundee and Newcastle S.S. Co. Ltd v. National Guarantee & Suretyship Association Ltd* (1881) 18 S.L.R. 685; *Bank of Scotland v. Morrison* (1911) S.C. 593.
[20] *Dawson v. Lawes*, above.
[21] See *Bank of Ireland v. Beresford* (1878) 6 Dow. 233 at 239. See also *Collins v. Gwynne* (1833) 9 Bing. 544; SC in error *sub. nom. Gwynne v. Burnell* (1835) 2 Bing. N.C. 7; 6 Bing. N.C. 453, HL. See also *R. v. Fay* (1878) 4 L.R. Ir. 606.
[22] *Hall v. Hadley* (1835) 2 A. & E. 758. See also *Palmer v. Sheridan-Bickers, The Times*, July 20, 1910.
[23] *Lawrence v. Walmsley* (1862) 12 C.B. (N.S.) 799.

not appear in the report) that he was then entitled to notice on order, if he wished it, to terminate the guarantee.[24]

Where it was stipulated that, before the surety was called on, the creditor "should avail himself to the utmost of any actual and bona fide security," it was held that this did not oblige him to bring an action upon a bill, given as such security, which was certain to be unproductive.[25] Where a guarantee was given to a mortgagee to cover any deficiency which might remain after the sale of the mortgaged property, it was held that this meant a completed sale, and that the guarantor could not be sued pending an action by the mortgagee upon a contract for sale, which was repudiated by the purchaser.[26]

Stipulation as to diligence to be expressed in guarantee

4–106	A stipulation that the creditor must exhaust any particular remedy against the principal before having recourse to the surety must be expressed in the guarantee. Thus oral evidence was held inadmissible to show that the indorsee of a bill of exchange drawn for the accommodation of the acceptor had taken the bill upon the terms of not calling upon the drawer until after certain securities to be deposited by the acceptor had been released.[27]

Notice of default

4–107	Upon the principle that it is the surety's duty to see that the principal performs the obligation guaranteed, the surety is not, apart from special stipulation, entitled to notice of the default.[28] Therefore, where the committee of a lunatic made default, and proceedings were taken and costs given against him, the surety for the committee was held liable for the costs (their undertaking extending to that), notwithstanding that they had received no notice of the default by reason of which costs were incurred.[29] "If they had no notice of it," said Lord Lyndhurst, "it was their own fault, for it was their duty to see that the committee duly passed his account".[29]

The right of the drawer or indorser of a bill to notice of dishonour is not an exception to this rule. Such a person is not by the law merchant liable at all until he has such notice.[30] However, a surety

[24] *Mountague v. Tidcombe* (1705) 2 Vern. 519. See *Phillips v. Foxall* (1872) L.R. 7 QB 666.
[25] *Musket v. Rogers* (1839) 8 Scott 51.
[26] *Moor v. Roberts* (1858) 3 C.B. (N.S.) 830.
[27] *Abrey v. Crux* (1869) L.R. 5 C.P. 37. See also *New London Credit Syndicate v. Neale* [1898] 2 QB 487; *Hitchings v. Northern Leather Co.* [1914] 3 K.B. 907.
[28] *Nares v. Rowles* (1811) 14 East. 510; *Stothert v. Goodfellow* (1832) 1 N. & M. 202. See also *Restatement*, security s.136 (1941): although American decisions have drawn a distinction between cases of specific debts and non-specific debts, this distinction is rejected by the *Restatement*. As to whether notice of default constituting "conclusive evidence" of liability under a guarantee is contrary to public policy see *Bache & Co. (London) Ltd v. Banques Vernes* [1973] 2 Lloyd's Rep. 437.
[29] *Re Lockey* (1845) 1 Ph. 509.
[30] *Warrington v. Furbor* (1807) 8 East. 242 at 245; *Black v. Ottoman Bank* (1862) 15 Moo. P.C. 472 at 484; *Duncan Fox & Co. v. North and South Wales Bank* (1880) 6 A.C. 1 at 13; *Carter v. White* (1883) 25 Ch D 666 at 671.

for payment of a bill or note by the acceptor, not being himself a party to the bill or having contracted to be treated as if he were, is not entitled to notice of dishonour for it is his duty to see that it is paid.[31]

A surety may, of course, contract that the receipt of notice, either generally or within a certain time of the default, shall be a condition precedent of his liability.[32] But an omission by the creditor to give notice as contemplated does not necessarily discharge the surety.[33] Where there was a surety for the payment by instalments of a loan granted by a society to one of its members, and one of the rules stated that where a member was four weeks in arrears, the committee were to communicate with the sureties, it was held that non-communication was no breach of the engagement of the surety, and he was not discharged.[34] In *Gordon v. Rae*,[35] where a surety, before executing the bond, took a memorandum to the effect that he was to be informed if the account guaranteed exceeded £1,000 and was not reduced within a month, it was held that omission to do this did not discharge her.[36]

Demand upon the surety before action

A surety has not, unless his contract so provides, any right to **4–108** require a demand to be made upon him before action. The right to a demand before liability can accrue is not inherent in the nature of suretyship and will not be implied unless expressly provided.[37] If a surety gives a bond conditioned to be void on the payment of a similar sum "on demand," or covenants or promises to pay the principal debt "on demand," a demand must be made upon him before he can be sued.[38] His obligation is to pay the collateral sum, and differs from a promise to pay on demand a present debt owing by the promisor.[39] In the latter case an action can be brought at once without any other demand than the writ.[40]

[31] *Warrington v. Furbor*, above; *Swinyard v. Bowes* (1816) 5 M. & S. 62; *Hitchcock v. Humfrey* (1843) 5 M. & Cr. 559; *Walton v. Mascall* (1844) 13 M. & W. 452; *Carter v. White* (1883) 25 Ch D 666.

[32] *Gordon v. Rae* (1858) 8 E. & B. 1065. And see *Clarke v. Wilson* (1838) 3 M. & W. 208.

[33] *Gordon v. Rae*, above. For a case where it did, see *Eshelby v. Federated European Bank* [1932] 1 K.B. 254, 423, CA.

[34] *Price v. Kirkham* (1864) 3 H. & C. 437.

[35] (1858) 8 E. & B. 1065.

[36] See, too, *Cooper v. Evans* (1867) L.R. 4 Eq. 45.

[37] *M.S. Fashions v. BCCI* [1993] Ch. 425.

[38] A surety has the right to have notice given to him in his capacity as a surety and not, *e.g.* as a director of the principal debtor. *Canadian Petrofina Ltd v. Motormart Ltd* (1969) 7 D.L.R. (3d) 330.

[39] *Re Brown's Estate, Brown v. Brown* [1893] 2 Ch. 300, following *Birks v. Trippet* (1666) 1 Williams' Saund. 32; *Bradford Old Bank v. Sutcliffe* [1918] 2 K.B. 833; *M.S. Fashions v. BCCI* [1993] Ch. 425. In *Esso Petroleum Co. Ltd v. Alstonbridge Properties Ltd* [1975] 1 W.L.R. 1474, Walton J. held that where a demand was required by the guarantee and which demand of its own intrinsic nature changed the liability of the guarantors from one to pay instalments to one to pay the whole amount guaranteed at once, it was an essential ingredient of any cause of action to recover the lump sum. *Cf. General Produce Co. v. United Bank Ltd* [1979] 2 Lloyd's Rep. 255.

[40] *Re Brown's Estate, Brown v. Brown* [1893] 2 Ch. 300; *M.S. Fashions v. BCCI* [1993] Ch. 425. And see *Norton v. Ellam* (1837) 2 M. & W. 461; *Jackson v. Ogg* (1859) Johns. 397; *Re George* (1890) 44 Ch D 629.

Standard form bank guarantees often contain "principal debtor" clauses which deem the guarantor to be a principal debtor. Such a clause has been held to obviate the need for any demand.[41]

Whereas Australian and Canadian authorities suggest that the surety should be given a period in which to pay after demand which should be such time as is reasonable in the circumstances, English case law has established a "mechanics of payment" test.[42] This test provides that the guarantor need only be given a reasonable opportunity of implementing whatever reasonable mechanics of payment he may need to discharge the debt.[43] This does not include time to raise the money.[44] In the ordinary case, the surety must have reasonable time within banking hours to make necessary arrangements to pay the debt.[45] However, if the surety makes it clear that he has no money with which to pay, no time need be given at all.[46]

A demand is sufficient if it requires a surety to pay what is due, without specifying a figure.[47]

4–109   If a surety joins with a principal in a promissory note payable on demand for money lent to the latter, the surety appearing on the face of the note as a principal, although known to have joined merely as surety, he can (notwithstanding the above rule) be sued without previous demand in the same way as the principal.[48] However, where a surety joined in such a note, and the payee gave a collateral memorandum that it was given to secure the banking account of the principal, the memorandum was treated as having the same effect as if it were a defeasance on the face of the note, and an action against the surety was held not maintainable until after demand made upon him.[49]

Where a surety joined in a lease to a third party and covenanted that the lessee should "at all times during the term pay the rent on the respective days" when it became due, and that in case the lessee should neglect to pay the rent for 40 days the defendant would pay it on demand, it was held that the earlier part of the covenant was

---

[41] *M.S. Fashions v. BCCI* [1993] Ch. 425; *Esso Petroleum Co. Ltd v. Alstonbridge Properties Ltd* [1975] 1 W.L.R. 1474 at 1483.

[42] *Bank of Baroda v. Panessar* [1987] Ch. 335 and authorities cited therein; *Sheppard & Cooper v. TSB (No. 2)* [1996] B.C.C. 965.

[43] *Bank of Baroda v. Panessar* [1987] Ch. 335.

[44] *ibid.*

[45] *Sheppard & Cooper v. TSB (No. 2)* [1996] B.C.C. 965.

[46] *ibid.* It was held that the time that needed to be given depended on the circumstances of the case. Although this is fine as a matter of common sense, it does, despite the protestations in the judgment to the contrary, depart from the simple "mechanics of payment" approach and introduce an element of uncertainty. It is suggested that the need for both a demand and the lapse of time can only be justified on the basis that they are both part of the "demand" condition precedent. For the purposes of a condition precedent, which should be construed as at the time the contract of suretyship is entered into, it is suggested that the certainty of the "mechanics of payment" test is desirable and that disputes about the circumstances of the demand should be avoided by not introducing such a further element.

[47] *Bank of Baroda v. Panessar* [1987] Ch. 335, followed in *NRG Vision Ltd v. Churchill* [1988] B.C.L.C. 624, where it was held that an offer in the demand to accept payment in instalments did not invalidate it, but the question of whether an excessive demand was valid was left open.

[48] *Ex p. Whitworth* (1841) 2 M.D. & De G. 158.

[49] *Hartland v. Jukes* (1863) 1 H. & C. 667.

qualified by the latter, and that the lessor could not sue the surety till after forty days' non-payment and demand made.[50] A guarantee for the prepayment of money which was in fact secured by mortgage, though it was not so stated in the guarantee, was held to become enforceable so as to set time running under the Statute of Limitations without notice to pay off the mortgage or demand upon the surety; but apparently it would not be so if the debt had been guaranteed as a mortgage debt.[51]

Other express conditions

The guarantor can, of course, by stipulation, interpose any other **4–110** condition precedent to his liability arising, as, for instance, that money shall be due from him to the principal on another account,[52] or that a certificate shall be given by a third party that the creditor has performed his part of the principal contract.[53] But where a building owner guaranteed the repayment of advances made to the builder "upon the completion" of the buildings "in accordance with the contract" between himself and the builder, it was held that he was liable when the buildings were, in fact, complete, though the builder could not have sued for want of a certificate of completion required by the contract.[54]

In *Associated Japanese Bank v. Credit du Nord*,[55] the creditor and surety were both informed by credit brokers that certain machines existed and on the strength of that entered into a guarantee in which the consideration was expressed to be the creditor's agreement to lease the machines. It was held in the light of this factual matrix that it was an express condition precedent that the machines should exist.

Implied conditions precedent to surety's liability

Cases may also, of course, arise, where the creditor is unable to **4–111** recover from the surety owing to non-fulfilment by him of a condition precedent being a necessary implication from the express terms of the contract between creditor and surety.[56]

In *Byblos Bank v. Al-Khudhairy*[57] the bank intended to take guarantees from the two principal investors in the corporate principal debtor, one of whom was the defendant. His guarantee was taken but the other was not. The Court of Appeal considered that the common contemplation of the bank and the defendant that the

---

[50] *Sicklemore v. Thistleton* (1817) 6 M. & S. 9.
[51] *Henton v. Paddison* (1893) 68 L.T. 405. See generally Chap. 10.
[52] *Hill v. Nuttall* (1864) 17 C.B. (N.S.) 262.
[53] See *Ex p. Ashwell* (1832) 2 Deac. & Ch. 281.
[54] *Lewis v. Hoare* (1881) 44 L.T. 66; *cf. Eshelby v. Federated European Bank* [1932] 1 K.B. 254, 423, CA.
[55] [1989] 1 W.L.R. 255.
[56] *Spencer v. Lotz* (1916) 32 T.L.R. 373; *Guy-Pell v. Foster* [1930] 2 Ch. 169.
[57] [1997] B.C.L.C. 232.

bank intended to take the other guarantee did not give rise to an implied condition precedent in favour of the defendant to the effect that his guarantee would be held in escrow till the other guarantee was executed. This was because the bank intended to take the other guarantee for its own protection and the fact that the execution of the other guarantee would have provided the defendant with valuable rights of contribution was not sufficient to create such an implication. Little short of an express mention by the defendant that he was signing on condition that the other guarantee would be taken would have sufficed to create such a condition precedent.

The position is very different where the form of the guarantee expressly shows that it is intended to be the guarantee of more than one party and one of the intended sureties does not sign.[58] The result is undoubtedly that the other proposed sureties are normally not liable, although the result has been analysed in different ways. In *James Graham Ltd v. Southgate-Sands*[59] the Court of Appeal held that this result arose not simply in equity, to which some of the cases had referred, but at law. That was a case where the other proposed guarantor's signature was forged. There could be no relief in equity because the creditor had no notice of the forgery, so that the case was distinguishable from situations where the further intended guarantor did not sign at all, and therefore the creditor was on notice of a defect. The Court of Appeal held that in such cases there was no contract at all in law. This can either be expressed by saying that the parties to the guarantee agreed to the suretyship of two parties and the creditor could not allege the suretyship of one, since that would be a different contract, or that there was an implied condition precedent to the effect that both sureties would sign or that they would become bound.

However, even where the form of the guarantee suggests that it is intended to be the guarantee of more than one party and one or more of the intended sureties do not sign, a guarantor will be liable if there is evidence to show that he was intended to be liable even if one or more others did not sign.[60]

In *Byblos Bank v. Al-Khudhairy*,[61] discussed above, the bank had also intended to take security over a third party deposit but did not do so. The fact that both the bank and the guarantor expected such security to be taken did not make the taking of such security an implied condition precedent to the guarantee. This approach was followed by the Court of Appeal in *TCB Ltd v. Gray*,[62] where it was held that the guarantor was liable despite an alleged failure to take

[58] *James Graham Ltd v. Southgate-Sands* [1986] QB 80, CA and the cases cited therein.
[59] [1986] QB 80, CA. See also *Hong Leong Finance Ltd v. Goy Khim Taik* [1994] 1 S.L.R. 366 (Singapore).
[60] *Taubmans Pty Ltd v. Loakes* [1991] 2 Qd. Rep. 109. See also *Walter & Morris Ltd v. Lymberis* [1965] S.A.S.R. 204.
[61] [1987] B.C.L.C. 232.
[62] [1988] 1 All E.R. 108, CA.

a valid debenture from another party. It was held that where a guarantor wished to make his guarantee dependent on the taking of some security he must establish that this formed part of the contract between him and the creditor.[63] The fact that the granting of the security was "part and parcel of the overall arrangements" was insufficient.[64] Moreover, clauses in the guarantee allowing the creditor to release security and insulating the guarantee from any defect in any security taken were considered to be contrary to the notion that the parties impliedly agreed that the taking of valid security was a condition precedent to the validity of the guarantee.[65]

In *Associated Japanese Bank v. Credit du Nord*,[66] referred to above in connection with express conditions precedent, an alternative ground of decision was that of an implied condition precedent.

Payment out of particular fund

Again, the promise may be only that the debt shall be paid out of **4–112** a fund of the debtor, and this either absolutely,[67] provided the fund exists,[68] or contingently upon there being no prior charges.[69] And if the fund does not exist, the surety is not liable, provided, of course, there has been no fraud by him, and no express or implied warranty that it does.[70] Thus, where three daughters agree to pay a debt of their mother "out of her estate at her decease," it was held that this was only a promise to pay out of what the mother might leave behind her available for the payment of her debts. It did not bind them to pay out of property of which the mother was tenant for life, with the remainder to the promisors, notwithstanding that it was shown that in fact (though the creditor did not appear to have notice of this) the mother had no other property.[70] Similarly, where a surety guaranteed payment of the price of bricks to be supplied to a Government contractor "when the amount of the contract is paid," and the contract was put an end to by the Government, owing to the default of the contractor (who was allowed for the work actually done, for which, however, he had been paid in advance by the consent of the plaintiff), the surety was held not liable for anything.[71]

---

[63] at 113F–H *per* Purchas L.J.
[64] at 115 E–F *per* Purchas L.J.
[65] at 112E and 115F *per* Purchas L.J.
[66] [1989] 1 W.L.R. 255.
[67] See *Stephens v. Pell* (1834) 2 C. & M. 710; *Brown v. Fletcher* (1876) 35 L.T. 165 *per* Bramwell B. arguendo; *Wilson v. Craven* (1841) 8 M. & W. 584; *Byblos Bank v. Al-Khudhairy* [1987] B.C.L.C. 232, CA.
[68] See *Brown v. Fletcher* (1876) 35 L.T. 165.
[69] See *Jupp v. Richardson* 26 L.J. Ex. 261.
[70] See n. 68, above.
[71] *Hemming v. Trenery* (1835) 2 C.M. & R. 385.

Admission by a judgment against principal

4–113   Unless it is admissible (*e.g.* under the Civil Evidence Act 1972), an admission by the principal debtor is no evidence against the surety.[72] Nor is he bound by a judgment or award against the principal.[73] This rule has, of course, no application to the admissibility of the accounts stated between the principal and creditor upon the question of appropriation of payments made by the principal. The effect of the accounts is in such cases the very issue to be tried.[74] But it has been held in Ireland that the books of a rate collector not deceased are evidence against his surety of the receipt of the money by the collector, at any rate where the surety bond was also conditioned for the correctness of the accounts.[75] However this may be, in an action against a surety for an officer or servant after the death of the principal, it is clear that evidence may be given of entries or ticks made by him in the books kept by him in the course of the duty the performance of which was guaranteed.[76] And even entries in a private book are admissible after his death on the ground that they were against interest,[77] a principle which, it seems, should also make receipts given by him to the debtors of his employers evidence against his sureties after his death.[78]
     It is common,[79] however, to make express provision for the surety being concluded by the admission of the principal, or by the result of proceedings against him or by the certificate of a third person.[80] But if the debt itself is irrecoverable for illegality no such certificate will make the surety liable.[80]
     Sureties for a liquidator, in the winding up of a company by or under the supervision of the court, ought to be allowed to attend at their own expense the taking of the accounts, and if the liquidator is known, when the taking of the accounts commences, to be bankrupt or unlikely to be able to pay over the balance found due, the sureties should have notice of the fact in order to enable them to attend.[81] Where under such circumstances the accounts were taken without such notice, the surety was allowed to re-open them

---

[72] *Evans v. Beattie* (1803) 5 Esp. 26; *Re Kitchin* (1881) 17 Ch D 668. In *Bruns v. Colocotronis, The Vasso* [1979] 2 Lloyd's Rep. 412, Robert Goff J. applied *Re Kitchin*, above, in holding that words guaranteeing the due performance of all the obligations of the principal debtor did not *per se* mean that the surety was bound by an arbitration award between creditor and principal debtor. At 418 the learned judge pointed out that to hold otherwise might result in the surety being bound by an award made in the absence of the principal debtor. Note also *Fisher v. P. G. Wellfair Ltd* (1981) 125 S.J. 413.

[73] *Re Kitchin* (1881) 17 Ch D 668.

[74] This was the question in *Lysaght v. Walker* (1831) 5 Bligh (N.S.) 1. The headnote would suggest that the general admissibility of accounts stated by the principal was affirmed in that case. But see case cited in the next note.

[75] *Guardians of Abbeyleix Union v. Sutcliffe* (1890) 26 L.R. Ir. 332.

[76] *Goss v. Watlington* (1821) 3 B. & B. 132; *Whitnash v. George* (1828) 8 B. & C. 556.

[77] *Middleton v. Melton* (1829) 5 M. & Ry 264.

[78] *Middleton v. Melton, ibid.*, questioning the dicta to the contrary in *Goss v. Watlington* (1821) 3 B. & B. 132.

[79] *e.g.* in guarantees given to banks for advances, in bonds for liquidators, etc.

[80] See *Swan v. Bank of Scotland* (1836) 10 Bligh (N.S.) 627.

[81] *Re Birmingham Brewing, Malting and Distillery Co.* (1883) 31 W.R. 415.

upon bringing into court the amount of the bond (in that case less than the balance due from the liquidator), with an undertaking to pay interest in respect of the delay, and paying the costs of the summons.[81]

Retainer/Rule in Cherry v. Boultbee (1839) 4 My. & Cr. 442

The executor of a creditor is entitled to retain the amount of the debt secured by the joint promissory note of the debtor and surety out of a legacy left by the creditor to the surety.[82] **4–114**

The creditor is not entitled to call upon the executors of a deceased surety to impound a fund to answer future claims of a contingent character.[83] But the executor of an obligor in a money bond, whose liability on the face of the bond was that of a principal, though in fact he was surety only, was held entitled to keep in hand the amount against creditors of inferior degree, though the debt was not yet payable, and though another obligor who was really the principal might possibly pay.[84]

---

[82] *Coates v. Coates* (1864) 33 Beav. 249. See also *Re Melton* [1918] 1 Ch. 37.
[83] *King v. Malcott* (1852) 9 Hare 692. *Cf. Antrobus v. Davidson* (1817) 3 Mer. 569.
[84] *Atkinson v. Grey* (1853) 1 Sm. & G. 577.

CHAPTER 5

MISREPRESENTATION AND CONCEALMENT

Mistake: general principles

5–01   A contract of guarantee can be set aside on account of the doctrine of mistake but different results may arise on account of the nature of the mistake which may be unilateral or mutual. The rules applicable to contracts generally will apply so that a fundamental mistake by all the three parties as to the nature of the contract of guarantee all having made a mistaken assumption as to some essential integral element of the subject matter of the contract will render the contract void at law and voidable in equity.[1]

Even if the mistake does not give rise to a finding of mistake in common law equity may relieve one of the parties of the burden of the contract by rescission or rectification.[2]

Common mistake

5–02   In *Associated Japanese Bank (International) Ltd v. Credit du Nord*,[3] the parties to a contract of guarantee namely the guarantor and the creditor both mistakenly believed that the subject matter of the guarantee existed whereas the principal debtor had in fact wrongfully represented that such was the case and the subject matter did not in fact exist. The guarantor successfully contended that existence of the subject matter was a condition precedent to the guarantee and to the guarantor's liability, but the court decided the issue on the basis of common mistake rendering the contract void at common law.

The same result would no doubt occur as a result of other types of mutual mistake such as mistake as to the identity of the parties to the main contract being guaranteed.[4]

---

[1] See *Bell v. Lever Brothers* [1932] A.C. 161.

[2] See, *e.g. Chitty on Contracts*, (27th ed.), Vol. 1, paras. 5–041 and 5–063 *et seq.* See also *Lloyds Bank v. Waterhouse* [1991] Fam. Law 23 for an example of a guarantee entered into by mistake.

[3] [1989] 1 W.L.R. 255, the Court also decided that by way of alternative relief that the guarantor was entitled to have the contract set aside on equitable grounds. For a critique of this decision see J. Carter "An Uncommon Mistake" [1991] 3 J.C.L. 237 suggesting that the effect of the decision should be confined to cases in which the subject matter does not exist and that the facts did not justify the finding of a condition precedent.

[4] See, *e.g. Provident Accident & White Cross Insurance Co. v. Dahne and White* [1937] 2 All E.R. 255; *De Brettes v. Goodman* (1855) 9 Moo. P.C. 466.

Unilateral mistake

In accordance with the general statements of principle set out **5–03** above if the guarantor claims that he was mistaken as to the existence of certain terms in his guarantee he may be able to seek relief in equity that it be set aside. However on the current state of English authorities it is suggested that a guarantor will be required to establish an actionable misrepresentation.[5] Even if a guarantor were able to establish his entitlement to equitable relief the right to rescind may be lost through such defences as affirmation, and the interposition of third party rights. Furthermore, there may be no justification for the guarantor avoiding any liability especially if he is able to be awarded rectification.[6]

Non est factum

There are very few reported English cases which have considered **5–04** the applicability of the doctrine of *non est factum* to a contract of guarantee.[7]

The leading decision of *Saunders v. Anglia Building Society*[8] established the modern boundaries of the doctrine namely that the signatory must have made a radical or fundamental mistake as to the nature or contents of the document which he signed, that he demonstrate that he took all reasonable precautions to determine the nature of the document and finally that he belongs to a class of persons deserving of protection, *i.e.* those under a severe disability such as blindness, illiteracy, etc.

On the basis of the last of these requirements it is highly unlikely that a surety in most cases will be able to avail himself of the doctrine. It is not thought that the recent developments with regard to those persons entitled to invoke protection on account of the existence of unconscionable transactions[9] will have affected this view. It follows that a typical surety will not be able to demonstrate that he failed to take all reasonable precautions to find out what the nature of the document was particularly if he shows that he was merely indifferent as to its contents.[10]

---

[5] For Commonwealth authority see, *e.g. Taylor v. Johnson* (1983) 151 C.L.R. 422 and *Royal Bank of Canada v. Hale* (1961) 30 C.L.R. (2d) 138; in the latter case there is a clear finding of misrepresentation.

[6] See, *e.g. Bank Negara Indonesia 1946 v. Taylor* [1995] C.L.C. 255.

[7] See, *e.g. Carlisle & Cumberland Banking Co. v. Bragg* [1911] 1 K.B. 489, *cf. Foster v. Mackinnon* (1869) L.R. 4 C.P. 709. *Carlisle & Cumberland* was overruled in *Saunders v. Anglia Building Society,* below.

[8] [1971] A.C. 1004 esp. at 1016 *per* Lord Reid.

[9] See below.

[10] As in *Avon Finance Co. v. Bridger* [1985] 2 All E.R. 281. See also *Lloyds Bank plc v. Waterhouse supra* in which it was suggested that a mistake by a guarantor as to the extent of his liability will not be sufficiently fundamental.

Misrepresentation and concealment: general principles

5–05   A surety is not bound by his contract if it was induced by any misrepresentation by the creditor whether fraudulently made or not of any fact known to him and material to be known to the surety.[11] Where the contract is voidable on this ground, the surety may have the contract set aside and any security pledged thereunder returned.[12]

It is no defence to claim that the surety might have found out the truth by making proper enquiry.[13]

Circumstances changing before completion

5–06   If circumstances calculated to influence a proposed surety are represented by a creditor as existing and they cease to exist before the guarantee is completed that must be notified to the surety.[14] If it is represented that it is intended that part of the risk will be borne by the creditor himself or by any specified party,[15] a subsequent abandonment of that intention if not communicated will destroy the validity of the guarantee.[16]

State of accounts with principal

5–07   A guarantee will fail if the creditor misrepresents to the surety the state of accounts between the principal and himself.[17] But a surety proposing to guarantee a banking account should inquire whether there is any adverse balance already existing; he is not entitled to assume there is not.[18]

---

[11] *London General Omnibus Co. v. Holloway* [1912] 2 K.B. 72 at 77; *Workington Harbour v. Trade Indemnity Co.* (1934) 49 Lloyd's L.R. 305; 49 Lloyd's L.R. 430, CA; 54 Lloyd's L.R. 103 HL; *Mackenzie v. Royal Bank of Canada* [1934] A.C. 468; *Ben Line v. Henreux* (1935) 52 Lloyd's L.R. 27 at 31, 32; *Levett v. Barclays Bank plc* [1995] 1 W.L.R. 1260. That the surety may have been induced to contract by the fraud of the principal is of course no defence unless the creditor is a party to the fraud: *Spencer v. Handley* (1842) 4 M. & Gr. 414: this decision confirms that the misrepresentation complained of does not have to be fraudulent or negligent to give rise to a remedy in rescission: see also *Small v. Currie* (1854) 2 Drew 102.
[12] *Mackenzie v. Royal Bank of Scotland* [1934] A.C. 1. The fact that the Bank acted on the faith of the guarantee did not preclude relief. See also as to this form of relief: *Cooper v. Joel* (1859) 27 Beav. 313; on appeal: (1859) 1 De G.F. & J. 240, *cf. Brooking v. Maudsley Son & Field* (1888) 338 Ch D 636.
[13] *Central Railway of Venezuela v. Kisch* [1887] L.R. 2, HL 99.
[14] *Davies v. London and Provincial Marine Insurance Co.* [1878] 8 Ch D 469; *Bank of Montreal v. Stuart* [1911] A.C. 120; *Hawes v. Bishop* [1909] 2 K.B. 390. The first of these decisions emphasises that although the misrepresentation may be minimal in its nature and extent it must at all times have been a material misrepresentation.
[15] *Evans v. Brembridge* (1855) 2 K. & J. 174; (1856) 8 De G.L. & G. 100 where a sole surety was misled into thinking he was one of two sureties.
[16] See *Tail v. Baring* (1864) 14 Giff. 405; 4 G.J. & S. 318; *cf. Hansard v. Lethbridge* (1892) 8 T.L.R. 346, CA; *Ellesmere Brewery Co. v. Cooper* [1896] 1 QB 75.
[17] *Blest v. Brown* (1862) 3 M. Giff. 450; 4 De G.F. & J. 367; *McKewan v. Thornton* (1861) 2 F. & F. 594.
[18] *Kirby v. Duke of Malborough* (1813) 2 M. & S. 518.

Mispresentation as to extent of liability

In the case of a guarantor who was led to believe that he was **5–08**
simply guaranteeing a bank loan but the guarantee in fact extended
to "all debts and liabilities direct or indirect" of the principal
debtor, the bank was prevented from recovering in respect of
"indirect liabilities".[19]

Misrepresentation by silence

Misrepresentation may of course be made by mere silence or **5–09**
concealment.[20] This may vitiate a security without it being wilful
and intentional or made with a view to an advantage being
gained by the creditor.[21] But a guarantee is not an insurance contract and there is no obligation upon the creditor to disclose to
the surety every circumstance within his knowledge material for
the surety to know.[22] The requirement in the earlier cases that the
creditor must disclose all known facts material to the risk was
abandoned because "no creditor could rely upon a contract of
guaranty unless he communicated to the proposed sureties everything relating to his dealing with the principal . . . ".[23] This
would be impracticable and in some cases, *e.g.* where there is a
banker/adviser relationship between creditor and principal, also a
breach of confidence.[24]

Despite earlier dicta to the contrary,[25] it now seems settled that
contracts of guarantee as opposed to insurance contracts[26] are not
uberrimae fidei and therefore non-disclosure to avoid a guarantee
must amount to misrepresentation.

---

[19] *Royal Bank of Canada v. Hall* (1961) 30 D.L.R. (2d) 138. The bank had taken assignments of other debts that the principal owed to other customers of the bank.

[20] As in *London General Omnibus Company v. Holloway* [1912] 2 Q.B. 72. In *Shidiak v. Bank of West Africa* [1964] N.N.L.R. 96 the guarantor was held entitled to rescind because the bank manager taking the guarantee knew that the guarantor was mistaken as to the amount involved but failed to disclose the true position.

[21] *Railton v. Matthews* (1844) 10 C. & F. 934; *Workington Harbour v. Trade Indemnity Co.*, above; *Mackenzie v. Royal Bank of Canada*, above; *Ben Line v. Henreux*, above.

[22] *Levett v. Barclays Bank plc* [1995] 1 W.L.R. 1260, applying *Hamilton v. Watson* (1845) 12 C. & F. 109; *North British Insurance Co. v. Lloyd* (1854) 10 Ex. Ch. 523; *Wythes v. Labouchere* (1859) 3 De G. & J. 593 at 609. See also *Pledge v. Buss* (1860) Johns 663; *Davies v. London and Provincial Marine Insurance Co.* (1878) 8 Ch D 469; *Lloyds Bank v. Harrison*, March 6, 1925, Legal Decisions Affecting Bankers 12, CA.

[23] *Lee v. Jones* (1863) 117 C.B. (N.S.) 482, *per* Lord Blackburn at 503.

[24] *Tournier v. National Provincial and Union Bank* [1924] 1 K.B. 461.

[25] *Owen v. Homan* (151) 3 Mac. & G. 378 at 397 (Lord Truro), a case affirmed on other grounds at 4 H.L.C. 997. Lord Truro's dictum was later disapproved: see *North British Insurance Co. v. Lloyd* (1854) 10 Exch. at 382 where it is pointed out that Lord Truro did not seem aware of *Hamilton v. Watson*, above, or *Pledge v. Buss*, above. The dictum of Tudor-Evans J. in *Wales v. Wadham* [1977] 1 W.L.R. at 214G, referring to suretyship as an example of a contract made *uberrimae fidei* appears to be *per incuriam*.

[26] The courts will look at the essence of the contract to see whether they are for insurance or they are guarantees in order to consider whether duty of the utmost good faith is required: *Seaton v. Heath* [1899] 1 Q.B. 782 at 794.

Misrepresentation by the principal debtor: no agency

5–10   As indicated above[27] if a creditor knows it is party to the fact that the guarantee has been entered into as a result of a misrepresentation made by the principal debtor to the surety the creditor cannot enforce the guarantee. Knowledge in this type of case is actual knowledge or recklessness.[28]

If the creditor is neither party to a misrepresentation nor aware of it liability may depend upon the question of whether the principal debtor is the agent of the creditor.[29] It is suggested that in such a case the surety will be required to demonstrate that he or she falls within that category of persons attracting protection under the principles established in *Barclays Bank v. O'Brien*,[30] *i.e.* that the relationship between the principal debtor and the surety was one known to the creditor to be one in which trust and confidence existed and one in which the transaction was manifestly disadvantageous to the surety.

Where the debt guaranteed is the result of fraud practised upon the principal by the creditor the surety may have the contract cancelled[31]; but he must make the principal a party in order that the whole transaction may be set aside.[32] Co-sureties are also necessary parties to an action by one surety to have the contract given up[33] but not a surety or sureties for a distinct part of the same debt.[34]

Misrepresentation by the principal debtor: agency

5–11   If the creditor merely requests the principal debtor to procure a guarantee or other security that fact of itself will not make the principal debtor the agent of the creditor.[35]

What matters must be disclosed

5–12   A creditor must reveal to the surety every fact which under the circumstances the surety would expect not to exist; for the omission to mention that such a fact does exist is an implied representation that it does.[36] But a banker taking a guarantee for an overdraft to a customer is not ordinarily bound to disclose to the intending surety the unsatisfactory character of a previous

---

[27] See above at 5–05.
[28] See *Spencer v. Handley* (1842) M. & G. 414. This will also cover so-called Nelsonian knowledge: see *Owen v. Homan*, above.
[29] See below at 5–11.
[30] See generally at Chapter 6.
[31] *Allan v. Houlden* (1843) 6 Beav. 148.
[32] *ibid.*
[33] *Allen v. Houlden*, above; *Ware v. Harwood* (1807) 1 Ves. 28 at 34, *cf. Coope v. Twynam* (1823) T. & R. 426.
[34] *Pendlebury v. Walker* (1841) 4 Y.C. Ex. 424.
[35] *Barclays Bank plc v. O'Brien* [1994] 1 A.C. 180; see also Scott L.J. at [1993] Q.B. 109 at 113.
[36] *Levett v. Barclays Bank plc* [1995] 1 W.L.R. 1260. It is a question of fact in each case as to which aspect or aspects of the underlying transaction must be disclosed: for an example of a somewhat

account of the customer or other matters generally affecting his financial credit[37] because dissatisfaction with a customer's credit is probably the reason for requiring the guarantee.[38] However, where the intending guarantor makes enquiries of the bank he must be given a "true honest and accurate answer" about any matters material to the giving of the guarantee.[39] If he is under a misapprehension which he communicated to the bank the bank has a duty to correct it.[40]

A guarantee given to a bank to cover the deficiency in produce to be consigned to the bank against bills drawn was held good notwithstanding that the bank had been informed that there would probably be a deficiency and had not communicated it to the sureties.[41]

In *North British Insurance Co. v. Lloyd*[42] it was held that on taking a guarantee for a loan a creditor was not bound to disclose that the guarantee was taken because another surety was desirous of retiring. At the end of the judgment it was observed that a surety may retire for other reasons than distrust of the debtor's position. In *Roper v. Cox*[43] a landlord took a guarantee for a tenant without disclosing that the latter had in a previous tenancy to him been in default with his rent and was still indebted to him for it. This was held to be no defence without an allegation of fraud. The building contract of an employer need not usually reveal to the contract or his surety the difficult nature of the site where under the contract this is a matter to be left to the skill and experience of the contractor.[44]

---

unusual set of facts where the duty was said to exist see *Burke v. Rogerson* (1866) 14 L.T. 780. For more modern examples see *Westpac Banking Corp. v. Robinson* (1990) A.C.S. 56—002 especially 59—035; *Shotter v. Westpac Banking Corp* [1988] 2 N.Z.L.R. 316 at 334. The older authorities reviewed largely in *Levett*, above, include *Hamilton v. Watson* (1845) 12 C. & F. 109 *per* Lord Campbell; *Lee v. Jones* (1864) 17 C.B. (N.S.) 482 at 503 at 504 *per* Blackburn J.; *Phillips v. Foxall* (1872) L.R. 7 QB 666. This obligation has been said to be subject to a "suitable opportunity to make the circumstances known": *Franklin Bank v. Cooper* (1853) 36 Maine 179 at 196.

[37] *Hamilton v. Watson*, above at 169; *Wythas v. Labouchere*, above at 609; *National Provincial Bank v. Glenusk* [1913] 3 K.B. 355; *Goodman v. National Bank of Australasia* (1968) 117 C.L.R. 17; 42 H.A.L.R. 110. But see *Small v. Currie* (1854) 2 Drew. 102 at 118. Perhaps an extreme boundary of this rule was reached in *Cooper v. National Provincial Bank* [1946] K.B. 1, where the Bank was held to be under no duty to disclose to the guarantor of a woman's account that her bankrupt husband was able to draw on the account or that the account had been operated irregularly in that the payment of properly issued cheques had been countermanded.

[38] See *Lee v. Jones*, above. Alternatively such matters can be described as being "extrinsic" to the guarantee: *London General Omnibus Co. Ltd v. Holloway*, above at 87. A third explanation is that it can be expected that the customer has properly explained the general position to the surety: *per* Sargant L.J. in *Lloyds Bank v. Harrison*, March 6, 1925, IV Legal Decisions Affecting Bankers 12 and 16. A fourth reason was suggested in the Scottish case of *Royal Bank of Scotland v. Greenshields* [1914] S.C. 259, *i.e.* that the bank is entitled to assume that the intending surety has made himself acquainted with the customer's financial position.

[39] *Westminster Bank Ltd v. Cond* [1940] 46 Con. Cas. 60; *O'Brien v. Australian and New Zealand Bank* (1971) 5 S.A.S.R. 347.

[40] *Royal Bank of Scotland v. Greenshields* [1914] S.C. 259.

[41] *Welton v. Somes* (1888) 5 P.L.R. 46; (1889) 5 T.L.R. 184.

[42] (1854) 10 Ex. Ch. A.T. 523.

[43] (1882) 10 L.R. Ir. 200.

[44] *Trade Indemnity Co. v. Workington Harbour and Dock Board* [1937] A.C. 1.

Existing indebtedness

5–13   But in some circumstances the fact of existing indebtedness may
be a matter to be naturally assumed not to exist and in such a case
disclosure must be made. In *Lee v. Jones*[45] merchants obtained a
guarantee for the payments over to them of the receipts of their
agents who sold for them upon a *del crederee* commission and was
recited in the guarantee to be employed on terms of settling with
them at short intervals. In fact he was at the date of the guarantee
in arrears with payment for coal sold. It was held that non-disclosure of these facts having regard for the recital was evidence of
fraud. "It depends", said Blackburn J. in the Exchequer Chamber,
"whether in such a transaction as that described in the agreement it
might not naturally be expected that the matters might have allowed
a balance of this extent to accumulate and might have allowed the
amount to stand over unsettled for so long a time".[46]

Previous misconduct of a servant

5–14   So too where a guarantee is taken for good behaviour, for
example by way of a fidelity bond, the employer must disclose any
previous misconduct of the principal in his office of which he is
aware. For it is not naturally to be expected that if he had miscon-
ducted himself to the employer's knowledge he would be continued
in the office.[47] And save where there is a continuing guarantee of
this sort the creditor must communicate any misconduct for which
the servant might be dismissed which he finds out during the
employment or he will lose the benefit of the guarantee in respect
of future misconduct.[48] If the employer knows facts which gave
him reason to believe that there has been misconduct and he does
not disclose them the surety is discharged.[49] The disclosure of
previous misconduct which the employer must make if he is aware
of it must be sufficiently complete to enable the surety to judge
whether he will assent to the servant being retained in office on his
guarantee; therefore it was held that notice of "default to a large
amount" was not enough where there had been falsification of
books and fabrication of entries.[50] It does not appear to have been
decided whether an employer must disclose to a guarantor misconduct of a servant in other positions of which he is aware.[51]

The holder of a fidelity guarantee does not by merely delaying to
communicate a defalcation to the surety lose his remedy against

---

[45] (1861) 14 C.B. (N.S.) 386; (1864) 17 C.B. (N.S.) 482.
[46] (1864) 17 C.B. (N.S.) at 505.
[47] *Smith v. Bank of Scotland* (1813) 1 Dow. 272 explained by Blackburn J. in *Lee v. Jones* (1864)
17 C.B. (N.S.) at 504; *Phillips v. Foxall* (1872) L.R. 7 QB 666.
[48] *Phillips v. Foxall*, above; *Sanderson v. Aston* (1873) L.R. 8 Ex. 73; *Enright v. Falvey* (1879) 4
L.R. Ir. 397.
[49] *Smith v. Bank of Scotland* (1813) 1 Dow. 272 *per* Lord Eldon.
[50] *Enright v. Falvey*, above.
[51] See however *Withes v. Labouchere* (1859) 3 De G & J. 593 at 609.

him for the defalcation provided he does not actively conceal it from him and the rights of the parties have not been altered.[52] A treatment of a defalcation in the books of the employer as a loan so as to prevent the other clerks knowing the fact does not discharge a surety either as a concealment from him or if not so intended by way of waiver or novation.[53] So a continuance of the employment or credit after a defalcation and without communicating it will not release the guarantor in respect of that defalcation.[54]

Secret arrangement as to application of advance

In *Hamilton v. Watson*[55] the surety guaranteed a cash credit. As **5–15** expected the cash was used to repay an existing debtor to the creditor's bank. Non-disclosure of the expected use of the cash did not release the surety. However, had there been a contractual obligation so to use the advance the creditor would have been bound to disclose it as "something between the creditor and the principal debtor which the surety would not naturally expect to take place".[56]

Hamilton v. Watson[57] was considered in *Levett v. Barclays Bank plc*[58] in which sureties had allowed treasury stock used by them to be used as security but on the express understanding that it would be returned to them unencumbered before the maturity date. The contractual arrangements between the debtor and the bank stipulated however that the treasury stock should be used to repay the loan. It was held that there was a duty owed to the sureties to disclose such contractual arrangements which made the principal contract materially different in a particularly disadvantageous respect from the circumstances which the sureties might naturally expect. Non-disclosure of such a term meant that the sureties would not have proceeded to provide the security if they had been aware of it.[59]

In *Stone v. Compton*[60] the mortgage securing the same sum as that covered by the guarantee was read over by the creditor's agent to the surety. It recited that the full sum was being advanced whereas it had been agreed that part of it should be applied to an old debt which the mortgage recited as paid. The Court of Common Pleas held that the creditor could not in law recover, though no

---

[52] *Peel v. Tatlock* (1799) 1 B. & P. 419.
[53] *Peel v. Tatlock*, above.
[54] *Montague v. Tidcombe* (1705) 2 Vern. 519.
[55] (1845) 12 C. F. 109.
[56] above at 119. See too *Pendlebury v. Walker* (1841) 4 Y. & C. Ex. 424; *Stone v. Compton* (1838) 5 Bing. N.C. 142; *Pidcock v. Bishop* (1825) 2 B. & C. 205; *Railton v. Matthews* (1844) 10 C. & F. 934, HL. See also the Scottish cases of *Wallace's Factor v. M'Kissock* (1898) 24 R. 642; *Sutherland v. W.M. Low & Co. Ltd* (1901) 3 F. 972.
[57] (1845) 12 C. & F. 109.
[58] [1995] 1 W.L.R. 1260.
[59] The court relied upon a passage regarding the applicable principles in *Commercial Bank of Australia Ltd v. Amadio* (1983) 151 C.L.R. 447 at 457. The *Levett* decision expressly left open what the position would have been if there had been "something less than a contractual arrangement" at 1277.
[60] (1833) 5 Bing. N.C. 142.

intention to defraud was suggested.[61] However there is no obligation to disclose to a surety an arrangement made by the debtor with
another surety to whom he is indebted for the payment of part of
that debt out of the monies to be raised on the guarantee.[62]

Other secret arrangements

5–16   Any private arrangement modifying what from the terms of his
guarantee the surety would take to be the transaction between the
principal and the creditor must be communicated to the surety,[63]
e.g. where a surety joins with the principal in a promissory note but
there was an understanding between the principal and the payee that
the note should not be enforced for five years and that interest at 10
per cent should be payable being secured by a distinct note of the
principal.[64] Where a surety guarantees to one of a number of
creditors repayment of an advance to be made by that creditor to
enable the debtor to pay a composition which the general body of
creditors has agreed to accept and the creditor making the advance
secretly arranges for and takes payment of his own debt in full, the
surety is entitled to be discharged.[65]

Non-disclosure after suretyship entered into

5–17   There is no general duty to inform the surety of change of
circumstances or default by the principal debtor after suretyship has
been entered into[66] unless some specific provision is made.

---

[61] But see *Greenfield v. Edwards* (1865) 2 De G.J. & S. 582.
[62] *Mackreth v. Walmesley* (1884) 51 L.T. 1 at 19.
[63] See *Especy v. Lake* (1852) 10 Hare 260, *cf. Walker v. Hardman* (1837) 4 C. & F. 258.
[64] *ibid.*
[65] *Pendlebury v. Walker* (1841) 4 Y. & C. Ex. 424.
[66] *National Provincial Bank v. Glanusk* [1913] 3 K.B. 335.

CHAPTER 6

ILLEGALITY DURESS AND UNDUE INFLUENCE[1]

Principal obligation illegal

A guarantee, like any other contract, may be void for illegality **6–01** which may affect either the debt itself guaranteed or only the guarantee. If the debt itself is void for illegality it cannot be recovered under the guarantee.[2] So guarantees have frequently been held void where given for a secret preference by a bankrupt or compounding debtor.[3]

A promise that a corporation shall do something beyond its legal powers is void.[4] On the other hand, a surety for the repayment of money borrowed by a company *ultra vires* is liable.[5]

This is apparently because an intention is imputed to guarantors in such a case to be bound irrespective of the fact that the company is not legally liable to carry out its obligations.[6] Sections 108 to 112 of the Companies Act 1989 (which came into force in July 1991) have modified the *ultra vires* doctrine at common law. In consequence a company's objects clause can be said no longer to have the effect of defining the company's capacity as far as third parties are concerned. However, the authority of directors is still affected by the provisions in the objects clause and they remain personally liable to the company for any loss arising out of *ultra vires* acts.[7] In

---

[1] See generally *Chitty on Contracts* (27th ed.), Vol. 1, Chapters 7 and 16: Treitel, *The Law of Contracts* (19th ed., 1995), Chapters 10 and 11.

[2] *Swan v. Bank of Scotland* (1836) 10 Bligh. (N.S.) 627; *Bentinck Ltd v. Cromwell Engineering Co.* [1971] 1 QB 324; *Heald v. O'Connor* [1971] 1 W.L.R. 497.

[3] *Jackman v. Mitchell* [1807] 13 Ves. 581; *Coleman v. Waller* (1829) 3 W. & J. 212; *McKewan v. Sanderson* [1875] L.R. 20 Eq. 65.

[4] *McGregor v. Dover and Deal Railway* (1852) 18 QB 618.

[5] *Chambers v. Manchester and Milford Railway* (1864) 5 B. & S. 588 at 612; *Yorkshire Railway Wagon Co. v. Maclure* (1881) 19 Ch D 478; *Garrard v. James* [1925] 1 Ch. 616. In the United States the distinction is drawn between contracts merely beyond the powers of corporation, *i.e.* a question of capacity where the surety is liable: *Gates v. Tebbets* 83 Neb. 573; 119 N.W. 1120 (1909); *Winn v. Sandford* 145 Mass. 302; 14 N.E. 119 (1887); *Maledon v. Leflone* 62 R. Ark. 387; 35 S.W. 1102 (1896); *Mitchell v. Zurn* 221 S.W. 754 (1920) and where the principal contract requires the performance of *mala in se*, or *mala prohibita* where the surety is discharged: see *Swift v. Beers* 3 N.Y. 70 (1849); *Basnight v. American Manufacturing Co.* 174 N.C. 206; 93 S.E. 734 (1917); *Edwards County v. Jennings* 89 Tex. 618; 35 S.W. 1053 (1896); *Pendleton v. Greever* 80 Okl. 35; 193 P. 885 (1920); *First National Bank v. Clark's Estate* 59 Colo. 455; 149 P. 612 (1915).

[6] See *Garrard v. James*, above at 250. It has been suggested that in reality such a contract of guarantee is one of indemnity: see *Jowitt v. Callaghan* (1938) 38 S.R. (N.S.W.) 512 at 518 *per* Jordan C.J. See also Steyn (1974) 90 L.Q.R. 246 at 250. Alternatively, it can be argued that the guarantor especially a director guarantor impliedly represents that the company has the requisite power to enter into the guarantee.

[7] The doctrine of *ultra vires* may affect bodies other than bodies corporate, *e.g.* local authorities. In *Credit Suisse v. Borough Council of Allerdale* [1995] 1 Lloyd's Rep. 315 it was held that the giving of a guarantee itself was *ultra vires*.

Heald v. O'Connor[8] Fisher J. suggested that the true distinction was not between guarantees of illegal and *ultra vires* contracts but between whether the guarantor undertook to pay only those sums which the principal debtor could lawfully be called on to pay and whether he undertook to pay those sums which the debtor promised to pay whether or not the principal debtor could lawfully be called upon to do so.[9]

If certain parts only of the principal contract are void, such as a contract made in restraint of trade so as to be capable of severance there seems no reason why the guarantee should not also be held valid to the same extent.[10]

Where a surety repays a debt which unknown to him or the principal was unenforceable (by reason of section 6 of the Money-lenders Act 1927) he was held entitled to recover from the principal.[11]

Illegal guarantee for legal debts

6–02   The guarantee may be illegal and void though the debt itself is enforceable as where it is given in order to induce the creditor to conceal the existence of the debt so as to deceive the Bankruptcy Court[12] or is given to stifle a prosecution.[13]

Wrongful court order

6–03   A guarantee may be valid even if the consideration takes the form of an irregular court order which is to be treated as valid unless and until set aside.[14]

Threat of prosecution

6–04   A mere promise not to institute a prosecution does not by itself make void for illegality a guarantee for which there is other con-sideration, *e.g.* forbearing a civil suit.[15] But where there is an agreement to stifle a prosecution the guarantee is void whether the

---

[8] [1979] 1 W.L.R. 497 (s.54 of the Companies Act 1948: illegal assistance to company to purchase own shares); the point was expressly left open in *Argo Caribbean Group v. Lewis* [1976] 2 Lloyd's Rep. 289. See also Cohn [1947] 10 M.L.R. 40. It may be that the question of the validity of the guarantee would turn on whether the guarantor knows or believes the contract to be binding on the principal debt: see Furmston (1961) 24 M.L.R. 644. See also *op. cit.* Steyn at 253. For a case similar to *Heald v. O'Connor* see *Yeoman Credit Ltd v. Latter* [1961] 1 W.L.R. 828.

[9] See also *Yeoman Credit Ltd v. Latter*, above.

[10] See *Citicorp Australia Ltd v. Hendry* [1985] 4 N.S.W.L.R. 1; [1984] A.C.L.D. 179.

[11] *Re Chetwynd's Estate* [1938] Ch. 13.

[12] *Coles v. Strick* (1850) 15 QB 2.

[13] *Cannon v. Rands* (1870) 23 L.T. 817; 11 Cox C.C. 631; *Seear v. Cohen* (1881) 45 L.T. 589; *Williams v. Bailey* (1866) L.R. 1 HL 200; *Davies v. London and Provincial Marine Insurance Co.* (1878) 8 Ch D 469; *Jones v. Merionethshire Building Society* [1891] 2 Ch. 587; [1892] 1 Ch. 173; *Osborn v. Robbins* 36 N.Y. 365 (1867).

[14] *Decouvreur v. Jordan, The Times*, May 25, 1987, CA.

[15] See *per* Bowen L.J. in *Jones v. Merionethshire Building Society* [1892] 1 Ch. 173 at 184.

alleged criminal was in fact guilty or not and whether the prosecution had in fact been stifled or not.[16] There is a distinction in the inference to be drawn[17] between cases where a debtor gives security for his own debt under apprehension of a prosecution and cases where by a threat to prosecute a debtor, a guarantee or security is obtained from a third person under no independent liability.[18] In the former case the circumstance that the security was obtained by a threat of prosecution does not of itself show there was an agreement not to prosecute and thus does not necessarily vitiate the security.[19] But threats addressed to a third person to which he yields almost necessarily show that the guarantee was given on the terms of there being no prosecution.[20] In many cases there is no other consideration which can be suggested.[21]

Undue pressure and duress

Where a security is obtained, by a threat of prosecution, from a father or other near relative of the suggested delinquent, it may also be invalid as extorted by undue influence or pressure.[22] Illegality alone will only enable the surety to resist and defend a demand upon a guarantee. If he claims that money must be repaid or that the security be returned to him, he must show undue influence or pressure.[23] Duress might also take the form of duress to goods, *i.e.* a threatened or actual seizure or destruction of goods but all forms of duress are now subsumed under the general heading of economic duress. It is well established that mere commercial pressure will not be sufficient: there must be coercion to will against the prospective guarantor in circumstances in which he had no alternative course open to him.[24] A critical question is whether the creditor hopes to exercise his rights and powers in a way which is not within his existing rights, so that the guarantor is left with no alternative but to execute the guarantee,[25] although there may be exceptional cases in which the creditor is guilty of extortionate demands even though they were contractually justifiable.[26]

6–05

---

[16] *Cannon v. Rands* (1870) 23 L.T. 817; 11 Cox C.C. 631; *Seear v. Cohen* (1881) 45 L.T. 589.

[17] See *per* Vaughan Williams J. in *Jones v. Merionethshire Building Society*, above at 594.

[18] *Flower v. Saddler* (1882) 9 Q.B.D. 83; 10 Q.B.D. 572 at 576.

[19] *ibid.* See the cases there cited and approved.

[20] *Jones v. Merionethshire Building Society*, above; *Seear v. Cohen*, above.

[21] See *Williams v. Bayley* (1866) L.R. 1 HL 200; *Flower v. Sadler*, above; *cf. Rourke v. Mealy* [1878] 4 L.R. Ir. 166; *Eldridge and Morris v. Taylor* [1931] 2 QB 416; *Temperance Loan Fund v. Ross* [1932] 1 QB 522.

[22] *Williams v. Bayley*, above; *Seear v. Cohen*, above; *Jones v. Merionethshire Building Society*, above; *Kaufman v. Gerson* [1904] 1 W.L.R. 591: see also *Mutual Finance Co. v. Wetton* [1937] 2 K.B. 389.

[23] *Jones v. Merionethshire Building Society*, above. But *cf. Davies v. London Marine Insurance Co.* (1878) 8 Ch D 469 at 477.

[24] See generally *Pao On v. Lau Yin Lang and Others* [1980] A.C. 614 as well as *Universe Tankships Inc. of Monrovia v. International Transport Workers' Federation* [1983] 1 A.C. 366.

[25] *cf. Wardley Australia Ltd v. McPharlin* (1984) 3 B.P.R. 9, 500 and *Shivas v. Bank of New Zealand* [1990] 2 N.Z.L.R. 327.

[26] *e.g.* as in *Mutual Finance Co. Ltd v. Wetton*, above.

Undue influence: general

6–06   A guarantee procured by undue influence to which the creditor is a party can be set aside.[27] Since the decision of the House of Lords in *Barclays Bank plc v. O'Brien*[28] it must be determined whether the undue influence is actual or presumed. In the case of the former it must be shown that coercion has been used or that one party has exercised a "dominating influence" over the other so as to affect the latter's independence of decision.[29] In such a case there is no requirement that the transaction being guaranteed was manifestly disadvantageous to the party or parties seeking to upset it.[30]

Presumed undue influence arises in cases in which the relationship between the parties is such as to raise a presumption that one party exerts influence over the party seeking to set aside the transaction, on account of the trust and confidence reposed by the latter party in him or her. Such a confidential relationship can be established in two ways. First, certain relationships give rise as a matter of law to a presumption that undue influence has been exercised.[31] Certain relationships are automatically included such as parent and child, and solicitor and client. This is considered in the following section.

If a complainant successfully demonstrates that presumed undue influence exists, the court will set aside the transaction in whole or in part[32] unless the party seeking to uphold it in turn can demonstrate that the party subject to the presumed undue influence entered into the transaction of his or her own free will. It follows that if there exists a relationship of trust and confidence between a creditor and a surety, there is no need to demonstrate actual undue influence. However, in both types of cases of presumed undue influence a surety will not be able to set aside the transaction on the ground of undue influence by the principal debtor unless the creditor had actual or constructive knowledge of the undue influence.[33]

Undue influence: confidential relationships

6–07   Those relationships which raise a presumption that undue influence has been exercised include normally that of solicitor and

---

[27] See below as to those circumstances in which a creditor may be affected by undue influence exercised by a third party.
[28] [1994] 1 A.C. 180. The House of Lords approved the differentiation drawn in *Bank of Credit and Commerce International SA v. Aboody* [1990] 1 QB 923 at 953 in which cases of actual undue influence were described as "Class 1" type cases and cases of presumed undue influence which were held to fall into types of cases known as "Class 2" cases which was further sub-divided into Classes 2A and 2B as described in the text.
[29] [1994] 1 A.C. 180 at 189.
[30] *CIBC Mortgages v. Pitt* [1994] 1 A.C. 200.
[31] *Barclays Bank plc v. O'Brien*, above at 189: these cases constitute Class 2A type cases.
[32] See below.
[33] *Barclays Bank plc v. O'Brien*, above at 195 *et seq.*; *CIBC Mortgages v. Pitt* [1990] A.C. 200. Cases in which it can be proved by the party seeking to set aside the contract that as a matter of fact the relationship was one of trust and confidence giving rise to a presumption of undue influence are described as Class 2B cases.

client,[34] doctor and patient,[35] and parent and child.[36] A husband and wife,[37] landlord and tenant[38] and principal and agent[39] will not fall within this class.

The categories of relationship which may give rise to a relationship of trust and confidence are however not exhaustive: co-habitees may be included especially if the relationship is long standing or if there are children.[40] There seems no reason why a relationship which has since the date of the transaction broken down should not also be included but no doubt the court would closely examine the limits of the relationship and its history as well as the motives of the surety in such a case. Even relationships which were neither of a family nor of a sexual nature might be included provided a showing of some degree of domination by one party over the other was made out.[41] However it is unlikely that a relationship of employee and employer let alone a purely commercial relationship would attract the operation of these principles.[42]

However neither husbands and wives nor bankers and customers fall within Class 2A: a banker can therefore explain the nature of a guarantee without giving rise to any presumption that undue influence has been exercised.[43] Only if a party seeking to set aside the transaction can go further and show that in fact there existed a relationship of trust and confidence will the presumption arise.[44]

Secondly, and following from the above even if the relationship is not one which normally raises a presumption of undue influence the party seeking to satisfy the transaction can in effect demonstrate presumed undue influence by showing that as a matter of fact the relationship was one of trust and confidence.[45]

Manifest disadvantage

In principle if a gift is made or an improvident transaction is **6–08** entered into undue influence is to be treated as having taken place

---

[34] See *Barclays Bank plc v. O'Brien* [1990] A.C. 180 at 189.
[35] *Dent v. Bennett* (1839) 4 My & Cr. 269; *Barclays Bank plc v. O'Brien*, above.
[36] It will be a question of fact whether the relationship continues after marriage. See, *e.g.* *Lancashire Loans Ltd v. Black* [1934] 1 K.B. 380. See generally *Re Pauling's Settlement Trust, Younghusband v. Coutts & Co.* [1964] Ch. 303 at 337: it is a question of fact and degree in each case.
[37] See *Bank of Montreal v. Stuart* [1911] A.C. 120.
[38] *Matthew v. Bobbins* (1980) 124 S.J. 479.
[39] See, *e.g. Coomber v. Coomber* [1911] 1 Ch. 723.
[40] *Midland Bank plc v. Massey* [1995] 1 All E.R. 929.
[41] See, *e.g. Ransom v. Leeder*, unreported, May 27, 1994, Judge Bromley Q.C..
[42] See, *e.g. Homes Bridging plc v. Berwin*, unreported, CAT No.0181 of 1994, February 24.
[43] *National Westminster Bank plc v. Morgan* [1985] A.C. 686 at 707.
[44] See *Lloyds Bank v. Bundy* [1975] QB 326 at 347. See also *National Westminster Bank plc v. Morgan*, above at 708, 709, where it was stressed that the court should examine the facts closely.
[45] *Barclays Bank plc v. O'Brien* [1990] 1 A.C. 180 at 189. In theory any relationship is susceptible to such a showing but clearly some will more readily lend themselves to this, *e.g.* wives, so-habitees and elderly relatives, see *e.g. Goldsworthy v. Brickell* [1987] Ch. 378 at 401 *per* Nourse L.J. and *Avon Finance Co. Ltd v. Bridger* [1985] 2 All E.R. 281.

in the case of relationships which attract the presumption of undue influence, *i.e.* Class 2A type cases.[46]

The presumption of undue influence will therefore be established if there is a showing that the transaction was manifestly disadvantageous to the guarantor. There is no need to demonstrate any manifest disadvantage if the case involves a showing of actual undue influence.[47]

In the case of a guarantee it is not enough to show that there is a risk that it will be called: what has to be shown is that the risk of enforcement outweighs the benefits which the surety would otherwise enjoy.[48] In general the risk of a guarantor losing his or her home will outweigh any indirect benefit or benefits which might be yielded from enjoying the income generated by the use of any advance made by the principal debtor.[49]

There should not be any fine or close evaluation[50] of the transaction to determine whether any disadvantage is manifest.[51] In the case of guarantees granted by a wife to support family businesses which otherwise are a source of income to them, this will not generally constitute a manifest disadvantage.

Undue influence by creditor

6–09   In the case of a bank guarantee it would be unusual for a creditor to be held responsible for exerting undue influence over a guarantor but the particular circumstances may show that such was in fact the case.[52]

Undue influence by principal debtor or by co-surety

6–10   It is not sufficient for a guarantor merely to show that the undue influence was committed by the principal debtor or by a co-surety. The guarantor must go further and show that the creditor is in law affected by such undue influence and also that in some way the creditor did not take reasonable steps to prevent the surety from acting under such undue influence.[53]

---

[46] See *Goldsworthy v. Brickell*, above at 401; *National Westminster Bank plc v. Morgan*, above at 704; *CIBC Mortgages v. Pitt*, above at 207–209.

[47] *CIBC Mortgages v. Pitt*, above at 209. For an example of a presumption of undue influence in the context of employer and Employee, see *Crédit Lyonnais Bank Nederland N.V. v. Barch* [1997] 1 All E.R. 144. For an example where both actual and presumed undue influence was exposed, see *Bank of Scotland v. Bennett* [1997] 1 F.L.R. 801.

[48] *Bank of Credit and Commerce International SA v. Aboody* [1990] 1 QB 923 especially at 965. The court must examine the circumstances closely which exist both at the time of the transaction and subsequently.

[49] See *Midland Bank plc v. Phillips* unreported March 14, 1986 CA, CAT No. 258 of 1986 and *Barclays Bank v. Kennedy* [1989] 1 F.L.R. 356.

[50] *cf. Cheese v. Thomas* [1994] 1 W.L.R. 129, not a suretyship case. See also *Barclays Bank Plc v. Sumner* [1996] 1 E.G.C.S. 65.

[51] *Bank of Credit and Commerce International SA v. Aboody* [1990] 1 QB 923 at 965.

[52] See, *e.g. Lloyds Bank v. Bundy* [1975] QB 336.

[53] For recent examples confirming this approach see *Coldunell Ltd v. Gallon* [1986] QB 1184; *Midland Bank plc v. Perry and Perry* [1988] 1 S.L.R. 161; *Midland Bank plc v. Shephard* [1988] 3 All E.R. 17; *Bank of Baroda v. Shah* [1988] 3 All E.R. 24.

In *Barclays Bank plc v. O'Brien*[54] the House of Lords confirmed that a creditor could be affected by the actions of the principal debtor either if the latter acted as the creditor's agent or the creditor had sufficient notice of the undue influence and did not take reasonable steps to prevent the surety from acting under it.

Undue influence by principal or co-surety as agent

It is clear that if the principal debtor who has exercised the undue   **6–11**
influence on a surety was the agent of the creditor, the guarantee signed in the wake of such undue influence will be voidable.[55] However if the creditor entrusts the principal debtor with the task of obtaining the surety's signature this will not of itself give rise to such an agency.[56] Even if agency is established, the terms of the agency may not be wide enough to cover the circumstances in which the act of undue influence relied upon occurred.[57] In most cases however a principal debtor in seeking the comfort of a guarantee will be acting on his own behalf and not on behalf of the creditor.[58]

Undue influence by a principal or co-surety: notice

If a creditor has actual[59] or constructive notice at the time the   **6–12**
guarantee is executed that it had been procured by the exercise of undue influence the creditor will not be allowed to enforce the transaction.[60] In *Barclays Bank plc v. O'Brien*[61] the House of Lords had to reconcile two differing lines of earlier authority namely the first which made no distinction between wives as sureties and other parties as sureties[62] and cases which treated wives as deserving of special treatment.[63] In the case of the first group it had been held that the guarantee could be upset only if the creditor had actual or

---

[54] [1994] 1 A.C. 180 at 189.

[55] *Barclays Bank plc v. O'Brien*, above at 191.

[56] *Barclays Bank plc v. O'Brien* [1993] QB 109 at 113 *per* Scott L.J.; [1994] 1 A.C. 180 at 194, 195.

[57] See *McCabe v. Skipton Building Society* (1994) S.L.T. 1272, a case involving fraudulent misrepresentation held not to have been by husband to his wife as surety, in his capacity as the bank's agent.

[58] The law has in effect been re-cast by *Barclays Bank plc v. O'Brien* [1994] 1 A.C. 180 at 191, and a host of earlier authorities running principally from *Turnbull & Co. v. Duval* [1902] 1 A.C. 429 to *Bank of Credit and Commerce International SA v. Aboody* [1990] 1 QB 923 can now be treated as overruled in this respect.

[59] The boundaries of actual notice in this area are not totally clearly defined. It is suggested that closing one's eyes to the obvious, *i.e.* so-called Nelsonian knowledge, should be included and there is some authority to suggest that if the circumstances were such as to lead a reasonable person to believe that fraud must have been used in order to obtain the guarantor's agreement to the transaction the creditor is bound to make enquiry, *Owen v. Homan* (1853) 4 HL Cas. 997 at 1034, 1035. There seems no reason why for present purposes undue influence should not be equated with fraud.

[60] *Barclays Bank plc v. O'Brien* [1994] 1 A.C. 180 at 191; *CIBC Mortgages v. Pitt* [1994] 1 A.C. 180 at 209.

[61] *ibid.*

[62] *e.g. Midland Bank v. Perry* (1987) F.L.R. 237; *Bank of Credit and Commerce International SA v. Aboody* [1990] 1 QB 923 and *Bank of Baroda v. Shah* [1988] 3 All E.R. 24.

[63] See *Kings North Trust v. Bell* [1986] 1 W.L.R. 119; *Barclays Bank v. Kennedy* [1989] 1 F.L.R. 356. See also *Avon Finance Co. v. Bridger* [1985] 2 All E.R. 281 extending the same principles to elderly relatives.

constructive knowledge of the relevant facts or that the principal debtor was an accredited agent: it was confirmed that other than in such cases the creditor did not need to ensure that the surety had an adequate understanding of the transaction.

In *Barclays Bank plc v. O'Brien* the House of Lords recognised that sureties should be afforded proper protection but held that creditors owed no special duty of care to any particular category of surety.[64] As already set out above a surety has to establish undue influence which would give the surety an equitable right to set the transaction aside as well as agency on the part of the creditor or actual or constructive knowledge by the creditor. The fact that the surety was inadequately informed or did not understand the true nature of the transaction does not justify upsetting the transaction. The creditor would have the requisite constructive knowledge if two conditions were satisfied namely: first, that the transaction was on its face one which lacked financial advantage for the surety[65]; and secondly, that there was a substantial risk that the debtor had committed a legal or equitable wrong, *e.g.* by virtue of the debtor and surety being to the creditor's knowledge in a relationship of trust and confidence.[66] Once the complainant had satisfied these two requirements then in order not to be affected by constructive knowledge of the surety's rights the creditor had to take reasonable steps to satisfy himself that the complainant entered into the transaction freely.

6–13   For present purposes a showing of lack of financial advantage does not necessarily involve consideration of the same matters as a showing of manifest disadvantage[67] although there may be an overlap in practice. The distinction is highlighted in cases where there is on the face of the transaction a joint benefit.

In *CIBC Mortgages v. Pitt*,[68] a transaction made in favour of a husband and wife jointly was not set aside despite proof of actual undue influence since the loan was ostensibly partly for the benefit of the wife who agreed to act as surety. There was therefore the clear presence of a financial benefit for the wife which could not put the creditor on enquiry.[69] The court should therefore look at the reality of the transaction so that even a loan ostensibly in favour of a husband might on further enquiry be seen to be in reality one made for the direct benefit of the wife.[70]

---

[64] [1994] 1 A.C. 180 at 195.

[65] See above.

[66] It is fair to note that the House of Lords clearly regarded the lack of financial advantage as the more critical of these two requirements.

[67] See above: a showing of manifest disadvantage is relevant strictly to a demonstration that there exists a presumed undue influence in cases where the relationship as such does not automatically give rise to the presumption.

[68] [1994] 1 A.C. 200.

[69] *CIBC Mortgages v. Pitt* [1994] A.C. 200 at 211.

[70] *e.g. Hedworth v. Scotlife Home Loans (No.2) Ltd* [1995] M.P.C. 91 demonstrating that the court will not shrink from considering the true nature of the transaction from the perspective of the surety if what was on the true face of the transaction did not properly represent the reality of the transaction, *cf. Goode Durrant Administration v. Biddulph* (1994) 26 H.L.R. 625.

Reasonable steps by the creditor

If the surety succeeds in proving that the transaction was not on **6–14**
its face to his or her financial advantage and further that there was
known to the creditor to be a relationship of trust and confidence,
the burden will shift to the creditor to prove that the guarantee was
given as a result of full free and informed thought by the guarantor.[71] This will commonly involve a demonstration by a creditor
that the guarantor had independent advice at the time of the transaction.[72] There is no necessity that such advice be legal.[73] Indeed it is
not even necessary always to demonstrate that independent advice
was given if there is other evidence to show that the surety had the
requisite understanding.[74] It is therefore important that the advice
emanates from a source which is not susceptible to any desire that
the transaction be concluded.

In *Barclays Bank plc v. O'Brien* the House of Lords set out
guidelines as to what might be regarded as sensible practical steps
in future transactions, namely the desirability of a private meeting
between the prospective guarantor and the creditor in the absence of
the principal debtor, at which the guarantor could be informed of
the extent of the liability being undertaken, the nature of the risks
and the need to take independent legal advice.[75]

The guidelines being prospective only, transactions entered into **6–15**
before the date of the decision of the House of Lords will not attract
precisely the same requirements and therefore it is suggested that
advising a prospective surety by letter or at a personal meeting of
the need to seek independent legal advice will generally discharge
the burden borne by a creditor in such cases.[76]

However both with regard to pre-*O'Brien* and post-*O'Brien*
transactions a creditor will also discharge the burden of ensuring
that the surety has been informed by the creditor of the need to seek
independent legal advice by showing that in fact the surety was in
receipt of such advice at the time of the transaction.[77]

With regard to post-*O'Brien* transactions only, a clause in the
relevant security documentation informing a surety of the need to
seek legal advice, that he or she had read the clause and that he or

---

[71] Alternatively, the creditor can attempt to prove that there was no undue influence which may
frequently be a difficult burden to discharge.

[72] The emphasis on full free and informed thought can be seen in such cases as *Zamet v. Hyman*
[1961] 1 W.L.R. 1442 at 1446 and *Allcard v. Skinner* (1887) 36 Ch D 245, 171.

[73] *Inche Noriah v. Shaik Allie Bin Omar* [1929] A.C. 127. See also *Re Coomber, Coomber v.
Coomber* [1911] 1 Ch. 723 at 730.

[74] *Inche Noriah v. Sheik Allie Bin Omar*, above at 135; *Re Brocklehurst's Estate, Hall v. Roberts*
[1978] Ch. 14.

[75] *Barclays Bank plc v. O'Brien* [1994] 1 A.C. 180 at 196. Note the terms of *Good Banking Code
of Practice* (1994 ed.), para. 14.1. On the approach set out by the House of Lords refusal by a surety to
seek independent advice following any meeting with a bank would presumably relieve the bank of
liability. See, *e.g. Coldunell v. Gallon* [1986] QB 1184 and *Bank of Baroda v. Shah* [1988] 3 All E.R. 24.

[76] See generally *Barclays Bank plc v. O'Brien* [1993] QB 109 especially at 139–140 *per* Scott
L.J.

[77] See *Banco Exterior International v. Mann* [1995] 1 All E.R. 936; *Midland Bank plc v. Serter*
[1995] 1 F.L.R. 1034; *Bank of Baroda v. Rayarel* [1995] 2 F.L.R. 376; *Barclays Bank Plc v. Thomson*
[1996] N.P.C. 155, CA.

she did not wish to do so would not, it is suggested, protect a creditor.

Decisions subsequent to *Barclays Bank plc v. O'Brien* however have expressed the view that the absence of a personal meeting is not fatal to the creditor's position and that the abiding consideration was whether the bank had taken reasonable steps to ensure that the surety's consent was properly obtained.[78] Often the bank can rely upon a certificate from the solicitor also signed by the surety to the effect that the nature and extent of the guarantee or other security was appreciated by the surety.[79]

6–16   Generally if the creditor is aware that the surety is in receipt of legal advice the creditor can safely assume that such advice is independent[80]; the same applies even if the creditor is aware that the surety is being advised by the same legal adviser as the principal debtor.[81] A bank is therefore entitled to assume that even in such a case the interests of the surety are being properly safeguarded.

If the creditor (as well as the borrower) should use the same legal adviser as the surety it is likely that that the creditor will be fixed with actual notice or knowledge of the fact that the surety may have received less than clear advice but the question is not settled.[82]

Although the present state of the law in the wake of *Barclays Bank plc v. O'Brien* is not entirely settled the Court of Appeal has recently given detailed guidance as to the duties of a solicitor when instructed by the wife in an *O'Brien* situation. The solicitor must be satisfied there is no improper influence and that the transaction can sensibly be entered into. If not, and a wife persists, the bank having been told as much, the solicitor should cease to act. It will usually be necessary for the solicitor to inform himself about the transaction, the amount of the debt, the reasons for the new advance or the bank's request for additional security. He may also have to probe the stability of the marriage.[83,84,85] Prudence however dictates that the advice contain a clear explanation of any of the more unusual aspects of the transaction involved.

---

[78] *Bank Melli Iran v. Samadi-Rad* [1995] 1 F.C.R. 465 at 474; *Massey v. Midland Bank* [1995] 1 All E.R. 939; *Banco Exterior International SA v. Mann*, above; *Midland Bank v. Serter*, above. See also Chandler "Undue Influence at the Function of Independent Advice". See also *Allied Irish Bank v. O'Byrne* [1995] 2 F.L.R. 325.

[79] *Midland Bank v. Serter*, above; *Banco Exterior International SA v. Mann*, above.

[80] *Bank of Baroda v. Shah*, above; *Banco Exterior v. Mann*, above.

[81] *Bank of Baroda v. Rayarel*, above *per* Hoffmann L.J. On this point earlier decisions such as *Allied Irish Bank v. Byrne*, *supra*, and *Bank Melli Iran v. Samadi-Rad*, above are to be treated as overruled.

[82] See *Halifax Mortgage Services Ltd v. Stepsky*, *The Times*, [1995] 4 All E.R. 656, suggesting that such knowledge would not always be imputed to the creditor in a situation where a solicitor was held to be acting only as agent for the surety and not for the creditor on being told why the money was required but the decision is difficult to reconcile with the Court of Appeal's views in *Bank of Baroda v. Rayarel*, above. *Cf. Midland Bank plc v. Taak*, unreported, CAT No.0084 of 1995.

[83] *Royal Bank of Scotland v. Etridge*, *The Times*, August 17 1998.

[84] It seems that in practice banks have ignored the view expressed by the House of Lords that the bank and the wife should have a separate meeting.

[85] The Court of Appeal stressed that a bank was not entitled to assume a solicitor had carried out his instructions to give full and proper advice, *Cooke v. National Westminster Bank Plc*, *The Times*, July 27 1998, approved.

In *Crédit Lyonnais Bank Nederland N.V. v. Barch*,[86] a case of employer and employee, in which a presumption of undue influence was held to arise, and where the transaction involving an unlimited guarantee was clearly to the disadvantage of the employee, the creditor was held to have been put on inquiry of the undue influence exerted by the employer. The Court of Appeal held that the creditor could only avoid the consequences of its suspicions if it had taken reasonable steps to allay such suspicions and the result of such steps must have been such as to allay those suspicions. On the facts, it was found that the creditor had not done enough. The Court of Appeal added that a person seeking to rebut the presumption of undue influence could only do so by showing that the complainant knew what he or she was doing and intended to do it. The giving of advice on its own would not necessarily be enough.

Creditor with no notice of undue influence

It follows from the above discussion that if a creditor has neither **6–17** actual nor constructive knowledge that a transanction on its face is not to the financial advantage of the surety[87] or that the debtor and surety are in a relationship of trust and confidence, there will be no requirement upon the creditor to ensure that the surety has the benefit of independent legal advice or has otherwise formed an independent and informed judgement.[88] Moreover it is suggested that in such circumstances the creditor is under no duty to explain the nature and contents of the guarantee to the prospective surety even if he is a customer.[89]

On the other hand should a creditor or its legal advisers attempt to explain the security documents to a surety and do so inadequately a duty of care may arise if the creditor voluntarily assumes the role of adviser or if that surety is a customer.[90] The operation is one of degree since fulfilment of the requirements stipulated by the House of Lords in *Barclays Bank plc v. O'Brien* will not of themselves put a creditor or his legal advisers in a position whereby they owe such a duty of care.[91]

Setting aside

In an appropriate case there exists a jurisdiction in the court to set **6–18** aside a transaction otherwise voidable at the instance of the surety on terms. Following the decision in *Barclays Bank plc v. O'Brien*

---

[86] [1997] 1 All E.R. 144.
[87] See above.
[88] See generally *Barclays Bank plc v. O'Brien* [1993] QB 109 at 126–127.
[89] See generally *O'Hara v. Allied Irish Banks Ltd* [1985] B.C.L.C. 52, *Barclays Bank v. Khaira* [1992] 1 W.L.R. 634–637; *Union Bank of Finland v. Lelakis* [1995] C.L.C. 27; *Cornish v. Midland Bank plc* [1985] 3 All E.R. 513 *per* Kerr L.J. at 522, 523, not followed in *Barclays Bank v. Khaira* but not considered in *Barclays Bank plc v. O'Brien*, above.
[90] See the discussion in the Court of Appeal in *Barclays Bank plc v. O'Brien* [1993] QB 109.
[91] See, *e.g. Midland Bank v. Kidwai* [1995] N.P.C. 81.

there was initially some doubt as to whether a transaction could be set aside in part, *e.g.* that a charge should be enforced to the extent of the limit which was the subject of misrepresentation by the principal debtor made to a wife acting as surety.[92] However in *Midland Bank v. Greene*[93] it was held that terms could be imposed on the grant of equitable relief to reflect an acceptance by a wife that the bank had a good security to the extent of the misrepresented limit. However the Court of Appeal in *TSB v. Camfield*[94] in turn held that the remedy was "all or nothing" save that the court recognised that terms could be imposed to ensure the proper application of restitution *in integrum*. The court also pointed out that generally a wife would have nothing which she could restore.

The test therefore is to consider what benefit the wife requires overall from the transaction.

---

[92] *Allied Irish Bank v. Byrne*, [1995] 2 F.L.R. 325, *per* Ferris J. who ruled that no partial setting aside could occur.

[93] [1994] 2 F.L.R. 827.

[94] [1995] 1 W.L.R. 430 followed in *Phillips Finance Co. v. Piddington* [1994] N.P.C. 155. In *Dunbar Bank plc v. Nadeem*, [1998] 3 All E.R. 876, the Court of Appeal stressed that if more than one transaction was involved, the precise extent of the enrichment needed to be determined in order to consider the requisite restitution. In some circumstances, the objectionable parts of a document can be severed, leaving the rest of the instrument enforceable, provided that doing so does not amount to reuniting the transaction: *Barclays Bank Plc v. Caplan, The Times*, December 12 1997.

CHAPTER 7

RIGHTS OF A SURETY

1. *General Principles*

The general principle here is the equity of the surety, subject to the   **7–01**
paramount right of the creditor to be paid, to have the creditor's
powers applied to produce an equitable result as between all persons liable.[1] The aim is to ensure that the person primarily liable
should bear the whole burden in relief of others,[2] or if there is a
deficiency that it should fall equally upon those with secondary
liability.[3] These rights of a surety do not depend upon any contract
involving the principal debtor or the sureties. Such rights depend
upon equitable principles of readjusting the inequal placing of
burdens upon persons or properties all equally liable at law[4]: " . . .
if, as between several persons or properties all equally liable at law
to the same demand, it would be equitable that the burden should
fall in a certain way, the Court will so far as possible, having regard
to the solvency of the different parties, see that if the burden is
placed inequitably by the exercise of the legal right, its incidence
should be afterwards readjusted."[5] A surety against whom judgment has been obtained by the creditor for the full amount of the
guarantee, even though he has paid nothing in respect of the
guarantee, can sue his co-sureties to compel them to contribute
towards the common liability.[6] Moreover, as soon as the surety
becomes liable, he can sue the principal debtor for an order to pay
the debt guaranteed so as to relieve the surety.[7]

2. *Surety's Equity Against Creditor*

There is some authority for suggesting that a surety also has an   **7–02**
equity against the creditor to prevent the creditor from bringing

---

[1] See *Dering v. Lord Winchelsea* (1787) 1 Cox. 318; 2 B. & P. 270; *Stirling v. Forrester* (1831) 3
Bligh 575; *Craythorne v. Swinburne* (1807) 14 Ves. 160; *Duncan Fox & Co. v. North and South Wales
Bank* (1880) 6 App. Cas. 1. Pennycurck J. in *Re Downer Enterprises Ltd* [1974] 1 W.L.R. 1460
considered on the basis of the *Duncan Fox* case that the rights of reimbursement and subrogation to
securities belonged not merely to sureties but to any person who paid a liability for which some other
party was ultimately responsible, *ibid.* 1468, 1469.
[2] *Anson v. Anson* [1953] 1 QB 636, especially at 641–642 where the rights of reimbursement
enjoyed by the surety are explained in terms of an implied term. But see the text and *cf. Brooks Wharf
& Bull Wharf Ltd v. Goodman Bros* [1937] 1 QB 523 at 544–545 *per* Lord Wright M.R. (enrichment
of principal debtor by the discharge of his liability).
[3] See *Duncan Fox & Co. v. North & South Wales Bank*, above *per* Lord Blackburn at 19, 20.
[4] See for approval of this passage *Whitham v. Bullock* [1939] 2 K.B. 81.
[5] *Craythorne v. Swinburne*, above at 165.
[6] *Wolmershausen v. Gullick* [1883] 2 Ch. 514.
[7] *ibid.* at 528.

down the whole weight of the debt upon the surety, although this view has been challenged.[8] Wright J. in *Wolmershausen v. Gullick*[9] considered by way of dictum that a surety could in equity "be controlled and prevented from enforcing its legal right inequitably against one alone of the sureties", even though the dictum was made in the context of a discussion regarding a guarantor's right to contribution from co-sureties. This, however, in his view was the point of having the creditor joined as party in *Dering v. Earl of Winchelsea*.[10] Lord Eldon in *Craythorne v. Swinburne*,[11] a commentary on *Dering v. Winchelsea* accepted that case as deciding that " . . . the creditor, who can call upon all, shall not be at liberty to fix one with payment of the whole debt . . . ".

The fourth edition of this book considered that in *Dering v. Winchelsea* the creditor was only made a party in order to compel him to receive the money which the co-sureties were called upon to pay and in order to obtain a discharge for all parties so that the surety's equity was primarily asserted against the co-sureties rather than against the creditor in order to control his remedies. The fourth edition also considered that a surety could not resist the demand of the creditor pending resort to the principal or his estate, on the basis of Sir John Romilly's judgment in *Jackson v. Digby*[12] and the House of Lords decision in *Ewart v. Latta*.[13] In the latter case, which concerned Scottish law but where the same principle was said to apply as in English law, it was said that a surety who had not paid could not compel the creditor to sue the principal debtor.[14] The underlying principle here is that a surety in default cannot dictate terms to the creditor. On that basis it would equally be the case that a surety could not compel the creditor to bring in co-sureties in an action against the surety.

7–03 Despite the considerable authority of the views examined in the fourth edition of this work[15] it is felt that it is still arguable that a surety has an equity on the basis of *Wolmershausen v. Gullick* and the authorities cited therein including the views of Lord Eldon, to stay a creditor attempting unfairly to place the whole burden of the debt upon the surety, at least in special circumstances, *e.g.* where there is a solvent principal debtor or solvent co-sureties who could easily be but are not joined in the action or where there is a security which could easily be realised to pay the whole debt. That would be more consonant with the rights a surety possessed in late Roman

---

[8] See O'Donovan & Phillips, *The Modern Contract of Guarantee* (3rd ed.) at pp. 536 *et seq.*
[9] [1993] 2 Ch. at 522.
[10] [1787] 1 Cox 318.
[11] (1807) 14 Ves. 160.
[12] (1854) 2 W.R. 540.
[13] (1865) 4 Macq. HL 983.
[14] *ibid.* at 989.
[15] And the criticisms set out in O'Donovan & Phillips, above.

law[16] and which passed into the Scottish and Continental legal systems. Lord Eldon himself changed his views on the matter: having appeared as counsel in *Dering v. Winchelsea* he was "much dissatisfied with the whole proceeding and with the judgment" but subsequently was "convinced that the decision was upon the right principles".[17]

Where the surety offers to pay the debt on condition that those remedies are made over to him, but the creditor refuses, the surety is entitled to pay the money into court and to bring an action for the assignment of the creditor's remedies.[18]

One situation in which the surety's equity has been held maintainable against the creditor is where the creditor has an opportunity to recover the debt from the principal debtor which will not be available to the surety. In *Cotton v. Blane*[19] it seems from the marginal note that the creditor was restrained from suing the surety, on the basis that the creditor but not the surety could have recovered the amount of the debt from another fund.[20] The principle appears to have been that the surety had an equity to compel the creditor to recover the debt from the alternative source. Relief was only granted upon the surety bringing money into court but this may have stemmed from possible doubts about the fund the creditor was to resort to. It is suggested that the case should be treated as analogous to the creditor's obligation to perfect a security which is held for the enforcement of the guaranteed obligation, but no distinction is drawn in the decisions based on the fact that the fund may have been provided by a third party as distinct from the principal debtor.

Where the creditor is in possession of a fund belonging to the **7–04** surety, the surety can insist on the creditor proceeding against the debtor or against the debtor's fund in relief of the surety's fund.[21]

A rather special situation where the surety can exercise his equity against the creditor is where the creditor obtains payment from a surety under duress or oppression. In *Law v. East India Co.*[22] the company compelled its servant, who was surety for another servant, to pay under duress. The company was ordered to replace the amount pending the ascertainment of the parties' rights.

---

[16] Rights of Discussion: See D.46.1, 1.17, 1.51 and 1.62; Cod. 8.41.1.5 and 1.19; Nov. 4, c.L. Rights of Division: Cod. 8.41, 1.2 and 1.21; Nov. 99 c.L.; G.3, 121, 122. In the USA a surety will not be able to restrain a creditor unless there are special circumstances, *e.g.* where a security can be realised without prejudicing the creditor but a failure to realise it would result in unusual hardship to the surety: Restatement, Security s.131 (1941).

[17] *Craythorne v. Swinburne* (1807) 14 Ves. 160.

[18] *Goddard v. Whyte* (1860) 2 Giff. 449.

[19] (1795) 2 Anstr. 544.

[20] The surety had guaranteed the performance of the charterers of an American vessel. The vessel was detained at Bordeaux under an embargo. The French National Convention resolved to compensate neutral owners. It seems that the surety was English and not a neutral whereas the creditor was a neutral and could claim compensation.

[21] See *Ex p. Goodman* (1818) 3 Madd. 373; *Re Westzinhaus* (1833) 5 B. & Ad. 817.

[22] (1799) 4 Ves. 824.

3. *Surety's Remedies Against Principal Debtor*

General principles: right to indemnity

7–05   A surety who was paid the debt can recover against the principal debtor for money paid to his use.[23] This is based upon the common law action for money paid and in turn is based upon an implied promise.[24] In equity, the surety has been given an order against a creditor for the assignment of the creditor's remedies against a principal debtor[25] or has even been given a direct right of recoupment.[26]

Even if the contract between the creditor and the principal debtor is unenforceable, *e.g.* through illegality, a surety can still claim an indemnity on payment.[27]

Cases analogous to suretyship

7–06   By analogy to the rights of a surety, any person liable only secondarily who performs under compulsion of law an obligation for which another is primarily liable has a right of recoupment against the person primarily liable.[28] Moreover the payment must have been reasonably necessary in the interests of the creditor or himself or both of them.[29] A common example is the position of an original lessee who has assigned the lease. If such an assignor is compelled to perform the covenants in the lease he can recover against the assignee, however remote, in possession of the land.[30]

---

[23] See *Morrice v. Redwyn* (1731) 2 Barnard 26; *Woffington v. Sparks* (1744) 2 Ves. Sen. 569; *Taylor v. Mills* (1777) 2 Cowp. 525; *Toussaint v. Martinnant* (1787) 2 Term. Rep. 100 at 105.

[24] In *Re A Debtor* [1937] Ch. 156, it was held that an implied contract arose at the time of the contract of suretyship. See also the discussion in *Anson v. Anson* [1953] 1 QB 636. *Anson v. Anson* also confirms that a husband's claim to an indemnity of his wife's debts on the making of any payments under such a guarantee will be presumed to constitute advances to his wife: see also *Re Salisbury-Jones* [1938] 2 All E.R. 459.

[25] See *Morgan v. Seymour* (1638) 1 Ch. R. 120; *Greerside v. Benson* (1745) 3 Atk. 248.

[26] Vin. Abr. Surety D.4. And see *Saunders v. Churchill ibid.* 2; *St John v. Holford ibid.* 6; *Hungerford v. Hungerford ibid.* 7. In *Brook's Wharf v. Goodman Bros* [1937] 1 K.B. 534 at 543 Lord Wright stated that the court decided on the circumstances of the case what was just and reasonable with regard to the relationship between the parties. Alternatively, the direct recourse can be seen as equitable subrogation to the creditor's singular to sue without express assignment. See *Brown Shipley & Co. Ltd v. Amalgamated Investment (Europe) BV* [1979] 1 Lloyd's Rep. 488 and *Re Walters Deed of Guarantee* [1933] Ch. 321 where a guarantor was subrogated to the rights of preference shareholders. In USA see *Re Dutcher* 213 F. 908 (1914), DC Wash. (subrogation of surety to preferential creditor's position), *Sanders v. Sanders* 49 Idaho 733; 291 P.1069 (1930) (surety subrogated to creditor's right to set aside fraudulent conveyance).

[27] *Re Chetwynd's Estate* [1938] Ch. 13 applied in *Argo Caribbean Group Ltd v. Lewis* [1976] 2 Lloyd's Rep. 289. See also *Alexander v. Vane* (1836) 1 M. & W. 511, *cf. Re Morris: Coneys v. Morris* [1922] 1 Ir. R. 81 but note that in that decision both the principal debtor as well as the surety were statute barred, in the case where the surety was not allowed to claim an indemnity.

[28] *per* Willes J. in *Roberts v. Crowe* (1872) L.R. 7 C.P. 629 at 637. See also *Duncan Fox & Co. v. North and South Wales Bank* (1886) App. Cas. 1 at 19.

[29] *Owen v. Tate* [1976] 1 QB 402 at 409–410. This is often described as an "officious" act or payment. But now *cf. The Zuhal K* [1987] 1 Lloyd's Rep. 151.

[30] *Moule v. Garrett* (1872) L.R. 5 Ex. 132; 7 Ex. 101; *Walker v. Bartlett* (1856) 18 C.B. 845. See also *Re Cleadon Trust* [1939] 1 Ch. 286; *Becton Dickinson Ltd v. Zwebner* [1989] Q.B. 208; *Selous Street Properties Ltd v. Oronel Fabrics Ltd* (1984) 270 E.G. 643.

Similarly a transferor of shares, if made contributory, can recover against a transferee.[31]

An analogous situation arises where the property of one person is lawfully seized for the debt of another,[32] *e.g.* in the case of distress for rent, where the right may be enforced against parties liable for rent even though they were not aware the property had been placed upon the premises, such as lessees, who had assigned their interest.[33]

The right in question being based on equitable principles founded upon the right of the surety to the creditor's remedies, it is suggested that the surety's remedy is not dependent upon the "principal's" knowledge of the "guarantee" situation.[34] However, a surety has no right against the person who agrees to indemnify the principal debtor in respect of that debt.[35]

In the case of bills of exchange, an indorser who pays can sue the acceptor.[36] Although the parties may not be known to each other, the acceptor should contemplate the likelihood of indorsers.[37] In *ex p. Bishop*[38] a bankrupt bill broker had deposited bills with the bank under a guarantee without indorsing them. The bank proved under the guarantee and were paid dividends. The bill broker's trustee in bankruptcy was held able to recover the sum paid by way of dividend from the acceptor. Cotton and James L.JJ. considered that an essential element of the decision was that the bill broker had authority, having regard to the original course of dealing, from the parties to the bill to deal with it under a covering guarantee. Cotton L.J. considered that mere compulsion to pay part of a bill of exchange will not necessarily entitle the person paying the bill to recover from the acceptor: the right to recovery arose only if the compulsion were undertaken at the request or implied request of the person primarily liable on the bill. In the case of an indorser, Cotton L.J. considered that he was impliedly authorised by the acceptor to endorse the bill over. Thesiger L.J. by contrast did not accept this view and even reserved his opinion as to whether a voluntary payment by a stranger of a debt did not "give him a right of action against the person who was liable to pay it", referring to the civil law and to the judgment of Willes J. in *Cook v. Lister.*[39]

7–07

---

[31] *Nevill's Case* (1870) L.R. 6 Ch. App. 43; *Roberts v. Crowe*, above, *Killock v. Entover* (1882) L.R. 8 QB 458.

[32] *Exall v. Partridge* (1799) 8 Term. Rep. 308; *Johnson v. Royal Mail Steam Packet Co.* (1867) L.R. 3 C.P. 38; *Edmunds v. Wallingford* (1885) 14 QBD. 811.

[33] *Exall v. Partridge*, above.

[34] See *Powers v. Nash* 37 Maine 322 (1853)

[35] *Re Law Courts Chambers Co.* (1889) 61 L.T. 669.

[36] See *Sleigh v. Sleigh* (1850) 5 Ex. Ch. 514; *Ex p. Bishop* (1880) 15 Ch D 400 at 410.

[37] See *Ex p. Bishop* above; *Duncan Fox & Co. v. North and South Wales Bank* (1880) 6 App. Cas. at 13, 14 *per* Lord Selborne.

[38] (1880) 15 Ch D 400.

[39] (1863) 13 C.B. (N.S.) 543 at 594. There Willes J. referred to the civil law rule that payment by a stranger in the name of the debtor might liberate the debtor from the demand; D.46.3.23, 53; J.3.29; G.3.168.

Where a creditor sues the principal debtor for the benefit of the surety, the principal debtor may set off in equity any set-off available against the surety.[40]

Express indemnity

7–08   In the case of an express contract of indemnity, the surety is bound to sue on such an agreement as distinct from any implied right or claim in restitution.[41] It is suggested that if such an express contract for indemnity were void or otherwise unenforceable, an implied right of indemnity would arise: indeed any implied rights would normally be excluded by virtue of the express contract. On the other hand, there would seem to be no reason why a claim in restitution should not lie[42] in the event of the express contract of indemnity being void, though the question as to whether the position would be the same if the contract of indemnity were merely unenforceable is open to doubt.[43]

Just as the surety's right to indemnity can be granted by express agreement it can be limited or even excluded in a similar way. If the contract between the principal debtor and the creditor places limits on the discharge of the principal liability before a certain period, the surety will not be entitled to an indemnity in respect of any payment made by him in advance of such date.[44]

Enforcement of indemnity

7–09   Subject to any agreement between the parties to the contrary[45] a surety's right to claim an indemnity from the principal debtor will not arise until a surety has paid the principal debt or some part of it.[46] It is open to the parties to agree that a right to indemnity can arise prior to the surety making payment,[47] but generally if the surety discharges the principal debt before the due date he will have no right to an indemnity until such time as the principal debtor could himself be sued.[48] It is suggested that a surety cannot bring forward the availability of his indemnity rights against the principal debtor by making an early or premature payment in favour of the creditor.[49]

---

[40] *Thornton v. Maynard* (1875) L.R. 10 C.P. 695.
[41] See, *e.g. Toussaint v. Martinnant* (1787) 2 Term. Rep. 100.
[42] See by way of analogy *Craven-Ellis v. Canons* [1936] 2 K.B. 403.
[43] See, *e.g. Britain v. Rossiter* (1879) 11 QBD 123, which suggests that no remedy will lie if the requirements of the Statute of Frauds are otherwise circumvented.
[44] See, *e.g. Bellingham v. Freer* (1837) 1 Moo. P.C. 333.
[45] *Spark v. Heslop* (1859) 1 El. & El. 563.
[46] *Stirling v. Forrester* (1821) 3 Bli. 575; *Re Fenton* [1931] 1 Ch. 85 at 113–114. A right of indemnity cannot arise after the time of payment.
[47] As in *Re Allen* [1896] 2 Ch. 345, where the surety's rights were held to sound in damages.
[48] *Coppin v. Gray* (1842) 1 Y. & C. Eq. 205; *Re Moss, ex p. Hallett* [1905] 2 K.B. 307.
[49] Under English law at least not in the absence of express agreement: but see *Drager v. Allison* (1958) 13 D.L.R. (2d) 204 at 216.

The surety who has discharged the principal debtor's obligation can be indemnified to the extent of any amount he has paid in reduction of the guaranteed debt. Consequently, in the case of co-sureties, whether their liability is joint, several or joint and several, each co-surety may recover the exact amount each will have paid. The surety will generally be entitled to claim interest on the sum he has paid from the date of payment[50] even though the underlying debt was paid free of interest.[51] It is thought that in practice the rate of interest to be awarded in any proceedings instituted by the surety would be in the discretion of the court.[52] However the surety can recover any additional loss and damages he may have been compelled to pay on account of non-payment of the principal debt.[53]

Where the principal debtor carries high interest and the surety knows that the principal disputes his liability to an indemnity, the surety should arguably pay the debt at once and stop the interest running: if he does not his right to interest may be reduced.[54] However, it is submitted that since the principal debtor is in any event primarily liable he should as between himself and the surety have paid the debt and cannot complain that the surety has not done so.

Quia timet proceedings

As soon as a definite sum has become payable from the surety to the creditor, the surety has a right to have it paid by the principal. The surety can in equity obtain an order directing the principal to pay such sum to the creditor. This remedy is available to the surety as long as the sum has become payable, even though no application has been made or is anticipated.[55] The surety's liability to the creditor for this purpose may be *qua* principal debtor rather than *qua* surety.[56]

7–10

---

[50] *Re Fox, Walker & Co., ex p. Bishop* (1880) 15 Ch D 400 at 421–422.

[51] *Re Swan's Estate* (1869) 4 Ir. Eq. 209, *cf. Rigby v. Macnamara* (1795) 2 Cox. 415; *Re Maria Anna & Steinbank Coal & Coke Company, Re McKewan's Case* (1877) 6 Ch D 447.

[52] *i.e.* under s.35A of the Supreme Court Act 1981.

[53] *Badeley v. Consolidated Bank* (1886) 34 Ch D 536 at 556.

[54] See *Hawkins v. Maltby* (1868) L.R. 6 Eq. 505 at 508.

[55] *per* Lord Keeper North in *Ranelagh v. Hayes* (1682) 1 Vern. 189; *Bechervaise v. Lewis* (1872) L.R. 7 C.P. 372, 377; *Ex p. Snowdon* (1881) 17 Ch D 44 at 47; *Ferguson v. Lipson* (1874) L.R. 14 Eq. 379; *Re Giles* [1896] 1 Ch. 956; *Ascherson v. Tredegar Dock Co.* [1909] 2 Ch. 401 (USA see: *Pavarini & Wyne Inc. v. Title Guarantee & Surety Co.* 36 App. D.C. 348 (1911); Canada, see *Double Diamond Bowling Supply Ltd v. Eglington Bowling Ltd* (1963) 39 D.L.R. (2d) 19). Once there is a debt there is no need for a "demand", a concept which is meaningless in this context, as opposed to a situation where a debt only accrues on demand, *per* Scrutton L.J. in *Bradford Old Bank v. Sutcliffe* [1918] 2 K.B. 833.

[56] In *Tate v. Crewdson* [1938] 1 Ch. 869, a bank lent money to joint borrowers who agreed to the principals *vis-à-vis* the bank but surety/principal *inter se*. The surety was given an order that the other repay since the surety was himself immediately liable as principal as against the bank. See also *Watt v. Mortlock* [1964] Ch. 84.

By contrast, until there is an ascertained sum due and owing by the surety,[57] the surety in the absence of any special agreement[58] has no right to such relief. Nor can he call upon the principal debtor to make provision for the payment of the creditor or to bring the money into court.[59]

For the surety's relief to exist it must be shown that a debt is payable, not merely that a demand has been made by a creditor, and that thereafter on the taking of accounts a debt may become due.[60]

It used to be the case that where a demand by the creditor was a condition precedent to the surety's liability, the surety would have no right against the principal before demand was made.[61] However, in *Thomas v. Nottingham Incorporated Football Club Ltd*,[62] Goff J. held that after the surety had given notice to the creditor of determination of the guarantee, he was entitled to call upon the principal debtor to pay. This was despite the fact that the surety was only liable on demand and no demand had been made. Goff J. thought it would be strange if the surety could not remove a cloud until it began to rain.

7–11   In the special situation of sureties to an administration bond, who had been told by the administrator that he intended to distribute the estate although he had been advised that there were liabilities still outstanding and not yet determined, the sureties were not entitled to bring a *quia timet* action restraining distribution and seeking administration by the court.[63]

It is arguable that on analogous grounds relief should be given to a surety of a bankrupt person or company being wound up if the trustee in bankruptcy or liquidator can be shown to be prejudicing the surety's position by, *e.g.* selling a security for the principal debt under value. However, the contrary is indicated by *Re Pratt*[64] where as between co-sureties it was agreed that one was primarily liable to the creditor. Both gave security to the creditor. Upon the bankruptcy of one it was held that the other had no right of action against the former as trustee in respect of a sale allegedly at an under value.

7–12   The special rules as to set-off in relation to bankruptcy and winding up laid down by section 323 of the Insolvency Act 1986

[57] *Re Ledgard* (1922) 66 S.J. 404; *Morrison v. Barking Chemicals Co.* [1919] 2 Ch. 325: see also *Hughes-Hallett v. Indian Mammoth Gold Mines Co.* (1882) 22 Ch D 561.
[58] *e.g.* a provision that the money shall be provided before it becomes payable to the creditor as in *Toussaint v. Martinnant* (1787) 2 T.R. 100.
[59] *Dale v. Lolley* (1808) Exch. Trin. T referred to in a note to *Nisbet v. Smith* (1789) 2 Bro. C.C. at 582. And see *Bellingham v. Freer* (1837) 1 Moo. P.C. 333; *Coppin v. Gray* (1842) 1 Y. & C. Eq. 205; *cf. Re Anderson-Berry* [1938] Ch. 290.
[60] *Antrobus v. Davidson* (1817) 3 Mer. 569; *Morrison v. Barking Chemicals Co.* [1919] 2 Ch. 325.
[61] *Bradford v. Gammon* [1925] Ch. 132.
[62] [1972] Ch. 596, not following *Bradford v. Gammon* and applying *Ascherson v. Tredegar Dock and Wharf Co.* [1909] 2 Ch. 401.
[63] *Re Anderson-Berry* [1928] Ch. 290.
[64] *Pratt's Trustee in Bankruptcy v. Pratt* [1936] 2 All E.R. 901. See also the Irish case of *Hiburnian Fire and General Insurance Co. v. Dorgan* [1941] I.R. 514.

and rule 4.90 of the Insolvency Rules 1986 respectively have been interpreted so as to prevent a surety who has not paid from setting off his indemnity against a liquidator of the principal debtor.[65] This seems to be based on the rule against double proof: the creditor not having been paid could have proved in the principal debtor's estate, which estate would then have been subject to double proof.

Wolmershausen v. Gullick[66] suggests that in any action by the surety to make the principal pay direct to the creditor, the creditor should be made a party. However, it is not vital that the creditor should be joined.[67]

The surety of a company can now, contrary to the previous position under *Re Vron Colliery Co.*[68] petition for winding up even before he has paid, on the basis of his being a contingent or prospective creditor within section 124(1) of the Insolvency Act 1986. The right to petition is based on the contingent or prospective right of indemnity; the *quia timet* right does not amount to a debt.[69]

Principal debtor covenants with surety to pay on given day

If the principal debtor covenants with the surety to pay the debt **7–13** upon a given day, the surety without paying may recover the whole sum from the principal debtor when the day has passed.[70] The surety in turn would be obliged to apply the money in payment of the debt.[71] If the principal debtor had already paid the creditor, the surety's damages for breach of covenant may be reducible to a nominal sum.[72]

Surety has given note to extinguish principal debt that has not paid thereon

There is disagreement in the authorities as to whether a surety **7–14** who was given his own promissory note in extinguishment of the principal debt can before paying pursue the principal debtor for

---

[65] *Re Fenton* [1931] 1 Ch. 85; *Barclays Bank Ltd v. TOSG Fund Ltd* [1984] 1 All E.R. 628. However, a surety who was paid part of the guaranteed debt can insist on set-off see *Stein v. Blake* [1996] 1 A.C. 243. Moreover, a surety who has paid in full prior to payment of any dividend to the creditor can himself prove and exercise all insolvency rights of set-off.

[66] [1893] 2 Ch. 514.

[67] He was not joined in *Tate v. Crewdson* [1938] Ch. 869; *Watt v. Mortlock* [1964] 1 Ch. 84 and *Thomas v. Nottingham Football Club Ltd* [1972] Ch. 596.

[68] (1882) 20 Ch D 442.

[69] *Re Mitchell* [1913] 1 Ch. 201.

[70] *Carr v. Roberts* (1833) 5 B. & Ad. 78; *Loosemore v. Radford* (1842) 9 M. & W. 657; *Carpenter v. Park* 19 Cal. App. 2d 567; 66 P. 2d 224 (1937); *Gustavson v. Koehler* 177 Minn. 115; 224 N.W. 699 (1929); *Re Allen* [1896] 2 Ch. 345. And see *Toussaint v. Martinnant* (1787) 2 T. R. 100; *Spark v. Heslop* (1859) 1 E. & E. 563; *Ashdown v. Ingamells* (1880) 5 Ex. D. 280; *Re Perkins* [1898] 2 Ch. 182. The whole sum of the debt is seen as a surety's quantum of loss in an action for breach of contract.

[71] *Loosemore v. Radford*, above at 658 *per* Parke B.; *cf. Re Richardson* [1911] 2 QB 705.

[72] *ibid. per* Alderson B.

money paid. It was held that he could in *Barclay v. Gooch*[73] by Lord
Kenyon. However in *Maxwell v. Jameson*[74] following *Taylor v.
Biggins*[75] an apparently contrary view was taken. Whilst in England
the balance of authority suggests that the mere giving of a promissory note by a surety cannot found an action against the principal
debtor for money paid, there is Irish authority for suggesting that
the handing over of a property can be the equivalent of payment in
this regard. Whatever the position in that regard in English law it is
submitted that the value of such property can be recovered by suing
the principal debtor for breach of the implied contract to
indemnity.[76]

Surety's right to prospective indemnity excluded by agreement

7–15   The surety's right to have the principal debtor pay off the creditor
as soon as the debt becomes payable can be excluded by agreement,
as set out above.[77] Alternatively exclusion may be implied from the
nature of the liability guaranteed. For example the surety for a
mortgage debt may be excluded from insisting upon the mortgagor
paying the mortgage debt on the day named in the covenant, on the
basis that the sense of the transaction involved the use of land as a
continuing security.[78] Likewise where the principal obligation is not
of a nature to be extinguished before a determinate period.[79]

The right to a prospective indemnity from the principal debtor
does not extend to the situation where the surety holds an indemnity
from a stranger. The surety cannot call upon the stranger to settle
the creditor's claim unless the surety shows that he is about to be
indemnified.[80] The reason for the distinction is that the stranger is
not, as the principal debtor is, the person in all events ultimately
liable to pay. However, in the case of an indemnity from a stranger,
if the surety has become liable but the stranger has not paid, the
surety may pursue *quia timet* to have the money provided by that
person before actual damage to the surety.[81]

---

[73] (1797) 2 Esp. 571, followed by the Court of Exchequer in Ireland in *McKenna v. Harnett* (1849)
13 Ir. L.R. 206 and referred to without disapproval by Pollock C.B. in *Rogers v. Maw* (1846) 15 M.
& W. 444 at 449.

[74] (1818) 2 B. & Ald. 51.

[75] (1802) 3 East. 169.

[76] *Fahey v. Frawley* (1890) 26 L.R. Ir. 78; *Gore v. Gore* [1901] 2 I.R. 269; *cf. Re Law Guarantee,
Liverpool Mortgage Insurance Company's Case* [1914] 2 Ch. 617; *British Dominions Insurance Co.
v. Duder* [1915] 2 QB 394; *Hope v. M'Gillivray* [1935] A.C. 1.

[77] See p. ???.

[78] *Hungerford v. Hungerford* Gilb. Eq. Ca. at 69.

[79] *Bellingham v. Freer* (1837) 1 Moo. P.C. 333 (applying civil law).

[80] See *Antrobus v. Davidson* (1817) 2 Mer. 569.

[81] *Wooldridge v. Norris* (1868) L.R. 6 Eq. 410. There the father of the principal debtor gave the
surety a bond and when the surety was called on, the surety was held entitled as against the father's
executors to an order that they raise and pay the sum demanded from the surety. See also *Re
Anderson-Berry* [1928] Ch. 290. It would seem that in such a case the surety would be under no
obligation to apply the money to pay off the creditor: see *Re Law Guarantee, Liverpool Mortgage
Insurance Company's Case* [1914] 2 Ch. 617.

Payments without suit

If there is no reasonable defence to the claim, the surety need not **7–16** wait to be sued but may pay the creditor as soon as the debt becomes due and recover over against the principal debtor on the basis of money paid.[82] Equity certainly regarded the surety as able to pay the debt at maturity and sue the principal debtor in the name of the creditor.[83]

Costs

A surety can recover from the principal debtor all costs, includ- **7–17** ing his own extra costs incurred in resisting the claim of the creditor.[84] This includes costs of a defence not expressly authorised by the principal debtor[85] unless there was clearly no defence.[86] Costs of execution by the creditor are not recoverable since the surety should have been paid on judgment.[87]

Compromise and notice to principal debtor

A surety may make a reasonable compromise of a doubtful **7–18** claim, and recover the amount from the principal debtor, even though he compromised without notice of the principal debtor.[88] The effect of lack of notice is only to allow in evidence by the principal that the surety acted unreasonably or that the principal might have obtained better terms.[89] If notice is given and the principal debtor ignores it, the surety is justified in taking any reasonable step towards testing or reducing the claim.[90]

Litigation for surety's benefit

A surety cannot claim the costs of litigation undertaken purely **7–19** for his benefit, *e.g.* to show that he has been discharged as between himself and the creditor.[91] By contrast a surety for bail may recover the costs of arresting an absconding principal even though the arrest is for the surety's benefit.[92]

---

[82] *Pitt v. Purssord* (1841) 8 M. & W. 538; *Broughton's Case* 5 Co. 23(b).

[83] *Swire v. Redman* (1876) 1 QBD. 536 at 541. *Cf.* rule in Canada: *Drager v. Allison* (1959) 19 D.L.R. 2(d) 431.

[84] *Ex p. Marshall* (1751) 1 Atk. 262; *Jones v. Brooke* (1812) 4 Taunt. 464; *Stratton v. Mathews* (1848) 3 Exch. 48; *Garrard v. Cottrell* (1847) 10 QB 679. Where recoverable costs are recovered by the surety in respect of his defence against the creditor on a common fund basis: *Howard v. Lovegrove* (1870) L.R. 6 Ex. 43. Now see *Gomba Holdings (U.K.) Ltd v. Minories Finance Limited (No. 2)* [1993] Ch. 171.

[85] *Smith v. Compton* (1832) 3 B. & Ad. 407; *Hornby v. Cardwell* (1881) 8 QBC. 329.

[86] *Roach v. Thompson* (1830) M. & M. 487; *Beech v. Jones* (1848) 5 C.B. 696.

[87] *Pierce v. Williams* (1854) 23 L.J. Ex. 322.

[88] *Smith v. Compton* (1832) 3 B. & Ad. 407, *cf. Webster v. Petre* (1879) 4 Ex. 127.

[89] *Smith v. Compton,* above.

[90] *Hornby v. Cardwell* (1881) 8 QBD. 329.

[91] *Re International Contract Co., Hughes' claim* (1872) L.R. 13 Eq. 623 at 624, 625 *per* Wickens V.C. and see *South v. Bloxam* (1865) 2 H. & M. 457.

[92] *Fisher v. Fallows* (1804) 5 Esp. 171.

Surety's executors

7–20   Where the principal debtor is a legatee under the surety's will, the surety's executors are entitled to retain the amount of the surety's claim plus reasonable interest, even if the surety's action would have been statute-barred. This applies even if the principal becomes bankrupt after the surety's death.[93] Similarly where the principal has executed a deed of assignment for the benefit of his creditors for payment according to the law of bankruptcy to which the creditor guaranteed has assented, the surety's executors can instead of proving in the creditor's place retain the amount of the debt out of the legacy payable to the principal.[94]

Death of principal debtor

7–21   A surety paying the debt even after the principal's death is entitled if the latter dies intestate to administration as a creditor.[95]

Release of principal debtor

7–22   Normally the release of the principal debtor will release the surety, unless a creditor expressly stipulates the contrary. Where there is a reservation of remedies against the surety, the surety will also retain his right over against the principal debtor notwithstanding the "release", which is in such cases seen as a mere covenant not to sue.[96]

Surety given security by principal debtor

7–23   A creditor can derive no benefit from securities given by the principal debtor to the surety, except perhaps where he can show a direct interest by contract or under a trust or unless both principal and surety are bankrupt and the rule in *Ex p. Waring* is found applicable.[97] In *Ex p. Rushworth*[98] a security had been given to the surety on trust to apply the proceeds to pay off the creditor. Lord Elton said that the creditor would have been entitled to call for its application accordingly. However, in *Wilding v. Richards*[99] where property was conveyed by the principal to the surety on trust to pay debts, it was held that the creditors, who had no notice of the conveyance, could not take advantage of it, but the surety could insist on retaining the property until the creditors were paid.

---

[93] *Re Watson* [1896] 1 Ch. 925.
[94] *Re Whitehouse* (1887) 37 Ch D 683.
[95] *Williams v. Jukes* (1864) 34 L.J.P. & M. 60.
[96] *Kearsley v. Cole* (1846) 16 M. & W. 128; *Cole v. Lynn* [1941] 1 K.B. 142.
[97] (1815) 19 Ves. 345. It had been thought that the creditor was generally entitled to such security: *Maure v. Harrison* (1692) 1 Eq. Ca. Ab. 93 and see *Wright v. Morley* (1805) 18 Ves. 12 at 22. However, this doctrine was not accepted by Lord Eldon in *Ex p. Waring* (1815) 19 Ves. 345 and has been shown to rest on no authority: *Re Walker* [1892] 1 Ch. 621.
[98] (1805) 10 Ves. 409 at 421.
[99] (1845) 1 Coll. 655.

As between himself and co-sureties, a surety must bring into account every security received by him from the principal.[1]

If a surety guarantees a composition, the deed may provide for the transfer of the principal's debtor's estate to the surety.[2] Where the surety is also a creditor and may possibly get payment in full out of the balance of the estate this will not necessarily make the deed bad.[3] However, a creditor guaranteeing a composition cannot stipulate secretly for payment in full[4] or any other preference.[5]

No creditor can impeach an assignment to a surety for a composition so long as the composition stands[6] or if the surety has paid the sum guaranteed.[7] However, an assignment to a surety who becomes bound in order to secure a fresh advance to enable the principal debtor to continue business is as valid as if it had been given to the creditor.[8]

Where a surety who has paid nothing has property made over to him by the principal debtor as a result of pressure by the surety to protect him from payments about to become due, the pressure may result in a finding that the assignment is a voidable preference, *i.e.* a finding that the principal debtor has been influenced by a desire to prefer the surety such as to constitute such a preference voidable by the liquidator or trustee in bankruptcy of the principal debtor under sections 239 or 340 of the Insolvency Act 1986.[9]

7–24

Where the surety guarantees the loan of money for a specific purpose only and the debtor in default of such use returns the money to the lender on the eve of bankruptcy, such money would not have passed to the trustee in bankruptcy and cannot be recovered from the lender.[10]

Loss of surety's rights under counter-guarantee

A surety should ensure that any securities given by the principal to support the agreement by the principal debtor to indemnify the surety are valid, *e.g* as to compliance under the bills of sale legislation.[11] If the surety seeks payment under a counter-guarantee, *e.g.* from the principal debtor's parent, this too may result in the surety's loss of rights including its ability to seek subrogation.[12]

7–25

---

[1] See below at para. 7–60.

[2] *Bissel v. Jones* (1878) L.R. 4 QB 49; *Ex p. Nicholson* (1877) L.R. 5 Ch. 332; *Latter v. White* (1870) L.R. 5 QB 622; 5 Hl. 578.

[3] *Ex p. Nicholson* (1870) L.R. 5 Ch. 332.

[4] *Wood v. Barker* (1865) L.R. 1 Eq. 139.

[5] See *Caldwell v. Parker* (1869) 3 Ir. R. Eq. 519.

[6] *Seymour v. Coulson* (1880) 5 QBD. 359.

[7] *Ex p. Burrell, Re Robinson* (1867) 1 Ch D 537.

[8] *Ex p. Hawswell, Re Hemingway* (1883) 23 Ch D 626 and see *Ex p. Defries, Re Myers* (1876) 35 L.T. 392.

[9] See generally *Re M. C. Bacon* [1991] Ch. 127.

[10] *Edwards v. Glyn* (1859) 2 E. & E. 29.

[11] See, *e.g. Hughes v. Little* (1886) 18 QBD. 32.

[12] *Brown-Shipley and Co. Ltd v. Amalgamated Investment (Europe) BV* [1979] 1 Lloyd's Rep. 488.

A secured creditor's right to exoneration

7–26   A person who charges his property to secure the debt of another is treated as a surety of the person whose debt is secured.[13] He can therefore seek to be exonerated by the principal debtor. A common example is where a jointly owned property is charged to secure the debt of one co-owner.[14] The rights of the guarantor do not simply reflect a right to seek an indemnity from the co-owner and joint mortgagee but also serve to grant the surety a priority right over the latter's joint interest.[15] The equity of exoneration here takes the form of a presumption which can be rebutted if it is shown that both parties in fact derived benefit from the charge.

4. *Surety's Rights to Securities Given by Principal Debtor to Creditor*

General principles

7–27   A surety paying off the debt is entitled to any securities given for the debt by the principal debtor to the creditor.[16] This right exists independently of contract and rests upon the surety's equity not to have the whole burden of debt thrown upon him by the creditor's choice not to resort to other remedies available to him.[17]

The right being based on equity, the surety has a right to them although he did not know of their existence when he made himself liable,[18] or even if they did not exist at that time.[19]

The surety's right to securities is not affected by payments by strangers and a stranger making such payments need not be made a party to proceedings to gain the benefit of the security.[20]

Formerly, the surety's right after payment to the benefit of securities was only to such securities as were not *ipso facto* extinguished by the payment.[21]

---

[13] See, *e.g. Re Conley* [1938] 2 All E.R. 127 at 131; *Barclays Bank plc v. O'Brien* [1994] 1 A.C. 180.

[14] *Re A Debtor (No. 24 of 1971), ex p. Marley v. Trustee of the Property of the Debtor* [1976] 1 W.L.R. 952; *Re Pittortou, ex p. Trustee of Property of Bankrupt* [1985] 1 W.L.R. 58.

[15] *Re Pittortou*, above at 61.

[16] *Morgan v. Seymour* (1638) 1 Ch. R. 120; *Ex p. Crisp* (1744) 1 Atk. 133; *Geerside v. Benson* (1745) 3 Atk. 248; *Mayhew v. Cricket* (1818) 2 Swanst. 185 at 191; *Goddard v. Whyte* (1860) 2 Giff. 449 at 452. This appears to include, in the case of a guarantor of a promissory note, a right to the assignment of the promissory note: *Armstrong v. Widmer* (1975) 65 D.L.R. (3d) 345.

[17] See Sir S. Romilly's argument in *Craythorne v. Swinburne* (1807) 14 Ves. at 162 approved by Lord Eldon; *per* Lord Eldon in *Aldrich v. Cooper* (1803) 8 Ves. at 389; *Duncan Fox & Co. v. North and South Wales Bank* (1879) 6 App. Cas. 1 at 12, 19; *Parsons v. Briddock* (1708) 2 Vern. 608; *Wright v. Morley* (1805) 18 Ves. at 22, 23.

[18] *Mayhew v. Cricket* (1818) 2 Swanst. 185 at 191; *Newton v. Chorlton* (1853) 10 Hare. 646 at 651; *Pearl v. Deacon* (1857) 24 Beav. 186; 1 De G. & J. 461; *Coates v. Coates* (1864) 33 Beav. 249; *Goddard v. Whyte* (1860) 2 Giff. 449; *Duncan Fox & Co. v. North and South Wales Bank* (1879) 6 App. Cas. 1; *Leicestershire Banking Co. Ltd v. Hawkins* (1900) 16 T.L.R. 317; *Re Jeffery's Policy* (1872) 20 W.R. 857.

[19] *Scott v. Knox* (1838) 2 Jo. Ex. Ir. 778.

[20] *Heyman v. Dubois* (1871) L.R. 13 Eq. 158; *Re Arcedeckne, Atkins v. Arcedeckne* (1883) 24 Ch D 709.

[21] The authorities and reasoning for this rule are set out in the third edition of this work at pp. 207–208.

The surety's right to subrogation has been described as a class right so as to bar any claim which might otherwise arise through mutuality, *e.g.* set off. A principal debtor cannot therefore set up against a paying co-surety the fact that the co-surety owes the principal debtor more than the amount paid by the co-surety in satisfaction of the overall debt.[22]

Mercantile Law Amendment Act 1856, s.5[23]

Under this section a surety who pays the debt is entitled to have **7–28** assigned to him any judgment or security held by the creditor, whether or not the judgment or security is deemed at law to have been satisfied by the payment. The surety is further entitled to the creditor's remedies and upon a proper indemnity to use the creditor's name in any action or other proceedings in order to obtain an indemnity from the principal debtor. The section also gives such rights to co-debtors such as co-sureties.[24]

The terms of the section make it clear that a surety cannot enforce the right of subrogation embodied in the section until payment or performance but the rights of the surety to security arise at the time the guarantee is given[25]; the surety also enjoys the right to marshal[26] by virtue of the fact that this right exists as from the time the guarantee is given.

Section 5 makes it clear that in order to become the assignee of all rights set out in the section, the surety must pay the entire debt. The authorities appear to support the view that irrespective of the statutory right, a surety will not be entitled to any right of subrogation if he has not satisfied the liability of the principal debtor, even though he has paid all he is liable to pay under the guarantee.[27] This question is considered further below.[28] It has, however, been suggested that the phrase "debt . . . of another" in the wording of section 5 refers to any part of the debt.[29]

The wording of section 5 however suggests that a person who satisfies the principal debtor's liabilities under a mistake of fact or law will not be entitled to rights of subrogation equivalent to those he would otherwise enjoy as a paying surety.[30]

---

[22] *A. E. Goodwin Ltd v. A. G. Heating Ltd* (1979) 7 A.C.L.R. 481. In the case of enforcement against co-surety see *Brown v. Cork* [1985] B.C.L.C. 363.

[23] 19 & 20 Vict. c.97. The text is set out in the Appendix.

[24] In this respect it recognises and enacts the position contained in the authorities: see Lord Blackburn in *Duncan Fox & Co. v. North and South Wales Bank* (1880) 6 App. Cas. 1 at 19.

[25] *Dixon v. Steel* [1901] 2 Ch. 602. This explains why a creditor must deal with security in a reasonable manner.

[26] See below at para. 7–33.

[27] *Re Howe, ex p. Brett* (1871) 6 Ch. App. 838 at 841, *per* Mellish L.J. This view has not been followed in Australia: *A. E. Goodwin Ltd v. A.G. Heating Ltd* (1979) 7 A.C.L.R. 481 at 487: see generally O'Donovan & Phillips, *The Modern Contract of Guarantee* (3rd ed.), at p. 654 *et seq.*

[28] See below.

[29] *Bayley v. Gibsons Ltd* [1993] 1 Tas. R. 385 *per* Zeeman J. at 400–401 with regard to the equivalent Australian provisions.

[30] *cf. Owen v. Tate* [1976] 1 QB 402, where there was no such mistake.

Under the section the surety is entitled to the benefit of a creditor's judgment without taking an assignment.[31] However execution cannot be issued without leave.[32]

A surety can bring an action for specific performance of the statutory right to an assignment[33] or for damages.

Co-debtors bound as principals vis-à-vis the creditor but as principal and surety inter se

7–29　　This is Lord Selborne's third class of suretyship as analysed in the House of Lords decision of *Duncan Fox & Co. v. North and South Wales Bank*.[34] In this third class the co-debtor contracts as principal with a creditor, but is in fact between himself and the other debtor a surety and will, upon giving notice to the creditor, have the rights of a surety as against a creditor *inter alia* with regard to securities.[35]

It seems that the status or agreement between such co-debtors constituting them surety and principal respectively can arise by inference or implication as well as by express agreement.[36]

Notice to the creditor can be given after the obligation is entered into and the principle applies even if the debtors contracted originally as principals *inter se* but later altered their positions, *e.g.* in the case of a retired partner.[37]

Conversely, where a surety stands *vis-à-vis* another surety in the position of a person primarily liable, that other surety has a surety's rights to the securities and remedies of the creditor.[38]

Surety's rights to securities given by persons other than the principal debtor

7–30　　The surety's right to the creditor's securities extends to wherever it is needed to make the giver pay his due proportion in situations where equities requiring the burden of the debt to be placed in a particular way.[39] For example, the principle applies to securities given by co-sureties[40] or by a partner of the debtor.[41]

---

[31] *Re M'Myn* (1886) 33 Ch D 575. The right in *Dearle v. Hall* (1828) 3 Russ. 1 will apply. See *e.g. Re Jason Construction Ltd* (1975) 25 A.L.R. (3d) 340.

[32] RSC, Ord. 46, r.2(1)(b); *Dale v. Powell* (1911) 105 L.T. 291 at 292; *Kayley v. Hothersall* [1925] 1 QB 607; *Brown v. Cork* [1985] B.C.L.C. 363 (co-sureties).

[33] *Dale v. Powell*, above; *Oddy v. Hallett* (1855) Cab. & El. 532.

[34] (1880) 6 App. Cas. 1 at 11 *et seq.*

[35] *Duncan Fox & Co. v. North and South Wales Bank* (1880) 6 App. Cas. 1 at 12.

[36] See, *e.g. Re Marley* [1976] 1 W.L.R. 952; *Re Pittortou* [1985] 1 W.L.R. 58.

[37] *Rouse v. Bradford Banking Co.* [1894] A.C. 586.

[38] *Parsons v. Briddock* (1708) 2 Vern. 608 approved in *Wright v. Morley* (1805) 2 A.C. Ves. at 22, 23. In *Hodgson v. Shaw* (1834) 3 My. & K. at 189, *Parsons v. Briddock* was treated as incorrectly decided by Lord Brougham and in *Armitage v. Baldwin* (1842) 5 Beav. 278 the opposite decision was reached on similar facts. However, the objection to the result in *Parsons v. Briddock* appears to have been based on there being no right to securities, etc., if the debt has been paid, a principle which is reversed by the Mercantile Law Amendment Act 1856.

[39] See Lord Blackburn in *Duncan Fox & Co. v. North & South Wales Bank* (1880) 6 App. Cas. 1 at 19.

[40] *Smith v. Wood* [1929] 1 Ch. 14.

[41] *Goddard v. Whyte* (1860) 2 Giff. 449.

However, a surety is not entitled to the benefit of a wrongful pledge by the principal debtor to the creditor of the property of a third person: on the contrary, that person will have the benefit of the guarantee to liberate his own property.[42]

Examples of particular securities

(i) Funds standing to the credit of the principal, but appro-   **7–31**
priated to a particular purpose under a contract.[43]

(ii) Lien on shares: sureties for a receiver of a testator's estate were held to be entitled to be recouped out of the receiver's shares, upon his default and upon payment by the sureties.[44]

(iii) Insurance policy: a surety for premiums was held to have a right to be reimbursed out of the policy monies.[45]

(iv) Lease: a surety for the performance of covenants is entitled to recoupment of the land in respect of any payments made by him on account of rent.[46]

(v) Vendor's lien on goods: a surety for the price of goods is entitled upon paying the vendor to the unpaid vendor's lien.[47] A similar lien is available to a broker acting for an unnamed buyer who is by the custom of the trade personally liable for the principal's default.[47]

(vi) Stoppage *in transitu*: a surety for the price of goods cannot stop them *in transitu* against the principal in his own name[48] but can perhaps stop them in the name of the seller who would in equity be bound to authorise or ratify such a stoppage.[49]

Guarantor for limited sum

A guarantor for a limited part of the principal debt is subrogated   **7–32**
to the same rights that the creditor has in respect of that amount and will be entitled to share in any securities held by the creditor for the whole amount.[50] There can be no such subrogation however to any

---

[42] *Ex p. Salting* (1883) 25 Ch D 148.
[43] *Re Sherry* (1884) 25 Ch D 692 at 702.
[44] *Brandon v. Brandon* (1859) 3 De G. & J. 524; see also *Glossop v. Harrison* (1814) 3 V. & B. 134.
[45] *Aylwin v. Witty* (1861) 30 L.J. Ch. 860.
[46] *Lord Harberton v. Bennett* (1829) Beat. 386.
[47] *Imperial Bank v. London & St Katherine's Dock Co.* (1877) 5 Ch D 195.
[48] *Siftken v. Wray* (1805) 6 Eact. 371.
[49] see *Imperial Bank*, above.
[50] *Goodwin v. Gray* (1874) 22 W.R. 312, applied in *Re Butler's Wharf* [1995] 2 B.C.L.C. 43. See also *Wade v. Coope* (1827) 2 Sim. 155 and *Butler's Wharf*, the court regarding the earlier decision of *Fairbrother v. Wodehouse* (1856) 23 Beav. 18 as doubtful.

security held by the creditor regarding any part of the debt to which the guarantee does not extend.

This principle reflects the critical distinction between the type of case here referred to namely where the surety guarantees only part of the debt, thereby giving rise to the right of subrogation referred to and where he guarantees the whole of the debt but pays only a limited amount, where there will be no such right until the creditor has been paid in full.[51]

Surety's right to have securities in creditor's hands marshalled in surety's favour

7–33   Where the surety has a security for a different debt which he can consolidate with that of the guaranteed debt, the surety would seem entitled to the benefit of the security.[52] However, a surety may not marshal in his favour securities held in respect of different debts or of a different part of the same debt,[53] unless on the other hand the securities can be consolidated.[54]

Where a surety guaranteed the general account of a customer of a bank and a bank subsequently made separate specific advances against particular securities it was held that the bank was entitled to and obliged to surrender them where those specific advances were repaid and that the surety's liability was not affected by their doing so.[55] But where a creditor who is owed his debts, one guaranteed one not, takes a security for both, the surety is entitled as against the creditor to the benefit of a proportion of the security.[56]

Priority of surety over subsequent encumbrances

7–34   The surety's right to the securities of the creditor is prior to that of later encumbrancers,[57] who are subject to the creditor's mortgage. This is on the basis that the surety stands in the place of the creditor he pays off and because the subsequent security is not lessened by the coming in.[58] Thus it does not seem material whether a subsequent encumbrancer had notice of the suretyship.

---

[51] See *Re Sass, ex p. National Provincial Bank of England* [1896] 2 QB 12.

[52] See *Praed v. Gardner* (1788) 2 Cox 86, discussed in *Duncan Fox & Co. v. North and South Wales Bank* (1880) 6 App. Cas. at 15; *Heyman v. Dubois* (1871) L.R. 13 Eq. 158. These cases also seem to show that a trustee in bankruptcy is bound by the equities upon which such marshalling is based.

[53] *Wade v. Coope* (1827) 2 Sim. 155; *Wilkinson v. London & County Banking Co.* (1884) 1 T.L.R. 63.

[54] This must be stipulated: see Law of Property Act 1925, s.93; see below at para. 7–36.

[55] *Wilkinson v. London & County Banking Co.*, above.

[56] *Perris v. Roberts* (1681) 1 Vern. 34; *Coates v. Coates* (1864) 33 Beav. 249; *Huggard v. Representative Church Body* (1916) 10 I.R. 1 at 19.

[57] *Drew v. Lockett* (1863) 32 Beav. 449; *Silk v. Eyre* (1875) 9 I.R. Eq. 393; *Alwin v. Witty* (1861) 30 L.J. Ch. 860; *Dawson v. Bank of Whitehaven* (1877) 4 Ch D 639.

[58] *Drew v. Lockett* (1863) 32 Beav. 449 at 505, 506.

Priority of surety over subsequent advances by creditors

After a period of uncertainty in the authorities[59] it has now been **7–35** established that the surety's right on payment to be recouped out of the creditor's securities cannot be postponed merely by the creditor giving further advances on those securities.[60] The principle here is that the surety is entitled to have all the securities preserved for him which were taken at the time of the suretyship or subsequently and the surety's position cannot be affected by the creditor granting further advances on the same security.[61]

The situation may be different where the terms of the security give the debtor the option of calling for further advances, on the basis that the surety should perhaps take the benefit of security with its obligation. Possibly the security would be apportioned rateably to the whole debt.

Consolidation against surety

The doctrine of consolidation permits a creditor, who holds two **7–36** mortgages made by the same mortgagor, to refuse to allow the mortgagor to redeem one mortgage without redeeming the other. The right to consolidate will only exist if stipulated for: Law of Property Act 1925, s.93.

Under the general principles already discussed, a creditor should not be entitled to consolidate in that way as against a surety. There is possible authority going in the opposite direction[62] although that decision appears to depend on the particular circumstances, where the surety knew that two separate mortgages were to be given for two loans, though he only granted one.

Where, after the guarantee has been given, the creditor takes a security which is at once subject to consolidation, *e.g.* where there is a prior or simultaneous charge for another debt, the right of consolidation should apply against a surety. This is on the basis that the principle regarding the preservation of securities for the benefit of the surety does not apply to securities which became subject to the doctrine of consolidation as soon as they were created.

Marshalling by surety for debt doubly secured

This problem arises where the guaranteed debt is secured by the **7–37** mortgage of two funds, one of which is also subject to a second mortgage. If a surety pays the debt, he is compelled to marshal the

---

[59] The contrary proposition had been held in *Williams v. Owen* (1843) 13 Sim. 597 followed in *Fairbrother v. Wodehouse* (1856) 23 Beav. 18 but see comments in para. 7–36.

[60] *Dawson v. Bank of Whitehaven*, above, reversed on another point 6 Ch. 218; *Forbes v. Jackson* (1882) 19 Ch D 615.

[61] *Forbes v. Jackson*, above.

[62] See *Farebrother v. Woodhouse* above but this case was regarded as of doubtful value in *Re Butlers Wharf Ltd* [1995] 2 B.C.L.C. 43. In any event the appeal in *Farebrother* was compromised.

securities in favour of the second mortgagee. Thus if the proceeds of the fund upon which there are two mortgages are applied in satisfaction of the guaranteed debt, the second mortgagee will be entitled to the balance of the other fund, after satisfaction of the first mortgage, to the extent of the value of the fund mortgaged to him.[63]

Person charging property for debt of another

7–38   A person charging his own property to secure the debt of another who charges his own property for that debt occupies the position of a surety.[64] He is moreover entitled to the benefit of the security upon the property of the principal and is entitled to have the debt discharged out of the principal's property.[65]

Where several persons charged their property by deposit of title deeds for the repayment of the company's debts to a person guaranteeing its overdraft, the mortgagors were entitled to have all the properties marshalled so as to cause any debt to fall rateably.[66]

Policies on life of principal debtor

7–39   A surety paying the debt is entitled to a policy on the life of a debtor if it has been provided as a security by or at the expense of a debtor in circumstances such that the policies are redeemable by the debtor and constitute a fund belonging to him in the hands of the creditor. However, if a creditor insures the life of a debtor on his own account he may keep and recoup upon the policies even though the debt is paid.[67]

Examples of securities not subject to subrogation: properties wrongfully charged for the debt of another

7–40   Apart from private insurance policies which have just been referred to no other rights which are purely personal by the creditor can pass to the surety.[68]

A person whose property is wrongfully though validly pledged by another to secure his own debt is entitled to have his property

---

[63] *South v. Bloxham* (1865) 2 H. & M. 457, *cf. Dixon v. Steel* [1901] 2 Ch. 602.

[64] See discussion above. See also *Re a Debtor, ex p. Marley v. Trustee of the Property of the Debtor* [1976] 1 W.L.R. 952. Here a father conveyed his property into the joint names of himself and his son so that it could be charged for the son's business debts. The father's position as a surety *vis-à-vis* the son's trustee in bankruptcy was conceded and the right of marshalling was held to exist as against the trustee.

[65] See *Dixon v. Steel*, above. This type of suretyship has an advantage over a suretyship by covenant that the surety has a charge from the date of execution of the relevant instruments, over the principles, properties to secure his right of indemnity.

[66] *Smith v. Wood* [1929] 1 Ch. 14. Thus the release of any one of the charges or its subjection to a prior charge without the agreement of the other mortgagors would lead to their discharge.

[67] *Dalby v. India & London Life Assurance Co.* (1854) 15 C.B. 365.

[68] *e.g.* rights of seizure or distraint: see *Chatterton v. McLean* [1951] 1 All E.R. 761 (hire purchase) and *Re Russell, Russell v. Shoolbred* (1885) 29 Ch. 254 (rent).

disencumbered out of any property of the debtor also pledged with the same debt,[69] or at the expense of any surety who may have guaranteed the payment of that debt.[70]

Surety's right to securities arises on payment

A surety is only entitled to the securities held by the creditor on   **7–41** paying the debt. Admission of a proof in bankruptcy is not equivalent to payment for this service, so that the surety is not entitled to the creditor's security merely on proof.[71] For present purposes and as indicated above, it is suggested that the present position in English law is that the surety is entitled to enforce his right to subrogation only when he has paid the entire debt owed to the creditor.[72] The surety may however tender the debt in return for the security. If the creditor refuses to give a security up, the surety may bring an action in order to compel the creditor to assign the securities to him.[73]

As long as the creditor is fully paid, a surety who is only paid part of the debt is still as against the principal entitled to the benefit of the creditor's securities.[74] For example, the trustee of a bankrupt surety whose estate had paid a dividend to the creditor, would be entitled to a charge on any property mortgaged to the creditor by the principal after the creditor had realised the balance of his debt out of it,[75] and before any encumbrances subsequent to the creditor.

Surety's right to securities limited to indemnity

A surety's right to use securities given to the creditor by the   **7–42** principal is limited to the recoupment of a surety's indemnity against the principal. If the surety makes terms with the creditor and settles the debt for a lesser sum, and then obtains an assignment of the creditor's securities, he cannot recover more from the principal than he has actually paid.[76]

Abandonment or waiver of surety's right to securities

A surety paying the debt may abandon the securities to which he   **7–43** thereby becomes entitled to the debtor. Alternatively, the paying

---

[69] *Ex p. Alston* (1868) L.R. 4 Ch. App. 168.
[70] *Ex p. Salting* (1883) 25 Ch. 148.
[71] *Ewart v. Latta* (1865) 4 Macq. 983; *ex p. Turquand* (1876) 3 Ch. D. 445, *cf. ex p. Brett* (1871) 6 Ch. App. 838.
[72] See above at para. 7–28. To the contrary is the Australian decision in *A. E. Goodwin Ltd v. A. G. Heating Ltd* (1971) 7 A.C.L.R. 481 especially at 487. It is certainly arguable that the surety should have some secured benefit on part payment if any to protect his right to an indemnity.
[73] *Goddard v. Whyte* (1860) 2 Giff. 449.
[74] *Gedye v. Matson* (1858) 25 Beav. 310, *i.e.* in order to recoup the indemnity due from the principal debtor.
[75] See *Ewart v. Latta*, above.
[76] *Reed v. Norris* (1837) 2 My. & Cr. 361, following *Ex p. Rushworth* (1805) 10 Ves. 409 and *Butcher v. Churchill* (1808) 14 Ves. Jun. 567. This rule now has statutory form in the proviso to s.5 of the Mercantile Law Amendment Act 1856.

surety may leave the security to the creditor to use in respect of any further debt which it may cover, and if the payment was made with that intention the principal debtor cannot insist that the payment be applied in redemption of the security.[77] Thus a surety may find that the terms of the guarantee provide that he shall not have the benefit of the securities.[78] However, the terms often found in guarantees that the creditor may treat the surety as a principal debtor and that the surety should not be discharged by any giving of time or act or omission of the creditor which would normally discharge a surety, do not disentitle the surety to the creditor's securities if and when the surety pays.[79] However a provision stating that the guarantee is in addition to other securities will not oust subrogation rights.[80]

A question may arise as to whether the surety has waived his right to enforce the creditor's security against the principal. The taking of a charge directly from the principal may possibly evince an intention to waive and disentitle the surety to the creditor's securities.[81] However if the surety took the charge from the principal in ignorance of the security given to the creditor, he cannot be taken to have intended to waive a right he did not know of.[82] It may be necessary for there to be an express rather than an implied release.[83]

Agreement between principal and creditor as to securities

7–44   A stipulation between the creditor and the principal debtor that the surety may not have the benefit of the securities upon payment would seem to be inoperative.[84] It may be possible, however, to prevent the surety having the benefit of the securities by stipulating that they can only be resorted to if both the principal and the surety fail to pay.

5. *Contribution Between Co-Sureties*

General

7–45   Where a co-surety pays the debt, or more than his proportion of it and the principal is insolvent, the co-surety is entitled to contribution from his fellow co-sureties to equalise the burden. It makes no difference whether the co-sureties are bound jointly or severally or jointly and severally. Nor does it matter whether the co-sureties are

---

[77] *Waugh v. Wren* (1862) 11 W.R. 244.
[78] *Midland Banking Co. v. Chambers* (1859) 4 Ch. at 398.
[79] *Re Kirkwoods Estate* (1878) 1 L.R. Ir. 108.
[80] *Re Butlers Wharf Ltd* [1995] 2 B.C.L.C. 43.
[81] *Cooper v. Jenkins* (1863) 32 Beav. 337.
[82] *Lake v. Brutton* (1856) 8 De G.M. & G. 440 at 451, 452.
[83] *Brandon v. Brandon* (1859) 3 De G. & G. 524.
[84] *cf. Steel v. Dixon* (1881) 17 Ch. D. 825.

bound by the same instrument or by separate instruments, whether in the same sum or different sums, whether at the same time or different times. Nor does it matter whether the surety paying the debt knows of the existence of any other sureties, since the rule of contribution does not depend upon agreement, express or implied, but upon an equity arising from the mere fact of the existence of co-sureties for the same debt owed to the same creditor.[85] Nor is it material that one surety agreed to become bound before another surety.[86]

The underlying principle of equity is that the creditor's remedies against the co-sureties should be applied so as to apportion the burden rateably. If the remedies have been applied otherwise, the court will, by employing the remedies of the creditor or otherwise, correct the inequity as between the co-sureties.[87]

Where any of the co-sureties are insolvent, the contributions of the others are proportionately increased.[88]

Contributing co-sureties must be sureties in the same degree

The equity depends upon the creditor's original ability (apart from any equity preventing him from doing so) to charge the co-surety from whom contribution is sought as much as the co-surety seeking contribution. Where this could not have been done there is no inequity to be remedied and no contribution. For example, where the surety's guarantee provides that he cannot be sued unless the other sureties may default, no right to contribution arises against him.[89] The surety in that position is in reality "a surety for the surety".[90] **7–46**

In the case of a bill of exchange given as a security for a person's debt whereas both the drawer and acceptor are sureties as regard the principal debtor, as between themselves the drawer is only surety

---

[85] *Dering v. Lord Winchelsea* (1787) 1 Cox. Eq. Cas. 318; *Craythorne v. Swinburne* (1807) 14 Ves. 160; *Re Ennis* [1893] 3 Ch. 238.

[86] See *e.g. Scholefield Goodman & Sons Ltd v. Zyngier* [1985] A.C. 562.

[87] The use of the creditor's remedies to obtain contribution between co-sureties was always recognised in Roman law: D.46.1.17; C.8.41.22. The principles upon which an English law is based are stated in the following authorities, namely: *Craythorne v. Swinburne*, above, especially at 162; *Stirling v. Forrester* (1821) 3 Bligh at 590 *per* Lord Redesdale; *Ex p. Stokes* (1848) De G. at 622; *Hartley v. O'Flaherty* Beatty 77 at 78; *Duncan Fox & Co. v. North and South Wales Bank* (1880) 6 App. Cas. 1 at 19; *Ward v. National Bank of New Zealand* (1883) 8 App. Cas. 755 at 765. The general view now is that principles of contribution represent an illustration of the broader principles of unjust enrichment.

[88] *Peter v. Rich* (1629) 1 Ch. R. 34; *Hole v. Harrison* (1673) 1 Ch. Ca. 246; *Lawson v. Wright* (1786) 1 Cox. Eq. Cas. 275; *Hitchman v. Stewart* (1855) 3 Drew. 271; *Dallas v. Walls* (1873) 29 L.T. 599; *Lowe v. Dixon* (1885) 16 Q.B.D. 455. The common law did not adjust the position to take insolvent co-sureties into account; *Batard v. Hawes* (1853) 2 E. & B. 287. Nor does Scottish law: *Buchanan v. Main* 3 F. 215 (1900).

[89] *Re Denton* [1904] 2 Ch. 178; *Craythorne v. Swinburne* (1807) 14 Ves. 160.

[90] *per* Lord Eldon in *Craythorne v. Swinburne*, above; referred to as a "sub-surety" in Restatement, Security s.145 (1941).

for the acceptor and is in the absence of contrary agreement, entitled to throw the loss on him.[91]

If, however, it can be shown that the parties who appear successively liable on the bill were intended as between themselves to be co-sureties in equal degree, contribution is recoverable by one against the other, irrespective of their places upon the bill.[92]

Where "a surety for the surety" is made to pay by the creditor, he can recoup himself from the surety.[93] The equities between them are not altered by the creditor's choice of whom he decided to sue.

If a surety pays off the creditor and demands the money from the debtor, who finds another surety, no right of contribution arises: the latter would have to pay the whole. The result may well be the same where the creditor, after the debt becomes due, presses the principal for payment and the debtor then finds a further surety,[94] unless the circumstances show that it was intended that the fresh surety would be co-ordinate with the liability of that of the existing guarantor and would not be that of a "mere surety for the surety", *i.e.* liable only upon the default of the original surety.

Time given to surety

7–47   The right to contribution is not affected by the fact that time is being given by the creditor to the claimant co-surety.[95]

Position at common law and in equity

7–48   It is doubtful whether the common law allowed any action for contribution between co-sureties prior to the beginning of the nineteenth century.[96] It was, however, enforceable in London by custom.[97] The common law courts eventually recognised the principle so as to permit an action for money paid to the use of the co-surety, the contribution calculated by reference to a crude division of the debt by the total number of sureties and now allowing for the

---

[91] *Ex p. Hunter* 2 Gl. & J. 7. In *Molson's Bank v. Korinsky* [1924] 4 D.L.R. 330 the endorser of the principal's promissory note payable to the bank was held not to be entitled to contribution from sureties of the sum ultimately due on the principal's account on the basis that he was a surety in a prior degree, following *Craythorne v. Swinburne*, above. See also the *Duncan Fox Case* (1818) 6 App. Cas. 1 *per* Lord Blackburn at 20.

[92] *Reynolds v. Wheeler* (1861) 10 C.V. (N.S.) 561; *Macdonald v. Whitfield* (1883) 8 A.C. 733; *Batson v. King* (1859) 4 H. & N. 739.

[93] *Re Denton*, above. Lord Eldon in *Craythorne v. Swinburne*, above, treated the surety as being in the position of a principal debtor with regard to the "surety for the surety". In *Fox v. Royal Bank of Canada* (1975) 59 D.L.R. (3d) 258 such a sub-surety was upon payment held to be subrogated to the creditor's rights against the principal and the sureties, with no right on the part of the sureties to contribution against him.

[94] *Parsons v. Briddock* (1708) 2 Vern. 608; *Armitage v. Baldwin* (1842) 5 Beav. 278.

[95] *Dunne v. Slee* (1817) 1 Moore 2. Nor does it matter that the payment from the claimant co-surety was exacted by the creditor upon a subsequent security given by that co-surety in aid of the creditor's remedies.

[96] Goff & Jones, *The Law of Restitution* (4th ed.) at p. 307.

[97] *Offley & Johnson's Case* (1584) 2 Leon. 166.

insolvency of any co-surety.[98] In equity, however, the solvent sureties had to make good the contributions of those unable to pay.[99] Since the fusion of common law and equity in England in 1873, the rule of equity prevails throughout the English Courts, and the common law action for money paid to the use of the co-surety has fallen into disuse.

Procedure

The proper course in England is now to sue for contribution in **7–49** the Chancery Division of the High Court joining the co-sureties and also the principal unless clearly insolvent. The rights of all can then be worked out in one inquiry.[1] It is perhaps desirable that the creditor be made a party in the event that the Court orders any payment to be made to him. Commonly, however, contribution will be claimed in third party proceedings whenever the sureties or some of them are already sued as defendants by the creditor.

Insolvency of principal

It would seem right in principle that a surety should not have a **7–50** contribution from a co-surety unless he can show that the principal debtor is insolvent or that there is some impediment in suing him.[2] It seems anomalous to permit an equitable remedy against co-sureties when recovery can be made against the principal, thereby relieving all the co-sureties.[3]

Moreover, each co-surety joined might himself sue the principal, thereby multiplying actions unnecessarily.

The Court of Appeal has confirmed the position that in an action for contribution between co-sureties the principal should be made a party unless it is proved or it can be inferred from the evidence that the principal is insolvent, or that there is other good reason why he should not be joined.[4]

Guarantees in varying amounts

It is important to distinguish between situations where different **7–51** sureties are liable for the same debt but in different maximum sums, when the contribution arises, and when different sureties are liable for different parts of the same debt, when it does not.[5]

---

[98] *Batard v. Hawes* (1853) 2 E. & B. 287.
[99] Goff & Jones, *op. cit.* at 307.
[1] *Lawson v. Wright* (1786) 1 Cox 275; *Hitchman v. Stewart* (1855) 3 Drew 271; *Hay v. Carter* [1935] Ch. 297. For the form of order see *Kent v. Abrahams* [1928] W.N. 266.
[2] *Dering v. Earl of Winchelsea* (1787) 1 Cox 318.
[3] But see *Cowell v. Edwards* (1800) 2 B. & P. 168.
[4] *Hay v. Carter* [1935] Ch. 397.
[5] *Pendlebury v. Walker* (1841) 4 Y. & C. (Ex.) 424.

The rule in suretyship cases where contribution arises, appears to be that sureties in varying amounts share the burden on a so-called "maximum liability" basis. In cases where the liabilities of the sureties are in limited amounts. Thus in *Ellesmere Brewery Co. v. Cooper*[6] there were four sureties, two at £50 each and two at £25 each. With a total liability of £48 it was assumed that the £50 sureties would bear £16 each and the £25 guarantors £8 each had they been held liable. The "independent liability" principle applicable, *e.g.* to indemnity insurance in England[7] would have divided liability between the two groups of sureties in the ratio 48:25, *i.e.* the principal's debt is borne in the proportions which each guarantor's limited liability bears to the total of the guarantors' limited liabilities.[8]

In practice where the creditor's claim is for the full amount each surety must pay up to the fixed limit of his liability but if the creditor's claim is for less than the full amount the sureties will share the burden on the so-called "maximum liability" basis. However this seems at odds with the principle that co-sureties should bear their burden rateably.[9]

A similar rateable method of division to the independent liability theory can apply in suretyship cases where one of the sureties has unlimited liability but the other's liability is in a limited amount.[10]

Payment in discharge of guarantee

7–52   Any payment made by a surety must be made in partial or total discharge of the guaranteed liability. In certain circumstances however, payment made to the principal debtor may constitute such a payment but in circumstances which demonstrate that it was not made for the general purposes of the principal debtor.[11]

---

[6] [1896] 1 Q.B. 75.

[7] *Commercial Union v. Hayden* [1977] 1 Q.B. 804.

[8] In the USA there is a division of opinion on this matter but generally speaking the maximum liability principle is followed, see *e.g. Malone v. Stewart* 235 Pa. 99; 83A. 607 (1912) *contra Burnett v. Millsaps* 59 Miss. 333 at 337 (1881). Where there are different groups of sureties or a group and an individual bound in different amounts, the general rule in the USA is to divide the demand first between the groups on a maximum liability basis and then within each group on the basis of the available sureties in the group: see, *e.g. United States Fidelity & Guaranty Co. v. Naylor* 237 F. 314 (1916).

[9] See *Ellesmere Brewery Co. v. Cooper*, above at 80–82. Indeed there is no rule in English law that the maximum liability basis must in all cases apply even in an insurance context. See *Commercial Union Assurance v. Hayden*, above.

[10] *i.e.* the guarantors who are liable to contribute to the common burden bear the debt equally up to the amount of their limited liability: see *Naumann v. Northcote*, unreported, February 7, 1978, CA: Transcript No. 7835.

[11] See the decision of the High Court of Australia in *Mahoney v. McManus* (1981) 55 A.J.L.R. 673 where it was held to be sufficient to give rise to a right of contribution that the co-surety had paid the principal in reduction of his liability under the guarantee, even though the amount paid was different from the principal debt and the principal's documentation demonstrated that the payment of the surety was a loan and not necessarily in reduction of the principal debt. This case is perhaps a good example of the operation of the principle of payments being made for a specific purpose.

Contributions varied by agreement

The right of contribution may be varied or even excluded by **7–53** agreement,[12] although it is unsatisfactory to infer such an agreement in the absence of a clear stipulation.[13]

Where a co-surety has joined at the request of the other surety, it is a question of fact in each case on what terms one asked the other to join.[14] It has been said that a surety induced by another surety to join, cannot be required to contribute, especially where the inducing surety had taken a security for himself only[15] but that dictum is probably limited to a situation where the facts warrant the inference that the additional surety was asked to join on that basis. A surety can resist a claim for contribution on the basis of the verbal promise of the co-surety to indemnify him, and the Statute of Frauds cannot be used to present such a defence to contribution.[16]

A clause in a guarantee that the surety will not "make a claim or enforce" his right to contribution will at least be sufficient to vary the surety's equitable right but will not mean that the parties have agreed not to seek relief from the Court.[17]

Sureties for different debts of a principal in different combinations may agree to share equally in certain events any liability which may be enforced against any of them, ousting any right of contribution which might arise on any particular debt.[18]

A co-surety has a defence to an action for contribution by a surety who induced him to join by fraud, although the inducing surety need not disclose any interest in the money to be raised.[19]

If a surety pays with the aid of a stranger, the two will be considered as one person and entitled between them to contribution against the co-surety.[20]

Sureties for different debts

There is no co-suretyship and no contribution between sureties **7–54** where sureties are bound for different debts. The same applies

---

[12] *Swain v. Wall* (1641) 1 Ch. R. 149. However the judge who is said to have decided this case seems to have died in 1638 or 1639: see Goff & Jones, *The Law of Restitution* (4th ed.) See also *Ellesmere Brewery Co. v. Cooper*, above and *Naumann v. Northcote*, above.

[13] In *Swain v. Wall* above, the three sureties agreed amongst themselves that they could pay in thirds. The creditor exacted the whole sum from one. One was insolvent. Hutton J. is reported to have accepted the proposition that each co-surety had agreed to pay only a third and therefore only a third could be recovered by contribution, leaving the paying surety to bear two-thirds. This result defeats the equitable principle of equalisation of the burden, based on the notion that it should not matter which surety the creditor chooses to sue.

[14] *Dune v. Walley* (1848) 2 Ex. Ch. 198 and see *Linguard v. Bromley* (1812) 1 V. & B. 114.

[15] per Lord Kenyon in *Turner v. Davies* (1796) 2 Esp. 478.

[16] *Rae v. Rae* (1857) 6 Ir. Ch. R. 490.

[17] *Hong Kong Bank of Australia Ltd v. Larobi Pty Ltd* (1991) 23 N.S.W.L.R. 593.

[18] See *Arcedeckne v. Lord Howard* (1872) 27 L.T. 194.

[19] *Mackreth v. Walmsley* (1884) 51 L.T. 19.

[20] See *Arcedeckne v. Lord Howard*, above.

where a single debt is guaranteed in distinct parts by different sureties.[21]

Death of a surety

7–55   Where the surviving surety pays, the right of contribution exists against the deceased surety's estate. This rests on the general basis that the surety's estate remains liable to contribute to the common liability which he was bound to. However this right of contribution requires the obligation to have been several and not merely joint, unless there was something beyond the mere fact of co-suretyship from which an agreement that a contribution should be payable out of the estate of a deceased surety may be inferred. At law the estate of a merely joint surety is discharged, and equity does not correct this by regarding the obligation as joint and several in the absence of special circumstances, *e.g.* mistake, partnership, prior extension of credit to the sureties where it was not the instrument that first created the liability.[22] There is some authority, however, for saying that the survivors of a number of joint sureties have a right to contribution in respect of the liability surviving to them by reason of an implied contract with the deceased.[23] However, whilst an agreement binding the estate of a surety may often readily be inferred from the dealings of the parties, it will not necessarily be implied. A surety might well desire that his own liability should cease at death, even if that means that the co-surety's liability could cease in the same way. The court should consider in particular the question whether the surety's estate would have been expected to benefit from the continuing liability.

When the right to contribution arises

7–56   A surety has no right of contribution until he has paid a larger sum than his proportion of the debt then actually due to the creditor.[24] It is only then that the surety has a debt as against the co-surety which will support a petition in bankruptcy.[25]

---

[21] See *Pendlebury v. Walker* (1841) 4 Y. & C. Ex. 242; and *Coope v. Twynam* (1823) T. & R. 426; *Collins v. Brosser* (1823) 1 B. & C. 682; *Ellis v. Emmanuel* (1876) 1 Ex. D. 157.

[22] Goff & Jones, *op. cit.* at 317 consider that a right of contribution may be available on the basis that there was a common obligation at some time in the past. They consider that in principle a contribution claim in equity should lie generally.

[23] By means of an action for money paid to the use of the deceased as executor: see *Ashby v. Ashby* (1827) 7 B. & C. 14 *per* Bayley J. The basis for this entitlement has been said to be by analogy with chattel-acquiring contracts, *i.e.* the guarantee could be said to ensure the continuity of a loan to the company: see *Prior v. Hembrow* (1841) 8 M. & W. 873. *Ashby v. Ashby* was applied in *Batard v. Hawes* (1853) 2 E. & B. 287.

[24] *Ex p. Gifford* (1802) 6 Ves. 805; *Davies v. Humphreys* (1840) 6 M. & W. 153; *Ex p. Snowdon* (1881) 17 Ch. D. 44. In *Davies v. Humphreys*, Parke B. felt that it "might be more convenient to require that the whole amount should be settled before the surety should be permitted to call upon each other, in order to prevent multiplicity of suits."

[25] *Ex p. Snowden*, above.

Where the surety has paid less than his share, but it becomes more by reason of the creditor's recovery from the principal debtor, a right to contribution arises.[26]

A surety paying more than his share of what is then due cannot insist on contribution if a larger sum may later become due.[27] Similarly, a surety who has paid the whole interest but less than half the principal sum cannot recover in respect of the interest by treating it separately.[28]

Once a surety has paid his share, contribution can be claimed as often as, by reason of further payments by the surety or the principal, the amount paid becomes greater than the surety's share.[29] Time begins to run under the Statute of Limitations in respect of each sum that might be claimed from the time to each portion arises.

Payment without being sued

A surety may pay as soon as the demand becomes due and claim **7–57** contribution.[30] If there is any doubt as to whether the sum is due, the surety should give notice to the co-sureties to defend, make terms or pay their proportions. If the co-sureties do not take any such action, the co-sureties will not be entitled to claim that the surety paid improperly.[31] The absence of notice permits the co-sureties to establish, if they can, that payment could have been resisted.[32] Contribution is of course not possible where a surety pays without being liable to the creditor.[33]

Claim before payment

Once judgment has been entered against the surety for more than **7–58** his proportion, he has the right, if recovery cannot be made against the principal, to bring an action in equity joining the co-sureties and the creditor to compel the co-sureties to pay their proportions.[34] Even before judgment is obtained it is possible to bring such an action if the creditor has a right to immediate payment from the surety.[35]

---

[26] *Davies v. Humphreys* (1840) 6 M. & W. 153.
[27] *Stirling v. Burdett* [1911] 2 Ch. 418.
[28] *Lever v. Pearce* (1888) W.N. 105.
[29] *Davies v. Humphreys*, above.
[30] *Pitt v. Purssord* (1841) 8 M. & W. 538.
[31] *Duffield v. Scott* (1789) 3 Term. Rep. 374 approved in *Jones v. Williams* (1841) 7 M. & W. at 501; *Pettman v. Keble* (1850) 9 C.B. 701.
[32] *Smith v. Compton* (1833) 3 B. & Ad. 407.
[33] *Barry v. Moroney* (1837) 8 Ir. R.C.L. 554; *Camberleg v. Lawson* (1857) 1 C.B. (N.S.) 709.
[34] *Wolmershausen v. Gullick* [1893] 2 Ch. 514. For the USA see *Davies v. First National Bank* 86 Or. 474; 161 P. 93; 168 P. 929 (1917). There it has also been suggested that a surety before payment may restrain a fraudulent conveyance by a co-surety: *Bowen v. Hoskins* 45 Miss. 183 (1871); *Pashby v. Mandigo* 42 Mich. 172; 3 N.W. 927 (1879). In Canada, it has been held that it is at least necessary that the surety should have been called on to pay more than his due: *Tucker v. Bennett* [1927] 2 D.L.R. 42 *per* Orde J.A. at 47–48.
[35] *ibid.*

It has been suggested that there is a possible pre-condition that the creditor must be threatening to make the surety liable for more than his share.[36]

Securities given by co-sureties to creditor

7–59   A surety is entitled in order to obtain contribution to any security given to the creditor by the co-surety.[37] Moreover, the creditor must not waste such security.[38]

Surety holding security or receiving payment from principal debtor

7–60   The surety's right to contribution from co-sureties is not affected by his having taken a bond for his security from the principal.[39] This is so even if the co-sureties are unaware of the security, if the surety only became a surety on the basis of having such a security and if it was agreed between the surety and the principal that the benefit of the security would not extend to the other sureties.[40] A security given by the principal to a surety to indemnify him against all liability in respect of his suretyship will in effect enure to the benefit of all the sureties until they are recouped in full (or the security is exhausted).[41] If the surety gives up such a security, he loses *pro tanto* his right to contribution.[42]

The same principle appears to apply to a payment by the principal to the surety, which must be shared with the co-sureties,[43] whereupon the surety will require a fresh claim for indemnity from the principal debtor.

A paying surety who takes over securities for the creditor will have to allow for the securities seeking contribution from co-sureties.[44] But where a surety insures the principal's life for the surety's benefit and pays the premiums himself, a co-surety cannot compel the surety to deliver up the policy.[45]

---

[36] But consider *Thomas v. Nottingham Inc. Football Club Ltd* [1972] Ch. 596 which suggests that *quia timet* relief is available to a surety against a principal debtor any time after the principal debt becomes repayable.

[37] *Ex p. Crisp* (1744) 1 Atk. 133 at 135; *Greerside v. Benson* (1745) 3 Atk. 248; *Stirling v. Forrester* (1831) 3 Bligh 575 at 590 citing *Dering v. Lord Winchelsea* (1787) 2 B. & P. 270; *Duncan Fox & Co. v. North & South Wales Bank* (1880) 6 App. Cas. 1 *per* Lord Blackburn at 19. Section 5, Mercantile Law Amendment Act 1856 puts this rule into statutory form in England.

[38] *Margretts v. Gregory* (1862) 6 L.T. 543.

[39] *Knight v. Hughes* (1828) 3 C. & P. 467; *Swain v. Wall* (1641) 1 Ch. 149.

[40] *Steel v. Dixon* (1881) 17 Ch. D. 825; *Re Arcedeckne, Atkins v. Arcedeckne* (1883) 24 Ch. D. 709.

[41] *Berridge v. Berridge* (1890) 44 Ch. D. 168.

[42] *Ramsey v. Lewis* 30 Barb. (N.Y.) 403 (1859).

[43] *Knights v. Hughes*, above, *cf. Steel v. Dixon*, above.

[44] *Re Arcedeckne, Atkins v. Arcedeckne* (1883) 24 Ch. D. 709.

[45] *Re Arcedeckne*, above; *Re Albert Life Assurance Co.* (1870) L.R. 11 Eq. 164 *per* Bacon V.C. at 172.

Surety consenting to time being given to the principal

A surety who agrees to time being given to the debtor loses, if the **7–61** time is given, his right to contribution from any sureties who have not agreed to it, for they would then be released.[46]

Co-surety's counterclaim against creditor

A co-surety is fully liable to contribution to a paying surety **7–62** regardless of any counterclaim the co-surety may have had against the creditor.[47]

Interest

A surety is entitled to charge interest[48] on the sum of contribution **7–63** due as from the date or dates when his payments became in excess of his proportion.[49] It does not matter that the principal debt did not carry interest.[50] Moreover, the surety who has paid his share can insist on his co-sureties exonerating him from further interest accrued to the creditor on the shares which they should have paid.[51]

Costs

A surety can seek contribution in respect of costs incurred in **7–64** reasonably resisting the creditors' claim.[52] This assumes that the proceedings were defended on grounds which would relieve the other co-sureties also, and not merely the defending surety on grounds personal to himself.[53]

---

[46] See *Way v. Hearn* (1860) 11 C.B. (N.S.) 774 and 781, 782. *Cf.* also *Sword v. Victoria Super Service Ltd* (1958) 15 D.L.R. (2d) 217; see *Greenwood v. Frances* [1899] 1 Q.B. 312 where the giving of time was authorised by the guarantee. Guarantees often contain stipulations permitting the creditor to give time without releasing any of the sureties. In Canada it has been held that the release by a surety of the principal's obligation to indemnify prevents such surety from seeking contribution from the co-surety who has thereby lost his right of indemnity: *Griffiths v. Wade* (1966) 60 D.L.R. (2d) 62, following the Massachussetts decision of *Hobart v. Stone* 10 Pick. 215 (1830).

[47] *Wilson v. Mitchell* [1939] 22 Q.B. 869 citing p. 139 of the third edition of this work and the cases of *Gillespie v. Torrance* 25 N.Y. 306 (1862) and *Newton v. Lee* 139 N.Y. 332 (1893).

[48] *Lawson v. Wright* (1786) 1 Cott. 275; *Hitchman v. Stewart* (1855) 3 Drew 271; *Ex p. Bishop* (1880) 15 Ch. D. 400.

[49] Not necessarily the same as the date of the payments: see *Davies v. Humphreys* (1840) 6 M. & W. 155.

[50] *Re Swan* (1869) 4 Ir. Req. 209, see above at p. ???.

[51] *per* Wright J. *ex relatione* M. Mackenzie, December 1902.

[52] In *Wolmershausen v. Gullick* [1893] 2 Ch. 514 at 529, 530, Wright J. allowed contribution for costs incurred in resisting the creditor's claim, which had been thereby materially reduced. The contrary was suggested by Lord Tenterden in *Knight v. Hughes* (1828) 3 C. & B. 467 but see also *Kemp v. Finden* (1844) 12 M. & W. 421, *Tindall v. Bell* (1843) 11 M. & W. 228; *Broom v. Hall* (1859) 7 C.B. (N.S.) 503.

[53] See *Re International Contract Co., Hughes' Claim* (1872) L.R. 13 Eq. 623 at 624 *per* Wickens V.-C.; *South v. Bloxam* (1865) 2 H. & M. 457.

CHAPTER 8

RELEASE OF THE SURETY BY DEALINGS WITH THE PRINCIPAL CONTRACT

Discharge of surety by release or giving time to principal

8–01   A surety is discharged by the creditor, without his consent, either releasing the principal debtor or entering into a binding arrangement with him to give him time. The ground upon which the surety is discharged being in both cases that his right at any time to pay the debt, and sue the principal in the name of the creditor, is interfered with.[1] In practice, guarantees often contain provisions attempting to exclude this rule.[2]

Basis of rule

8–02   The theory is that the creditor cannot place his remedies at the disposal of the surety without a breach of his arrangement with the principal not to sue him. To carry out that arrangement, it is necessary that the right of the surety to take action against the principal should be suspended.[3] And as this cannot be done without his consent, he is held discharged altogether.[4]

A surety is also discharged if the creditor agrees with the principal not to receive the money from the surety since this is inconsistent with the right of the surety to pay the debt and sue the principal.[5] It has been held by a majority of the Court of Appeal that the doctrine has no application where the surety has agreed with the principal not to require him to pay until the surety is himself sued; but this view, though not formally overruled, was questioned in the House of Lords in the same case.[6]

---

[1] See *Nisbet v. Smith* (1789) 2 Bro. C.C. 579; *Samuell v. Howarth* (1817) 3 Mer. 272; *Orme v. Young* (1815) Holt. N.P.C. 84; *Price v. Kirkham* (1864) 3 H. & C. 437 at 442; *Bailey v. Edwards* (1864) 4 B. & S. 761 at 771; *Swire v. Redman* (1876) 1 Q.B.D. 536. It is necessary carefully to distinguish the cases discussed in this chapter, from cases where the transaction amounts to a payment of the debt by the principal. For the importance of the distinction see *Perry v. National Provincial Bank* [1910] 1 Ch. 464. The absurdity of the application of this rule with regard to agreements to give time where the surety's interests are not harmed is pointed out by Glanville Williams in *Joint Obligations* (1949) at p. 124 and Cardozo in *Law and Literature* (1931) at p. 51 as well as in *The Nature of The Judicial Process* (1933) at pp. 153 and 154.
[2] See *e.g.* Appendix 1.
[3] See *per* Lord Eldon C.J. in *English v. Darley* (1800) 2 B. &. P. at 62; *per* Best C.J. in *Philpot v. Briant* (1828) 4 Bing. 717 at 719; *Ex p. Gifford* (1802) 6 Ves. 804; *Neville v. Glendinning* (1816) 7 Taunt. 126; *Davies v. Stainbank* (1855) 6 De G.n. & G. 679 at 689, 696; *North v. Wakefield* (1849) 13 QB 536 at 541; *Webb v. Hewitt* (1857) 3 K. & J. 438 at 442; *Bateson v. Gosling* (1871) L.R. 7 C.P. 9 at 14; *Cragoe v. Jones* (1873) L.R. Ex. 81 at 83.
[4] See *Combe v. Woolf* (1832) 8 Bing. 156 at 163.
[5] *Oriental Financial Corporation v. Overend Gurney & Co.* (1871) 7 Ch. App. 142 at 152; (1874) L.R.7 HL 348 at 358.
[6] *Rouse v. Bradford Banking Co.* [1894] 2 Ch. 32; [1894] A.C. 586.

Doctrine does not apply to quasi-sureties

The doctrine releasing a surety when time is given to a principal   **8–03**
debtor does not apply to persons not sureties but who merely
occupy positions of secondary liability.[7]

Actual damage to surety not material

The surety is discharged however short may have been the time   **8–04**
given, and whether or not the arrangement in fact operated to the
advantage or disadvantage of the surety.[8] An analogy with the cases
on variation might have suggested an exception where it is clear
without enquiry[9] that the matter is not substantial or can only be
beneficial to the surety.[10]

Sureties contracting as principals but where one is a surety

The rule as to the effect of giving time is not confined to sureties   **8–05**
contracting as such, but extends to those who undertake what is in
form a principal liability, but is in fact only assumed to secure the
consideration for another. Such persons are released, if the creditor
gives time or releases the principal, after notice of the true relations
of the parties, whether he had that notice at the time of taking the
surety or not. For example, a person who gives a bond or promissory note for the debt of another, or who becomes a party, either as
acceptor or as indorser, to a bill of exchange for the accommodation
of another, in order that the other may obtain money upon it, is
released if the holder, after notice of these facts, gives time to the
principal debtor or person accommodated. This applies even though
in the case of a bill the accommodation party may upon the bill
appear to be liable in a prior degree for the party accommodated, as
where he is acceptor and the party accommodated the drawer.

Debtors originally principals may become sureties

The doctrine extends further, even to those who, having con-   **8–06**
tracted as and being in fact principals, afterwards by arrangement
with another principal become sureties as between themselves and

---

[7] *Way v. Hearn* (1862) 11 C.B. (N.S.) 774; *British Airways v. Parish* [1979] 2 Lloyd's Rep. 361
(director liable for company debt because name of company misdescribed contrary to s.108 Companies Act 1948). Nor does it apply to a surety who undertakes to be liable as a principal: *Reed v.
Lowndes* (1857) 23 Beav. 361.

[8] *Rees v. Berrington* (1789) 2 Ves. 540; *Bowmaker v. Moore* (1819) 3 Price 214; 7 Price 223;
Samuell v. Howarth (1817) 3 Mer. 272; *Oakley v. Pasheller* (1836) 4 C. & F. 207 at 224, 233; *Bailey
v. Edwards* (1864) 4 B. & S. 761; *Wilson v. Lloyd* (1873) L.R. 16 Eq. 60 at 71; *Polak v. Everett* (1876)
1 Q.B.D. 669; *Holme v. Brunskill* (1878) 3 Q.B.D. 495 at 505; *Ward v. National Bank of New Zealand*
(1883) 8 A.C. 755 at 763; *Re Darwen & Pearce* [1927] 1 Ch. 178 at 183–185.

[9] *Holme v. Brunskill,* above.

[10] *National Bank of Nigeria Ltd v. Awolesi* [1964] 1 W.L.R. 1311, PC; *Hydro Electric Power
Commission v. Fidelity Insurance Co.* (1937) 4 D.L.R. 626; *Bell v. National Forest Production Ltd*
(1964) 45 D.L.R. (2d) 249; 47 W.W.R. 449; *Nelson Fisheries Ltd v. Boese* [1975] 2 N.Z.L.R. 233.

that other, if the creditor before the time is given, has notice of that fact.[11] A partner, therefore, who retires taking a covenant from the continuing partners that they will pay the debts and indemnify him, becomes a mere surety of such of the creditors of the firm as have notice of the dissolution deed.[12] A proviso in that deed to the effect however that he is not to be entitled to call upon the continuing partners to pay off the debts so long as he has kept indemnified does not apparently deprive him of his discharge if the time is given to the continuing partners.[13]

But the rule under discussion has no application to cases where the relation of principal and surety does not exist, but one person indemnifies another against loss which may accrue from credit given to another.[14]

Delay no discharge

8–07   A surety is only discharged if a binding agreement is made between a creditor and the principal that time should be given to the principal. Mere delay, therefore, by the creditor in suing the principal does not discharge the surety.[15] It is the surety's business to see whether the principal pays, and not that of the creditor.[16]

Although a surety is not discharged by the mere failure of the creditor to press for payment, even though this may pressure the surety,[17] it is equally clear that a binding agreement to give time discharges the surety even though, as often happens, he suffers no harm.[18]

Forms of giving time

8–08   It is immaterial what form the giving of time takes, so long as there is a binding agreement by the creditor to suspend his rights. Thus, agreeing to take payment by instalments,[19] taking a bill or note payable on a future date,[20] accepting a new bill in lieu of

---

[11] *Rouse v. Bradford Banking Company* [1894] 2 Ch. 32; [1894] A.C. 586; *Goldfarb v. Bartlett* [1920] 1 K.B. 639.

[12] *Rouse v. Bradford Banking Company*, above.

[13] See *Rouse v. Bradford Banking Company*, above. The House of Lords was evidently of this opinion and would have overruled the opinion to the contrary expressed in the Court of Appeal [1894] 2 Ch. 32. But *cf. Oakford v. European and American Steam Shipping Co. Ltd* (1863) 1 H. & M. 182.

[14] See *Way v. Hearn* (1862) 11 C.B. (N.S.) 774.

[15] *Shepherd v. Beecher* (1725) 2 P.W. 288; *Ex p. Mure* (1788) 2 Cox 63 at 74; *Walwyn v. St. Quentin* (1797) 1 B. & P. 652; *Wright v. Simpson* (1802) 6 Ves. 714 at 734; *Trent Navigation Co. v. Harley* (1808) 10 East 34; *Goring v. Edmunds* (1829) 6 Bing. 94; *Brickwood v. Annis* (1814) 4 Taunt. 614; *Orme v. Young* (1815) Holt N.P.C. 84; *Perfect v. Musgrove* (1818) 6 Price 111; *Bell v. Banks* (1841) 3 M. & Gr. 258; *Eyre v. Everett* (1826) 2 Russ. 381; *Heath v. Key* (1827) 1 Y. & J. 434; *Clarke v. Wilson* (1838) 3 M. & W. 208; *Price v. Kirkham* (1864) 3 H. & C. 437.

[16] *Wright v. Simpson*, above. This is also the view of the case law in most states of the USA.

[17] *e.g.* if the principal becomes insolvent: *Trent Navigation Co. v. Harley* (1808) 10 East 34.

[18] *Petty v. Cooke* (1874) L.R. 6 QB 790 at 795 *per* Blackburn J.

[19] *Clarke v. Henty* (1838) 3 Y. & Ce. 187. See *Tyson v. Cox* (1823) T. & R. 395.

[20] *Rees v. Berrington* (1795) 2 Ves. 540; *Samuell v. Howarth* (1817) 3 Mer. 272.

payment,[21] renewing a promissory note[22] or obtaining judgment by consent with a stay of execution beyond the date when in the regular course judgment could have been obtained,[23] discharge to the surety. An agreement to accept the proceeds of the sale of ships at sea and others then about to be built[24] is a giving of time. But taking a security for the payment of the debt at a future time, with the reservation of the right to proceed at any time upon the original demand, does not discharge the surety.[25] Equally, taking a bill of sale for the debt does not affect the liability of the surety, even though the property assigned is not to be seized until after a certain time, if the personal liability of the debtor is not postponed.[26]

Where a mortgage, in which the defendant had joined as a surety, was assigned, and a new covenant entered into by the mortgagor with the assignee to pay the amount together with further advances at a future day, it was held that this put an end to the right to sue on a covenant in the first mortgage, and that the surety was therefore discharged, notwithstanding that the "full benefit of the covenants" in the first mortgage was expressed to be assigned.[27] So where a mortgage was taken for a debt already secured by an accommodation acceptance with a covenant for payment at a later date, the acceptor was discharged.[28] But where it was intended that the promissory note of the debtor and sureties and also a mortgage by the debtor and others, should be taken, and that the promissory note should be collateral to the mortgage, the sureties in the promissory note were not discharged by the taking of the mortgage, though it contained a covenant by the debtor to pay at a later date.[29]

The receipt of interest before it is due amounts to a contract not to sue for the principal until the date arrives when that debt would have been payable, and is therefore a giving of time and discharges the surety,[30] unless it is part of an understanding that, notwithstanding the payment in advance, the right to sue is reserved.[31]

Binding agreement necessary

In order that there may be a giving of time so as to discharge a surety, there must be an agreement legally binding to that effect.[32] **8–09**

---

[21] *Goldfarb v. Bartlett* [1920] 1 K.B. 639.
[22] *Provisional Bank of Ireland v. Fisher* (1919) 2 Ir.R. 249.
[23] *Whitfield v. Hodges* (1836) 1 M. & W. 679; *Croft v. Johnson* (1814) 5 Taunt. 319.
[24] *Davies v. Stainbank* (1855) 6 De.G.M. & G.679.
[25] *Lindsay v. Lord Downes* (1840) 2 Ir.Eq.R. 307. See *Pearl v. Deacon* (1857) 24 Beav. 186; 1 De.G. & J. 461.
[26] *Twopenny v. Young* (1824) 3 B. & G. 208 but *cf. Searles v. Finch* (1891) 7 T.L.R. 253.
[27] *Bolton v. Buckenham* [1891] 1 Q.B. 278.
[28] *Munster v. Leinster Bank v. France* (1889) 24 L.R. Ir. 82.
[29] *Boaler v. Mayor* (1865) 19 C.B. (N.S.) 76.
[30] *Blake v. White* (1835) Y. & C. Eq. 420.
[31] *Rayner v. Fussey* (1859) 28 L.J. Ex. 132.
[32] See *per* Lord Eldon in *Samuell v. Howarth* (1817) 3 Mer. 272 at 278; *Heath v. Key* (1827) 1 Y. & J. 434.

Therefore, if a further security is given by the principal which may induce the creditor to forbear, this does not discharge the surety if the creditor does not bind himself to the forbear.[33] Nor does any obligation merely binding on the honour of the creditor.[34] Where there was an overdraft for £50,000 for which a surety was liable, and the principal requested the bank to allow it to be increased to £53,046 until March 14, to which the bank assented, it was held in the House of Lords that the only legal effect of this was to oblige the bank to honour drafts up to that amount until March 14, and that the bank did not contract not to claim the £50,000 before that day; consequently the surety was not discharged.[35] A mere promise by the debtor of interest[36] or of interest at an increased rate[37] if the debt is not pressed, followed by payment accordingly, does not show there has been such a giving of time as to discharge a surety, because it remains optional with the creditor whether in order to earn the interest he should let the debt run on. In the same way, if the agreement is to give time provided certain things are done by the debtor, which he does not do, the surety is not discharged. For example, where the debtor was to give a bill and goods for the balance due, and he gave a bill but not the goods, the taking of the bill was held to be conditional and there was no discharge of a surety.[38] Similarly where time was promised if £100 was sent by return of post but only £80 was sent.[39]

8–10   If the creditor merely intimates to the debtor that he will accept a composition if the other creditors do, and promises to hold his hand while the debtor approaches them, this is no binding agreement to give time, and the surety is not discharged.[40]

The same result will follow if a creditor signs an agreement to take a composition provided all of the other creditors come in and they do not come in.[41] If, however, the proviso is only to operate by way of defeasance on failure to carry out certain arrangements, and in the meantime the creditor is debarred from suing, the surety will be discharged.[42] A promise by the creditor not to enforce the debt for a certain time, if arrears of interest and expenses were paid up, is not binding because of lack of consideration and does not discharge the surety.[43]

---

[33] *Bell v. Bankes* (1841) 3 M. & Gr. 258.
[34] *Ladbrook v. Hewett* (1832) 1 Dowl. 488. And see *Tucker v. Laing* (1856) 2 K. & J. 745.
[35] *Rouse v. Bradford Banking Co.* [1894] A.C. 586, reversing on this point the Court of Appeal [1892] 2 Ch. 32.
[36] *Arundel Bank v. Goble* cited in *Philpot v. Bryant* (1828) 2 Bing. 717 at 721.
[37] *York City & County Banking Co. v. Bainbridge* (1880) 43 L.T. 732.
[38] *Vernon v. Turley* (1836) 1 M. & W. 316.
[39] *Badnall v. Samuel* (1817) 3 Price 521.
[40] *Brickwood v. Annis* (1814) 5 Taunt 614.
[41] See *Lewis v. Jones* (1852) 4 B. & C. 506.
[42] *Bailey v. Edwards* (1864) 4 B. & S. 761.
[43] *Tucker v. Laing* (1856) 2 K. & J. 745. However, consideration should be given to the possible application of estoppel applying so as to make the promise binding: see *Central London Property Trust Ltd v. Hightrees House Ltd* [1947] K.B. 130, and subsequent cases on equitable estoppel.

Remedy against principal must be actually postponed

A surety is not discharged unless the remedy against the principal   **8–11**
is, in a practical sense, postponed. Thus if an action is commenced
against the principal and judgment agreed on terms that no execution issues until a day earlier than judgment could have been
obtained in the usual course of the courts, the surety is not discharged.[44] And even where it is agreed that if instalments are
regularly paid, the stay of execution is to continue beyond that
period, the surety is not discharged if default is made on the
payment of an instalment (so that the whole becomes due) before
that period expires.[45]

Giving time in respect of one of several debts

Where a surety is liable for several distinct debts, duties or   **8–12**
obligations, time given in respect of one of them, the position of the
surety with regard to the remainder not being altered, will not
discharge a surety as to the remainder. In *Croydon Commercial Gas
Co. v. Dickinson*[46] where the principal had contracted to buy the
by-products of a gas company, and there was a surety for payment
of the price monthly, and time was given in respect of one month's
supply, it was held in the Court of Appeal[47] that the surety was
discharged only as to that monthly payment, as his position in
reference to the contract as a whole was not varied, though the
effect of the arrangement was to cause the indebtedness to accumulate. Similar considerations apply when the guarantee is for the
performance of several duties[48] or distinct contracts.[49] Where there
was a continuing guarantee for the price of the goods to be supplied, and an amount having become due, time was given in respect
of that amount without prejudice to the creditor's rights in respect
of future supplies, it was held that the surety remained liable in
respect of future supplies.[50] However, the giving of time, followed
by an agreement to take instalments and a variation of the terms of
the principal debt has been held to release a surety, not only as to
the payments for which time had been given, but as to the whole
debt. The circumstances were such that what had been done
"directly or by its consequences wholly altered the situation of the

[44] *Ladbrooke v. Hewitt* (1832) 1 Dowl. 488; *Hulme v. Coles* (1827) 2 Sim. 12; *Whitfield v. Hodges* (1836) 1 M. & W. 679; *Jay v. Warren* (1824) 1 C. & P. 532.
[45] *Price v. Edmunds* (1829) 10 B. & C. at 578; *Bowsfield v. Tower* (1812) 4 Taunt 456; *Croft v. Johnson* (1814) 5 Taunt 319.
[46] (1876) 1 C.P.D. 707; (1876) 2 C.P.D. 46. See also *Davies v. Stainbank* (1855) 6 De.G.M. & G. 679 at 689; *Provincial Bank v. Cussen* (1886) 18 L.R.Ir. 302; *Midland Motor Showrooms v. Newman* [1929] 2 K.B. 256.
[47] (1876) 2 C.P.D. 46.
[48] *Skillet v. Fletcher* (1867) L.R. 1 C.P. 217; (1867) 2 C.P. 469.
[49] *Harrison v. Seymour* (1866) L.R. 1 C.P. 518.
[50] *Bingham v. Corbett* (1864) 34 L.J.Q.B. 37; the principal paid the amount in respect of which time had been given.

surety".[51] A surety for the payment of the premiums on a policy deposited by a debtor with his creditor was held discharged by the creditor releasing the debtor from his personal liability upon the original debt, and agreeing to look only to the policy.[52]

Power to give credit may be implied

8–13   A guarantee for the price of goods supplied involves the usual trade credit being given, and this will not discharge a surety as a giving of time.[53] It seems, too, that the creditor is entitled to give, not merely the usual trade credit, but the credit usual as between him and the debtor[54] on the theory the surety ought to enquire into the nature of the dealings before he assents to guarantee. It is probably a question in each case what latitude it was fairly in the contemplation of the surety to allow to the creditor under the circumstances. The surety would clearly not be bound to allow any dealings which he would not expect might naturally take place.[55] But the creditor cannot allow a long time to elapse and then give the agreed or trade credit, for this in effect is granting more than that credit.[56]

Time given expiring before surety's liability arises

8–14   Where the liability of a surety is only to come into being upon the happening of a condition (*e.g.* after demand) he is not discharged by time having been given, where it has expired before his liability arose.[57] An agreement by the creditor with a stranger[58] or with another surety[59] to give time to the principal does not discharge the surety.

Time given after payment by surety

8–15   If a surety, on being applied to, pays part of the debt in satisfaction of the whole of his liability, and the creditor afterwards releases the debtor, the surety has no ground of complaint, because his right of action against the debtor in respect of the payment made has already attached and is not interfered with.[60]

---

[51] *per* Sir John Leach V.C. in *Eyre v. Bartrop* (1818) 3 Madd. 221.
[52] *Lowes v. Maughom* (1884) C. & E. 340.
[53] *Samuell v. Howarth* (1817) 3 Mer. 272; *Combe v. Woolf* (1832) 8 Bing. 156; *Allan v. Kenning* (1833) 9 Bing. 618; *Re Fox Walker & Co., ex p. Bishop* (1880) 15 Ch D 400.
[54] *Simpson v. Manley* (1831) 2 C. & J. 12; *Combe v. Woolf*, above, *Howell v. Jones* (1834) 1 C.M. & R. 97 at 107.
[55] *cf. Lee v. Jones* (1864) 17 C.B. (N.S.) 482 at 503.
[56] *cf. Holl v. Hadley* (1828) 5 Bing. 54; *Combe v. Woolf*, above, *Howell v. Jones*, above.
[57] *Prendergast v. Devey* (1821) 6 Madd. 124. See S.C. at law, *sub nom. Davey v. Prendergrass* (1821) 5 B. & Ald. 187 at 190.
[58] *Frazer v. Jordan* (1858) 8 E. & B. 303, following *Lyon v. Holt* (1839) 5 M. & W. 250.
[59] *Clarke v. Birley* (1889) 41 Ch D 422 *cf. Cross v. Sprigg* (1850) 2 Mac. & Gl. 113.
[60] *Reade v. Lowndes* (1857) 23 Beav. 361 at 367, 368. See *Ex p. Bishop* (1880) 15 Ch D 400 at 407, 415.

Time given after surety undertakes principal liability

Where, on being applied to, the surety gives a fresh undertaking   **8–16**
to pay, by way of a note of his own[61] or a covenant by himself,[62] or
makes an arrangement by which the creditor is to obtain satisfaction
from securities provided by the surety,[63] he may be held to have
come under a principal liability to pay. In that case he will not be
discharged by dealings between a creditor and the original
principal.

Time given after judgment against surety

It has been held[64] that time given to the principal after judgment   **8–17**
against both the surety and the principal does not discharge the
surety, and there seems no difference between this case and the case
of judgment recovered against the surety only. But where a joint
and several judgment has been obtained against both principal and
surety, and one of them is actually released, both are discharged on
the ordinary principles applicable to judgments.[65]

Reservation of remedy against surety

The doctrine under which a surety is discharged by an agreement   **8–18**
on the part of the creditor either not to sue, or to give time to the
principal debtor, does not apply if it is made a condition of the
agreement that the rights of the creditor to sue or receive the money
from[66] the surety are reserved. The principle upon which the surety
is released rests on the basis that if a surety is not released he will
be able to sue the principal for an indemnity and that will be a fraud
on the principal.[67] Where the creditor reserves the rights against a
surety, in the agreement with the principal, the principal knows that
he will be exposed to a claim by the surety for an indemnity and the
surety is therefore not discharged.[68] This being the principle on
which the reservation operates, it is unnecessary that the surety
should be a party to or have notice of it.[69]

---

[61] *Hall v. Hutchons* (1830) 3 M. & K. 426.
[62] *Defries v. Smith* (1862) 10 W.L.R. 189.
[63] *Reade v. Lowndes* (1857) 23 Beav. 361.
[64] *Re a Debtor* [1913] 3 K.B. 11. See also *Pole v. Ford* (1819) 2 Chit. 125; *Bray v. Manson* (1841)
8 M. & W. 668; *Jenkins v. Robertson* (1854) 2 Drew 351. See also references at n. 1 above.
[65] See, *e.g. Re E.W.A.* [1901] 2 K.B. 642.
[66] See *Philpot v. Briant* (1828) 4 Bing. 717 at 719; *Oriental Financial Corporation v. Overend
Gurney & Co.* (1871) L.R. 7 Ch. App. 142 at 152; 7 HL 348 at 358.
[67] *per* Mellish L.J. in *Nevill's Case* (1870) 6 Ch. App. 43 at 47.
[68] *Ex p. Glendinning* (1819) Buck. 517; *Ex p. Gifford* (1802) 6 Ves. 805; *Baultbee v. Stubbs* (1811)
18 Ves. 20; *Kearsley v. Cole* (1846) 16 N. & W. 128; *Nichols v. Norris* (1831) 3 B. & Ad. 41, note;
North v. Wakefield (1849) 13 QB 536 at 541; *Price v. Barker* (1855) 4 E. & B. 760; *Bailey v. Edwards*
(1864) 4 B. & S. 761 at 774; *Webb v. Hewitt* (1857) 3 K. & L. 438 at 442; *Bateson v. Gosling* (1871)
L.R. 7 C.P. 9 at 14; *Cragoe v. Jones* (1873) L.R. 8 Ex. 81 at 83, 84; *Muir v. Crawford* (1875) L.R.
2 H.L.Sc. 456 *cf Bellingham v. Freer* (1837) 1 Moo. P.C. 333.
[69] See *Webb v. Hewitt* (1857) K. & J. 438 at 442. Unless the guarantee requires that such notice be
given. See *Guinness Mahon & Co. v. London Enterprise Investments Ltd* [1995] 4 Bank L.R. 185.

Reservation incompatible with actual release

8–19   Where, however, the creditor actually releases the principal, there is no room for any reservation or remedies against a surety.[70]

Similarly no such reservation can have effect where another debtor is accepted in the place of the debtor guaranteed.[71] But the presence of such a reservation is frequently a reason for construing words of release (if the intention absolutely to put an end to the debt is not apparent)[72] as a mere covenant not to sue,[73] in which case no such repugnancy arises.[74]

However, if there is no doubt as to the intention absolutely to extinguish the debt, it is a release, and any sureties or co-debtors are discharged.[75] In *Metropolitan Bank of England v. Coppee*[76] it seems to have been assumed that the withdrawal of execution under a *fi. fa.* discharges a surety *in toto*. A similar result will follow from a withdrawal of a bankruptcy petition on terms.[77] It may, however, be that the true principle of these decisions is not that discussed in this chapter, but that the transaction amounted to accord and satisfaction which is equivalent to the payment of the debt.[78]

Accepting from principal composition outside bankruptcy law discharges surety

8–20   Since *Ex p. Smith*[79] it has been settled that a voluntary composition outside the bankruptcy law giving time to the debtor or reducing his liability discharges the surety, unless there is in the deed a reservation of the remedies against sureties.[80] In that case the debtor remains open at the suit of the surety to the original demand of the

---

[70] See *Commercial Bank of Tasmania v. Jones* [1893] A.C. 313 at 316. But see *Perry v. National Provincial Bank* [1910] 1 Ch. 464 where the Court of Appeal said that *Jones* was perhaps in conflict with earlier authority. The question is whether a reservation arises in the event of the release or novation leaves the guarantor in a position of secondary liability for the primary liability. It is suggested that such an express clause will generally be upheld. See also *Webb v. Hewitt* (1857) 3 K. & J. 438 *Cf. Bolton v. Buckenham* [1891] 1 QB 278.
[71] See previous note. *Cf. Bradford Old Bank v. Sutcliffe* [1918] 2 K.B. 833.
[72] See *Webb v. Hewitt*, above.
[73] *Solly v. Forbes* (1820) 2 B. & V. 38; *Thompson v. Lack* (1846) 3 C.B. 540; *North v. Wakefield* (1849) 13 QB 536; *Price v. Barker* (1855) 4 E. & B. 760; *Willis v. DeCastro* (1858) 4 C.B. (M.S.) 216; 27 L.J.C.P. 243; *Keyes v. Elkins* (1864) 5 B. & S. 240; *Muir v. Crawford* (1875) L.R. 2 HL Sc. 456; *Hooper v. Marshall* (1869) L.R. 5 C.P.4; *Bateson v. Gosling* (1871) L.R. 7 C.P. 9; *Re Armitage, ex p. Good* (1877) 5 Ch D 46; *Duck v. Mayeu* [1892] 2 QB 511.
[74] *Kearsley v. Cole* (1846) 16 N. & W. 128 at 136; *Price v. Barker* (1855) 4 E. & B. 760 at 777; *Owen v. Homan* (1851) 4 H.L.C. 997 at 1037; *Muir v. Crawford* (1875) L.R. 2 H.L. Sc. 456; *Jones v. Whitaker* (1887) 57 L.T. 216; *Cole v. Lynn* [1942] 1 K.B. 142.
[75] *Cheetham v. Ward* (1797) 1 B. & P. 630; *Nicholson v. Revill* (1836) 4 A. & E. 675; *Gholson v. Savin* 137 Ohio. St. 551; 31 N.E.(2d) 858 (1941).
[76] [1985] 12 T.L.R. 129, 258 *cf. Mayhew v. Crickett* (1818) 2 Swanst. 185; *Williams v. Price* (1824) 1 S. & S. 581.
[77] See *Re E.W.A.* [1901] 2 K.B. 642.
[78] See *Perry v. National Provincial Bank* [1910] 1 Ch. 464.
[79] (1789) 3 Bro. C.C.J., followed in *Ex p. Wilson* (1805) 11 Ves. 410; *Ex p. Glendinning* (1819) Buck. 517; *Ex p. Carstairs* (1820) Buck. 560; *Lewis v. Jones* (1825) 4 B. & C. 506; *Craigoe v. Jones* (1873) L.R. 8 Ex. 81.
[80] *Ex p. Glendinning*, above, *Ex p. Carstairs*, above; *Kearsley v. Cole* (1846) 16 M. & W. 128; *Bateson v. Gosling* (1871) L.R. 7 C.P. 9.

creditor, notwithstanding the provisions for giving time or reducing the debt which the deed may contain.[81] In such cases the operation of the deed, though containing words of release, is often held to be that of a covenant not to sue only.[82] But where all the property of the debtor was assigned absolutely to a creditor in consideration of a release and the payment by that creditor of a composition to all the others, this was held a release notwithstanding the reservation of the remedies against a surety.[83]

And where the creditor made a secret bargain with the principal that he should be paid in full, notwithstanding the composition, the effect of this being, on ordinary principles, that the creditor could thereafter claim against the principal neither the debt nor the composition, the surety was held discharged notwithstanding a reservation in the composition deed of remedies against him.[84]

Contributories in winding-up of company

Where the holder of shares at the date of the winding-up of the **8–21** company agreed with the liquidator, under sanction of the court, that upon paying certain sums and surrendering all his interest in the company he should be discharged from all calls, with the proviso that nothing in the agreement should prejudice the right of another liquidator against any other contributories, whether as past or present members or otherwise, it was held that a former holder of the same shares was not discharged.[85] And in such a case the former holder being made liable can recover over against his transferee, notwithstanding the agreement.[86]

Discharge of principal in bankruptcy, dissolution of company

In the case of an individual, discharge from his bankruptcy will **8–22** not release any person from liability acting as surety for that individual as principal or any such person in the nature of such a surety.[87] The basic principle is that any release or indulgence to the

---

[81] *Kearsley v. Cole* above; *Close v. Close* (1853) 4 De. G. M. & G. 176; *Green v. Wynn* (1868) L.R. 4 Ch. 20; *Re Whitehouse* (1887) 37 Ch. D. 683.

[82] *Green v. Wynn*, above; *Bateson v. Gosling* (1871) L.R. 7 C.P. 9; *Re Whitehouse*, above.

[83] *Webb v. Hewitt* (1857) 3 K. & J. 438. See also *Muir v. Crawford* (1875) L.R. 2 H.L. Sc. 456 at 459. Even where there is an absolute release under a voluntary composition, the reservation of remedies against sureties may perhaps not be, from every point of view, nugatory. If any of the creditors party to the arrangement were secured by guarantees, there might, so far as the sureties' rights were concerned, retain them by the consent of the sureties. It might be considered that such retention of such securities would be a fraud upon the other creditors and void. The authorities have been reviewed in *Johnson v. Davies* [1998] 2 All E.R. 649 in which the Court of Appeal held that whether a term is a voluntary arrangement under the Insolvency Act 1988 releases a jointly liable ex-debtor depends on the true construction of the arrangement and on the surrounding circumstances.

[84] *Mayhew v. Boyes* (1910) 103 L.T. 1.

[85] *Nevill's Case* (1870) L.R. 6 Ch. App. 43.

[86] *Roberts v. Crowe* (1872) L.R. 7 C.P. 629.

[87] s.281(7) Insolvency Act 1986. *Hooper v. Marshall* (1869) L.R. 5 C.P. 4; *Ex p. Jacobs* (1875) L.R. 10 Ch. App. 211.

principal is an act of the law[88]; nor, where the principal is a company, does the adoption of a scheme of arrangement under section 425 and following of the Companies Act 1985 affect the liability of sureties.[89] The position is that the surety cannot complain of what is not the act of the creditor but, as said above, an act arising by operation of law: and the debtor cannot complain because he is entirely freed by the discharge and the liability of the surety does not mean a recourse against himself.[90] Such recourse cannot be preserved and the doctrine of the reservation of remedies against sureties is wholly inapplicable.[91]

Nor can the surety who has not paid the debt in any way interfere with the dealings of the creditor with the bankrupt under the Insolvency Act 1986 or the Companies Act 1985.[92] His right is, upon the relevant statutory provisions being invoked, to pay off the creditor and intervene in his place in the proceedings.[93]

8–23   In the case of voluntary arrangements under Part VIII of the 1986 Act, these are expressed to include both compositions in satisfaction of a debtor's debts as well as schemes of arrangement. In the case of the latter, section 16(20) of the Bankruptcy Act 1914 formerly treated them as having the same effect as a discharge granted in bankruptcy. Although there is no express provision in the Insolvency Act 1986 that a voluntary arrangement discharges the debtor, it has been held that a surety will not necessarily be discharged on a voluntary arrangement coming into effect.[94] But if, by an arrangement outside the insolvency or company legislation, a debtor is expressed to be discharged as if he had been the subject of a bankruptcy order without any express reservation or remedies against sureties, the latter, unless they consented, are discharged, for a discharge in bankruptcy is a discharge from the demand even at the suit of the surety and this if produced by the voluntary act of the creditor, must discharge the surety.[95]

As in the case of a surety for a bankrupt under section 281(7) of the Insolvency Act 1986 whose liability will not be released on the principal's discharge, a surety for a principal which is a corporation and which is later dissolved will not be released.[96]

A surety for the upkeep of a policy of insurance on the life of the principal pledged to the creditor to secure the debt is however

---

[88] *Ex p. Jacobs*, above; see also *Ellis v. Wilmot* (1874) L.R. 10 Exch. 10; *Ex p. Wilson* (1805) 11 Ves. 410; *Provincial Bank v. Cussen* (1886) 16 L.R.Ir. 382. And *cf. English v. Darley* (1800) 2 B. & P. 61 at 62; *Browne v. Carr* (1831) 7 Bing. 508.

[89] *Re London Chartered Bank of Australia* [1893] 3 Ch. 540, decided under the Joint Stock Companies Agreement Act 1870. *Cf. Mortgage Insurance Corporation v. Pound* (1894) 64 L.J.Q.B. 394; 65 L.J.Q.B. 129. See also *Dane v. Mortgage Insurance Corporation* [1894] 1 Q.B. 54.

[90] *Ex p. Jacobs*, above; *Cragoe v. Jones* (1873) L.R. 8 Ex. 81.

[91] *Ex p. Jacobs*, above; *Re London Chartered Bank of Australia*, above.

[92] *Browne v. Carr* (1831) 7 Bing. 508; *Ellis v. Wilmot* (1874) L.R. 10 Ex. Ch. 10.

[93] *ibid.*

[94] *R.A. Securities Ltd v. Mercantile Credit Co. Ltd* [1994] B.C.C. 599. In *Johnson v. Davies* [1998] 2 All E.R. 649, the Court of Appeal confirmed that it is a matter of construction of the arrangement as to whether a discharge of a jointly liable co-debtor is effective by the terms of the particular arrangement.

[95] *Cragoe v. Jones* (1873) L.R. 8 Ex. Ch. 81.

[96] *Re Fitzgeorge, ex p. Robson* [1905] 1 K.B. 462.

discharged if the creditor values the policy and proves in the
bankruptcy of a principal for the balance.[97] On the other hand a
surety for the payment of interest until repayment of the principal
has been held not to be discharged by the dissolution of the
principal, which is a corporation.[98] It would have been different if
the obligation had been to pay interest so long as the principal may
remain due.[99]

What reservation of remedies is effectual

In order to prevent an argument for giving time from discharging
sureties, it must be so worded as to show that it was intended only
to apply to suits for the benefit of the creditor, and to expect from
its operation suits at the instance of sureties and on their behalf.[1]
And this exception may be unqualified. Therefore, where time was
given to the debtors to enable them to carry out certain proposals,
and the remedy against the sureties was reserved in the event of the
proposals not being carried out, the sureties were discharged,
because until that event was determined the creditor could not
without breach of contract allow the surety to sue the debtors.[2] In
the same way, if the arrangement with the principal is expressed to
the effect that he shall have the respite in any case, a reservation of
rights against sureties might be rejected as repugnant.[3]

8–24

Assent of surety to composition

A surety will remain liable even if there is no reservation of his
liability on the face of a composition deed, release or agreement in
writing not to sue, where it was made at his request and with his
agreement to remain liable notwithstanding,[4] at any rate unless it is
shown that the agreement was kept secret from the other creditors.[5]
In such a case the liability of the surety must be without recourse to
the principal. It was laid down generally in *Ex p. Glendinning*[6] that
a reservation arises against the surety on a release to the principal
must appear on the face of the release.[7] This rule, however, can

8–25

---

[97] *Re Moss* [1905] 2 K.B. 307. See also *Bank of Montreal v. McFatridge* (1958) 14 D.L.R. (2d) 552. affirmed (1959) 17 D.L.R. (2d) 557; *Quainos v. NZ Breweries Ltd* [1991] 1 N.Z.L.R. 161.
[98] *Re Fitzgeorge, ex p. Robson,* above.
[99] *Re Moss,* above. See also *Re Forester,* unreported, but referred to in [1919] 2 Ch. 159. In *Re Moss* the surety was released because on the wording employed there ceased upon the bankruptcy to be any sums due from the principal which the surety had guaranteed. The bankruptcy of the principal does not normally itself release the surety: see also *Bank of Montreal v. McFatridge,* above where *Re Moss* was distinguished.
[1] *Bailey v. Edwards* (1864) 4 B. & S. 761 *per* Blackburn J. at 774.
[2] *Bailey v. Edwards,* above.
[3] See *Webb v. Hewitt* (1857) 3 K. & J. 438; *Wilson v. Lloyd* (1873) L.R. 13 Eq. 60 (overruled on the main point in *Ex p. Jacobs* (1875) L.R. 10 Ch. App. 211).
[4] *Davidson v. McGregor* (1841) 8 M. & W. 755; *Poole v. Willats* (1869) L.R. 4 Q.B. 630.
[5] *Davidson v. McGregor,* above.
[6] (1819) Buck. 517.
[7] See too *Lewis v. Jones* (1825) 4 B. & C. 506; *Wyke v. Rogers* (1852) 1 De G. M. & G. 408 but *cf. Pring v. Clarkson* (1822) 1 B. & C. 14.

apparently only apply where the reservation is to be given effect to as a term of the contract with the principal debtor.[8] If the continuance of the liability of the surety is assented to by the surety, this can be proved dehors the instrument.

Guarantee authorising giving of time

8–26   The surety remains bound where either the guarantee authorises the indulgence which has been given to the principal[9] or the surety has assented to it at the time,[10] or even upon hearing of it afterwards has ratified it or promised to pay notwithstanding.[11] Where a guarantee expressly provides that the creditor may give time or enter into a composition with a debtor, the right of the creditor against the surety remains by virtue of that clause, whether the latter is precluded from having any remedy over against the debtor or not.[12]

The result is the same as in cases where the surety, though he remains liable himself, is prevented by express provision such as section 281(7) of the Insolvency Act 1986 from recovering over against the principal.[13] Where a surety guaranteed payments to be made within 14 days from the close of each month, unless the creditor "should by writing allow a longer time for payment" it was held that this did not enable the creditor to enlarge the time for a payment out of the 14 days that expired, and the liability had attached.[14]

Compositions amounting to payment by the principal

8–27   There is, however, a distinction between compositions which operate merely as a discharge of the principal debtor and compositions where there is an accord and satisfaction of the debt or part of the debt. Thus in *Perry v. National Provincial Bank*[15] the plaintiff as surety mortgaged certain property to the defendants to secure the principal's overdraft. The mortgage deeds provided that the defendants should be at liberty to compound with the principal without

---

[8] See the note to *Lewis v. Jones* above at 515, 516; *Smith v. Winter* (1838) 4 M. & W. 454; *Davidson v. McGregor* (1841) 8 M. & W. 755.

[9] See *Cooper v. Smith* (1838) 4 M. & W. 519; *Union Bank of Manchester v. Beech* (1865) 3 H. & C. 672; *Perry v. National Provincial Bank* [1910] 1 Ch. 464 *cf. Rouse v. Bradford Banking Co.* [1894] 2 Ch. 32; [1894] A.C. 586. Such a provision is common.

[10] *Clarke v. Devlin* (1803) 3 B. & P. 363; *Tyson v. Cox* (1823) T. & R. 395; *Davidson v. McGregor* (1841) 8 M. & W. 755; *Ex p. Harvey* (1854) 4 De G. N. & G. 881; *Atkins v. Revell* (1860) 1 De. G. F. & J. 360.

[11] *Mayhew v. Crickett* (1818) 2 Swanst. 185; *Smith v. Winter* (1838) 4 M. & W. 454. The reference in the judgments in the latter case to the assent being given was held so to allege. *Mayhew v. Crickett* shows that the assent would have been effectual though given later.

[12] *Cooper v. Smith*, above; *Union Bank of Manchester v. Beech* (1865) 3 H. & C. 672.

[13] *Hooper v. Marshall* (1869) L.R. 5 C.P. 4.

[14] *Croydon Gas Co. v. Dickinson* (1876) 1 C.P.D. 707; (1876) 2 C.P.D. 46.

[15] [1910] 1 Ch. 464.

affecting their rights against the plaintiff. Subsequently, the principal being insolvent, a company was formed to acquire the principal's property, and the defendants agreed to take debentures from that company at the rate of 25 shillings worth of debentures for every £1 of debt not secured by mortgages of the principal's own property in full satisfaction of their whole claim against the principal. It was held by the Court of Appeal that this transaction amounted to payment by the principal of that portion of the debt in respect of which the debentures had been issued, and that the plaintiff's property was not liable in respect of that portion of the debt; but that as to the residue of the debt, there had been no payment but merely a discharge of the principal under a composition, and that therefore the plaintiff's property remained liable.

Surety not discharged by loss of recourse to principal, unless due to act or omission of creditor contrary to duty to surety

A guarantee is not put an end to by reason of the debt becoming   **8–28** unenforceable against the principal by reason of matters happening subsequently, unless it is due to an act or omission of the creditor contrary to his duty to the surety.[16] Thus a surety is liable although the claim against the principal be barred by the Statute of Limitations[17] or by reason of the bankruptcy of the principal.[18]

Since the discharge of a surety by time given to the principal rests upon the basis that it is against good faith for the creditor to make such an arrangement, where the creditor in good faith receives payment from the principal, which payment is afterwards set aside as a voidable preference, the surety is not discharged. However, the effect is that his right to intervene is suspended, for the creditor could not have refused to accept the payment.[19] Where the creditor releases the surety on the representation of the surety (resulting from the fraud of the debtor but unknown to the surety) that the debt is covered by a security which the debtor has given to the creditor, the creditor, when the fraud is discovered, is entitled to set aside the release, though in the meantime, of course, the surety's right of recourse to the debtor has been in abeyance.[20] Where a contractor for works by fraud obtained a certificate of completion from the engineer, and was paid his retention money, the surety was not released.[21] This was on the basis that a surety cannot claim to be discharged on the ground that his position has been altered by the conduct of the creditor where that conduct has been caused by

---

[16] Similarly in the USA inaction, even if resulting in the claim being unenforceable, *e.g.* by reason of the Statute of Limitations, does not release the surety: see, *e.g. Fidelity & Casualty Co. of New York v. Lackland* 175 Va. 178; 8 S.E. (2d) 306 (1940).

[17] *Carter v. White* (1883) 25 Ch.D. 666.

[18] *Bank of Montreal v. McFatridge* (1958) 14 D.L.R. (2d) 552, affirmed (1959) 17 D.L.R. (2d) 557.

[19] *Pritchard v. Hitchcock* (1843) 6 M.Gr. 151; *Petty v. Cooke* (1871) L.R. 6 Q.B. 790.

[20] *Scholefield v. Templer* (1859) 4 De G. & J. 429.

[21] *Kingston-upon-Hull v. Harding* [1892] 2 Q.B. 494.

a fraudulent act or omission against which the surety guaranteed him.[22]

Where the creditor promised the principal without consideration that time would be allowed him for payment, and the surety, hearing this, abandoned a negotiation to get the money raised elsewhere for the principal, it was held that the surety was not discharged, though circumstances which had arisen in the meantime had made it impossible for that negotiation to be renewed.[23] Unless he has been misled by the creditor, a surety cannot escape from his guarantee by reason that, in the belief that there was nothing outstanding upon it, he has given up a right of indemnity over and against the third party.[24]

Death of a debtor jointly bound

8–29   If a surety contracts jointly only with his principal or another surety, and the surety dies before the principal or the co-surety, his debt will be discharged.[25] However, a promise by such a surety in his lifetime to pay the debt himself in consideration of the joint demand being forborne might be enforceable against the estate.[26]

Giving time to principal under disability

8–30   It has never been decided, nor has the point apparently ever been discussed, whether a surety for a person under disability is discharged by the creditor purporting to give time to the so-called principal. It is certain that, whether the so-called surety is in theory to be held liable as a principal or by way of estoppel,[27] he has, in fact, no recourse against the principal. Thus he has the enjoyment of none of those rights against the principal which are held infringed by the creditor giving time, and may therefore be said to have no cause to complain. On the other hand, if the basis of his liability is that he is estopped from setting up the disability of the principal, the creditor, perhaps, should likewise take no advantage of that circumstance. The rule discharging the surety where time is given does not depend upon the proof of actual damage to the surety; and he could urge that he might, notwithstanding the disability, have got the debt paid by or on behalf of the principal had his position not been weakened by the indulgence of the creditor. It would not be difficult to imagine cases of real hardship to a surety under such circumstances. But, as an absolute rule of law, the

[22] *ibid, per* Bowen L.J. at 504.
[23] *Tucker v. Laing* (1856) 2 K. & J. 745.
[24] *Oxley v. Young* (1796) 2 H.Bl. 613.
[25] *cf. Jones v. Beech* (1851) 2 De G.M. & G. 886; *Brookes v. Stuart* (1839) 1 Beav. 512. For a criticism of this rule see Glanville Williams *Joint Obligations* (1949), pp. 63 *et seq.*, where exceptions are also discussed.
[26] *Tucker v. Laing* (1856) 2 K. & J. 745.
[27] See above Chaps 1 and 4.

principle by which a surety is discharged by time being given to the principal is perhaps not likely to receive an extension.

Rescission of contract by creditor upon repudiatory breach by principal debtor

Where the victim of a repudiatory breach exercises his right to **8–31** treat the contract as rescinded, this does not amount to a fresh agreement or to any variation so as to discharge a surety from the defaulting party's performance.[28] In this situation, the guarantor's obligation does not cease but is transmuted by operation of law into an obligation to compensate the creditor for the loss suffered by the breach.[29] A discharge of the guarantor in this situation would mean the creditor would lose the guarantor when he most needed him.[30] A guarantor is not released in such a situation even where arguably the acceptance of the repudiation seems detrimental to the position of the creditor or surety.[31]

---

[28] *Moschi v. Lep Air Services Ltd* [1973] A.C. 331; the rescinding party was merely exercising a right conferred by the original contract.

[29] The House of Lords in *Moschi*, above refer to the third edition of this work, p. 143 with approval for the proposition that the guarantor's obligation was to see that the debtor paid or performed his obligations to the creditor: see Lord Diplock at 348C, Lord Kilbrandon at 359B. Upon the guarantor's failure to perform this primary obligation, there arose a secondary obligation on the guarantor to pay the amount of the creditor's loss, *per* Lord Diplock at 351B.

[30] *Moschi v. Lep* above, *per* Lord Simon at 355C.

[31] In *Chatterton v. MacLean* [1951] 1 All E.R. 761 the acceptance of the hirer's repudiation by a creditor under a hire purchase agreement meant that he lost the right to repossess the vehicle hired. The guarantor was not released.

CHAPTER 9

LOSS OF SECURITIES AND CO-SURETIES

General principles

9–01 Since a surety is entitled to contribution from every co-surety and to the benefit of every security held by the creditor, an allowance must always be made to the surety for every right of contribution or security lost by the fault of the creditor. The relief to which he is entitled in respect is however of a different kind from that which is accorded him where his remedies upon the principal obligation itself are interfered with. Unless the obtaining of a co-surety or a security is a condition express or implied or his undertaking the liability of surety, he is not discharged absolutely, but is only entitled to an allowance commensurate with the value of the protection lost to him. In *Carter v. White*[1] Cotton L.J. said:

> "The principle is this: that if there is a contract express or implied that the creditor should acquire or preserve any right against the debtor, and the creditor deprives himself of the right which he has stipulated to acquire, or does anything to release any right which he has, that discharges the surety; but where there is no such contract, and he only has a right to perfect what he has in his hand, which he does not do, that does not release the surety unless he can show that he has received some injury in consequence of the creditor's conduct."

In such an event the surety is only released *pro tanto*. A similar principle applies to the release of or failure to obtain co-sureties.

In such cases a surety will be released *pro tanto* whenever the creditor's dealings only affect the amount for which the surety will be liable should the principal default: in effect the surety is discharged to the extent of the loss he has suffered. On the other hand, if the creditor's conduct results in a variation of the risk of default and more usually where the creditor has committed a breach of a

---

[1] (1884) 25 Ch D 666 at 670. See also *Dale v. Powell* (1911) 105 L.T. 291. A similar principle is generally accepted in the USA, see, *e.g. Morton v. Dillon* (1894) 90 Va. 592; 19 S.E. 654 and in Canada as to which see *Rose v. Afterberger* (1969) 9 D.L.R. (3d) 42. However Manitoba (RSM 1970 M-120) and Saskatachewan (RSF 1965 C73) have legislated to limit the surety's defence to the extent of his prejudice. For an unsuccessful attempt to exclude this principle by a clause in a guarantee see *Dowling v. Ditanda* (1975) 236 E.G. 485.

190

condition of the guarantee, the surety will be released absolutely.[2]

Where instrument of suretyship reveals security

Where the instrument which the surety signs reveals that a **9–02** certain security has been or is to be given, or a certain co-surety has joined or is to join, he is only liable, as surety, for a principal liability so secured or so additionally guaranteed. And if the security is not taken or after being taken is surrendered, or the co-surety does not join or after joining is released, the surety first named is not bound. Thus a surety for performance of covenants in a deed granting land with rent reserved was held discharged from liability for rent in arrears by the grantor accepting a reconveyance of the land, notwithstanding that the land was not worth the annual rent for which the surety was liable and the reconveyance was therefore a relief to the surety.[3] Similarly a surety who guarantees performance of a contract for works by joining as surety in the instrument constituting the contract is discharged absolutely if the owner prematurely advances the retention money to the contractor[4] or does not insure the works according to the contract.[5]

A surety joining as such in a deed by which the debtor agreed to pay a certain sum, and gave a charge on book debts to cover it, was, upon the release of the charge, liberated *in toto* without reference to the value of the debts.[6] Where a debtor assigned a policy to his creditor by way of security for the debt, engaging to pay the premiums, and the latter engagement was guaranteed by a surety and the creditor subsequently released the debtor from his personal liability for the original debt, looking only to the policy, it was held that the surety was discharged.[7] Where a surety agreed to join the principal in a joint and several bond on having a counter-bond, and the principal never executed the bond, though he gave the counter-bond, the surety was held entitled to have the bond given up and cancelled.[8] But where a surety executed a bond from the form of which it appeared that the principal was to execute it too, and on the faith that he would do so and the principal never did so, but executed an agreement under seal which gave the creditor the same

---

[2] For examples of situations in which a surety was released only *pro tanto* see *Wulff v. Jay* (1872) L.R. 7 Q.B. 756 (failure to register a security and to take possession); *Rainbow v. Juggins* (1880) 5 Q.B.D. 422 (failure to pay insurance premiums on a policy securing the principal debt). *Cf. Smith v. Wood* [1929] 1 Ch. 14 (absolute release: loss of rights of marshalling); *Watts v. Shuttleworth* (1861) 7 H. & N. 353 as to which see below. For a full review of these principles see *China & South Seas Bank Ltd v. Tan* [1990] 1 A.C. 536.

[3] *Lord Harberton v. Bennett* (1829) Beatt. 386 at 389.

[4] *General Steam Navigation Co. v. Rolt* (1858) C.B. (M.S.) 550, *cf. Kingston-upon-Hull v. Harding* [1892] 2 QB 494.

[5] *Watts v. Shuttleworth* (1861) 7 H. & N. 353.

[6] *Polak v. Everett* (1876) 1 Q.B.D. 669 especially at 775; *Smith v. Wood* [1939] 1 Ch. 14, *cf. Berg v. Rogerson* [1866] 14 L.T. 708. In the United States see *Foerderer v. Moors* 91 F. 476 (CA Pa. 1898).

[7] *Lowes v. Maughan* (1884) 6 C. & E. 340.

[8] *Bonser v. Cox* (1841) 4 Beav. 379.

remedy as the bond would have done, it was held that the surety was bound.[9] Where sureties covenanted to make good the deficiency which should remain after the realisation of certain securities recited to be held by the creditor, and it turned out that one of those securities had never been acquired, it was held that the sureties were discharged, and that they were not were not estopped by the recital.[10] Sureties for the payment of future calls on shares will be discharged if, on non-payment by the holders, the company, as it is entitled to do, forfeits the shares, since by such act the sureties lose the lien on the shares which they would have on payment.[11]

A creditor is under no duty to seek additional security from the principal at least in the absence of a clear contractual stipulation to that effect, *e.g.* by way of condition precedent.[12]

Guarantee showing intended co-surety

9–03   On similar principles a surety is not bound if the instrument when signed by him is drawn in a form showing himself and another or others as intended joint and several guarantors and any intended surety does not sign.[13] It is immaterial by whom the instrument was prepared[14] or whether the surety omitted was solvent or not.[15] In such cases the creditor must show that the surety consented to dispense with the execution of the document by the other or others.[16] The rule is an equitable one and is applicable even though the surety who has executed did not execute as an escrow and is consequently bound at law.[17] The principle is that the arrangement to which the surety consented to become a party has been left uncompleted and has, in equity, never become binding upon him. He is entitled therefore to have the instrument given up to be cancelled, and not merely to have relief to the extent of the contribution which the other surety might have been compelled to pay in his relief.[18] Thus if a surety who signs for a smaller amount than the form of the instrument indicated he was to sign for, the sureties

---

[9] *Cooper v. Evans* (1867) L.R. 4 Eq. 45.

[10] *Coyte v. Elphick* (1874) 22 W.R. 54.

[11] *Re Darwen and Pearce* [1929] 1 Ch. 176.

[12] *e.g.* in a recital as in *ANZ Banking Group Ltd v. Beneficial Finance Corp. Ltd* [1983] 1 N.S.W.L.R. 199, *cf. Byblos Bank SAL v. Al-Khudhairy* (1986) 2 B.C.C. 99, 549.

[13] *Evans v. Bremridge* (1852) 2 K. & J. 174: on appeal 8 De G.N. & G. 100; *Hansard v. Lethbridge* (1892) 8 T.L.R. 346; *Fitzgerald v. McCowan* (1898) 2 Ir.R. 1; *National Provincial Bank v. Brackenbury* (1906) 22 T.L.R. 797; *James Graham & Co. (Timber) Ltd v. Southgate Sands* [1986] QB 80.

[14] *Hansard v. Lethbridge*, above.

[15] *Fitzgerald v. McCowan*, above.

[16] *Hansard v. Lethbridge*, above. This decision in the Court of Appeal settled the law, see however *Cumberledge v. Lawson* (1857) 1 C.B. (N.S.) 709; *Coyte v. Elphick* (1874) 22 W.R. 541 at 543 and 544. The rule may operate harshly upon the creditor where the joinder of the other surety was a matter really insisted upon by him and afterwards waived and was never in fact made a point of by the surety who signed first. See *Traill v. Gibbons* (1861) 2 F. & F. 358; *Horne v. Ramsdale* (1842) 9 M. & W. 329.

[17] *Evans v. Bremridge*, above. And see *Elliott v. Davis* (1800) 2 B. & B. 338, *Cumberledge v. Lawson* (1857) 1 C.B. (N.S.) 709; *Underhill v. Horwood* (1804) 1 Ves. 209 at 225 and 226.

[18] See *per* Wood V.-C. in *Evans v. Bremridge*, above at 185.

who signed before him are discharged.[19] And the further result has been to follow in such a case, in as much as the surety who signed for the reduced amount himself only agreed to be liable if the other sureties were also liable, their release, owing to the alteration introduced by him, liberates him too.

The rights of a surety to his discharge upon this principle would apparently not be affected by the fact that he has, by some independent arrangement between himself and the intended co-surety obtained a right over against him; for he is entitled to insist that the latter should become liable to the creditor by the same instrument as himself or one equivalent to it.[20]

Securities and co-sureties existing at the same time

The mere circumstance that at the time when the surety became **9–04** bound there exists, to the knowledge of the surety, another surety for the same debt, or a security available to the creditor which is collateral, and the surrender of which does not, therefore, alter the contract itself, performance of which is guaranteed, does not necessarily establish that it is an implied term of the contract of suretyship that this protection shall remain for the benefit of the surety so as to bring the case within the principle cited from *Carter v. White*.[21] The maintenance of such protection must in such cases expressly be made a condition.

Existing co-sureties

Thus, to take the cases relating to co-sureties, it has been held **9–05** that mere knowledge by the surety who signed that the creditor is insisting on having the additional liability of another surety will not suffice,[22] even though in his own mind the surety signing relied upon it,[23] and still less the mere existence of the co-surety at the time when the surety is seeking relief became bound.[24]

Existing securities

The same rule holds in the case of securities. In *Taylor v. Bank of* **9–06** *New South Wales*[25] a surety guaranteed bank advances "on the faith of" a mortgage securing such advances. The Privy Council held that a surety was entitled to allege that the creditor has mishandled part of the mortgaged property. However, even if the surety had made out such an allegation he would not have been entirely

---

[19] *Ellesmere Brewery Co. v. Cooper* [1896] 1 Q.B. 75.
[20] See *Bonser v. Cox* (1841) 4 Beav. 379; *Cooper v. Evans* (1867) L.R. 4 Eq. 45.
[21] (1884) 25 Ch D at 670: above at p. 9.01.
[22] *Traill v. Gibbons* (1861) 2 F. & F. 358.
[23] See *Cumberledge v. Lawson* (1857) 1 C.B. (N.S.) 709; *Dallas v. Walls* (1873) 29 L.T. 599.
[24] *Ward v. National Bank of New Zealand* (1883) 8 App. Cas. 755, see especially at 759.
[25] (1886) 11 App.Cas. 596.

discharged. The principle is that where the creditor has by his own act, rendered unavailable part of the security to the benefit of which the surety was entitled, the latter is only discharged *pro tanto*.[26]

There is however a dictum of Blackburn J. in *Polak v. Everett*[27] to the effect that the surety is discharged absolutely if the creditor abandons rights which he held "when the surety entered into the suretyship" or, as the Law Journal reports it "rights which the surety acquires under the original bargain" as opposed to "rights acquired by him under some subsequent collateral security".[28] This passage does not, it is submitted, lay down the principle that the surety impliedly contracts for collateral securities merely because they exist when he becomes bound.[29] This would be at variance with *Ward v. National Bank of New Zealand*.[30]

Where Act of Parliament requires several sureties

9–07   If, under an Act of Parliament, a bond is required to be taken with two sureties, and it is taken with one only, it is not therefore void at law.[31] Nor, if it was not drawn in a form to indicate that the second surety was to join, would it apparently be voidable in equity.[32]

Release of a co-surety whose liability was a condition

9–08   If a surety, whose liability is an essential condition of the liability of another surety, signs the instrument, but is afterwards released, or becomes entitled to discharge by virtue of any equitable principle,[33] the surety is discharged in the same way as if the first had never become bound.[34]

Rules applicable to joint debtors

9–09   Where the sureties have become jointly or jointly and severally bound and one is released absolutely, the other is discharged at common law and independently of the equitable rule now under consideration, upon the principle that the discharge of a joint debtor

---

[26] *Pearl v. Deacon* (1857) 24 Beav. 186; 1 De G. & J. 461. For the facts see the report in Beavan.
[27] (1876) 1 Q.B.D. 669 at 676, *cf. Rainbow v. Juggins* (1880) 5 Q.B.D. 138 at 142.
[28] 45 L.I.QB 365 at 373.
[29] This was the basis upon which *Newton v. Chorlton* (1853) 10 Hare 646, the general right of a surety to securities was explained. But the reasoning in that case cannot be considered as lawful. See *Pledge v. Buss* (1860) Johns.
[30] (1883) 8 App. Cas. 755 especially at 759. See also *R. v. Fay* (1878) 4 L.R. Ir. 606.
[31] *Peppin v. Cooper* (1819) 2 B. & Ald. 431.
[32] *cf. Bank of Ireland v. Beresford (1818) 6 Dow.* 233.
[33] *Ellesmere Brewery Co. v. Cooper* [1896] 1 Q.B. 75.
[34] *Ward v. National Bank of New Zealand* (1883) 8 App. Cas. 755 at 765; *Evans v. Bremridge* (1855) 2 K. & J. 174, 185; *Ellesmere Brewery Co. v. Cooper*, above. See also *James Graham & Co. (Timber) Ltd v. Southgate Sands* [1986] Q.B. 80.

discharges all.[35] The principle applies, moreover, if one surety is released after joint and several judgment against the two co-sureties.[36]

Release of persons analogous to co-sureties

Where several persons charge their properties by the deposit of **9–10** title deeds with the repayment of any sum due from a company to one guaranteeing its overdraft, and the title deeds of one depositor are subsequently released, all the others are absolutely discharged on the principle that the release affects the right to have all the properties marshalled so as to cause the debt to fall rateably.[37]

Express stipulation for another surety

Even where it does not appear from the form of the instrument **9–11** signed by a surety that others are to join also, the surety signing will be discharged if it was orally made a condition that another should join and he does not, or after joining is released.[38]

Express stipulation for security

Where again the surety expressly stipulates for a security the **9–12** taking or maintaining of it according to the stipulation is an essential condition of his liability.[39]

Conduct of creditor causing loss of security

A surety is not discharged absolutely by the loss of a security or **9–13** of a co-surety even if stipulated for by him unless that loss is brought about either by the wilful act of the creditor or by his

---

[35] *Nicholson v. Revill* (1836) 4 A. & E. 675; *Re E.W.A.* [1901] 2 K.B. 642; *Deanplan Ltd v. Mahmoud* [1993] Ch. 151. So judgment against one of two co-sureties bound jointly used to put an end to the right of action against the other; but not judgment on a cheque given by one for the joint debt. *Wegg & Prosser v. Evans* [1958] 1 Q.B. 103. But now see the Civil Liability (Contribution) Act 1978, s.3 which prevents judgment against one joint debtor releasing another joint debtor.

[36] *Re E.W.A.*, above. For criticism of this see Glanville Williams, *Joint Obligations* (1949) at pp. 117, 135–137.

[37] *Smith v. Wood* [1929] 1 Ch. 14. Lords Hanworth M.R. and Sankey L.J. treated the case as determined by authorities which established that the sureties released where the creditor has varied the principal obligations. *Cf.* the reasons given by Russell L.J. who also points out at p. 31 that the deed returned to the depositor had not been released from the charge but had been subjected to a prior charge of £600.

[38] *Leaf v. Gibbs* (1830) 4 C. & B. 466; *Traill v. Gibbons* (1861) 2 F. & F. 358; *Barry v. Moroney* (1873) 8 Ir. R.C.L. 554; Ex. Ch. reversing C.P. 7 Ir.R.C.L. 110. See also *Stirling v. Forrester* (1821) 3 Bligh 575; *Cooper v. Twynam* (1823) T. & R. 426 at 429; *Dallas v. Walls* (1873) 29 L.T. 599; *Ex p. Harding* (1879) 12 Ch D 557 at 564; *Ward v. National Bank of New Zealand* (1883) 8 App. Cas. 755 at 765.

[39] *Watson v. Alcock* (1853) 1 Sm. & G. 319; on appeal for De G.M. & G. 242. The security being under seal, this defence had failed at law. See *Parker v. Watson* (1853) 8 Exch. 404, *cf.* see also *Jephson v. Mounsell* (1847) 10 Ir. Eq. R. 38, 132.

neglect to take some step which the surety had stipulated he should take.[40]

Where the creditor, by neglecting to comply with the Ships Register Act, lost the benefit of the assignment of two ships recited in the surety bond, the surety was only discharged *pro tanto*.[41] Similarly where he neglected to give notice of an equitable assignment by way of security[42] to register a bill of sale[43] or to value a security in bankruptcy,[44] although in each case the security was part of the surety's contract. Where a surety joined in a contract for the execution of works which the creditor was to insure, the surety was discharged absolutely by his omission to insure.[45] Whenever the obtaining of a security for the liability of another as co-surety is an essential term of the surety's contract, of course the mere omission by the creditor to do so discharges the last named surety.[46]

Mere neglect may give rise to discharge pro tanto

9–14   Where the question is not of the absolute discharge of the surety, but merely of an allowance *pro tanto* in respect of the loss of a security or of a right to contribution, the distinction between a wilful act of abandonment and a mere negligent omission disappears. With regard to securities, whenever taken, the creditor is chargeable in relief of the surety with everything which, but for his wilful neglect or default he might have recovered by means of the security.[47] A typical illustration of the duty borne by the creditor with regard to securities granted in respect of the debt guaranteed is the duty to perfect such security: any neglect to register a security will generally discharge the surety *pro tanto*.

Where the surety by wilful negligence wasted goods upon which he had a bill of sale as security for the debt, so that they did not realise the full value, the surety was discharged to the extent of the waste.[48] So, also, if the creditor destroys the security by the exercise

---

[40] See generally *Polak v. Everett* (1876) 1 Q.B.D. 669 at 672; *Carter v. White* (1883) 25 Ch D 666 at 670; *Rainbow v. Juggins* (1880) 5 QBD. 138 at 142; *R. v. Fay* (1878) 4 L.R. Ir. 606; *Re Darwen and Pearce* [1927] 1 Ch. 176 at 187 and now see *China and South Seas Bank Ltd v. Tan* [1990] 1 A.C. 536.

[41] *Capel v. Butler* (1835) 2 S. & S. 457.

[42] *Strange v. Fooks* (1863) 4 Giff. 408. In Scotland, the negligence of a creditor in allowing a third party to obtain priority over the security was held to discharge the surety: *Fleming v. Thomson* (1826) 2 W. & S. 277 HL Sc.

[43] *Wulff v. Jay* (1872) L.R. 7 QB 756.

[44] *Rainbow v. Juggins* (1880) 5 QBD 138, 422.

[45] *Watts v. Shuttleworth* (1861) 5 H. & N. 235; 7 H. & N. 235.

[46] *Bonser v. Cox* (1841) 4 Beav. 379; *Coyte v. Elphick* (1874) 22 W.R. 541; *Evans v. Bremridge* (1855) 2 K. & J. 174 on appeal 8 De G. & G. 100; *Hansard v. Lethbridge* (1892) 8 T.L.R. 346.

[47] *Capel v. Butler* (1825) 2 S. & S. 457; *Strange v. Fooks* (1863) 4 Giff. 408; *Mutual Loan Fund v. Sudlow* (1858) 5 C.B. (N.S.) 449; *Wulff v. Jay* (1872) L.R. 7 QB 756; *Polak v. Everett* (1876) 1 QBD 669 at 675; *Rainbow v. Juggins* (1880) 5 QBD 138; *Taylor v. Bank of New South Wales* (1886) 11 App. Cas. 596.

[48] *Mutual Loan Fund v. Sudlow*, above, *cf. Margrett v. Gregory* (1862) 10 W.R. 630.

of a paramount right, *e.g.* by distraining for rent furniture mortgaged to secure the advance guaranteed by the surety, the latter is
entitled to a discharge *pro tanto*.[49] But giving a further advance on
the security does not discharge a surety, for his right is not interfered with,[50] nor will the fact that the creditor has allowed the
security for the principal debt to fall in value.[51]

Creditor's duty to surety

In general a creditor is only obliged to deal in a reasonable   **9–15**
manner with any security granted in respect of the guaranteed
debt.[52] Consequently mere inactivity in that respect will not discharge a surety; the obligation of the creditor is to ensure that the
realisation of the security achieves the maximum benefit.[53]

Although it has been held by the Court of Appeal that a creditor
may be regarded as owing a duty of care to sureties with regard to
the negligent realisation of such security,[54] it is suggested that the
true position is best characterised by the Privy Council in *China
and South Seas Bank Ltd v. Tan*.[55] Although a creditor owes no duty
to exercise any power of sale he may enjoy over the mortgaged
security, a surety will be discharged if the creditor commits an act
which is injurious to the interests of the surety or if the creditor acts
inconsistently with a surety's rights so as to discharge the surety *pro
tanto*, or, alternatively if the creditor is in breach of any obligation
express or implied towards the surety in which event the surety will
be absolutely discharged.[56] The Privy Council confirmed that there
was no room for implying a duty of care as distinct from the
applicability of well established equitable principles.[57]

It follows that as there exists no general duty to enforce securities, a creditor may choose the time and manner in which to
exercise his power of sale. Should the creditor elect not to do so the
surety retains the right to pay off the creditor and have the security
assigned to him in order to forestall any diminution in value.[58]

---

[49] *Pearl v. Deacon* (1857) 24 Beav. 116; De G. & J. 461.
[50] *York City and County Banking Co. v. Bainbridge* (1886) 43 L.T. 732.
[51] *China and South Seas Bank Ltd v. Tan* [1990] 1 A.C. 536.
[52] *Mutual Loan Fund v. Sudlow*, above; *China and South Seas Bank Ltd v. Tan*, above.
[53] *Gosling v. Gaskell* [1879] A.C. 575; *Cuckmere Brick Co. v. Mutual Finance Ltd* [1971] Ch. 949;
Gomba Holdings (UK) Ltd v. Homan [1986] B.C.L.C. 331. See also *Downsview Nominees Ltd v. First
City Corporation Ltd* [1993] B.C.C. 46.
[54] *Standard Chartered v. Walker* [1982] 1 W.L.R. 1410 disapproving *Barclays Bank Ltd v. Thienel*
(1978) 247 E.G. 385. The *Standard Chartered* decision has been applied in *American Express
International Banking Corporation v. Hurely* [1986] 3 All E.R. 564; *Gomba Holdings (UK) Ltd v.
Homan*, above; *Shamji v. Johnson Matthey Bankers Ltd* [1986] B.C.L.C. 278 especially at 283;
National Bank of Greece SA v. Pinos Shipping Co. (The "Maria") (No.3) P [1988] 2 Lloyd's Rep.
126.
[55] [1990] A.C. 536.
[56] The Privy Council expressly approved the reasoning in the earlier decisions of *Wulff v. Jay*
(1872) 7 Lr. 7 QB 756 and *Watts v. Shuttleworth* (1860) 5 H. & N. 235.
[57] See also *Barclays Bank v. Quincecare* [1988] F.L.R. 166 and *Palk v. Mortgage Services Funding
plc* [1993] Ch. 330.
[58] *China and South Seas Bank Ltd v. Tan*, above *per* Lord Templeman at p. 545.

Loss of security only avails surety by act or omission of creditor

9–16   The loss of a security must, if it is to relieve the security to any extent be due to some act or omission of the creditor. As stated in the previous section the creditor is not bound to preserve securities at his peril. Thus in *Wheatley v. Bastow*[59] a solicitor by the unauthorised use of the names of the parties in the case got hold of a fund in court over which the creditor had a security. It was held that the surety was not discharged, just as if a pledge had been stolen. Similarly, where a creditor surrenders to the trustees in bankruptcy of the principal debtor securities which he could not have successfully retained, the surety was not relieved.[60]

Where debt is assigned

9–17   A surety is not discharged if the debt and guarantee are assigned and he receives no notice of the assignment, nor if the creditor assigns the debt and no notice of assignment is given by the assignee either to the surety or to perfect the assignee's title to a security.[61] In such a case the assignor remains the only creditor known to the parties, and if any payment is made upon the security or by the surety to the original creditor, the assignee is bound by it, and no harm can be suffered by the surety.

Sale of part of security in due course of management

9–18   A sale by a mortgagor, with the consent of the mortgagee, of some livestock mortgaged with a run of 4,000 acres, the mortgagor being in possession, and the sale being in the due course of management, does not affect the liability of a surety for the mortgagor who became bound on the failure of the mortgage.[62]

Relief by discharge of co-surety to extent of contribution

9–19   The relief to which a surety is entitled where the creditor releases a co-surety is (putting aside the special cases where he is thereby discharged absolutely upon principles already discussed) limited to the extent of the contribution he could have claimed from the surety released.[63] Since the surety has no right to contribution until he has

---

[59] (1855) 7 De G.M. & G. 261.

[60] *Hardwick v. Wright* (1865) 35 Beav. 133. Contrast the voluntary surrender of a security to the debtor himself: *Rose v. Aftenberger* [1970] 1 Q.R. 546.

[61] *Wheatley v. Bastow*, above; *Bradford Old Bank v. Sutcliffe* [1918] 2 K.B. 833. It is however suggested that a novation will discharge a surety: see *Commercial Bank of Tasmania v. Jones* [1893] A.C. 313.

[62] *Taylor v. Bank of New South Wales* (1886) 11 App. Cas. 596. In Australia it has been held that the mere fact of sale of property comprised in a bill of sale given by the principal as security for a loan does not operate to discharge the guarantor of the loan: *Tooth & Co. Ltd v. Lapin* (1936) 53 W.N. (N.S.W.) 224.

[63] *Ex p. Gifford* (1802) 6 Ves. 805; *Ward v. National Bank of New Zealand* (1883) 8 App. Cas. 755; *Re Wolmershausen* (1890) 62 L.T. 541; *Stirling v. Forrester* (1821) Bligh. 575.

paid more than his share,[64] he remains liable to the extent of that share despite the release of a co-surety.[65] Where two independent sureties each guarantee a floating account to the extent of a certain sum, the release of one will not relieve the other at all if the balance owing is more than the aggregate amount of the two guarantees.[66]

If a surety guaranteeing a particular part of the debt is released, that does not relieve in any respect a surety engaged for a different part.[67]

Release of a surety after payment by another

If a surety has already paid more than his share before the **9–20** co-surety is released, he will not apparently be entitled to a return of the excess, for his right to contribution is vested and not interfered with.[68]

Application of payments by principal where one surety has been released

If one of two sureties is discharged without any reservation of **9–21** rights against the other, the creditor is, it seems, to be treated as having taken upon himself the position of the surety discharged.[69] On this basis the creditor should give and possibly receive, as the discharged surety would have done, credit for the proper proportion of any payment made by the principal in relief of the guarantors. The sum borne by the surety not discharged is therefore (where each surety is liable for half the total debt) half the debt left after the payments by the principal.[70] This was the order in *Stirling v. Forrester.*[71] But any payments made by the surety discharged may be applied by the creditor in discharge of that share of the liability which the surety discharged would have borne and as to which the other surety's relief. This is involved in the decision in *Ex p. Gifford*[72] where the surety undischarged unsuccessfully contended that though he had not paid more than his share, he was entitled to a proportion of the composition paid by the other.

---

[64] See above in chapter entitled "Rights of Surety" when a right to contribution arises.
[65] *Ex p. Gifford*, above; *Ward v. National Bank of New Zealand*, above.
[66] *Ward v. National Bank of New Zealand*, above at 766; see also *Wolmershausen v. Wolmershausen* (1890) 62 L.T. 541.
[67] See *Coope v. Twynam* (1823) 1 T. & R. 425; *Pendlebury v. Walker* (1841) 4 Y. & C. Ex. 424; and see *Stirling v. Forrester* (1831) 3 Bligh. 575 *per* Lord Eldon at 592.
[68] See *Reade v. Lowndes* (1857) 23 Beav. 361 at 367 and 368.
[69] See *per* Lord Redesdale in *Stirling v. Forrester*, above at 590.
[70] See above in Chap. 7, in section entitled "Surety holding security or receiving payment from principal debtor", at para. 7–60.
[71] (1821) 3 Bligh. 575.
[72] (1802) 6 Ves. 805.

Where remedy of creditor against surety is statute barred

9–22   There is no reason for suggesting that the liability of a surety is affected by the circumstance that time has run under the Statute of Limitation in favour of a co-surety.[73] The latter will doubtless remain open to the demand of the former for contribution,[74] although as against the demand of the creditor he has a defence.

Giving time to co-sureties

9–23   It has never been suggested that a surety is discharged by time being given to a co-surety. The doctrine which prevails where time is given to the principal seems wholly inapplicable. At the same time it would seem an injustice if a creditor after bargaining to give time to a surety were to be allowed while that time is running to sue another surety for more than his share or even to accept it from him and so turn him for contribution upon the surety to whom time has been given.[75]

And if this is so, and the former surety could prove that he has been indemnified by the delay (as for instance by the other surety in the meantime becoming insolvent) it is possible that he ought to be allowed the amount of this damage. But the point seems never to have arisen.[76]

Discharge of surety with reservation of rights against others

9–24   A discharge of a surety with a reservation of the creditor's rights against co-sureties operates to preserve intact the right of the latter, when sued, to have contribution from the first surety, notwithstanding the so-called "discharge".[77] And it was pointed out by Lord Eldon in *Ex p. Gifford*[78] that a discharge on these terms is a much more real advantage to a co-surety than to a principal debtor; the principal will, notwithstanding his discharge, be had recourse to as soon as any surety is made to pay anything; but a co-surety who has obtained such a qualified discharge is safe until some other surety pays more than his share. However, when a creditor surrenders his right of proof in the bankruptcy of a surety, reserving his rights against another surety, the latter will be entitled to an allowance to

---

[73] See as to the effect of time running in favour of the principal; see below at Chap. 10.

[74] See generally *Wolmershausen v. Gullick* [1893] 2 Ch. 514.

[75] See above Chap. 8: Release of surety: section entitled "Giving time in respect of one several debts" at para. 8–12.

[76] But see *Clarke v. Birley* (1889) 41 Ch D 422 suggesting that the guarantor is not released by the creditor promising a co-surety that time will be given to the principal debtor.

[77] It requires clear words to reserve against the co-sureties: the release of one surety with a reservation against sureties and persons liable to pay the released party's debts proved ineffective in *Liverpool Corn Trade Association v. Hurst* [1936] 2 All E.R. 309 since on a literal reading the co-sureties did not come within those categories.

[78] (1802) 5 Ves. 805. See also *Commercial Bank of Australia v. Official Assignee* [1893] A.C. 181.

the extent of the sum by which he would have been relieved had the creditor's right of proof been exercised.[79] A release of a co-surety with a reservation of a right to sue another co-surety, such right to be exercised for the benefit of the co-surety released, is equivalent to an absolute release.[80]

Where surety entitled to relief express promises to pay

If a surety entitled to equitable relief owing to the release of a co-surety or a security afterwards expressly promises to pay notwithstanding, this promise would appear to be binding and not open to objection as being without consideration.[81]   **9–25**

---

[79] *Re Wolmershausen* (1890) 62 L.T. 541.
[80] *Hallet v. Taylor* (1921) 6 Lloyd's L.R. 417.
[81] *Mayhew v. Crickett* (1818) 2 Swanst. 185.

CHAPTER 10

STATUTES OF LIMITATION

1. *As to Claims Against a Surety*

When time begins to run

10–01 Time begins to run under the Statutes of Limitation[1] in favour of a surety from the date of the accrual of the cause of action; that is to say from the date on which the surety may have been sued.[2] Where there are successive breaches, the time runs anew in respect of each breach, from the time when it occurred, so that the remedy against the surety may be barred in respect of earlier breaches, but remain available as to later ones. And this will apply even in the case of a bond.

Where a surety is only liable to pay after demand,[3] time does not begin to run till after it has been made.[4] Once a demand has been made and the limitation period has begun, the creditor cannot restart it by making a fresh demand for a larger sum which includes the sum originally demanded.[5]

In *Wright v. New Zealand Farmers Co-operative Association of Canterbury Ltd*[6] the Privy Council held that under the guarantees there involved, the repayment of every debit balance was guaranteed as it was constituted from time to time by the excess of total

---

[1] The Limitation Acts 1939 to 1980. The relevant rules are: actions founded on simple contract cannot be brought after six years following accrual of the cause of action (s.5 of the 1980 Act); where a loan is made which contains no specific date for repayment and does not effectively make the obligation to repay conditional on demand or the occurrence of some other event, time will only begin to run under s.5 when the creditor makes a demand in writing for repayment (s.6) except that where a debtor enters into a "collateral obligation" to pay the amount of the debt (*e.g.* a promissory note as security, but not, it is submitted, a guarantee) either on or before a fixed or determinable date, or effectively on demand, time will run against the creditor from the date of making the loan (s.6(2)); actions upon a specialty (*i.e.* contract or other obligation contained in a document under seal) cannot be brought after 12 years from the accrual of the cause of action (s.8); the limitation period for claiming contribution under the Civil Liability (Contribution) Act 1978 is two years (s.10); and the general period of limitation relating to mortgages or other charges on property (whether real or personal) is 12 years (s.20). The Law Commission's Consultation Paper No. 151 (January 6, 1998) suggests a reform of the periods so as to provide for a unified limitation period of 3 years from the date the plaintiff discovers or ought to discover that he has a legal claim, subject to a 10-year long stop period from the relevant act or omission (30 years for personal injury).
[2] *Colvin v. Buckle* (1841) 8 M. & W. 680; *Holl v. Hadley* (1835) 2 A. & E. 758.
[3] See above.
[4] *Hartland v. Jukes* (1863) 1 H. & C. 667; *Re Brown* [1893] 2 Ch. 300; *Romain v. Scuba T.V. Ltd* [1996] 3 W.L.R. 117 at 123E.
[5] *ANZ v. Douyglas Morris Investments Pty Ltd* [1992] 1 Qd.R. 478.
[6] [1939] A.C. 439. The Privy Council expressed no views on the correctness of *Parr's Banking Co. v. Yates* [1898] 2 QB 460 which had suggested that in the case of a continuing guarantee, a cause of action arises as at the date of each advance, *sed quaere*. Cf. *Hartland v. Jukes*, above, not cited in *Parr's* case.

debits over total credits, and therefore the time which had expired since any individual debt was incurred was immaterial, and the period of limitation could run only from the time at which the balance guaranteed and sued for had been constituted.

Where a guarantee is given in consideration of forbearance to sue the debtor, time commences to run not later than when the time of forbearance expires; and this if not defined will be a reasonable time.[7] Where the surety is not to be liable till after measures taken against the debtor, a reasonable time for taking these measures must elapse before time begins to run against the surety.[8] When the surety was to become liable in the event of pending transactions with the principal showing a certain result, time was held to run as soon as all the facts were ascertained on which an adjustment could have been made; notwithstanding that, owing to disputes and litigation, no such adjustment had been made until long afterwards.[9]

Application of legacy by creditor to surety to statute-barred liability

The executors of the creditor are entitled to apply in payment of the debt a legacy left to the surety by their testator, even though an action to recover the debt would be statute-barred.[10] **10–02**

Interest

Interest expressly guaranteed is recoverable, if it has accrued within six years, though the principal money is statute-barred.[11] **10–03**

Surety for mortgage debt

The obligation of a surety for a mortgage debt who gives a separate bond is not statute-barred until after the lapse of 12 years.[12] Whether this is also the case where the surety joins in the covenant in a mortgage deed is not definitely settled. The question arose, but was not finally dealt with in *Re Frisby*.[13] **10–04**

Where principal alone protected by statute

A surety, whose liability is not itself barred by any statute of limitation, remains liable, notwithstanding that the remedy against **10–05**

---

[7] See *Henton v. Paddison* (1893) 68 L.T. 405.
[8] *Holl v. Hadley* (1835) 2 A. & E. 758.
[9] *Colvin v. Buckle* (1841) 8 M. & W. 680.
[10] *Coates v. Coates* (1864) 33 Beav. 249.
[11] *Parr's Banking Co. v. Yates* [1898] 2 QB 460; *Wright v. New Zealand Farmers Co-operative Association of Canterbury Ltd* [1939] A.C. 439; Limitation Act 1980, s.29(6). See also *Commercial Bank of Australia Ltd v. Colonial Finance* (1906) 4 C.L.R. 57 at 69.
[12] Limitation Act 1980, s.20. Formerly the limitation period prescribed by the Real Property Limitation Act 1874, s.8 was 20 years. *Re Powers* (1885) 30 Ch D 291. *Cf. Re Wolmershausen* (1890) 62 L.T. 541; *Barnes v. Glenton* [1899] 1 QB 885.
[13] (1889) 43 Ch D 106. See also *Barnes v. Glenton*, above. *Cf. Colonial Investment & Loan Co. v. Martin* [1928] 3 D.L.R. 784.

the principal may be barred.[14] Thus, where securities were deposited to secure payment of bills, and the bills became statute-barred, the charge remained.[15]

Effect of payment or acknowledgment by principal

10–06　　The effect upon the running of time under the Statutes of Limitation in favour of a surety of a payment or acknowledgment by the principal must be considered to some extent with reference to the statutory provision which, in the particular case, applies to the liability of the surety.

Surety by simple contract

10–07　　In the Limitation Act 1623, which formerly applied to sureties liable by simple contract, there was no provision making time run afresh after a payment or acknowledgment; and the doctrine that a payment or acknowledgment interrupts the running of the Act rested upon the theory that it was evidence of a new promise to pay. Therefore a payment or acknowledgment by one person, unless the circumstances were such that it must have been regarded as payment for another, could not keep alive the remedy against that other. There appeared to be nothing in the relation of principal and surety itself which made payment or acknowledgment by the principal binding as a payment or acknowledgment by the surety.[16] Before Lord Tenterden's Act,[17] either a payment or any other acknowledgment by a principal liable jointly with the surety, or jointly and severally, would have prevented time running in favour of the surety, on the principle that a payment or acknowledgment by one joint debtor was a payment or acknowledgment by all.[18] This was altered as regards an acknowledgment by Lord Tenterden's Act, and as regards a payment by the Mercantile Law Amendment Act 1856. By section 14 of the latter Act it was provided that no co-debtor should lose the benefit of the Statutes by reason only of payment by any principal, interest or other money by another

---

[14] *Carter v. White* (1884) 25 Ch D 666. But *cf. Re Powers* (1885) 30 Ch D 291 at 295, 297. This question is considered by the British Columbia Law Reform Commission Report on Consumer Guarantees (1979) where it is recommended that a guarantor should be able to rely on the principal debtor's defence. *Semble* such may already be the position in British Columbia itself. See British Columbia Limitations Act S.B.C. 1975 (c.37), s.9(1).

[15] *Carter v. White*, above. See also *Manning v. Phelps* (1854) 10 Exch. 59. *Cf. Re Powers*, above, where Cotton L.J. at 295 seems to imply that a bond conditioned for the payment of a mortgage debt would only remain enforceable so long as the rights of the mortgagee are not barred by the Statute of Limitations. See also *Re Frisby* (1890) 43 Ch D 106. Therefore payment by the principal debtor will interrupt the running of the limitation period on the contract of guarantee, *cf. Re Thomson* [1927] 2 D.L.R. 254.

[16] See *Re Wolmershausen* (1890) 62 L.T. 541; *Henton v. Paddison* (1893) 68 L.T. 405.

[17] Statute of Frauds Amendment Act 1828. See Appendix 2.

[18] *Whitcomb v. Whiting* (1781) 2 Dougl. 652.

co-debtor. And in *Cockrill v. Sparkes*,[19] it was held that payment of a composition by a principal debtor to the creditor with the assent of the surety, such assent being given with a view only of preventing the surety being discharged by the acceptance of the composition, and not amounting to any acknowledgment by the surety, was a "payment only" within this section, and that the remedy against the surety was statute-barred.

Now the effect of these provisions as reproduced in sections 29(5), 29(6) and 31 of the Limitation Act 1980 is to make time run afresh in the case of an acknowledgment of debt and not to create a fresh cause of action.[20] Subject to pay payments of interest being treated as payments in respect of the principal debt,[21] after the limitation period is extinguished, any acknowledgment or payment subsequently made will not create a fresh cause of action.[22] Section 31 of the 1980 Act applies the provisions of section 29 to persons other than the acknowledgor or maker of the part payment in particular cases. Subsections 31(6) and (7) provide respectively that an acknowledgment of a debt shall bind the acknowledgor and his "successors" but not other persons[23] and that a payment made in respect of any debt shall bind all persons liable in respect of the debt or claim. Therefore part payment of a debt by the principal debtor will cause a re-accrual of the limitation period against the surety[24] and payment of interest by a surety will make time run against the principal debtor.[25]

Surety by mortgage

The period of limitation for actions to recover moneys secured by a mortgage or charge to recover proceeds of the sale of land is in general 12 years,[26] which is the period also applicable to specialties.[27] A period is reckoned from the date when the right to receive the money accrued.[28] **10–08**

If in a mortgage deed the mortgagor and surety jointly and severally covenant for repayment of the mortgage debt, the above

---

[19] (1863) 1 H. & C. 699; *Re Powers* (1885) 30 Ch D 291 at 295; *Re Wolmershausen* (1890) 62 L.T. 541; *Bradford Old Bank v. Sutcliffe* [1918] 2 K.B. 833 at 839, 848. And *cf. Henton v. Paddison* (1893) 68 L.T. 405.

[20] *Bush v. Stevens* [1963] 1 QB 1. Note, too, s.30 of the Act providing for the formalities regarding acknowledgments and part payments and dealing with questions of agency. See *Wright v. Pepin* [1954] 1 W.L.R. 635.

[21] s.29(6).

[22] s.29(7).

[23] "Successor" is defined in s.31(9) for present purposes as a person on whom the liability in respect of the debt or claim may "devolve" whether on death or bankruptcy or disposition of property and would not therefore appear to include a surety.

[24] See *Re Powers* (1885) 30 Ch D 291.

[25] See *Re Seager's Estate* (1857) 26 L.J. Ch. App. 809.

[26] Limitation Act 1980, s.20.

[27] Limitation Act 1980, s.8. For a review of the law prior to the Limitation Act 1939 see the third edition of this work at pp. 301–305.

[28] Limitation Act 1980, s.20(1)–(4)..

provisions will not apparently apply to an action against the surety.[29]

As has been seen, under the Limitation Acts 1939 to 1980 the period of limitation is postponed where the proper person either makes a payment in respect of a debt, or acknowledges the claim.[30] And in neither case will the part payment be treated as a fresh promise to pay.[31]

Effect of payment or acknowledgment by co-surety

10–09   The effect of part payment or acknowledgment by a co-surety upon the running of the statute in favour of a surety will apparently be the same as—at least it cannot be greater than—the effect of part payments or acknowledgments by the principal.

2. *As to Claims by the Surety Against the Principal*

When time begins to run

10–10   A surety has ordinarily six years from the time when payment was made by him in which to sue the principal, there being before payment no breach of the contract of indemnity.[32] Thus the right over of an accommodation acceptor against the drawer is not barred till six years from payment by him of the bill.[33] But time begins to run against an indorser, whose remedy is upon the bill, in favour of the drawer, as soon as the bill is dishonoured.[34] If a principal expressly covenants with a surety, not only to indemnify him, but positively to pay the debt at the due date, there is a breach if the debt is not paid as soon as the due date is reached, and the statute begins to run from that moment.[35]

---

[29] *Re Frisby* (1889) 43 Ch D 106; *Re Powers* (1885) 30 Ch D 291. See also *Re Wolmershausen* (1890) 62 L.T. 541 at 544 *per* Stirling J. At p. 303 of the third edition it was pointed out that there exists a distinction between those cases where, by virtue of one bond or covenant, several persons claiming under the obligor or covenantor, or their property, are all liable to the debt (see, *e.g. Roddam v. Morley* (1857) 1 De G. & J. 1; *Dibb v. Walker* [1893] 2 Ch. 429; *Barclay v. Owen* (1889) 60 L.T. 220) and the case of a surety by several bond or covenant, where there are in effect two debtors. See *Re Powers* (1885) 30 Ch D 291 at 295 *per* Cotton L.J. Nor does the case of a bond or covenant for payment of money by another appear to be affected by the considerations applicable where a mortgage is given by a surety, and is expressed to be redeemable on payment by the principal and the latter makes payments on account of the mortgage money or interest, which payments will keep the mortgage alive. See *Lewin v. Wilson* (1886) 11 App. Cas. 639. Further where a surety has given a mortgage of his property expressed to be redeemable upon payment by the principal, payments by the latter will keep alive the remedy of the creditor against the land under s.31(2) of the Limitation Act 1980. But note that s.31(2) makes no reference to acknowledgments.
[30] Limitation Act 1980, s.29(5) and (7). See text in preceding section.
[31] *ibid. Re Powers* (1885) 30 Ch D 291; *Re Frisby* (1889) 43 Ch D 106.
[32] *Considine v. Considine* (1846) 9 Ir. L.R. 400; *Angrove v. Tippett* (1865) 11 L.T. 708. If a surety satisfies a debt which has become statute-barred as against him, he cannot recover the money from the principal: *Re Morris* [1922] 1 I.R. 81 and 136.
[33] *Angrove v. Tippett*, above.
[34] *Webster v. Kirk* (1852) 17 QB 944.
[35] *Carr v. Roberts* (1833) 5 B. & Ad. 78.

Time runs separately in respect of each payment by surety

A right of action against the principal accrues to a surety *toties* **10–11**
quoties for every amount he pays under the guarantee and he can
therefore only recover from the principal such payments as have
been made within six years before action.[36]

It follows from what has already been said that the principal may
remain liable at the suit of the surety after he has obtained a defence
founded on the statute against the creditor, and this apparently even
though the creditor does not sue the surety till after the principal
debt is barred.[37]

3. *As to Claim by a Surety Against a Co-surety*

When time begins to run

The right of a surety to recover contribution from a co-surety **10–12**
does not stand upon quite the same footing as his right to recover
over against the principal. No claim for contribution accrues till a
surety has paid more than his share of what is unpaid by the
debtor,[38] or perhaps, if his estate is being administered by the court,
from the time that his liability is ascertained.[39] As soon as the
surety has paid his share he can sue his co-sureties *toties quoties* for
every further payment made by him.[40]

If a surety more than six years before action has paid a portion of
the debt not exceeding his share, and the principal has paid the residue within six years, the limitation period will not run from the
payment by the surety but from the payment of the residue by the
principal, if until the latter date the surety has not paid more than
his share.[41]

In an action for contribution, there can be recovered not half
what the plaintiff has paid within six years, but the whole amount,
whenever paid, that has been paid by the plaintiff in excess of his
share, provided that nothing be recovered in respect of what has
been in excess for more than six years.

Where claim by creditor against co-surety is statute-barred

The right of a surety to contribution from a co-surety is appar- **10–13**
ently not affected by the circumstance that at the time of his suing
for contribution, the right of the creditor to recover from the

---

[36] *Davies v. Humphreys* (1840) 6 M. & W. 153 at 167.
[37] See *Wolmershausen v. Gullick* [1893] 2 Ch. 514.
[38] *Ex p. Gifford* (1802) 6 Ves. 805; *Ex p. Snowdon* (1881) 17 Ch D 44; *Gardner v. Brooke* (1897)
2 I.R. 6. Note the provisions of Limitation Act 1980, s.10 providing a two-year limitation period in
respect of the right to recover contribution under s.1 of the Civil Liability (Contribution) Act
1978.
[39] See *Wolmershausen v. Gullick* [1893] 2 Ch. 514; *Robinson v. Harkin* [1896] 2 Ch. 415.
[40] *Davies v. Humphreys* (1840) 6 M. & W. 153 at 169.
[41] *Davies v. Humphreys*, above.

co-surety is statute-barred,[42] nor even that such right was so barred when the creditor sued the surety who seeks contribution, inasmuch as this would not seemingly affect the liability of the last-named surety. It may be open to question, however, whether where the sureties are bound by separate instruments, and the right to contribution rests entirely on their common though independent liability,[43] one of them paying at a time when the other had become protected by the statute, would be entitled to contribution. At any rate, it would hardly seem reasonable that there should be contribution if the surety paying had (as might happen) only become surety after the other had obtained the protection of the Limitation Acts.

Whether statute can ever run against surety before payment

10–14   It is submitted that the existence of a right in the surety before payment to take equitable proceedings to compel the principal or a co-surety to pay, as the case may be, the whole or the proper proportion of the debt, can have no affect on the time when the statute begins to run against him. The statute would seem to have no direct application to a claim in that form; and if the surety pays and immediately afterwards sues principal or co-surety for money paid, it is hard to see how a defence founded on the statute could be supported by evidence that more than six years before proceedings might have been taken *quia timet* in equity. Where, however, a surety before payment sued a co-surety who resisted the claim on the ground that as against him the creditor's claim was statute-barred, Wright J. said that even if the statute could begin to run against the plaintiff before payment, at any rate it did not run till the plaintiff's liability, which had been disputed, was ascertained.[44]

---

[42] See *Wolmershausen v. Gullick* [1893] 2 Ch. 514.
[43] See above.
[44] See *Wolmershausen v. Gullick* [1893] 2 Ch. 514.

CHAPTER 11

BANKRUPTCY

1. *Rights of Creditor in Bankruptcy of Principal*

Rule against double proof

This rule represents the most important aspect of a principal debt-   **11–01**
or's insolvency in that it addresses a situation in which both the
creditor and the surety seek to prove in the same insolvency. The
rule against double proof for what is in effect the same debt is in
substance a rule against the receipt of two dividends.[1]

Although the liability of a surety is co-extensive with that of the
principal debtor,[2] the surety's claim remains contingent until he has
paid the debt at which time his right to recover an indemnity from
the principal debtor will arise. The real effect of the rule against
double proof is therefore to insulate the principal's estate from a
claim by the surety at least so long as the surety has not discharged
the whole of the guaranteed debt.[3]

If on the other hand the surety pays the whole of the principal
debt, he will be subrogated to the creditor's proof. Should the
creditor already have submitted a proof the creditor will then
become a trustee for the surety in respect of any dividends that he
as creditor should receive from the principal's estate.[4]

If a surety pays only part of the guaranteed debt, the position
depends upon whether the guarantee is in respect of the whole or
only part of the debt.[5] If a guarantor pays that part which he has
guaranteed, he is entitled to lodge a proof in respect of the amount
that he has paid.[6]

In accordance with the general principles set out above, he
becomes subrogated to the creditor's right to prove for that part. In
such circumstances there can be no breach of the rule against

---

[1] See *Re Oriental Commercial Bank* (1871) L.R. 7 Ch. 99; *Re Moss, ex p. Hallett* [1905] 2 K.B.;
Re Fenton [1931] 1 Ch. 85; *Barclays Bank Ltd v. TOSG Trust Fund Ltd* [1984] A.C. 626 (Court of
Appeal judgment at 630).
[2] See generally above.
[3] *Re Fenton* [1931] 1 Ch. 75, especially at 118–120; *Barclays Bank Ltd v. TOSG Trust Fund Ltd*
[1984] A.C. 626, CA.
[4] *Ex p. Rushforth* (1805) 10 Ves. 409 at 414; *Re Sass* [1896] 2 QB 12 at 15.
[5] See above. The typical instance of a guarantee for a fluctuating balance with a limit upon liability
will be treated for these purposes as a guarantee of only part of the debt. See generally *Barclays Bank
Ltd v. TOSG Trust Fund Ltd* [1984] A.C. 626, CA, especially at 644.
[6] *Re Sass* [1896] 2 QB 12 and 15.

209

double proof. If the creditor has already lodged a proof for the full amount of his claim, he should either reduce it to reflect the amount satisfied by the surety or if he is already in receipt of dividends, hold the appropriate amount on trust for the surety.[7]

11–02   If on the other hand, the surety has paid to the extent of his liability, he cannot prove in competition with the creditor, as long as any amount remains unrecovered by the creditor: in such circumstances the creditor can prove for the whole debt.[8]

There seems to be no distinction for these purposes between cases in which the creditor seeks to recover first merely any unpaid balance from the guarantor and those in which he claims the entire amount against the surety: the abiding guideline is that the creditor cannot finally recover more than 100 pence in the pound in respect of the principal debt. The position is nowadays somewhat academic since most modern guarantees will expressly curtail the ability of the surety to prove or to recover any dividends from the principal debtor's estate until the creditor has recovered all outstanding liabilities in full.

If the guarantee on its proper construction is a guarantee of the whole debt rather than a guarantee of only part of the debt, the question arises whether the creditor can prove in the bankruptcy of the principal for the full extent of the debt even though a surety may have made payments in discharge of the principal's liability prior to the bankruptcy of the principal. The view that he can is indorsed by the Northern Irish decision of *Ulster Bank Ltd v. Lambe*.[9]

There is also a question whether any recoveries made by the creditor from the principal debtor (including realisations of security) following the principal's bankruptcy, but before proof, will reduce the amount of the creditor's proof, subject to the qualification already made that the creditor cannot recover more than 100 pence in the pound so that any surplus is held on trust for the surety.[10]

There is some debate concerning the moment at which the rule against double proof applies, *i.e.* at the time of the lodging of this proof by the creditor[11] or at the time that a dividend is paid to the creditor.[12]

---

[7] For a good illustration of these principles see *Westpac Banking Corp. v. Gollin & Co. Ltd* [1988] V.R. 397.

[8] *Barclays Bank Ltd v. TOSG Trust Fund Ltd* [1984] A.C. 626, CA.

[9] [1966] N.I. 161. This decision was followed in *Westpac Banking Corp. v. Gollin & Co. Ltd* [1988] V.R. 397. The older authority of *MacKinnon's Trustee v. Bank of Scotland* [1915] S.C. 411 is to the contrary. The fourth edition of this work at p. 199 was also to the opposite effect, relying on cases dealing with bills of exchange. Those cases were distinguished as being restricted to bills in *Re Houlder* [1928] 1 Ch. 212, although no good rationale for the distinction has been suggested. See also *Re Suss* [1896] 2 Q.B. 12. It may still be arguable that the principle which requires deduction, set out in the fourth edition, is correct and is not limited to bills: see *Ex p. Taylor* (1857) 1 De G. & J. 302, CA, where the principle is described as a general rule in bankruptcy.

[10] See references in n. 9.

[11] So that a surety has not paid in full prior to that moment will be excluded. This view finds expression in *Re Fenton* [1931] 1 Ch. 85 at 118 and was indirectly advanced albeit without this authority then existing in the fourth edition of this work at p. 202.

[12] As stated above, the better view is that the rule against double proof is a rule against the receipt of a double dividend.

It is suggested that the latter view is preferable being supported **11–03**
by at least one modern decision at the Court of Appeal.[13] A potent
reason for adopting this view is that it has regard to the procedural
nature of the lodging of a proof.[14,15]

The creditor who holds a guarantee is not a "secured creditor"

The rules as to valuing and surrendering securities held by the **11–04**
creditor do not apply to a guarantee or to a charge on the property
of a third person.[16] It makes no difference to this that the surety has
a security on the principal's estate.[17]

If the principal has pledged to the creditor bills on which third
parties remain liable to the principal, reserving to himself the right
to redeem them, this is a security upon the principal's property
which must be valued or surrendered.[18]

However, bills endorsed and transferred to the creditor need not
be valued or surrendered,[19] unless it can be shown that despite the
endorsement, the transaction was intended to be merely a
deposit.[20]

The creditor need never value bills in his hands accepted for the
principal's accommodation, since provision of such bills is not a
security on any property of the principal. The principal has none of
the bills and the acceptor is merely a surety.[21]

Subsequent bankruptcy of the principal who has entered into a composition guaranteed by sureties

Where the principal defaults in the terms of a composition and **11–05**
becomes bankrupt, the creditor can prove for the full amount of the
debt allowing for anything received from the principal or the surety
under the composition.[22] The creditor is not confined to the amount
unpaid in the composition, even though a surety for an instalment
may have paid and may not be entitled to recover the payment.[23]

---

[13] *Barclays Bank Ltd v. TOSG Trust Fund Ltd* [1984] A.C. 626, CA, at 638.
[14] The history of the procedure is set out in *Re Amalgamated Investment and Property Co Ltd*
[1985] 1 Ch. 349.
[15] [1996] A.C. 243. See also *MS Fashions Ltd v. BCCI SA* [1993] Ch. 425.
[16] *Ex p. Parr* (1811) 1 Rose 76; *Ex p. Goodman* (1818) 3 Madd. 373; *Ex p. Biddulph* (1849) 3 De
G. & S. 587; *Ex p. Shepherd* (1841) 2 M.D. & De G. 204.
[17] *Midland Bank & Co. v. Chambers* (1869) L.R. 7 Eq. 179; 4 Ch. App. 398, *cf. Re Melton* [1918]
1 Ch. 37.
[18] *Ex p. Rushforth* (1805) 10 Ves. at 419; *Ex p. Toogood* (1812) 19 Ves. 32; *Ex p. Britten* (1833)
3 D. & Ch. 35; *Ex p. Schofield* (1879) 12 Ch D 337.
[19] *Ex p. Schofield*, above.
[20] See n.17 above.
[21] *Ex p. Schofield*, above.
[22] *Ex p. Gilbey* (1878) 8 Ch D 248.
[23] *ibid.*

The rule in Ex p. Waring[24]

11–06   Property which is in a bankrupt's possession for a specific purpose is not normally available for division among the creditors. Thus where the principal and the surety are both bankrupt[25] and the principal has deposited with the surety security in respect of the debt, a creditor of the principal is entitled to have the security applied in the discharge of the principal's debt.[26]

This is not because the creditor has any lien or equity but in order to work out the equities between the two insolvent estates. The security having been realised for the creditor's benefit, he is then entitled to prove in the surety's bankruptcy for the balance of the debt.

The so-called rule in *Ex p. Waring*[27] is drawn from the realm of negotiable instruments. If a drawer of a negotiable instrument deposits a fund with the acceptor in order to satisfy the drawer's liability to the holder, the latter is entitled in the event of the insolvency of each of the acceptor and the drawer to apply that fund in satisfaction of the holder's claim. It will not be available for the creditors of the acceptor generally. As explained above, the same principles apply to ordinary guarantees.[28]

An alternative solution has been found in Scotland where the creditor is restricted to proving in the surety's bankruptcy and the surety's estate can indemnify itself out of the security in respect of the dividends paid to the creditor.[29]

Where the principal and the surety are both bankrupt

11–07   In a case in which both the principal and the surety are bankrupt, the creditor can prove against each for the full amount owing at the date of the proof and can take and keep dividends limited to a total of 100 pence in the pound.[30]

A creditor who is owed a number of debts guaranteed by different sureties is limited to keeping 100 pence in the pound in respect of each debt. He cannot attempt to accumulate dividends beyond that limit in order to achieve 100 pence in the pound on the aggregate indebtedness.[31]

If a creditor obtains more than 100 pence in the pound he will hold the excess on trust for any guarantor who pays.[32]

---

[24] (1815) 19 Ves. 345.
[25] See below at 11–07.
[26] (1815) 19 Ves. 345.
[27] *ibid.*
[28] See in particular *Ex p. Dever (No. 2)* (1885) 14 QBD 611.
[29] *Royal Bank of Scotland v. Commercial Bank of Scotland* (1882) 7 App. Cas. 366 at 367.
[30] *Ex p. Gilbey* (1878) 8 Ch D 248; *Re Sass* [1896] 2 QB 12; *Re Rees* (1881) 17 Ch D 98.
[31] *Ex p. Rushworth* (1805) 10 Ves. at 417; *Cooper v. Pepys* (1741) 1 Atk. 107; *Ex p. Wildman* (1750) *ibid.* 109: *Ex p. Royal Bank of Scotland* (1815) 19 Ves. 310; *Re Blakeley* (1892) 9 Morr. 173; *Ex p. Turquand* (1876) 3 Ch D 445 at 450.
[32] *Westpac Banking Corp. v. Gollin & Co. Ltd* [1988] V.R. 397 especially at 403.

However most modern guarantees will expressly allow the creditor to retain the benefit of all dividends, payable out of the principal's estate in priority to the guarantor and will provide that the guarantee covers the amount remaining due after payment of such dividends often describing such sum as "the ultimate balance". In the case of the guarantee of part of a debt there will normally be a provision (being a so-called non-competition clause) where the guarantor in effect waives all rights to prove in competition with the creditor.[33]

Payments by a guarantor made prior to and after the principal's bankruptcy

As indicated above, in the case of payments made by or on behalf **11–08** of the guarantor prior to the date of the bankruptcy of the principal debtor, there is a question as to whether credit should be given for such sums except in the case of a guarantee of part of the debt. In the latter case there is a separate debt for which the guarantor is liable and which is reduced.[34]

However in the case of a guarantee which is treated as a guarantee of the whole debt, it is not clear whether any reduction for payments made prior to the bankruptcy of the principal debt need be made. If the creditor recovers more than is required in respect of the debt owed to him he will hold the balance on trust for the surety.

Sums received by the creditor after the principal's bankruptcy (as well as the proceeds of the realisation of any security given by the surety realised after that date) do not require the creditor to reduce his proof in the bankruptcy of the principal.[35]

It is irrelevant for this purpose whether the principal receives the sum in question before or after the date of his lodging a proof in the principal's bankruptcy.[36]

As in the case of payments received by him prior to the principal's bankruptcy, the creditor will hold any surplus on trust for the guarantor who has paid.[37]

In the case of a guarantee for part of the debt, the creditor may not apply such payment against that part of the debt which is not covered by the guarantee. In such a case, the guarantor will receive the benefit of any dividend paid by the principal debtor which

---

[33] See *Barclays Bank Ltd v. TOSG Trust Fund Ltd* [1984] A.C. 626 at 644. See also *Midland Bank & Co. v. Chambers* (1869) L.R. 4 Ch.App. 398.
[34] *Ulster Bank Ltd v. Lambe* [1966] N.I. 161. *Cf. McKinnon's Trustee v. Bank of Scotland* 1915 S.C. 411. The *Ulster Bank* decision has been approved in Australia by *Westpac Banking Corp. v. Gollin & Co. Ltd* [1988] V.R. 397 especially at 406, 407 and 409.
[35] *Ulster Bank Ltd v. Lambe*, above.
[36] *Re Rees* (1881) 17 Ch D 98; *Re Sass* [1896] 2 QB 12.
[37] *Westpac Banking Corp. v. Gollin & Co. Ltd*, above.

should be applied to the whole debt so that the guarantor receives a corresponding benefit from the dividend.

2. *Rights of Creditor in the Bankruptcy of a Surety*

Proof

11–09   The creditor clearly has a right of proof for any amount due and payable by the surety at the date of the surety's bankruptcy. As explained in the preceding section, the creditor can lodge his proof in the estate of the insolvent surety even though he also lodges a proof for a similar amount in the estate of the principal and in the estates of any co-sureties, provided that each of those parties is liable for the whole debt and that he, the creditor, does not receive more than 100 pence in the pound.[38] Proof in the surety's state is reduced by any receipts, realisations of securities, or receipts of dividends from the principal's estate.[39]

Where several sureties are jointly and severally liable for the whole debt, the creditor may prove in the bankruptcy of one for the whole amount owing at the time of the bankruptcy order against the surety without giving credit for sums received from other sureties between the date of the bankruptcy order and proof again provided that in all he does not recover more than 100 in the pound.[40]

11–10   The creditor who receives a security from some of a number of sureties is not obliged to apply the security in order to reduce his proof in the bankruptcy of another surety. This is so even though the security was a deposit of money in a suspense account which the creditor could at any time apply for the payment of the debt.[41]

If the surety has guaranteed only part of the debt as distinct from having guaranteed the whole debt subject to a financial limit, it is initially for the creditor to appropriate any sums received from the principal debtor. The trustee in bankruptcy of the surety has no entitlement to compel the creditor to apply such sums to reduce the overall debt otherwise covered by the guarantee.[42]

The creditor can prove in the bankruptcy of the guarantor in respect of the guarantor's liability under the guarantee even though the liability is merely contingent[43] as in the typical case where the liability does not crystallise until a demand has been made.

---

[38] See, *e.g. Ex p. Rushforth* (1886) 10 Ves. 409.

[39] *Re Blakeley* (1892) 2 Morr. 173; *Re Houlder* [1929] 1 Ch. 205; *Re Amalgamated Investments & Property Co. Ltd* [1985] 1 Ch. 349; see also *Westpac Banking Corp. v. Gollin & Co. Ltd* [1988] V.R. 397.

[40] *Re Houlder*, above; *Re Amalgamated Investments & Property Co. Ltd*, above; see also *Ulster Bank v. Lambe* [1966] N.I. 161.

[41] *Commercial Bank of Australia v. Official Assignee* [1893] A.C. 181.

[42] Invariably a well-drawn guarantee would allow the creditor to appropriate any such payment in any way the creditor thinks fit: see generally *Re Sherry* (1884) 24 Ch D 692.

[43] See Insolvency Rules 1986, r.12.3(1).

A proof can also be lodged even where the principal debtor being a company has been dissolved.[44]

Interest

Subject to the specific wording of the guarantee, a creditor is in general not able to prove for interest after the date of insolvency of the principal debtor: this is because no interest is recoverable after the relevant date by the creditor as a provable debt.[45] No interest accruing after the surety's bankruptcy can be recoverable as a provable debt.[46]   **11–11**

Payment by the principal debtor prior to the date of the creditor's proof

As a general rule,[47] any payments made by or on behalf of the principal debtor prior to the date of the submission by the creditor of his proof in the surety's insolvency will reduce the amount of the debt provided such payments are appropriated to the overall debt.   **11–12**

In the case of a guarantee for the whole debt, coupled with a limit on the guarantor's liability, this will produce a corresponding reduction in the creditors proof.[48] In the case of a guarantor being liable for part of the debt, whether the creditor's proof should be reduced depends upon whether and if so how the creditor appropriates payment received. This in turn will depend on whether the guarantee contains provisions expressly entitling the creditor to appropriate the payment to a non-guaranteed portion of the debt or in such other ways as he thinks fit.[49]

The application of the proceeds of the realisation of any security follows the principles set out in the above paragraphs. However in the case of a security granted in respect of the guarantee of part only of the debt, the proceeds must in general be appropriated so as to effect a corresponding reduction in the creditor's proof.[50]

No allowance for co-surety or collateral securities

The creditor can prove for the full amount without having to make over any collateral securities, since the surety's right to these   **11–13**

---

[44] *Re Fitzgeorge* [1905] 1 K.B. 462.
[45] See generally s.189 of the Insolvency Act 1986.
[46] *ibid.*
[47] See *Re Houlder* [1929] 1 Ch. 205 at 209; *Re Blakeley* (1892) 9 Morr. 173; *Re Amalgated Investments & Property Co. Ltd* [1985] Ch. 349.
[48] *ibid.*
[49] See generally *Re Sherry* (1984) 25 Ch D 692; see also *Raikes v. Todd* (1838) 8 Ad. & E. 844.
[50] See generally *Bank of Adelaide v. Lorden* (1970) 45 A.L.J.R. 49.

arises only upon payment in full.[51] The creditor may also prove even though he is giving up his remedies against a co-surety.[52]

However in that case the dividends are limited to the amount which the surety would have had to bear allowing for the contribution for the allocated so-surety which has been lost.[53]

There exists an apparently anomalous exception to the general principle otherwise illustrated by *Re Houlder*[54] to the effect that the creditor can prove for the whole debt irrespective of payments received otherwise than from the principal debtor in the case of bills of exchange. In the latter case, while the holder may prove against the estates of all persons liable on a bill, he must deduct in his proof all sums received from or dividends declared from the estates of all other persons liable and not only from the estate of the person principally liable.[55]

Bankruptcy of the surety from whom nothing is yet due

11–14   The creditor can under the Insolvency Act 1986 prove in the bankruptcy of the surety in respect of his contingent debt in practically every case,[56] though the estimate of the amount may often be very difficult.

3. *Enforcement of Securities by Creditor*

11–15 If a guarantor grants a security in favour of the creditor and in respect of the sums owed by the principal debtor, realisation by the creditor of such security will reduce the guarantor's liability accordingly. The liability of any other co-surety will not benefit from a corresponding reduction. If, on the other hand, security is taken by the creditor directly from the principal debtor, the proceeds of that security must be applied in reduction of the indebtedness only of the principal debtor.

It follows that a creditor will generally have no right to attach any security which the guarantor has himself taken, *e.g.* by way of counter-security, from the principal debtor in respect of the contingent liability of the guarantor. In such a case the creditor will

---

[51] *Ewart v. Latta* (1865) 4 Macq. HL 983.
[52] *Ex p. Gifford* (1802) 6 Ves. 805.
[53] *ibid.*
[54] [1929] 1 Ch. 205.
[55] See *Re Amalgamated Investment & Property Co. Ltd* [1985] Ch. 349. In the case of a bill of exchange this may because those occupying the position of sureties are responsible only for part of the debt as distinct from the whole debt.
[56] See *Hardy v. Fothergill* (1888) 13 App. Cas. 356; *Wolmershausen v. Gullick* [1893] 2 Ch. 514; *Re Fitzgeorge* [1905] 1 K.B. 462; see generally Insolvency Act 1986 and r.13.12 of the Insolvency Rules 1986.

have only an unsecured claim against the principal debtor or the right to prove as such in the insolvency in the principal debtor.[57]

The principal exceptions to the principle that a creditor cannot enforce collateral securities held either by the principal debtor or by the guarantor are first the rule as *Ex p. Waring*,[58] and secondly by circumstances in which the surety in effect holds the security as trustee for the creditor.[59]

4. *Rights of a Surety in the Bankruptcy of the Principal*

Proof generally

Payments made by the surety to the creditor and dividends paid **11–16** in the surety's bankruptcy to the creditor can, provided no double proof results, be proved for in the principal's bankruptcy.[60]

Under section 382(1) and (3) of the Insolvency Act 1986, a surety can prove in respect of every debt or liability, in respect of which the principal may become subject after the commencement of the bankruptcy (including after his discharge) by reason of any obligation incurred prior to bankruptcy and such a debt or liability can be present or future, certain or contingent, fixed or liquidated in amount, capable of being ascertained by fixed rules or as a matter of opinion. By section 281(1) of the 1986 Act the principal is similarly protected in respect of such claims upon his discharge. A surety's right to *quia timet* relief[61] does not however constitute an existing accrued debt though the surety may be entitled to prove *qua* contingent or prospective creditor.[62] The surety's right is however subject to the rule against double proof[63]: the surety cannot prove if the creditor is proving for the debt himself.

As stated above,[64] the rule against double proof is to prevent the payment of more than one dividend in respect of what is in substance the same debt.[65] It is only if the guarantee is restricted to part of the principal's debt that the surety will be entitled to prove in the principal's bankruptcy on payment by the surety of that part.[66] In

---

[57] See, *e.g. Re Standard Insurance & Co. Ltd (in liq.) and the Companies Act 1936* [1970] 1 N.S.W.L.R. 392, especially at 396.

[58] Dealt with above at 11–06.

[59] As appears to be the case in *Re Richardson* [1911] 2 K.B. 705.

[60] See generally *Hardy v. Fothergill* (1883) 13 App. Cas. 351; *Wolmershausen v. Gullick* [1893] 2 Ch. 514; *Re Fitzgeorge* [1905] 1 K.B. 462, Insolvency Act 1986, s.382. In general terms the guarantor can prove for his contingent claim which would need to be the subject of an estimate by the principal's trustee in bankruptcy or he might prove for any sum he had in fact paid in discharge of the principal debtor's liability which would be a liquidated claim based on the right indemnity as in such cases in *Hardy v. Fothergill*, above and *Wolmershausen v. Gullick*, above.

[61] See above.

[62] *Re Mitchell* [1913] 1 Ch. 201.

[63] See above at 11–01.

[64] *ibid.*

[65] See generally *Re Oriental Commercial Bank* (1871) L.R. 7 Ch. App. 99, especially at 101 *per* Mellish L.J. See also *Re Fenton* [1931] 1 Ch. 85.

[66] See, *e.g. Re Sass* [1896] 2 K.B. 12. For a discussion on the relevant principles in this respect see above.

such a case there is no longer one debt and the rule against double proof will not apply.

Modern guarantees contain a number of provisions designed to strengthen the creditor's position. There might be a provision prohibiting the surety from lodging any right of proof of the bankruptcy of the principal debtor until the claims of the creditor have been wholly satisfied: this is often to be described as a non-competition clause. Alternatively the guarantor may not be allowed to prove in respect of any debt owed by the principal debtor to the guarantor, not being restricted to the guaranteed debt.[67]

When can the guarantor prove?

11–17   There is no infringement of the rule against double proof if the creditor is satisfied by the payment from the surety: if the creditor has been paid, the surety will inherit the benefit of the creditor's proof.[68] Consequently the guarantor in such a case would recover all dividends previously paid to the creditor[69] and would in addition be entitled to receive future dividends to the extent of recouping himself for such part of the 100 pence in the pound he may have paid.[70] However in accordance with the principles set out above, if the guarantee is for the whole debt, the surety will not be entitled to any dividends in the bankruptcy of the principal debtor until the creditor has received payment in full.

If the surety and the principal are both bankrupt, no proof can be made on behalf of the surety's estate in respect of dividends declared out of the surety's estate after proof by the creditor in the principal's estate.[71]

But once the situation arises that the creditor receives 100 pence in the pound from the aggregate dividends paid out of the surety's and the principal's estate, the surety's estate can claim the benefit of future dividends receivable as a result of the creditor's proof.[72] In *Ex p. Whittaker*[73] it was left open whether a surety for a present liquidated debt could prove before payment, but it was held that any such proof would be in respect of a contingent debt.

History of proof

11–18   Before the Bankruptcy Act 1809, the surety could only prove (and the bankrupt receive his discharge) in respect of money actually paid by the surety to the creditor before the principal's

---

[67] Another alternative is to provide that any sums received in respect of such proof are to be held on trust for the creditor.
[68] *Re Whitehouse* (1887) 27 Ch D 689 especially at 695.
[69] *ibid.*
[70] *Ex p. Turquand, Re Fothergill* (1876) 3 Ch D 445.
[71] *Ex p. European Bank* (1871) L.R. 7 Ch. App. 99.
[72] *Re Whitehouse* (1887) 37 Ch D 683.
[73] (1891) 3 W.R. 400.

bankruptcy.[74] If the surety paid the whole debt after the creditor had proved, the surety became entitled to the benefit of the creditor's proof.[75]

If the surety paid the debt after the bankruptcy but before the creditor's proof, the creditor could not prove[76] and the surety was wholly deprived of the benefit of any dividend in the principal's bankruptcy, while the bankrupt did not receive a discharge from the surety's claim. The courts of equity intervened to permit the surety to pay the money into court and compel the creditor to prove before exacting payment from the surety.[77] It was then provided by section 8 of the Bankruptcy Act 1809 as re-enacted in section 52 of the Bankruptcy Act 1825 and, subsequently in section 173 of the Bankruptcy Act 1849 that where the surety pays after the commencement of the bankruptcy, he was entitled to the benefit of the creditor's proof or if the creditor had not proved, he could prove in his own name but not disturbing passed dividends.

Prior to the Bankruptcy Act 1914, if the surety paid part only of the debt after the principal's bankruptcy but before proof by the creditor, neither the surety nor the creditor could prove in respect of that part; the creditor could not prove because he had received payment, the surety because he had paid after bankruptcy and not in full discharge of the debt. The principal remained liable to the surety after the principal's discharge from bankruptcy. However under section 30 of the Bankruptcy Act 1914 the surety could prove in such a case, since it was a debt to which the bankrupt became subject before his discharge by reason of an obligation incurred prior to the operative date of the bankruptcy namely, the receiving order. The same principle is in turn reflected in the provisions of section 382, especially section 382(1)(b), of the Insolvency Act 1986.

The only other situation in which the 1914 Act might have extended the surety's right to prove is where the creditor permanently covenants not to sue the principal, while reserving his remedy against the surety. The surety may now be entitled to have his contingent liability valued even though he could not prove for the whole amount as a liquidated sum.[78] Under the Bankruptcy Act 1914 and now the Insolvency Act 1986, where the creditor has proved, the surety's only right upon payment to the creditor is to stand wholly or partly in the place of the creditor for dividends,[79]

11–19

---

[74] *Taylor v. Mills* (1777) 2 Cowp. 525; *Paul v. Jones* (1789) 1 R.R. 599; *Howis v. Wiggins* (1792) 4 T.R. 724.

[75] *Ex p. Rushworth* (1805) 10 Ves. 409 at 417, 419 (Lord Eldon); *Wright v. Morley* (1805) 11 Ves. at 23.

[76] *Cooper v. Pepys* (1741) 1 Atk. 107; *Ex p. Royal Bank of Scotland* (1815) 2 Rose 1977; *Ex p. Leers* (1802) 6 Ves. 644; *Ex p. Taylor* (1857) 1 De G. & J. 302.

[77] See *Ex p. Taylor,* above *per* Turner L.J. at 308; *Wright v. Simpson* (1892) 6 Ves. at 734; *Ex p. Rushforth,* above at 414; *Philips v. Smith* referred to in 10 Ves. at 412.

[78] *Ex p. Whittaker* (1891) 39 W.R. 400.

[79] See *Re Pyke* (1910) 55 S.J. 109. He may also have the right to prove for interest in certain circumstances.

and the surety will only have this right if the creditor has been paid in full.[80]

If the surety holds a security upon the principal debtor's estate, the surety's ability to benefit from the creditor's proof in the principal's estate is limited to the sum by which the debt (or its guaranteed part) exceeds the security. If the creditor proves and takes dividends for the whole debt and the surety realises the security, the surety will have to restore to the estate the amount by which the dividends paid exceed the dividends which would have been paid to the surety by which the debt was greater than the value of the security.[81] Where, however, the creditor by the terms of the guarantee can take all dividends from the principal's estate and hold the surety liable to the full extent of the guarantee, proof by the creditor does not affect any security held by the surety over the principal's estate.[82]

In short, while the surety may prove for a liability which remains contingent at the date of the principal debtor's insolvency, the surety will only be entitled to the dividend provided he pays the whole of the principal debt. If the surety pays off the principal debt before an account is taken in the insolvency of the principal debtor, under section 323 of the Insolvency Act 1986 in the case of bankruptcy and under rule 4.90 of the Insolvency Rules in the case of liquidation, then the surety will be entitled to a statutory set-off. This is because the surety's claim being a provable debt is capable of being subject to the express terms of these statutory provisions.

Set-off: The guarantor's right of set-off in insolvency of the principal debtor

11–20   If a surety pays the creditor on demand pursuant to a guarantee entered into prior to the bankruptcy of the principal, the creditor can set off such payment against debts owed to the principal pursuant to the provisions regarding insolvency set-off, *i.e.* section 323 of the Insolvency Act 1986 in the case of bankruptcy and rule 4.90 of the Insolvency Rules 1986 in the case of liquidations. These provisions require an account to be taken of all those sums due from one party to the other in respect of all mutual dealings between them. In *Stein v. Blake*[83] the House of Lords confirmed that the account taken in the context of insolvency set-off is mandatory, self-executing and that it operates as at the date of the insolvency but with the benefit

---

[80] *Ex p. Turquand* (1876) 3 Ch. D 445. It was held in that case that debentures issued to creditors under a scheme of arrangement by a company formed under the scheme to take over the business of the debtors were to be treated as dividends, and that a surety who had only paid part of the debt was not therefore entitled to a proportion of them.

[81] *Baines v. Wright* (1885) 15 Q.B.D. 202; 16 Q.B.D. 330.

[82] *Midland Banking Co. v. Chambers* (1869) L.R. 7 Eq. 179; 4 Ch. App. 398; *Re Melton* [1918] 1 Ch. 37; *Re Lennard* [1934] Ch. 235.

[83] [1986] A.C. 243.

of hindsight so that contingencies which have matured after that date by the time the account comes to be taken are to be included in the account.[84] The relevant date for the purpose of the above principles is in the case of bankruptcy, the making of the bankruptcy order, and in the case of liquidations, the commencement of the winding-up.[85]

It follows that if the guarantor has paid the creditor under the guarantee prior to the relevant date, he will be entitled to a set-off.[86]

If the surety who is merely under a contingent obligation to pay at the relevant date subsequently pays off the creditor, then the surety will be allowed to set-off his claim for an indemnity against a debt enforceable by the insolvent principal against the surety. The fact that the surety's right is merely contingent does not prevent insolvency set-off arising. This analysis has been reinforced by the House of Lords decision in *Stein v. Blake*.[87]

The House of Lords in *Stein v. Blake* also rejected the suggestion[88] that separate cross claims required for set-off did not cease to exist until the statutory account had been taken.[89] In other words the basis for allowing a surety's contingent claim to be admitted for set-off is to treat the contingency as being due at the relevant date by virtue of subsequent events. The mutual credits, debits or dealings available for set-off do not survive the relevant date as separate cross claims.[90]

Where the surety has made no actual payment to the creditor, he **11–21** cannot set-off his contingent liability as at the relevant date against debts due to the principal. This is despite the fact that the surety's debt arises out of mutual dealings and is otherwise a provable debt. This was decided by *Re Fenton*[91] on the basis that such set-off would infringe the rule against double proof since it was always open to the creditor to prove.

There appears to be an exception to the operation of the rule against double proof in the case of the personal representatives of a deceased guarantor invoking a similar right in the bankruptcy of the principal debtor to recoup amounts paid by then in discharge of the guaranteed debt. This is dealt with elsewhere.[92] On analysis however this is not a case in which mutual debts are involved and

[84] *per* Lord Hoffmann at p. 252, the term "due" in this respect did not mean due at the time when the account came to be taken but means treated as having been owing at the bankruptcy date with the benefit of hindsight and given the necessary estimates prescribed by the bankruptcy laws.

[85] Generally either the date of the resolution of winding-up voluntarily or the date of the presentation of a winding-up petition.

[86] *Re Fenton* [1931] 1 Ch. 85.

[87] See n. 83.

[88] The suggestion was made most explicit in *Day & Dent. Constructions (Pty) v. North Australian Properties (Pty) Ltd* (1981) 150 C.L.R. 85.

[89] The House of Lords in this respect endorsed the earlier decision of *Farley v. Housing and Commercial Developments Ltd* [1984] B.C.L.C. 442.

[90] [1986] A.C. 243 and especially at 252, 253.

[91] [1931] 1 Ch. 85.

[92] See in particular *Re Melton* [1931] 1 Ch. 85 and *Re Watson* [1896] 1 Ch. 925.

correspondingly there is no room for the operation of the rule against double proof. This is to be contrasted with the situation in which the guarantor pays the creditor in full after the principal debtor's insolvency but before the creditor has lodged a proof. In such a case the rule against double proof has no role to play but the resulting debts that are owed by the principal to the surety should be available for set-off principally because the debt arose out of prior dealings between the parties.[93] In *Re Waite*[94] the principal claimed to set-off a debt owed to him by the surety against a judgment obtained by the surety's trustee in bankruptcy enforcing the surety's rights to be indemnified by the principal against sums paid by the surety as guarantor of debts owed to the principal. No set-off was allowed in respect of payments made after the relevant date of the bankruptcy (*i.e.* under the then bankruptcy principles, the date of the receiving order) that being the date at which the respective rights of the parties were crystallised. The decision can now be regarded as being subject to the House of Lords' view in *Stein v. Blake*[95] to the effect that contingent debts can in all cases, unless there is a special reason to the contrary such as the rule against double proof, be set-off.[96] This may have undermined the authority of *Re Waite*.

11–22   In *Re Charge Card Services Ltd*,[97] it was held that a contingent claim could be employed in a set-off provided that it was exclusively referable to a prior agreement between the parties to the proposed set-off. In the case of a principal debtor's obligation to indemnify the surety in the context of a guarantee, it is arguable that the obligation in question is not referable to a contract between the principal debtor and the guarantor.[98] The contract of guarantee does not normally bind a principal debtor. On the other hand this may be too narrow an approach to adopt: it may be enough to show that there were mutual dealings, or at least a prior transaction of some sort which would normally or in the ordinary course of business result in such a liability. The latter analysis would therefore be wide enough to cover the case of the surety who pays the creditor following the principal's insolvency.[99]

Creditor proving prior to payment by the surety

11–23   If the guarantor has paid the creditor in full after the creditor has proved in the principal's insolvency, it is debatable whether set-off should be allowed between the surety's claim for an indemnity and

---

[93] Note that both s.323(3) of the 1986 Act as well as r.4.90(3) qualify the right of set-off by providing sums due *from* the insolvent party may not be included in the account for set-off if the creditor had notice at the time the sum became due that a bankruptcy petition was pending.
[94] *Re a Debtor (No. 66 of 1955)* (1956) 1 W.L.R. 1226.
[95] See n. 91.
[96] See also *Hiley v. The People's Prudential Assurance Co. Ltd* (1938) 60 C.L.R. 496–497 *per* Dixon J. It is arguable that the availability of set-off in the case of contingent debts was recognised in the English authorities prior to *Re Waite, e.g. Jones v. Mossop* (1844) 3 Hare. 568 at 571; *Re Taylor, ex p. Norvell* [1910] 1 K.B. 642 and *Baker v. Lloyds Bank Ltd* [1920] 2 K.B. 327.
[97] [1987] 1 Ch. 150 esp. 189–190.
[98] See Derham, *Set-off* (2nd ed.) at p. 235.
[99] Note Hobson L.J. in *Re Waite*, above at 1327.

the liability borne by the surety to the debtor. Even though the guarantor may have a provable debt he is subrogated to the creditor's proof but this does not of itself justify treating the creditor's proof as the surety's proof for all purposes. The fact that the surety's entitlement to the creditor's proof is arguably exclusively referable to an obligation incurred before the bankruptcy should not alter that analysis.

Payment by the surety with notice to serve act of bankruptcy

Where the surety gives a guarantee for the debts of the principal **11–24** with notice of an available act of bankruptcy by the principal, it seems that the surety cannot prove in the principal's bankruptcy for contribution in respect of monies paid to the creditor.[1] This is so even though the principal debt was incurred before the act of bankruptcy and therefore the creditor could have proved if the surety had not paid.

Interest

The surety cannot prove in the principal's bankruptcy for money **11–25** paid by the surety to the creditor as interest on the principal debt accrued due after the commencement of the bankruptcy where the debt was payable at the date of the bankruptcy.[2] Where, however, the debt is payable at a future date with interest in the meantime, the surety is entitled to value his ability for interest at the rate for which he is liable and to prove for and take full dividends on that value and also to prove for the principal as a present debt subject to a rebate on the dividends calculated from the declaration of the dividend to the date would have been payable.[3]

Where the principal and surety are partners[4]

In *Lacey v. Hill*,[5] a partner in a banking firm deposited in a **11–26** separate account at the bank moneys received by him as treasurer of a public body. Another partner has surety for the treasurer's responsibilities to the body. The partnership became bankrupt although the separate estate of the surety was solvent. The solvent estate of the surety was not allowed to prove against the separate estate of the treasurer since the dividend would have gone to enlarge the estates of the joint estate which was in reality primarily liable for the money deposited.

---

[1] *Farhall v. Farhall* (1871) 7 Ch. App. 123.
[2] *Re International Contract Co., Hughes' claim* (1872) L.R. 13 Eq. 623.
[3] *Re Browne & Windgrove, ex p. Adore* [1891] 2 QB 574; *Re Theo Garvin Ltd* [1969] 1 Ch. 264. See also *Re Evans* (1897) 4 Mans. 114.
[4] For an extensive treatment of bankruptcy as it affects partnerships, see *Lindey & Banks on Partnership* (17th ed., 1995), Chap. 27.
[5] (1872) L.R. 8, Ch. App. 441.

Proof by persons in positions analogous to suretyship

11–27   The principles applicable to proof by sureties should extend to all persons in analogous positions, *i.e.* where a person is secondarily liable under a liability for which another person is also liable whether or not the former is strictly speaking a surety. Examples are an accommodation acceptor,[6] the drawer[7] or indorser[8] of a bill of exchange, and also a retired partner[9] or solvent partner paying the whole partnership debt[10] and an executor liable for the default of a co-executor.[11] Examples of cases where the suretyship analogy has not been applied include an undertenant whose goods were distrained for rent due from his immediate lessor[12] and a lessee who incurred expenses by reason of the non-observance of covenants by the assignee.[13]

5. *Rights of Surety in Bankruptcy of Co-surety: Proof in Co-surety's Bankruptcy*

11–28 The surety can in principle prove in respect of his future claim against a co-surety.[14] However, the rule against double proof will prevent the surety from proving in his co-surety's insolvency in respect of the proving surety's liability for sums for which the creditor cannot be debarred from proving. Indeed the terms of the guarantee may expressly prevent the surety from proving at all until the creditor receives payment in full or it may allow the surety to prove but require the surety to hold any dividends on trust on behalf of the creditor.

The surety, however, has the right to stand in the shoes of the creditor in respect of dividends.[15]

Rights of the surety to benefit of creditor's proof in co-surety's estate

11–29   Where a co-surety is bankrupt and the creditor proves for the whole debt, if the surety pays the creditor more than the surety's share, the surety (or his trustee in bankruptcy) is entitled, once a creditor has been paid 100 pence in the pound to the benefit of the creditor's proof. The surety may use the creditor's proof to take dividends up to the amount of the surety's right to contribution.[16] If,

---

[6] *Stedman v. Martinnant* (1811) 3 East. 427, *cf. Filbey v. Lawford* (1841) 3 M. & Gr. 468, *cf. Re Evans* (1807) 76 L.T. 530.
[7] *Ex p. Lobbon* (1810) 17 Ves. 334.
[8] *Haugh v. Jackson* (1838) 3 M. & W. 598.
[9] *Wood v. Dodgson* (1913) 2 M. & S. 195.
[10] *Ex p. Yonge* (1814) 3 V. & B. 31 at 40; *Ex p. Watson* (1815) 4 Madd. 477; *Aflalo v. Foudrinier* (1829) 6 Bing. 306.
[11] *Lincoln v. White* (1841) 4 Beav. 427.
[12] *Hoare v. White* (1857) 3 Jur. (N.S.) 445.
[13] *Hardy v. Fothergill* (188) 3 App. Cas. 351.
[14] *Wolmershausen v. Gullick* [1893] 2 Ch. 514. See also *Re Lennard* [1934] Ch. 235.
[15] *Ex p. Stokes* (1848) De G. 618.
[16] *ibid. Re Parker, Morgan v. Hill* [1894] 3 Ch. 400.

however, the creditor has not proved when the surety pays and then proves in his own right for compensation, it seems that proof can only be made in respect of the amount which could be recovered in compensation.[17] Where the surety pays the debt he should always see that proof is made on the estate of any insolvent co-surety in the name of the creditor for the whole debt. This right is confirmed by section 5 of the Mercantile Law Amendment Act 1856.

The operation of section 5 will not be affected by any assignment which the creditor may have entered into with regard to the benefit of the debt or of the proof to the surety.[18] If a co-surety receives dividends in excess of his rateable share he will be bound to share them accordingly with his co-sureties or give credit.[19] If a co-surety has discharged the whole debt himself and then proves in his own name as distinct from that of the creditor, his proof is limited to his share.

Discharge

Discharge of a co-surety from bankruptcy may not necessarily **11–30** relieve him from his liability to contribute. If the liability to contribute arises through an event which does not normally need to discharge, *e.g.* a breach of trust, the co-surety will not be released from his liability to contribute.

---

[17] *Re Parker*, above.
[18] *Re M'Myn, Lightbown v. M'Myn* (1886) 33 Ch D 575.
[19] *Re Hendry, ex p. Murphy* [1905] S.A.L.R. 116.

CHAPTER 12

WINDING-UP AND RECEIVERS

Insolvency Rules

12–01 Prior to the Insolvency Act 1986 the rules obtaining in bankruptcy as to the debts provable and as to the valuation of future and contingent claims were to be observed in the winding-up of insolvent companies.[1] There is therefore no provision currently in force to require the application of any of the bankruptcy rules *per se* in the case of the winding-up of companies. The rules which determine the categories of debt provable in a winding-up are self-contained and are now to be found in the Insolvency Rules 1986.[2]

Briefly the rules in question provide for the attribution of an estimated value to any debt which by reason of its being subject to a contingency or for any other reason, does not bear a certain value.[3] The estimate of valuation may be made by the liquidator but in difficult cases or in cases of dispute may be referred to the court under section 168 (3) or (5) of the Insolvency Act 1986.[4]

Every company liable by way of guarantee and every company for which a guarantee has been given would seem, therefore, if wound-up and insolvent, to be open at the instance of the creditor or surety respectively to the same proof as might have been made against its assets had it been an individual adjudged bankrupt. This includes the rules as to set-off and reference should be made to Chapter 11 on this point.

Disclaimer

12–02 The rules concerning the operation of disclaimer upon the rights of sureties are dealt with elsewhere.[5]

However, rent may come to be paid during a winding-up by a person secondarily liable to pay it. That person will therefore be entitled to be indemnified by the company and if the rent were to rank as an expense of the winding-up if the liquidator paid it

---

[1] ss.611 and 612 of the Companies Act 1985 repealed by the Insolvency Acts 1985 and 1986.
[2] See Insolvency Rules 1986, in particular r.12.3 as amended.
[3] Insolvency Rules, r.4.86.
[4] This is of particular relevance to the complication of an unliquidation claim in court against the company. Formerly if the company was insolvent, demands in the nature of unliquidated damages were not provable unless they arose by reason of a contract or by reason of breach of trust.
[5] See generally Chap. 14.

himself, the person paying the rent will be subrogated to the landlord's right to be indemnified out of the company's assets. The amount of his indemnity claim against the company will rank as a pre-preferential expense of winding-up.

Company not insolvent

The rules regarding disclaimer in the Insolvency Act 1986[6] will **12–03** not apply where the company being wound-up is not insolvent. In that case the creditor will apparently have the right to have impounded before any money is distributed amongst the shareholders a sum sufficient to satisfy, if invested at interest, any ascertained payments that will become due, such as future instalments of rent.[7]

It would seem reasonable that, if the creditor did not avail himself of any such right, the surety who would be certain to have to pay, the company being about to be dissolved and the assets distributed to the shareholders, ought to have such rights. Whether the creditor could claim any similar right in respect of future liabilities as for breaches of covenant to repair, must be treated as open. The question arose in *Gooch v. London Banking Association*[8] but that case was compromised. It was suggested in argument that the company impliedly agreed to maintain capital to assume the liability assumed by the covenants[9] and that the lessor could claim a sum as for breach of this agreement. If so, perhaps a surety for the company could in some cases take the same position.

It would appear that if the surety for a company in liquidation though not insolvent has the above-mentioned rights against the company, the creditor would have similar rights against a surety company in the same position. In the various authorities no allowance seems to have been made for possible payments by assignees of the lease. In either case, as the money would only be impounded, and would be released if no payment became due, no ultimate injustice would be done to the company by the omission to make such allowance.

Preferential payments

A surety for the company's liability for preferential debts may, as **12–04** to payment, stand in the place of the payee[10] and will be entitled in the winding-up to the payee's right to preferential payment under section 175 of the Insolvency Act 1986.[11]

---

[6] See s.178 and following.
[7] *Oppenheimer v. The British & Foreign etc. Bank* (1877) 6 Ch. 744; *Gooch v. London Banking Association* (1885) 32 Ch D 41, *cf. Re Telegraph Construction Co.* (1870) L.R. 10 Eq. 384.
[8] Above, and see also *James Smith & Son v. Goodman* [1986] Ch. 216 at 227, 235.
[9] *cf. per* Jessel M.R. in *Re National Funds Assurance Co.* (1878) 10 Ch. 118 at 127.
[10] *Re Lamplugh Iron Ore Co.* [1927] Ch. 308.
[11] *ibid.*

Effect of liquidation

12–05   As in the case of bankruptcy, the liquidation of a company will not release the surety for a company's obligations.[12]

Effect of receivership

12–06   There is no reason to suppose that the appointment out of court of a receiver by a debenture holder, even in the case of an insolvent company, would have the consequence of discharging a surety.

A receiver appointed by a debenture holder of a company owes no duty of care to the guarantor of the company's indebtedness to realise the assets of the company in relation to which he is appointed, at a fair market value. In *China and South Sea Bank Ltd v. Tan*[13] the Privy Council held that a surety would be discharged if the creditor or the receiver had committed an act which was injurious to the interests of the surety or had acted inconsistently with the surety's rights or had otherwise breached an obligation. Generally a creditor and any receiver are entitled to choose their own time for sale though they are also obliged to make reasonable and proper arrangements for the sale and to take reasonable care to obtain the true market value or the best price reasonably obtainable at the time that the sale does take place.[14]

Liability for mutual guarantees

12–07   In *Ford & Carter Ltd v. Midland Bank Ltd*[15] a question arose as to whether the plaintiff company in liquidation had entered into a pre-existing mutual guarantee with five other related companies. The authorised signatures of the plaintiff company were added to a document containing the signatures given on behalf of the related companies but no fresh signatures were sought from the previous party to the guarantees. The House of Lords rejected the argument that as a matter of construction, the initial mutual liability could automatically and unilaterally extend to a fresh signatory albeit of the same corporate group, and secondly, and reversing the view of the Court of Appeal, that the liabilities of the other companies had been incurred through the agency of an officer common to all companies. The House of Lords stressed that whenever creditors became involved, as in this case, the separate legal existence of the companies in the group had to be respected.

---

[12] *Re Fitzgeorge* [1905] 1 K.B. 462. In *Re London Chartered Bank of Australia* [1983] 3 Ch. 540 there is the suggestion that the liquidation of a company had the same effect on a surety's liability as the bankruptcy of an individual.
[13] [1990] A.C. 536.
[14] See generally *Cuckmere Brick v. Mutual Finance* [1971] Ch. 949; *Standard Chartered Bank v. Walker* [1962] 1 W.L.R. 1410.
[15] (1979) 129 N.L.J. 543, HL.

CHAPTER 13

BILLS OF EXCHANGE AND NEGOTIABLE INSTRUMENTS

1. *General*

The drawer of an ordinary bill of exchange is not, strictly speaking, **13–01**
a surety for the acceptor, who will remain primarily liable, although
the position of a person liable on a bill is clearly analogous to that
either of principal debtor or surety to the holder.[1]

Bills of Exchange and the Statute of Frauds

Difficulties have frequently arisen under the Statute of Frauds **13–02**
when a bill of exchange has merely been indorsed with the name of
a person other than the drawee, and to whom the bill has not been
negotiated, as guarantor for the acceptor. To a holder a due course
both by the law merchant[2] and by virtue of section 56 of the Bills
of Exchange Act 1882,[3] such a person incurs the liabilities of an
indorser and no question of the Statute of Frauds arises. Similarly,
it appears that if a bill so indorsed is otherwise properly completed,
such an indorser is liable to the drawer on default by the acceptor.[4]
Oral evidence is admissible to show that the indorsee put his
signature to the bill with the intention of being liable as guarantor
to the drawer of payments by the acceptor.[5] If, on the other hand,
the evidence is insufficient to establish this,[6] or the bill was incomplete when indorsed and the circumstances are such that section 20
of the Bills of Exchange Act does not apply, then an attempt to
render the indorser liable apart from the law merchant and the Bills

---

[1] See *Re Conley* [1938] 2 All E.R. 127 at 131 *per* Lord Green M.R., citing *Duncan Fox & Co. v. North & South Wales Bank* (1880) 6 App. Cas. 1. See above and generally *Byles on Bills of Exchange* (16th ed., 1988), Chap. 33; *Chalmers & Guest on Bills of Exchange* (14th ed., 1991), pp. 448–461. See also *Horne v. Rouquette* (1878) 3 QBD 514 at 518 *per* Brett L.J.
[2] *Steele v. M'Kinlay* (1880) 5 App. Cas. 754 at 769, 782; *McDonald v. Nash* [1924] A.C. 625 at 632, 650.
[3] *McDonald v. Nash*, above. Section 56 provides that where a person signs a bill otherwise than as drawer or acceptor, he thereby incurs the liability of an indorser to a holder in due course. See *G. & H. Montage v. Irvani* [1988] 1 W.L.R. 1285 at 1294; [1990] 1 W.L.R. 667, CA.
[4] *McDonald v. Nash*, above; *McCall v. Hargreaves* [1932] 2 K.B. 423; *G. & H. Montage v. Irvani* [1988] 1 W.L.R. 1285 at 1294; [1990] 1 W.L.R. 667 at 672–3, CA. *Cf. Singer v. Elliott* (1888) 4 T.L.R. 524.
[5] *Steele v. M'Kinlay* (1880) 5 App. Cas. 754; *MacDonald v. Whitfield* (1883) 8 App. Cas. at 749; *McDonald v. Nash*, above; *Elliott v. Bax-Ironside* [1925] 2 J.B. 301; *G. & H. Montage v. Irvani* [1990] 1 W.L.R. 667 at 679, CA.
[6] *Steele v. M'Kinlay*, above.

of Exchange Act will fail, unless there is writing to satisfy the Statute of Frauds.[7]

Where a bill is indorsed by the drawer and by his indorsee back again to the drawer, it may be shown by oral evidence that the intermediate party indorsed as surety so as to enable the indorsee, though himself also the drawer, to sue such indorser—a right which he would not have if the indorser had been holder of the bill.[8] Similarly where the payee indorses to the drawer for the same purpose.[9]

Consideration

13–03   On the same principle whereby the granting of credit will be sufficient consideration for a guarantee to secure a further debt which may in the future be due,[10] the obtaining of bill stamps and drawing bills thereon will be sufficient consideration to support a guarantee of bills to be drawn.[11]

Accommodation bills

13–04   It has already been noted[12] that the rights of a surety depend not upon contract but upon notice, and that even notice given to the creditor after the contract has been entered into is sufficient. On this principle, an accommodation party to a bill of exchange is, from the time when the relation to the parties is notified to the holder, entitled to be regarded as surety only for the party accommodated, notwithstanding that upon the bill he is liable in a prior degree to the other, as where a bill is accepted for the accommodation of the drawer.[13]

An accommodation party to a bill is defined by section 28(1) of the Bills of Exchange Act 1882 as a person who has signed a bill as drawer, acceptor or indorser, without receiving value therefor,

---

[7] *Jenkins v. Coomber* [1898] 2 QB 168; *Shaw v. Holland* [1913] 2 K.B. 15. It is extremely difficult, if not impossible, to reconcile these two cases and *Singer v. Elliott* (1888) 4 T.L.R. 524 with the decisions as to the filling up of an incomplete bill indorsed by way of guarantee under s.20 of the Bills of Exchange Act 1882 in *Glenie v. Bruce-Smith* [1908] 1 K.B. 268; *Re Gooch* [1921] 2 K.B. 593; *Bernardi v. National Sales Corporation* [1931] 2 K.B. 188; *McCall v. Hargreaves* [1932] 2 K.B. 423. It is submitted, following the opinion of Goddard J. in the last named case that *Jenkins v. Coomber* and *Shaw v. Holland*, above, are no longer good law. This appears to be borne out by *Yeoman Credit Ltd v. Gregory* [1963] 1 W.L.R. 343. See Byles, *op. cit.*, at pp. 198 *et seq.* especially at 202–204, where the problem is extensively discussed. See also *G. & H. Montage v. Irvani* [1988] 1 W.L.R. 1285 at 1294.

[8] *Wilkinson v. Unwin* (1881) 7 QBD 736. See also *Re Gooch*, above; *Yeoman Credit Ltd v. Gregory*, above.

[9] *Holmes v. Durkee* (1883) C.B. & E. 23.

[10] See above, p. 9.

[11] *Bluck v. Gompertz* (1852) 7 Exch. 862.

[12] See above.

[13] *Oriental Finance Corporation v. Overend Gurney & Co.* (1874) L.R. 7 HL 348. See too *Davies v. Stainbank* (1855) 6 De G.M. & G. 679; *Pooley v. Harrandine* (1857) 7 E. & B. 431; *Greenough v. McLelland* (1860) 30 L.J.QB 15. The recognition of accommodation bills was much regretted by many judges, including Lord Eldon. See *Bank of Ireland v. Beresford* (1818) 6 Dow. 233; *Ex p. Glendinning* (1819) Buck. 517; and *cf. Fentum v. Pocock* (1813) 5 Taunt. 192; *Nichols v. Norris* (1831) 3 B. & Ad. 41, note; *Harrison v. Courtauld* (1832) 3 B. & Ad. 36.

and for the purpose of lending his name to some other person. Section 28(2) provides that he will be liable on a bill to a holder for value and that it is immaterial, when such holder took the bill that he knew such party to be an accommodation party or not.[14] The underlying intention to a transaction whereby one party signs without consideration for the accommodation of another is that the latter should be at liberty to raise money, *e.g.* by negotiating the bill, but should be in a position to meet the bill if called on at maturity.[15] By virtue of the foregoing provisions in the 1882 Act, a bill will only be a true accommodation bill when the accommodation party signs as acceptor and not in any other capacity.[16] If the party who is accommodated is in default in failing to provide funds to meet the bill at maturity, he must indemnify the acceptor or other party compelled to pay the holder.[17]

A holder who has made advances on an accommodation bill without discounting it outright, with or without notice, can recover no more than the amount of the advances[18]; although, if the accommodation party is bankrupt, the holder, if he took without notice, can prove for the full amount and take dividends to the extent of his advances.[19] This rule applies where the bill has been indorsed to the creditor as security for a debt, and rests upon the principle that the excess would be recovered only for the indorser or depositor who, as the party accommodated, would have no right to recover anything.[20]

Contribution

Two or more persons agreeing to becoming parties to an instrument for the accommodation of a third party will be treated as co-sureties entitled to contribution *inter se* irrespective of the order **13–05**

[14] See generally *Oriental Finance Corporation v. Overend Gurney & Co.*, above, affirmed *sub. nom. Overend Gurney & Co. (Liquidators) v. Oriental Finance Corporation (Liquidators)* (1874) L.R. 7 HL 348.
[15] *Sleigh v. Sleigh* (1850) 5 Exch. 514. See the discussion in Byles, *op. cit.*, at pp. 221, 222.
[16] *Scott v. Lifford* (1808) 1 Camp. 246. The maker of an accommodation note will on similar principles be a surety. See *Bechervaise v. Lewis* (1872) L.R. 7 C.P. 372.
[17] The acceptor will also enjoy the right to benefit from securities belonging to the party accommodated in the hands of the holder. See *Bechervaise v. Lewis*, above; *cf. Duncan Fox & Co. v. North and South Wales Bank* (1880) 6 App. Cas. 1. The indemnity may be extended to include the rights of an action fought unsuccessfully against the holder. See *Bagnall v. Andrews* (1830) 7 Bing. 217 at 222 *per* Tindal C.J. *Cf. Beech v. Jones* (1848) 5 C.B. 696. See also *Garrard v. Cottrell* (1847) 10 QB 679; *Hammond & Co. v. Bussey* (1887) 20 QBD 79. For the manner in which the indemnity is enforced, see *Sleigh v. Sleigh* (1850) 5 Exch. 514 and *Re Fox Walker & Co., ex. Bishop* (1880) 15 Ch D 400.
[18] *Wiffen v. Roberts* (1795) 1 Esp. 261 (note however the caution expressed by Byles, *op. cit.*, at p. 226 on this decision); *Smith v. Knox* (1880) 3 Esp. 46; *Charles v. Marsden* (1808) 1 Taunt. 224; *Simpson v. Clarke* (1835) 2 C.M. & R. 342; *Ex p. Newton* (1880) 16 Ch D 330. Quite apart from the provisions of s.28(2) of the 1882 Act, it is no defence to an action upon an accommodation bill that it was negotiated when overdue, unless the negotiation was a fraud upon the accommodation party. *Charles v. Marsden*, above; *Sturtevant v. Ford* (1842) 4 M. & G. 101; *Re Overend Gurney & Co., ex p. Swan* (1868) L.R. 8 Eq. 344.
[19] *Ex p. Newton*, above.
[20] *ibid.* at 336.

of priority of their names on the instrument.[21] Further an accommodation party will be entitled to contribution from another such party even though he was unaware of the latter's capacity when he became such a party.[22]

Discharge[23]

13–06   Generally the holder of a bill of exchange need not actively or diligently pursue the acceptor, but if he extinguishes or suspends his right of action against the acceptor, or contracts with the latter so to do, the drawer and indorsers will be released, in the absence of agreement to the contrary, *e.g.* where it is agreed that judgment is to be given to the holder in the case of default, on the same terms as those to which he would otherwise have been entitled, the drawer is not released.[24]

A covenant not to sue the acceptor will generally discharge the drawer and indorsers, unless such agreement is made without consideration.[25] Similarly, an acceptor, known only by the holder to be a surety, will be released if the holder gives time to the party accommodated.[26]

The taking of a fresh bill from the acceptor in lieu of a dishonoured bill will similarly discharge the other parties, unless it is given as a second or collateral security.[27]

However, no release of the indorser will be effected if he consents to it,[28] and this will be so if the consent is expressed or can be inferred after the state of facts giving rise to the release.[29]

Aval

13–07   In continental systems, a stranger to a bill can undertake liability as a guarantor by signing it. This known as an *aval* and is not recognised in English law.[30]

---

[21] *Reynolds v. Wheeler* (1861) 30 L.J.C.P. 350 approved in *Macdonald v. Whitfield* (1883) 8 App. Cas. 733; *Godsell v. Lloyd* (1911) 27 T.L.R. 383; *Lacombe v. Labonte* (1920) Q.R. 59 S.C. 17. Note too *Dering v. Winchelsea* (1880) 2 B. & P. 270; *Mayhew v. Crickett* (1818) 2 Swanst. 185 for the general rules regarding contribution showing that there will still be mutual contribution even though the same debt be secured by different instruments executed by different sureties.
[22] *Reynolds v. Wheeler*, above. See the other cases cited in the preceding note.
[23] See generally Chap. 8 where several of the cases cited there involve the rights of holders of bills, *e.g. Moss v. Hall* (1850) 5 Ex. 46; *Philpot v. Briant* (1828) 4 Bing. 717; *Clarke v. Birley* (1888) 41 Ch D 422.
[24] *Kennard v. Knott* (1842) 4 M. & G. 474; *Michael v. Myers* (1843) 6 M. & G. 702. *Cf. Rayner v. Fussey* (1859) 28 L.J. Exch 132. See also *Abrey v. Crux* (1869) L.R. 5 C.P. 37.
[25] See, *e.g. Arundel Bank v. Goble* (1816) 2 Chit. 364; *Clarke v. Birley* (1888) 41 Ch D 422.
[26] See *Re Acraman, ex p. Webster* (1847) De G. 414.
[27] *Gordon v. Calvert* (1828) 4 Russ. 581; *Calvert v Gordon* (1828) 7 B. & C. 09. See also *Twopenny v. Young* (1824) 3 B. & C. 208; *Bedford v. Deakin* (1818) 2 B. & Ald. 210.
[28] See, *e.g. Clark v. Devlin* (1803) 3 B. & P. 363.
[29] See, *e.g. Stevens v. Lynch* (1810) 12 East. 38. *Cf. Withall v. Masterman* (1809) 2 Camp. 179.
[30] *per* Lord Blackburn in *Steele v. M'Kinlay* (1880) 5 App. Cas. 754 at 772, citing *Jackson v. Hudson* (1810) 2 Camp. 447 at 448. See also *Moti & Co. v. Cassim's Trustee* [1924] A.D. 720 (South Africa). In South Africa, Roman-Dutch law recognises the principle of the *aval*. See generally Cowen, *Law of Negotiable Instruments in South Africa* (1966), Chap. 13; the Geneva Convention (Uniform Law on Bills of Exchange and Promissory Notes: Convention No. 3313: Geneva, June 7, 1930) upon which continental and some other systems are based and which expressly provides for

The Statute of Frauds requires guarantees in English law to be in writing.[31] Moreover an *aval* is a security which passes with the bill and therefore breaches the necessity in English law to have privity between the surety and the creditor.

However, as has already been discussed above, section 56 of the Bills of Exchange Act 1882 imposes the liability of an indorser upon a stranger signing a bill regardless of the question of the Statute of Frauds.

The equivalent of section 56 in Canada has been held in *Robinson v. Mann*[32] to have introduced the principle of the *aval* into English law.[33] In Australia in *Ferrier v. Stewart*[34] the equivalent provision of section 56 of the English statute was held to make a stranger liable where she had indorsed the bill at the payee's insistence, the latter subsequently indorsing his name both above and below hers. The stranger was estopped from denying either that she was an indorser or that the payee was a holder in due course.[35]

2. *Cross Acceptances and Bankruptcy*

Specific exchange of acceptances

The simple case of one accommodation bill does not differ from an ordinary guarantee: namely, the accommodating party, even though he may be an acceptor of the bill, is entitled as between himself and the party accommodated to have it taken up by the latter and be indemnified against his liability upon it. However, where two parties enter into a specific exchange of accommodation acceptances, each acceptance is regarded as being the consideration for the other, and each acceptor is bound to pay his own acceptance, his remedy being against the drawer on the other bill and not as surety in the bill accepted.[36] It was finally settled that the drawer holding the bill accepted by the other party might prove in the bankruptcy of the acceptor, provided the counter acceptance was taken up.[37]

13–08

---

avals in Chap. IV, Art 30, 31, 32. However, the English courts may give effect to an *aval* valid under a foreign law applicable to the instrument: *G. & H. Montage v. Irvani* [1988] 1 W.L.R. 1285; [1990] 1 W.L.R. 667, CA.

[31] See generally Chap. 3.

[32] (1901) 31 S.C.R. 484.

[33] At p. 486. See also *Grant v. Scott* (1919) 59 S.C.R. 227 at 230 and see discussion in Byles, *op. cit.*, pp. 204 *et seq.*

[34] (1912) 15 C.L.R. 32.

[35] See to similar effect in New Zealand *Cook v. Fenton* (1892) 11 N.Z.L.R. 505; *Erickssen v. Bunting* (1901) 20 N.Z.L.R. 388.

[36] *Rolfe v. Caslon* (1795) 2 H.Bl. 571; *Cowley v. Dunlop* (1798) 7 Term Rep. 565; *Buckler v. Buttirant* (1802) 3 East 72.

[37] See *Re Bowness and Padmore* (1789) 1 *Cooke's Bankruptcy Laws* (8th ed.), p. 183; *Ex p. Rawson* (1821) Jac. 274 *per* Lord Eldon at 279. The history of this development is set out at pp. 329–330 of the third edition of this work. See also Byles, *op. cit* at pp. 466–467.

Acceptances not specifically exchanged

13–09   Where, however, two parties have mutually accommodated each other, but have not specifically exchanged acceptances, one in consideration of the other, all the bills must be treated as strictly accommodation bills, and the acceptor paying any of them can prove upon the footing that he has made such payment as surety.[38]

Double bankruptcy

13–10   Where acceptances for mutual accommodations have been exchanged between two persons both of whom are bankrupt, neither trustee can prove against the other estate in respect of any of such bills which may have remained in the hands of the bankrupt whose estate he represents, until the holders of all the bills have been paid in full. This is so even though, by reason of the unequal negotiation of bills by the two parties, greater damage arises out of the accommodation transactions to one estate than to the other.[39]

This rule also applies to prevent a proof being made on behalf of the estate of a bankrupt who has given accommodation acceptances (which have been discounted and are outstanding) against the estate of the drawer of other accommodation bills on a third party given that drawer to the acceptor of the first-named accommodation bills in exchange for such acceptances.[40]

The rule in Ex p. Walker

13–11   The basis of this rule, as set out in the previous paragraph, appears to be that the only ascertainable debt which could arise between the parties out of the mutual accommodation transactions is in respect of the balance which would result if both parties remained solvent and the bills duly met and accounts adjusted.[41] Otherwise the proportion in which the liability will fall on the two estates will depend upon the respective dividends which they may pay, resulting in a possible double proof, *i.e.* a proof by the party accommodating, in addition to a proof by the holders of the bills. Proof should therefore be allowable only in respect of any balance outstanding as between the parties or bills actually paid.[42]

---

[38] See *Ex p. Read* (1822) 1 Gl. & J. 224.

[39] *Ex p. Walker* (1798) 4 Ves. 373; *Ex p. Earle* (1801) 5 Ves. 833.

[40] *Ex p. Solarte* (1832) 2 D. & Ch. 261 explained in *Ex p. Solarte* (1834) 3 D. & Ch. 419. Note too *Sarratt v. Austin* (1811) 4 Taunt 200. Byles, *op. cit.*, at p. 466 suggests that s.382(3) of the Insolvency Act 1986 and Insolvency Rules, r.13.12(3) may enable a party to prove a bill not yet due as a contingent debt even though his own counter-bill remains undue and unpaid.

[41] Lord Eldon who argued *Ex p. Walker* (1798) 4 Ves. 373 before Lord Loughborough, who in turn applied the rule in *Ex p. Earle* (1801) 5 Ves. 833, said later that none of the counsel in the case understood the judgment. See *Ex p. Rawson* (1821) Jac. 274 at 278.

[42] See *Ex p. Read* (1822) 1 Gl. & J. 224; *Ex p. Macredie* (1873) L.R. 8 Ch. 533.

Where one estate shows a surplus

In *Ex p. Rawson*[43] it was stated by Lord Eldon that in the event **13–12**
of there being a surplus upon the estate suffering less than the other,
owing to the accommodation given, the rule in *Ex p. Walker* would
not apply but relief would be given to the other estate out of the
surplus.[44]

Rule inapplicable except in cases of cross-accommodation

The rule in *Ex p. Walker* will also not apply where one party only **13–13**
has given accommodation paper[45] and secondly where the person
that seeks to prove is not the same as the person who made the
arrangement for the exchange of acceptances.[46]

Where A gave B his own accommodation acceptances and B
then indorsed them to C in exchange for acceptances of C, and all
three became bankrupt, it was held that, though no proof could be
made on behalf of the estate of C against the estate of B (with
whom he had made the exchange) as indorser of the acceptances of
A in the hands of C at the date of his bankruptcy, this did not
prevent such proof being made against the estate of A, the acceptor,
even though first there had been cross-acceptances by B to A,
which were outstanding, and secondly dividends were kept in hand
pending the final adjustment of the equities between the three
estates.[47]

The estate of a bankrupt indorser may stand in the place of the
holder, after the latter has received 100 pence in the pound, for any
future dividends upon the estate of the acceptor to the extent of
dividends already paid to the holder by the estate of the indorser,
even though the bill was received by the indorser from a previous
holder in exchange merely for his own acceptance given to that
holder.[48]

Proof on bills of exchange generally

If a bill is indorsed by a debtor as security for the debt the **13–14**
indorsee can prove in the bankruptcy of the acceptor for the full
amount of the bill, even though less may be owing to him from the
indorser. This is true, at any rate if he took without notice, even

[43] (1821) Jac. 274.
[44] (1798) 4 Ves. 373. Except in the case of a surplus, Lord Eldon did not question the rule in *Ex p. Walker* and it was further followed in *Ex p. Solarte* (1834) 3 D. & Ch. 419 and *Ex p. Laforest* (1833) 2 D. & Ch. 199.
[45] *Ex p. Metcalfe* (1805) 11 Ves. 404.
[46] *Ex p. Cama* (1874) L.R. 9 Ch. App. 686 at 689. See also *Ex p. Macredie* (1873) L.R. 8 Ch. 535 at 539.
[47] See *Ex p. Solarte* (1832) 2 D. & Ch. 261 explained in *Ex p. Solarte* (1834) 3 D. & Ch. 419. *Cf. Ex p. Metcalfe* (1805) 11 Ves. 404.
[48] *Ex p. Greenwood* (1834) Buck. 237.

though the bill was accepted for accommodation,[49] or, if for value, even though, as between drawer and acceptor, less than the full amount of the bill would be recoverable.[50] If one person, to secure the debt of another, accepts or indorses a bill direct to the creditor, no more can be proved against his estate than the amount of the debt secured.[51]

If an accommodation bill is indorsed to his creditor by the party accommodated, the creditor having notice that it was an accommodation bill, it may be that the creditor can only prove against the party accommodating for the amount due to him from the indorser.[52] If the benefit of a guarantee for payment of a promissory note is transferred with the note, the transferee cannot prove in the bankruptcy of the guarantor but he can claim that the amount of the guarantee be brought into the account between the parties to it, and he can stand in the place of the transferor in respect of any balance found due to him to the extent of the guarantee.[53]

---

[49] *Ex p. Moxham* (1802) 6 Ves. 449; *Ex p. Philips* (1840) 1 M.D. & De G. 232; *Ex p. Newton* (1880) 16 Ch. D. 330.
[50] *Ex p. Newton,* above.
[51] *Ex p. Reader* (1819) Buck 381.
[52] See *Ex p. Gomersall* (1875) 1 Ch D 137 at 142. This in substance would be the same case as *Ex p. Reader,* above. *Ex p. Newton* (1880) 16 Ch D 330 does not deal with such a case to which it is probable that the dicta in the *Gomersall* case were confirmed. The latter case really turned on the fact that the bills were, to the knowledge of the holder, issued fraudulently in contemplation of bankruptcy by both drawer and acceptor. See same case in the House of Lords, *sub nom. Jones v. Gordon* (1887) 2 App. Cas. 616.
[53] *Re Barrington* (1804) 2 Sch. & Lef. 112. *Cf. Re Barned's Banking Co.* (1871) L.R. 6 Ch. 338.

CHAPTER 14

LANDLORD AND TENANT

General: continuation of liability

In the case of a business tenancy protected under Part II of the **14–01**
Landlord and Tenant Act 1954, most of the contractual terms survive
the contractual termination date of the lease.[1] However, unless the
contrary is specifically agreed, the surety's obligations will end at
the contractual termination date.[2] This applies to future rent or
breaches of the lease but a surety remains liable for past breaches.[3]

If the underlying agreement is varied then in accordance with the
principle in *Holme v. Brunskill*,[4] the guarantor will be released. A
clause in the guarantee of a lease that the guarantor would be liable
for a tenant's default "notwithstanding . . . any other act or thing
whereby but for that provision the guarantor would have been
released" was held not to be wide enough to cover the situation
where the obligations of the lessee were extended beyond those
originally guaranteed.[5]

It is not uncommon for a well drafted guarantee of the obligations of a lessee or assignee to contain a covenant by the landlord
to give notice of any proposed variation to the guarantor on the
basis that should the guarantor not object in writing within a stated
period the guarantor will be deemed to be bound.[6]

The lease may contain a covenant by the surety that a tenant will
pay the rent on the due dates and that if the tenant fails to make
payment the surety will have to pay (a) after default by the tenant
following a specified number of days as well as (b) "on demand".
Such terms and words construed in such a way as to override the
general words of liability and to make the period of default by the
tenant and the demand upon the surety pre-conditions of the surety's
liability.[7]

---

[1] Section 24 of the Landlord and Tenant Act 1954; *Bolton Engineering Ltd v. Graham and Sons Ltd*
[1967] 1 QB 159.
[2] *Junction Estates Ltd v. Cope* [1974] 28 P. & C.R. 482; *Plesser v. Davis* (1983) 267 E.G. 1039;
Associated Dairies v. Pierce (1982) 265 E.G. 127. A creditor may be able to rely upon a covenant in
the guarantee so as to extend it to any renewed lease: see, *e.g. Verdi La Fontana Pty Ltd v. Mabrook
Pty Ltd* [1992] N.S.W. Conv. R. 59,606.
[3] *ibid.*
[4] (1878) 3 QBD 495.
[5] *West Horndon Industrial Park v. Phoenix Timber* [1995] N.P.C. 42, *cf. Metropolitan Property Co.
(Regis) Ltd v. Bartholomew and Another* [1994] 14 E.G. 143, an example of the variation embodied
within the original guaranteed obligation.
[6] *B. M. Samuels Finance Group plc v. Beechmanor* [1993] E.G.C.S. 97.
[7] *Sicklemore v. Thistleton* (1817) 6 M. & S. 9.

Revocation

14–02   The surety under a lease cannot normally revoke his guarantee since the consideration has moved once and for all[8]; however, in the case of a weekly tenancy it has been held that the guarantee is revocable.[9]

In the case of a yearly tenancy the surety may face the unenviable prospect of indeterminate liability if neither party to the lease wishes to give notice. It is an undecided question here whether the surety can compel the termination of the principal liability by requiring the giving of notice under the lease. Clearly a surety should attempt to require express provision for this.

Assignment of lease

14–03   Neither the assignment of the lease in the absence of an express release nor the covenant by an assignee to a lease with the landlord to pay all rent reserved by the lease will release the surety. Indeed in the latter case the assignee will assume a primary obligation.[10] A surety will then generally be liable according to the terms of any such assignment so that normally he will remain liable for rent and other covenants undertaken by the first assignee even after the licence to assign[11]; on the other hand if the guarantee is only in respect of a period in which the lease is vested in the tenant the guarantor will be released.[12]

Transfer of freehold reversion

14–04   It is now well established that if a covenant by the surety "touches and concerns the land" the benefit of the surety's covenant will pass automatically to the assignee of the reversion without the need for a separate assignment.[13] In *P & A Swift Investments v. Combined English Stores Group plc* [1989] A.C. 643, the House of Lords held that whether a covenant touched or concerned the land depended upon the covenant satisfying three conditions, namely that it was beneficial only to the reversioner for the time being, secondly that it affected the nature, quality, and mode of user or value of the reversioner's land and finally that it was not personal in nature. Consequently a covenant by a surety guaranteeing that a

---

[8] *Lloyds v. Harper* (1886) 16 Ch D 290 at 319.
[9] *Wingfield v. De St Croix* (1919) 35 T.L.R. 432.
[10] See, *e.g. Baynton v. Morgan* (1888) 22 Q.B.D. 74.
[11] *Estates Gazette Ltd v. Benjamin Restaurants Ltd* [1994] 1 W.L.R. 1529.
[12] *Johnsey Estates v. Webb* [1990] 19 E.G. 84. However, the release of the guarantor of an assignee will not release the tenant: *Allied London Investments Ltd v. Hambro Life Assurance Ltd* [1985] 274 E.G. 148.
[13] *Kumar v. Dunning* [1989] 1 QB 193; *P & A Swift Investments v. Combined English Stores Group plc* [1989] A.C. 643, *cf.* English authorities such as *Pineman Ltd v. Welbeck International Ltd* [1984] 272 E.G. 1168 and *Re Distributors and Warehousing Ltd* [1986] B.C.L.C. 129 reflecting the views in *Sacher Investments v. Forma Stereo Consultants Pty Ltd* [1976] 1 N.S.W.L.R. 5 to the contrary.

tenant's covenants which touched or concerned the land be performed and observed had itself to be a covenant which touched and concerned the land.[14]

Rent review

A surety for rent will generally have no right to participate in a **14–05** rent review. It is suggested that the surety should be permitted to compel the tenant to participate in the review or to allow the surety to participate in the tenant's name. Even if the lease is later assigned a suitably drafted clause could make the guarantor the attorney both for the tenant and (by means of an undertaking to procure such an eventuality) for the assignee. Alternatively the guarantor can insist on a contractual right to participate in his own name.

Relief from forfeiture

A surety for rent in the ordinary way has no right to seek relief **14–06** from forfeiture.[15] Suitable provision can be made enabling the surety to act in the principal's name. Alternatively the tenant can covenant to assign the lease to a surety should the tenant default. This has been held to be an agreement for an underlease within section 146(5) of the Law of Property Act enabling the surety to apply for relief from forfeitures.[16] The surety should ensure that he is served by the landlord with copies of all notices otherwise served on the tenant.

Substitute guarantor

In general a surety will remain liable throughout the term of the **14–07** lease which will cover liability arising in respect of the obligations of assignees of the lease. It will therefore be prudent for him to make provision that on giving reasonable notice to the landlord he can revoke his guarantee on procuring a suitable substitute guarantor, the landlord in turn undertaking to give his consent to such a substitution (not to be unreasonably withheld).[17]

---

[14] In *Kumar v. Dunning*, above the surety's covenant was given in the assignment as distinct from on the grant of the lease as in *Swift Investments*. See Lord Oliver at pp. 640–642 in *Swift Investments* who described the surety's covenant and repairing obligation as being one to procure that the tenant in turn procured that the premises be kept in repair.

[15] With the possible exception of a case where a tenant agrees that if called upon he will execute a mortgage of the lease in the surety's favour: see *Re Good's Lease* [1954] 1 W.L.R. 309.

[16] *Re Good's Lease* [1954] 1 W.L.R. 309.

[17] For a similar type of clause, see, *e.g. Grovewood (IE) Ltd v. Lundy Properties Ltd and Others* [1993] E.G.C.S. 168. The surety's release should not precede the provision of the substitute surety.

Disclaimer

14–08   A trustee in bankruptcy may disclaim a bankrupt's lease under section 315 of the Insolvency Act 1986 just as a liquidator may disclaim under section 178 of that Act. On being struck off the register under section 652 of the Companies Act 1985 a company's property including any lease will vest in the Crown as *bona vacantia* under section 654 and the Crown can also disclaim under section 656 of that Act. Although there are differences between disclaimer as effected by an officeholder[18] and a disclaimer as effected by the Crown, both involve the operation of section 178(4) of the Insolvency Act 1986 which provides that a disclaimer:

    (a) operates to determine as from the date of disclaimer the rights, interests and liabilities of the insolvent company in or in respect of the property disclaimed; but

    (b) does not, except in so far as is necessary for the purpose of releasing the company from any liability affect the rights or liabilities of any other person.

Any person sustaining loss or damage in consequence of the operation of a disclaimer can prove in the bankruptcy or in the liquidation. The effect of the disclaimer is to determine the interests of the person whose interests have been disclaimed in the lease and to release him and his estate from all future liability thereunder including any liability to pay rent for any period after the disclaimer as well as to impose a statutory liability on the part of his estate to compensate any person injured by the disclaimer including the landlord.

14–09   These principles were exhaustively considered by the House of Lords in *Hindcastle Ltd v. Barbara Attenborough Associates Ltd.*[19] In the *Hindcastle* decision it was held that in the case of leases granted before January 1, 1996[20] the effect of a disclaimer under section 178 is that the termination of an insolvent company tenant's liabilities does not affect the obligations to the landlord of the guarantor of the company whether the company was original tenant or assignee. The House of Lords confirmed that if the insolvent party was the original tenant the disclaimer determined not only the tenant's obligations but also the lease itself.[21] In the case of a sub-tenant determination of his sub-tenancy is not necessary to free the tenant from his liabilities.[22] Consequently a sub-tenant may

---

[18] Neither an administrative receiver nor an administrator can disclaim.

[19] [1997] A.C. 70.

[20] Being the date of the coming into force of the Landlord and Tenant (Covenants) Act 1995 which in general terms provides that where a tenant lawfully assigns premises demised to him he will be released from any covenant or covenants falling to be complied with by the tenant of the premises.

[21] Lord Nicholls at 87. See *Re Morrish, ex p. Hart Dyke* (1882) 21 Ch D 410 *per* Jessel M.R. at 425.

[22] Lord Nicholls at 89.

apply to the court for an order under section 181 of the Insolvency Act 1986 that the lease be vested in him.[23]

The sub-tenant will therefore hold his estate on the same terms and subject to the same rights and obligations which would otherwise be applicable as if the tenant's obligations had continued.

Until the House of Lords' decision in *Hindcastle* it had been held **14–10** that a disclaimer by a trustee in bankruptcy or a liquidator of a lease held by the principal debtor released the surety.[24] Four main grounds had been advanced in support of such a result. First it was argued that on disclaimer the lease determined and no future rent could be payable. However, if it was also to be argued on this point that there was no logical distinction between the position of an original tenant and that of a guarantor, this offended the plain language of section 178(4)(b). Secondly, it had been maintained[25] that the release of the debtor discharged the guarantor. This however again failed to take into account the effect of the critical words in section 178(4)(b) of the 1986 Act set out above. Thirdly, the House of Lords made it clear that in order to release the insolvent party it was sufficient only to extinguish the insolvent party's liability to indemnify the guarantor. It was not necessary to go further and release the guarantor from his liability to the lessor. Fourthly, it had been maintained that the deprivation of a surety's right of indemnity effectively left him without a remedy; the House of Lords confirmed that whilst the surety might not be released he enjoyed a right to prove as a creditor and if necessary seek a vesting order.[26]

As a means of mitigating the rigour of the rule that a surety was released on disclaimer, it had been held in *Re Katherine et Cie*[27] that the court would not exercise its discretion in favour of granting leave to disclaim in the event that release of the surety was likely to prejudice the landlord's rights to recover substantial sums from any surety even if the land had become *bona vacantia*.

In the case of the disclaimer on the insolvency of an assignee or **14–11** of a sub-tenant,[28] the effect of the House of Lords' decision in *Hindcastle* was in effect to approve the decision of Megarry V.-C. in *Warnford Investments v. Duckworth*[29] in holding that in the case of the insolvency of an assignee the obligations of the original

---

[23] *Re A. E. Realisations (1985) Ltd* [1988] 1 W.L.R. 200 applying *Re Finley, ex p. Clothworkers Co.* (1888) 21 Q.B.D. 475. On the other hand the sub-tenancy will terminate if the lease is forfeited subject to the ability to seek relief or if either landlord or tenant served a notice to quit.

[24] *Stacey v. Hill* [1901] 1 QB 660; *D. Morris & Sons Ltd v. Jeffreys* [1933] 429 T.L.R. 76. The correctness of *Stacey v. Hill* was apparently confirmed in *Murphy v. Sawyer-Hoare and others* [1983] 2 E.G.L.R. 67.

[25] *per* Collins L.J. in *Stacey v. Hill* at 666.

[26] Or an overriding lease under s.19 of the Landlord and Tenant (Covenants) Act 1995 applicable to existing leases at the time of the coming into force of that Act.

[27] [1932] 1 Ch. 70.

[28] Note that a disclaimer by a trustee in bankruptcy of an insolvent assignee disclaims both his interests under the licence to assign and also the interests of the bankrupt in the lease itself: see *MEPC plc v. Scottish Amicable* [1993] N.P.C. 44.

[29] [1979] 1 Ch. 127.

tenant survived any disclaimer and to confirm that the law was reflected in the House of Lords' own earlier decision in *Hill v. East and West India Dock Co.*[30]

Disclaimer: no leave required

14–12   The disclaimer provisions in the 1986 Act removed the earlier requirement that an office holder was required to obtain the court's leave to disclaim. Any challenge to a decision to disclaim can now only be made on the basis that a liquidator or trustee in bankruptcy has acted in a way in which no reasonable liquidator or trustee in bankruptcy could have acted, *i.e.* a challenge as to the *bona fides* of the office holder or a finding that the decision to disclaim was in some way perverse.[31]

In any event in cases decided before the *Hindcastle* decision it had been held that a disclaimer will effect the release of the guarantor from any liability which might accrue in the future under a lease and that even in respect of any liability for breaches such a liability was not a liability in respect of the disclaimed property within the vesting provisions, *i.e.* section 181(2)(b) of the Insolvency Act 1986. Consequently a surety would have no *locus standi* to apply for such an order.[32] It follows that a surety remaining liable for rent accruing after the date of the disclaimer will have *locus standi* to be able to apply for a vesting order. However, such rights may not prevail as against other parties such as the original tenant (in the case of an assignee's insolvency) or a current assignee.[33] Overall and subject to any contrary terms in the guarantee a surety should be in no better position than if he took a lease directly from a landlord on the same terms as the original lease of which he was guarantor.

Disclaimer by Crown

14–13   The Crown can disclaim a lease following the dissolution of a company. In the light of the House of Lords' decision in *Hindcastle* if a company is subsequently restored to the register the surety's liability should not also thereby be revived.[34] If on disclaimer the surety is no longer released at least as to future arrears of rent there

---

[30] (1884) L.R. 9 App. Cas. 448 which had considered the language in the Bankruptcy Act 1869 which was similar to that in s.178(4) save for the language now found in s.178(4)(b). For a critical view of the applicable principles see *Tempany v. Royal Liver Trustees Ltd* (1985) 1 B.C.C. 364.

[31] See, *e.g. Re Hans Place Ltd* [1992] B.C.C. 737: see generally *Leon v. York-o-Matic Ltd* [1966] 1 W.L.R. 1450.

[32] *Re No. 1 London Ltd* [1991] B.C.L.C. 501; *Re Yarmarine (IW) Ltd* [1992] B.C.C. 28: these cases involved a disclaimer by the Crown.

[33] See *Re AE Realisations Ltd* [1988] 1 W.L.R. 200.

[34] *cf. Allied Dunbar plc v. Fowle* [1994] 1 E.G.L.R. 122 where it was held that a disclaimer constituted a "disposition" within the meaning of s.655 of the Companies Act 1985 entitling an assignee to compensation from the Crown.

is no need to consider whether revival of a surety's liability is required.

Discharge of other party's liability

Where one person may be forced to discharge a liability which **14–14** belongs primarily to another party there will on recognised principles[35] be a right of reimbursement sometimes thought of as being akin to suretyship. For example where a sub-lessee is compelled to pay sums to the head lessor in respect of rent due from the intermediate landlord the sub-lessee may deduct such sums from his rent to the intermediate landlord.[36] Moreover it would seem that a person in the sub-lessee's position can claim to be subrogated to the head landlord's securities and rights as against the intermediate landlord.[37] In *Re Downer Enterprises Ltd*[38] the lease was assigned to the plaintiff and then by him on to a company which went into liquidation. The plaintiff on paying the arrears of rent was held entitled to be subrogated to the landlord's rights and in the circumstances of the case to have part of the arrears paid out of the company's assets as an expense of the winding-up. This was because as between the plaintiff and the company the company was ultimately liable.[39]

Securities held by a landlord

By the rules of equity and under section 5 of the Mercantile Law **14–15** Amendment Act 1856, the paying surety is entitled to any remedies and any securities held by the landlord over the tenant and his property in order to enforce the surety's right to contribution. However, the landlord's right to distrain for rent has been held to be neither one of the "remedies of the creditor" nor a "security" within the section.[40] On the other hand, a surety for the performance of covenants in a lease is entitled to be recouped out of the land in respect of payments made on account of rent.[41]

Mesne profits

A guarantor of rent and the performance of a lessee's covenants **14–16** will not be held liable for mesne profits, or in general matters

---

[35] See Goff & Jones, *The Law of Restitution* (4th ed.) at pp. 343 *et seq.*
[36] *Carter v. Carter* (1827) 7 L.J. (O.S.) C.P. 141.
[37] *Re Downer Enterprises Ltd* [1974] 1 W.L.R. 1480 *per* Pennycuick J. at 1468C.
[38] *ibid.*
[39] Pennycuick J. considered at 1468 that the principles embodied in *Duncan Fox and Co. v. North and South Wales Bank* (1880) L.R. 6 App.Cas. 1 by Lord Selborne at 16 and Lord Blackburn at 19 applied not only to guarantees but to any situation of primary and secondary liability, the sense of "primary" meaning alternative liability.
[40] *Re Russell* (1885) 29 Ch D 254.
[41] *Lord Harberton v. Bennett* (1829) Beat. p. 386. This right is subject to the paramount rights of the landlord to obtain payment of future rent and to enforce covenants; *ibid.* at p. 388.

arising after the termination of the lease.[42] Nevertheless, he will be held liable for breach of a covenant to yield up possession.[43]

Privity

14–17   There must be privity of contract between a creditor and a surety in order to make the latter liable. Accordingly, where a guarantor's covenant is with a lessor and its "successors and assigns," this was of itself insufficient to enable the lessor to sue without an assignment of the benefit of a guarantee.[44] It has since been established that the benefit of a guarantee will pass with the reversion so that the lessor can sue without any specific assignment of the benefit of the guarantee.[45]

Non-disclosure

14–18   Although bound to give truthful answers to questions put to him regarding a tenant for whom a surety is taken,[46] the lessor is under no positive duty to disclose material facts affecting the tenant's reliability, *e.g.* the fact that the tenant still owed rent to the lessor from the previous tenancy,[47] unless the circumstances are such that the surety might naturally have expected those facts not to arise.[48]

---

[42] *Associated Dairies v. Pierce* (1981) 259 E.G. 562.
[43] *ibid.*
[44] *Sacher Investments Pty Ltd v. Forma Stereo Consultants Pty Ltd* [1976] 1 N.S.W. L.R. 5, followed in England in *Pinemain Ltd v. Welbeck International Ltd* [1984] 272 E.G. 1168 and *Re Distributors and Warehousing Ltd* [1986] B.C.L.C. 129.
[45] See para. 14–04 above.
[46] See above.
[47] *Roper v. Cox* (1882) 10 L.R.Ir. 200.
[48] See above.

CHAPTER 15

BUILDING CONTRACTS[1]

General

A guarantee may relate to the performance of any party to a **15–01** building contract. The standard forms of building contract such as the JCT form[2] do not provide for sureties so that typically a guarantee will be a collateral document, *e.g.* in the form of some sort of bond.[3] As in other types of guarantees the need for writing is present, unless the surety's promise can be construed as an indemnity reflecting primary liability.[4]

Non-disclosure

The employer's duty (if any) on the making of any implied **15–02** representation to the surety, *e.g.* as to the nature of contracted works to be performed or as to the prevailing conditions, will depend upon the particular circumstances of each transaction.[5] If the employer has not disclosed that the works are to be executed under the joint supervision of his own surveyor and the surveyor of an undisclosed third party, a surety will be released.[6] The guarantor is said to look in the usual situation no further than the skill and experience of the contractor[7] and there is no duty on the employer to reveal difficulty in the terrain.

Extent of liability

In the case of a guarantee of the contractor's performance, the **15–03** surety's liability will in normal circumstances be interpreted to cover only the building works and not any other, albeit related, transactions with the employer, *e.g.* a loan to enable the contractor to carry out or complete the work.[8] The situation may be otherwise where the surety knows of the related transaction, *e.g.* where it is made a term of the building contract or is contained in a collateral

---

[1] See also *Keating on Building Contracts* (6th ed., 1995).
[2] *e.g.* the JCT Standard Form of Building Contract (1980 Edition).
[3] As to which see generally Chap. 17.
[4] *Lakeman v. Mountstephen* (1874) L.R. 7 HL 17.
[5] *Trade Indemnity Co. v. Workington Harbour & Dock Board* [1937] A.C. 1. With regard to the question of the fitness of the site, the employer does not usually warrant this to the contractor: see *Appleby v. Myers* (1987) L.R. 2 C.P. 651. The court may imply a term for further payments where the difficult nature of the site requires further work.
[6] *Stiff v. Eastbourne Local Board* (1986) 20 L.T. 339, *cf. Russell v. Trickett* (1965) 13 L.T. 280.
[7] *Trade Indemnity Co. v. Workington Harbour & Dock Board*, above.
[8] *Trade Indemnity Co. v. Workington Harbour & Dock Board*, above.

document which accompanies it. Again, where a surety guarantees the building works his guarantee is not normally construed so as to extend to the consequences of the contractor's fraud.[9] However, the contractor's fraud is not necessarily a defence for the surety, if on the true construction of the guarantee the guaranteed liability has arisen.[10]

Completion of performance

15–04   The usual rule is that when the principal debtor has completed his performance the surety is discharged. In building terms the performance may be "complete" but the building contract may require the architect to certify certain stages of completion by means of a certificate, *e.g.* in the JCT form.[11] Where a building contract, unlike the JCT form, does not specify any stage or stages of certified completion, actual completion may be taken as complete performance by the contractor of the principal obligation so as to discharge the surety.[12] Where the building contract specifies certain stages of certified completion but the guarantee is silent as to which stage is meant, it is submitted that the final certificate should be taken as the stage of complete performance for the purpose of the guarantee.

Discharge otherwise than by completion

15–05   From time to time the building contract may determine, not according to the provisions of the agreement, but by virtue of a repudiatory breach by one party accepted by the other. This type of determination will not release the surety of the repudiating party, who remains liable for the losses caused by the repudiation.[13] Nor is a surety of a contractor bound by the contractor fraudulently obtaining a final certificate.[14]

However, repudiation of the principal contract by the beneficiary of the contract of guarantee, *i.e.* normally the creditor, as distinct from repudiation by the principal debtor, will if it is accepted, generally discharge a surety. A non-repudiatory breach will not without more do so.[15]

Another possible cause of the discharge of a surety for the contractor other than by performance is where there has been some material non-disclosure by the employer which alters the nature of

---

[9] *Kingston-upon-Hill v. Harding* (1982) 2 QB 494, CA. The guarantor guaranteed that the contractor would "well and truly" execute the contract and this was held to apply to a situation where the certificate of completion was obtained by fraudulent concealment of defects.

[10] *Kingston-upon-Hill v. Harding*, above.

[11] *e.g.* under clause 17 of the JCT Standard Form of Building Contract (1980 Edition).

[12] *Lewis v. Hoare* (1881) 44 L.T. 66, HL.

[13] *Moschi v. Lep Air Services Ltd* [1973] A.C. 331, HL. See generally Chapters 4 and 8.

[14] *Kingston-upon-Hill v. Harding*, above.

[15] *National Westminster Bank v. Riley* [1986] B.C.L.C. 268, CA. Discharge will depend upon whether there has been a "non-substantial" departure from a term of the principal contract which in that case was found to have been incorporated within the guarantee.

an important quality of the work to be executed, *e.g.* where the employer has failed to disclose that the supervision of the work was to be shared with a surveyor of an outside party.[16] However, where the contract itself anticipates possible difficulties, *e.g.* by warning the contractor itself to make proper inspections of the site, unexpected difficulties arising from the nature of the site may not enable the surety to treat himself as discharged.[17]

As in other situations, conduct by the creditor which prejudices the surety's position will discharge the surety.[18] For example, a surety for a contractor will be discharged where the employer has a contractual duty but fails to carry it out, *e.g.* a duty to superintend the work[18] or to insure the works against fire.[19] Moreover where the building contract provides for the retention of sums which act both as security for completion and as a form of pressure upon the contractor, a premature payment to the contractor without his surety's consent will discharge the surety.[20]

A surety may also be released by variations in the contractual obligations agreed between the employer and the contractor without the surety's consent, *e.g.* extension of the contraction time for performance.[21] It should be remembered that a standard form building contract will normally make express provision for extension of time.

Guarantee of employer's payment

Where a surety guarantees payment by the employer of the contract price, the contractor in the absence of provision for stage payments cannot normally recover against a surety unless he can show entire completion.[22] However, in a case where a guarantor has guaranteed payment for the building works by instalments, and the employers fail to make payment, giving the contractors the right to rescind, which they exercise, the guarantor will be held liable to pay the accrued instalment.[23] The guarantors had there contended that the contractor's rescission terminated the contract and destroyed their right to recover the instalments as opposed to recovery of damages. They argued moreover that such damages were not recoverable under the guarantee as sums "due or to become due" under the contract. The House of Lords rejected these arguments on the basis that (a) the instalments accrued due prior to rescission were

15–06

---

[16] *Stiff v. Eastbourne Local Board* (1869) 20 L.T. 339.
[17] *Trade Indemnity Co. v. Workington Harbour & Dock Board*, above.
[18] *Kingston-upon-Hill Corporation v. Harding*, above.
[19] *Watts v. Shuttleworth* (1861) 7 H. & N. 353.
[20] *Calvert v. London Dock Co.* (1838) 2 Keen. 638; L.J. Ch. 90; 48 E.R. 774.
[21] See, *e.g. Rees v. Berrington* (1795) 2 Ves.Jan. 540; *Harrison v. Seymour* (1866) L.R. 1 C.P. 518.
[22] *Eshelby v. Federated European Bank Ltd* [1932] 1 QB 432, CA.
[23] *Hyundai Heavy Industries Co. Ltd v. Papadopoulos* [1980] 1 W.L.R. 1129 (shipbuilding contract).

recoverable from the employer and therefore due under the guarantee, alternatively (b) the object of the guarantee was to enable recovery of the instalments irrespective of the position between the contractor and employer.

Procedure

15–07   It used to be the case that where the surety had entered into a bond for a contractor's performance, and the bond was in the nature of a guarantee,[24] as soon as the contractor committed a breach, the employer could sue the surety and claim judgment for the whole amount of the bond as long as some damage occasioned by the breach could be shown.[25] Execution could only issue for the amount of damages proved, but the judgment remained as security for the recovery of damages for future breaches.[26] This is however no longer the case. Judgment can only be obtained for a declaration as to the breach and for such damage as can be proved.[27]

---

[24] *Workington Harbour & Dock Trade v. Trade Indemnity Co. (No. 2)* (1938) 2 All E.R. 101, HL *per* Lord Atkin at 105: see now *Trafalgar House Construction (Regions) Ltd v. General Surety & Guarantee Co.* [1996] A.C. 199.
[25] *ibid.*
[26] *ibid.*
[27] *Bold v. BGK Metals* (unreported, Gibson J., May 21, 1997).

CHAPTER 16

CONSUMER CREDIT

Introduction

The Consumer Credit Act 1974[1] was enacted to reflect the fact **16–01**
that in many modern commercial contexts, the notion of freedom of
contract is more imaginary than real. Without abolishing the dis-
crepancy in bargaining power it has imposed certain formalities and
standards of disclosure which must be satisfied to render a transaction enforceable.

Definitions

Continuing the tradition laid down in earlier hire purchase legis- **16–02**
lation, the 1974 Act makes no distinction between contracts of
guarantee and contracts of indemnity.[2] "Security" is defined in
section 189(1) as:

" . . . a mortgage, charge, pledge, bond, debenture, indemnity,
guarantee, bill, note or other right provided by the debtor or
hirer, or at his request (express or implied), to secure the
carrying out of the obligations of the debtor or hirer under the
agreement."

A surety is defined as one by whom any security as above defined
is provided or the person to whom his rights and duties in relation
to the security have passed by assignment or operation of law.[3] This
is a widely drawn definition and can obviously include not only
guarantors and indemnifiers, but even the debtor or hirer himself.

Scope of the Act

The Act regulates the supplying of credit not exceeding £15,000[4] **16–03**
to individuals (including sole traders and partnerships) in the form

---

[1] For the background to the Act see the Report of the Committee on Consumer Credit (The
Crowther Report) Cmnd. 4596 (1974), and generally Guest & Lloyd, *The Encyclopaedia of Consumer Credit Law* (1975). The Act was brought fully into force on May 19, 1985. Note too the
increasing importance of distinguishing between commercial and consumer guarantees as to which
see, *e.g.* British Columbia Law Reform Commission Report on Guarantees of Consumer Debts 1979
("British Columbia Report"). So-called recourse agreements are excluded from the British Columbia
Report. The relevant sections of the 1974 Act are set out in Appendix 2.
[2] See, *e.g.* Hire Purchase Act 1965. Note s.113(7) of the Act which ensures that where a debtor or
hirer is for example, a minor, any contract of indemnity will not be unenforceable merely by reason
of his minority, as if it would be if it were a contract of guarantee.
[3] Section 189(1) of the Act.
[4] Consumer Credit (Increase of Monetary Limits) Order 1983 (S.I. 1983 No. 1878).

of so-called consumer credit agreements[5] and consumer hire agreements.[6] The Act also imposes a system of licensing in respect of credit and hire businesses dealing with such agreements.[7] It further regulates the form and content of such agreements[8] and modifies the common law rules in respect of those to whom notice of withdrawal may be given and the consequences of withdrawal.

Formal requirements

16–04　　Under the Act, any security provided by a party other than the debtor or hirer, including a guarantee or indemnity, must be expressed in writing and signed by the surety or his agent.[9] Such a document, which must embody all the terms of the security except implied terms and be readily legible, is called "security instrument".[10] Detailed requirements as to the precise form of guarantees and indemnities that are provided at the express or implied request of the debtor or hirer are prescribed by the Consumer Credit (Guarantees and Indemnities) Regulations 1983.[11]

　　The surety is also naturally entitled to receive a copy of the security instrument, when the document is presented or sent for the purposes of being signed by him or on his behalf.[12] He should also be provided with a copy of the executed credit or hire agreement.[13]

Effect of non-compliance

16–05　　Where a security has not been expressed in writing, or where it is improperly executed in that the security instrument is not in the prescribed form, or copies of either the security instrument or the regulated agreement has not been provided to the surety, the security is enforceable against the surety only with leave of the court.[14] The court will dismiss an application for an enforcement order if and only if it considers it just to do so taking into account

---

[5] Defined in section 8 of the Act.

[6] Defined in section 15 of the Act, *e.g.* ordinary domestic rental agreements.

[7] See Part III of the Act (see ss.21 *et seq.*).

[8] See sections 60 *et seq.* of the Act. *Cf.* the recommendations of the British Columbia Report.

[9] sections 105(1), (4) and (6) of the Act.

[10] sections 105(2) and (4) of the Act.

[11] S.I. 1983 No. 1556, which came into operation on May 19, 1985. It does not apply to all security instruments as that term is defined in the Act, but only to documents expressing a guarantee or indemnity in writing. The Regulations specify, for example, forms of words for the heading of such documents and require, *inter alia*, that a statement of rights of sureties in a specified form be included.

[12] section 105(4)(d) of the Act. Such a copy must comply with the Consumer Credit (Cancellation Notices and Copies of Documents) Regulations 1983 (S.I. 1983 No. 1557).

[13] section 105(5) of the Act. Where the security is provided after or at the same time as the regulated agreement, the surety must be given a copy of the agreement at the time the security is provided. Where the security is provided before the regulated agreement is made, a copy of the executed agreement must be given to the surety within seven days of the making of the regulated agreement.

[14] section 105(7) of the Act.

the prejudice caused by the contravention and the degree of culpability for it, as well as the wide powers to compensate the surety conferred on the court.[15] Beyond this general provision, the factors which ought to be taken into account by the court in exercising its discretion are not set out.[16] If an application is dismissed, on other than technical grounds,[17] the security will be "ineffective".[18]

Ineffective securities

Section 106 of the Act provides that where under any provision **16–06** of the Act that section is applied to any security provided in relation to a regulated agreement then:

(a) the security, so far as it is so provided, shall be treated as never having effect[19];

(b) any property lodged with the creditor or owners solely for the purposes of the security as so provided shall be returned by him forthwith;

(c) the creditor or owner shall take any necessary action to remove or cancel an entry in any register, so far as the entry relates to the security as so provided; and

(d) any amount received by the creditor or owner on realisation of the security shall, so far as it is referrable to the security agreement, be repaid to the surety.[20]

Continuing obligations to supply information

Both a creditor under a regulated agreement for fixed-sum **16–07** credit[21] or running-account credit,[22] and the owner under a regulated consumer hire agreement, in relation to which a security is

---

[15] section 127 of the Act, which applies not only to applications under s.105(7), but also, for example, to those under s.65(1). Under s.127(2), in making an enforcement order, the court may reduce or discharge the sum payable by a surety. See also s.135 and s.136.

[16] The British Columbia Report, as to which see n. 1 above, recommends that any judicial determination be conducted on an "objective" basis to ascertain whether the guarantor ought not to have been misled by any formal irregularities.

[17] See sections 189(1) and (5) of the Act.

[18] section 105(8) of the Act, applying s.106.

[19] See also *Orakpo v. Manson Investments Ltd* [1978] A.C. 95 which effectively frustrated an attempt to assert an unpaid vendor's lien by way of subrogation in the case of a security made unenforceable by the Money Lenders Act 1927. The 1927 Act has now been repealed and replaced by the 1974 Act.

[20] section 106 of the Act would apply not only where there has been a contravention of s.105, above, but also where, for example, a regulated agreement is cancelled under s.69(1) or terminated under s.91, or where a court dismisses an application for an order under s.65(1) for the enforcement of an improperly executed agreement (s.113(3)). See generally Guest & Lloyd, *op. cit.*

[21] Defined in sections 10(1) and 189(1) of the Act, *e.g.* bank loans or hire purchase transactions.

[22] *ibid., e.g.* bank overdrafts, shop budget accounts or credit cards.

required, must within 12 working days[23] after receiving a request in writing to that effect from a surety, as well as the statutory fee,[24] give the latter a statement of account as between himself and the hirer, in the same terms as the statement given to the debtor or hirer.[25] The creditor or owner must also give the surety first a copy of the executed agreement if any, and any other document referred to in it, and a copy of the security instrument, if any.[26] Any failure to comply will prevent the creditor from enforcing the security while the default continues and will, after one month's default, constitute a criminal offence.[27] Non-commercial agreements are exempt.[28]

A statement made by a creditor or owner under these provisions is, in principle, binding on him.[29] Where a party seeks to rely on such a statement in proceedings however, and the statement is incorrect, the court may direct such relief as seems just in favour of the creditor or owner.[30]

Termination

16–08   Section 98(1) of the Act provides that a creditor or hirer is not entitled to terminate a regulated agreement except by or after giving the debtor seven days' notice of termination, but that section will not apply to termination by reason of any breach by the debtor or hirer of the agreement.[31] In cases of breach, a default notice must be served.[32] Section 76(1) provides that a creditor or owner is not entitled to enforce a term of a regulated agreement by (a) demanding earlier payment of any sum, or (b) recovering possession of any goods or land, or (c) treating any right conferred on the debtor or hirer by the agreement as terminated, restricted or deferred, except by or after giving the debtor or hirer not less than seven days' notice of his intention to do so. Copies of notices under sections 76(1) and 98(1), as well as default notices, must be served on any surety.[33] Failure to comply means that the security is enforceable against the surety on an order of the court only.[34]

[23] Consumer Credit (Prescribed Periods for Giving Information) Regulations 1983 (S.I. 1983 No. 1569).

[24] At present, 50p: Consumer Credit (Increase of Monetary Amounts) Order (S.I. 1983 No. 1571).

[25] sections 107–109 of the Act. For the requirements regarding the contents of such statements, see sections 77 *et seq* of the Act.

[26] *ibid.*

[27] *ibid.*

[28] Defined in section 189(1) of the Act as not made by a creditor or owner in the course of a business carried on by him.

[29] section 172(1) of the Act.

[30] section 172(3) of the Act.

[31] section 98(6) of the Act.

[32] The need for and content of a default notice are set out in sections 87, 88 *et seq.* of the Act.

[33] section 111(1) of the Act. The form of each type of notice is prescribed by the Consumer Credit (Enforcement, Default and Termination Notices) Regulations 1983 S.I. 1983 No. 1561).

[34] section 111(2) of the Act. Section 127, for which see above, is applicable. Section 173 forbids contracting out of the protection afforded by the Act.

Disclosure

The question of disclosure in guarantees is dealt with in detail **16–09** elsewhere,[35] but the Consumer Credit Act 1974 imposes no specific duty of disclosure on either creditor or principal debtor to ensure for example that the guarantor is acquainted with whatever other indebtedness the debtor may have or indeed with every term of the principal transaction[36] either before or during the currency of the guarantee.

---

[35] See Chap. 5 above.
[36] *cf.* British Columbia Consumer Protection Act S.B.C. 1977, section 12 of that Act is discussed in the British Columbia Report, which recommends that a consumer guarantee be treated as one of *uberrimae fidei.*

CHAPTER 17

PERFORMANCE BONDS

Nature of bonds

17–01   Performance or guarantee bonds[1] are here dealt with given their increasing importance in modern commerce, especially in construction and international sales contracts where they represent the means whereby surety companies or banks will guarantee performance in accordance with the provisions of the requisite contract.[2]

A performance bond[3] will also act as an assurance of the financial stability of the contractor and is a means of ensuring total execution of the contract should he fail to perform whether through his own default or not. A distinction is in practice drawn between performance bonds issued by surety companies[4] and those issued by banks or other financial institutions. In the case of the former, there is a guarantee in the event of the contractor's failure causing loss; in the case of the latter there is often an undertaking to pay money, in the event of breach or in certain cases upon presentation of certain documents or even upon a mere formal demand.[5]

A performance bond[6] is an undertaking given by a bank, insur-

---

[1] *cf.* usage in the United States where the term "surety bond" is frequently given to an indemnity granted by a surety company which undertakes in effect to perform the contract, as distinct from merely making payment in the event of non-performance by a contractor. See generally McNeill Stokes, *International Construction Contracts* (New York, McGraw Hill, 1980). Bid bonds are given at the pre-tender stage and advance payment bonds are for the due repayment as the work proceeds of advance payments made to secure plant or equipment or for financing purposes. Other types of bonds include, *e.g.* in building cases, maintenance, materials and labour bonds.

[2] As to the nature and commercial advantages of performance bonds see G. Andrews and R. Millet, *Law of Guarantees* (2nd ed., 1995), pp. 451–453.

[3] The practice of bonding grew out of the relationship of master and servant and the desire of the former to safeguard his secrets or goods from being stolen or passed on to another employer. In due course buyers, in the sense used later in the text, who awarded large contracts out of public funds became concerned to ensure first that bidders for such contracts had sufficient technical and financial ability to undertake the property involved and further that the contracts would subsequently be fulfilled satisfactorily in accordance with their terms and conditions. Moreover a buyer might want to be certain that any payment made to a contractor was used for the purposes of the contract and not, for example, as part of a contractor's working capital. These various forms of undertakings or assurances have come to be known as bid bonds, performance bonds and advance payment bonds respectively and as suggested in the text the term "Guarantee Bond" can be used in respect of any one of these entities. Specimen bonds are contained in Appendix 1.

[4] The House of Lords has recently held that a deed described as a bond was a guarantee rather than an unconditional performance bond entitling the surety to raise any set-off open to the principal debtor: *Trafalgar House Construction (Regions) Ltd v. General Surety & Guarantee Co. Ltd* [1995] 3 All E.R. 737, HL; see also *The Wardens and Commonalty of the Mystery of Mercers of the City of London v. New Hampshire Insurance Co.* [1992] 2 Lloyd's Rep. 365, CA.

[5] Although the courts are inclined to construe in a performance bond on demand an additional obligation to assert a breach: *I.E. Contractors Ltd v. Lloyds Bank plc* [1990] 2 Lloyd's Rep. 496; *Esal (Commodities) Ltd and Reltor Ltd v. Oriental Credit Ltd and Wells Fargo Bank NA* [1985] 2 Lloyd's Rep. 546.

[6] A demand guarantee is defined in Art. 2(a) of the I.C.C.'s Uniform Rules for Demand Guarantees, I.C.C. Publication 458 published in October 1992. See Guide to the URDG, I.C.C. Publication 510, Goode.

ance company or other party (the guarantor) at the request of a tenderer or contractor (the principal or seller) to a party inviting the tender or entering into a contract of purchase (the beneficiary or buyer) whereby the guarantor undertakes in the event of default by the seller in the performance of the latter's obligations under the tender or contract to pay the buyer up to a limit of a stated sum of money or to arrange for performance of the relevant obligations under the tender or contract.

The transaction therefore involves agreement first between the guarantor and buyer (the guarantee or bond), secondly between seller and buyer (the contract of sale or purchase) and thirdly between guarantor and seller (the counter-indemnity). Normally the contract of sale will precede the issue of the bond, followed by the execution of the counter-indemnity.[7] The nature of the undertaking given by the guarantor is sometimes described as "conditional" since he will only pay the buyer on condition that the latter proves or establishes default by the seller.[8]

It is implicit in the nature of a performance bond that in the absence of clear contractual words to a different effect there will be an accounting between the parties at some stage after the bond has been called, in the sense that their rights and obligations will be determined at some future date.[9]

Conditional or unconditional bond?

In deciding whether a bond is conditional or unconditional the court will consider the overall purpose of the contractual relationship.[10] However the courts tend to treat the bond as unconditional if there is evidence that this was its intention even though there are indications to the contrary elsewhere in the document. In *Esal Commodities Ltd and Reltor Ltd v. Oriental Credit Ltd*[11] a bank "undertook to pay the said amount on your written demand in the event that the supplier fails to execute the written performance". It was held that the latter words did not alter the fact that the moneys were payable upon a written demand. **17–02**

---

[7] Except in the case of a bid bond, where there will probably be no executed contract of sale. For an illustration of the operation of a performance bond and counter-indemnity in the context of a building contract see *General Surety & Guarantee Co. Ltd v. Francis Parker Ltd* (1977) 6 Build. L.R. 16 *per* Donaldson J. This case shows that in any case of ambiguity a bond will not be construed so as to be enforceable without proof of default in the discharge of the bonded obligation.

[8] This is to be contrasted with so-called unconditional bonds discussed in the authorities referred to in the text below. Such bonds are commonly used abroad, especially in the Middle East where the guarantor is required to pay the buyer on first demand without any need by the latter to prove any default by the seller.

[9] In order to displace this usual implication as to subsequent accounting between the parties clear words are required: *Cargill International SA v. Bangladesh Sugar & Food Industries Corp.* [1998] 1 W.L.R. 461, CA. In that case it was held that although the contract provided that the buyer forfeit the performance bond in certain circumstances this did not displace the general rule.

[10] *Attaleia Marine Co. Ltd v. Bimeh Iran (Iran Insurance Co.)* [1993] 2 Lloyd's Rep. 497 at 502.

[11] [1985] 2 Lloyd's Rep. 546. See also *I.E. Contractors v. Lloyds Bank plc and Rafidain Bank* [1990] 2 Lloyd's Rep. 496.

Unconditional bonds

17–03   The risks incurred by a seller in providing unconditional bonds[12] have been illustrated in four English decisions. In *R. D. Harbottle (Mercantile) Ltd v. National Westminster Bank Ltd*[13] performance bonds providing security to Egyptian buyers for the fulfilment by the plaintiffs, who were English sellers, of the latter's obligations under various contracts for the supply of goods were taken with Egyptian banks. The bonds provided payment would be made on first demand by the buyers without proof of any breach of contract by the plaintiffs or any other safeguard against abuse by the buyers. Kerr J. in discharging interim injunctions against *inter alia* the English bank which confirmed the latter's guarantees stated[14]:

> "It is only in exceptional cases that the courts will interfere with the machinery of irrevocable obligations assumed by banks. They are the life-blood of international commerce. Such obligations are treated as collateral to the underlying rights and obligations between the merchants at either end of the banking chain. Except possibly in clear cases of fraud of which the banks have notice, the courts will leave the merchants to settle their disputes under the contracts by litigation or arbitration as available to them or stipulated in the contracts."[15]

On the facts the result appears to have been inevitable given the manner in which the plaintiffs had there agreed to enter into the particular commitments.[16] In various passages in his judgment[17] Kerr J. suggests that only "established frauds" would be a sufficient reason not to pay.[18]

17–04   In *Howe-Richardson Scale Co. Ltd v. Polimex-Cekop*[19] and *Edward Owen Engineering Ltd v. Barclays Bank International Ltd*[20] English suppliers again entered into contracts for the supply of goods to be paid by irrevocable letters of credit confirmed by

[12] See n. 8 above.
[13] [1978] QB 146.
[14] At p. 155G.
[15] This unwillingness to grant injunctive relief is evident in the case law: *Bolvinter SA v. Chase Manhattan Bank NA* [1984] 1 All E.R. 351N.
[16] The learned judge adopted a similar approach to the so-called "conclusive evidence" provision in the counter-guarantee given by the plaintiffs to their own English bank, applying *Bache & Co. (London) Ltd v. Banques Vernes* [1973] 2 Lloyd's Rep. 431.
[17] See, *e.g.* pp. 155F and 155G. *Cf. Edward Owen Engineering Ltd v. Barclays Bank International Ltd* [1978] 1 Lloyd's Rep. 166 at 172, 173, *per* Lord Denning M.R. and Browne L.J.
[18] The only defendant before the court in the *Harbottle* case was the plaintiffs' own bank in England, against whom there was no allegation of fraud. See also *Discount Records Ltd v. Barclays Bank* [1975] 1 W.L.R. 315. Making a demand in order to put financial pressure upon the contractor will probably not be held to be fraud enabling the court to intervene. See *Wood Hall Ltd v. The Pipeline Authority* (1979) 53 A.L.J.R. 487.
[19] [1978] 1 Lloyd's Rep. 161.
[20] [1978] 1 Lloyd's Rep. 166. In the U.S., see *Szteyn v. J. Henry Schroder* 31 N.Y.S. (2d) 631 (1941). See also *Emerson Electric Industries Controls v. Bank of America* (Court of Appeal Transcript 79442, July 10, 1979) (alleged frustration of sale contract held not to affect implementation of bond).

their English banks. In both cases it was a condition precedent to the execution of such contracts first that the buyers had to establish a letter of credit in the suppliers' favour and further that the suppliers had to provide the buyers with unconditional performance bonds, as to which first requirement for differing reasons the buyers failed to open the requisite letters of credit on each supplier refusing to proceed with its contract on the basis of non-performance by each buyer resulting in the latter calling in the bonds. Interim injunctions were again sought by the suppliers to restrain their respective banks from paying out under the bonds and the English banks succeeded in the Court of Appeal in the *Howe-Richardson* case in resisting the granting of any such injunction and in the *Edward Owen* decision, in discharging an injunction previously preventing them from paying a Libyan bank and seller the amount stipulated under the bond.

In the latter case[21] Lord Denning M.R. characterised performance bonds as "virtually promissory notes on demand". He added[22]:

> "So long as the Libyan customers make an honest demand, the banks are bound to pay: and the banks will rarely, if ever, be in a position to learn whether the demand is honest or not . . . . All this leads to the conclusion that the performance guarantee stands on a similar footing to a letter of credit. A bank which gives a performance guarantee must honour the guarantee according to its terms . . . the bank must pay according to its guarantee, on demand, if so stipulated, without proof or conditions. The only exception is when there is a clear fraud of which the bank has notice."[23]

In *Intraco Ltd v. Notis Shipping Corporation*[24] the Court of Appeal applied *Howe-Richardson* to a situation where the purchasers of a ship tried to restrain the sellers from calling for payment from the bank under the bond for part of the purchase price. Without proof of fraud, the court held payment could not be stopped by attempting to restrain the sellers from calling upon the bond. However, Parker J. was willing to grant a *Mareva*[25] injunction freezing the proceeds of the bonds. The Court of Appeal discharged the *Mareva* injunction on the basis that the bond was payable in Greece and not within the jurisdiction.[26] **17–05**

---

[21] At 171.
[22] Geoffrey Lane L.J. (at 175) agreed that performance bonds have much more the characteristics of a promissory note than of a guarantee.
[23] Browne L.J. at 173 stated that the fraud had to be "very clearly established".
[24] [1981] 2 Lloyd's Rep. 256.
[25] [1975] 2 Lloyd's Rep. 509, CA.
[26] Donaldson L.J. said that since a bank guarantee is to be treated as cash when a bank pays and the cash is received by the beneficiary, it should be subject to the same restraints as any other of his cash assets.

In the recent case *Kvaerner John Brown Ltd v. Midland Bank plc & Another*[27] Cresswell J. granted an injunction restraining the defendant bank from making a payment. In that case, the certificate which was included by the beneficiary with the demand stated that it had given the seller notice in accordance with the agreement. Cresswell J. held that as no notice had in fact been given the demand was manifestly untrue and known to be untrue and fell within the category of "clear and obvious fraud of which the bank had notice".

It is clear from the case law that to obtain an injunction against a paying bank on the basis of a fraudulent demand a plaintiff must show that (i) the beneficiary has no right to payment under the underlying contract; (ii) the beneficiary has no genuine belief in such right[28]; and (iii) the bank is aware of the beneficiary's fraud at the time of payment or else reckless, in that the only realistic inference to be drawn in the circumstances is that the demand was fraudulently made. To prove the fraud there has to be strong corroborative evidence, mere assertion of fraud is not enough.[29]

Even if these obstacles are surmounted a plaintiff may face further difficulties in obtaining an injunction preventing a bank satisfying a demand under the performance bond. The courts can only intervene by way of injunction in order to prevent the alleged breach of a legal duty owed by the defendant to the plaintiff. It is difficult to identify the cause of action that founds the fraud exception.[30]

In order to evade the problems associated with obtaining injunctions against a paying bank courts have utilised different routes. In *Themehelp Ltd v. West*[31] an injunction was granted against the beneficiary restraining him from presenting the documents. Waite L.J. held:

> "In a case where fraud is raised as between the parties to the main transaction at an early stage . . . before any question of the enforcement of the guarantee (as between the beneficiary and the guarantor) has yet arisen at all . . . it does not seem to me that the slightest threat is involved to the autonomy of the performance guarantee if the beneficiary is injuncted from

---

[27] [1998] C.L.C. 446.

[28] Lack of honest belief is sufficient fraud: *State Trading Corp. of India Ltd v. E. D. & F. Man (Sugar) Ltd per* Lord Denning M.R. [1981] Com. L.R. 35; *United Trading Corp. SA v. Allied Arab Bank Ltd* [1985] 2 Lloyd's Rep. 554n at 559. The evidence must be such that fraud is the only realistic inference: *United Trading Corp. SA v. Allied Arab Bank Ltd* [1985] 2 Lloyd's Rep. 554n at 565. It is clear that the beneficiary must be given an opportunity to answer the allegations of fraud: *Bolvinter Oil SA v. Chase Manhattan Bank NA* [1984] 1 Lloyd's Rep. 251 at 257.

[29] *United Trading Corp. SA v. Allied Arab Bank Ltd* [1985] 2 Lloyd's Rep. 554 at 561 approved in *Kvaerner John Brown v. Midland Bank plc* [1998] C.L.C. 446 at 449E.

[30] In *United Trading Corp. SA v. Allied Arab Bank Ltd* [1985] 2 Lloyd's Rep. 554n the Court of Appeal held that it was arguable that all banks in the chain owe a duty of care to the party ultimately liable at the end of the chain not to pay out on a performance bond if there is clear evidence of fraud. In *Group Josi Re* [1996] 1 W.L.R. 1155 Staughton L.J. held at 1160 that there was a cause of action or alternatively it was a case where a cause of action was unnecessary.

[31] [1995] 4 All E.R. 215.

enforcing it in proceedings to which the guarantor is not a party."[32]

Another approach which has found favour in other jurisdictions **17–06** is to grant an injunction restraining the beneficiary from receiving payment after a demand has been made.[33]

The risk inherent in agreeing to the issue of unconditional bonds is therefore that the bond may be unfairly called by the beneficiary and yet there may be no adequate redress under the contractual terms of the transaction which gave rise to the bond.[34]

It is suggested that such a risk can be minimised by the inclusion of clauses designed, for example, first to prevent any claim being met by the guarantor unless accompanied by a court or arbitration award[35] in a party's favour, secondly to specify the precise documentation required to accompany claims by the beneficiary,[36] and thirdly to stress the importance of the bond being returned to the guarantor on a definite expiry date.[37]

Article 9 of the I.C.C. Uniform Rules for Contract Guarantees[38] assumes that the bond will provide for documentary proof for a claim in default of which an arbitral or court award will be required for the bond to be called. Article 9 may be excluded by agreement. Article 5 assumes the provision of an expiry date for the bond and Article 6 provides for the return of a guarantee which ceases to be valid.

Article 20(a) of the I.C.C. Uniform Rules for Demand Guarantees[39] requires that any demand for payment must be in writing and be supported by a written statement stating (i) that the principal is in breach of his obligations under the underlying contract, and (ii) the respect in which the principal is in breach. Articles 22 to 26 contain expiry provisions.

---

[32] *cf.* the different view taken by Phillips J. at first instance in *Deutsche Ruckversicherung AG v. Walbrook Insurance Co. Ltd* [1994] 4 All E.R. 181 who considered that the same test should apply whether or not the injunction was being sought against the bank or the beneficiary; affirmed in the Court of Appeal *Re Group Josi* [1996] 1 W.L.R. 1152 *per* Staughton L.J. at 1161H-1162B.

[33] *Kvaerner Singapore Pte Ltd v. UDL Shipbuilding (Singapore) Pte Ltd* [1993] S.L.R. 350.

[34] It is not possible to imply a term that the bond will only be called upon where there is reasonable and just cause to complain of default: *State Trading Corp. of India Ltd v. E. D. & F. Man (Sugar) Ltd* (See above) *per* Lord Denning M.R. An honest belief on the part of the buyer permits him to call on the bond.

[35] *e.g.* by reference to the I.C.C. (International Chamber of Commerce) Rules of Conciliation and Arbitration. For an example of a claim under I.C.C. Rules see *Dalmia Dairy Industries Ltd v. National Bank of Pakistan* [1978] 2 Lloyd's Rep. 223.

[36] This appears to be a principal reason as to why many banks object to using conditional bonds.

[37] Even if the buyer accepts the expiry date of the date for returning the bond he may well, as was shown in the *Harbottle* case, insist on the validity date being extended by threatening to call on the bond if such extension is not granted.

[38] First Edition, (1978) I.C.C. Publication No. 325.

[39] I.C.C. Publication No. 458 which does not replace the 1978 I.C.C. Uniform Rules for Contract Guarantees which remains in force.

CHAPTER 18

STAMP DUTY

18–01 There is no longer any statutory requirement for the memorandum of a guarantee not under seal to be subject to stamp duty[1]; nor is there any requirement to stamp a guarantee under seal.[2]

18–02 Notwithstanding the fact that a guarantee is not itself liable to duty, it may comprise the whole or part of the stampable consideration for another transaction. For example, it is not uncommon on a sale of business for the parties to the contract to exclude debtors and creditors from the transfer in order to mitigate stamp duty. The purchaser will instead collect any debts as agent for the vendor and use the money to discharge liabilities of the business which are not being assumed by the purchaser. If the purchaser "guarantees" that he will pay any excess of liabilities in the event that the debts are insufficient, for the purposes of ascertaining the stamp duty on the transfer of the business, this will be treated as the assumption of all the liabilities of the business[3] and will increase the stampable consideration thus defeating the object of the agency agreement. If the vendor requires some protection, the purchaser can give an indemnity for the anticipated deficiency thus limiting the exposure under section 57.

---

[1] *i.e.* by the Stamp Act 1981, s.1, Sched. 1, "Agreement or any Memorandum of an Agreement etc.", now repealed; see Finance Act 1970, s.32(a), Sched. 7, para. 1(2)(a).
[2] *ibid.* Sched. 1, "Deed of any kind whatsoever, etc.", now repealed; see Finance Act 1985, s.85(1), Sched. 24, para. (e).
[3] *ibid.*, s.57.

CHAPTER 19

CONFLICT OF LAWS

Where a guarantee is given in one country to secure obligations **19–01**
which have been contracted or are to be contracted, and that
guarantee is to be fulfilled in another country,[1] two questions about
the conflict of laws arise: (i) by what law is the guarantee itself to
have effect; and (ii) by what law is it to be determined whether the
principal obligation has been fulfilled.

By what law is the guarantee to have effect?

The first question must be answered in accordance with the same **19–02**
rules which are applicable to any contract. In respect of contracts
which were made on or after April 1, 1991, the law governing
contractual obligations is determined by the provisions of the Rome
Convention on the Law Applicable to Contractual Obligations to
which effect has been given by the Contracts (Applicable Law) Act
1990.[2]

In determining the applicable law, the general rule is that a
guarantee is governed by the law which has been chosen by the
parties,[3] unless there are issues relevant to the situation which are
connected with the rules of a country from which there can be no
derogation by contract.[4]

The choice of law of the parties may be implied. For example,
where a contract is governed by a particular law, it is generally
inferred that the parties to a guarantee of the obligations which arise
under it intended that the guarantee should be governed by the same
law, in particular where the guarantor and the party whose performance is guaranteed are connected.[5] However, such an inference is
not normally drawn where the guarantee is issued by a bank in the
form of a performance bond, which is an instrument which is in
many ways similar to a letter of credit.[6]

---

[1] As to the conflict of laws where the question is between co-sureties as to contribution, see
American Surety Co. v. Wrightson (1910) 103 L.T. 663, where at 665 it is suggested that the *lex fori*
should determine questions of contribution. The basis of this suggestion is questioned in Dicey and
Morris, *The Conflict of Laws* (12th ed., 1993), at p. 218.
[2] For a further discussion of the conflict of laws rules applicable to contracts, see Dicey and Morris,
op. cit., Chap. 32 at pp. 1187 *et seq.*
[3] Dicey and Morris, *op. cit.*, Rule 175.
[4] Dicey and Morris, *op. cit.*, Rule 177.
[5] *Broken Hill Pty Co. Ltd v. Xenakis* [1982] 2 Ll. Rep. 140; *Turkiye Is Bankasi A.S. v. Bank of China*
[1993] 1 Ll. Rep. 132; *Wahda Bank v. Arab Bank plc* [1996] 1 Ll. Rep. 470.
[6] *Attock Cement Co. Ltd v. Romanian Bank for Foreign Trade* [1989] 1 W.L.R. 1147.

Where the parties have not chosen the applicable law, the guarantee is governed by the law of the country with which it is most closely connected.[7] Under the Rome Convention,[8] there is a presumption that the guarantee is most closely connected to the law of the country in which the surety is resident or incorporated, or in which the surety has his/her principal place of business, and not the country in which the surety has to make payment to the creditor.

19–03　　The existence and validity of the contract should also generally be determined by the law chosen by the parties, or, in default of such agreement, the law of the country with which the guarantee is most closely connected. However, a party may rely upon the law of his/her habitual residence to establish that he/she did not consent to the guarantee if it appears from the circumstances that it would not be reasonable to determine the effect of his/her conduct in accordance with this general rule.[9]

The law which applies to the guarantee governs, in particular, the interpretation of the guarantee, its performance, the consequences of default, the determination of liability, and the question of discharge from the guarantee.[10]

In determining any question of the capacity of an individual to enter into the guarantee, the court will have regard to the law of the country with which the contract is most closely connected, or the law of his/her domicile and residence. However, if the parties to the guarantee are in the same country, an individual may not rely upon his/her incapacity under the law of some other country with which the contract is most closely connected or in which he/she is domiciled and resident, unless the other party was aware of the incapacity at the time of the conclusion of the guarantee, or was not aware of this incapacity as a result of negligence.[11]

By what law is it to be determined whether the principal obligation has been fulfilled?

19–04　　The second question which may arise is which law will be applied when there is a question whether the principal obligation has been fulfilled. Where the contract of guarantee is governed by a different law from that which governs the principal obligation between the creditor and the principal debtor, the parties to the guarantee would prima facie contemplate that the question of fulfilment of the principal obligation (as between the parties to it) would remain governed by the law which governs that principal obligation. Authority supports this prima facie view.

---

[7] Dicey and Morris, *op. cit.*, Rule 176.
[8] As was the case with the earlier position at common law, see *Ex p. Littlejohn* (1843) 2 M.D. & De G. 182.
[9] Dicey and Morris, *op. cit.*, Rule 178.
[10] Dicey and Morris, *op. cit.*, Rule 180.
[11] Dicey and Morris, *op. cit.*, Rule 181.

The Privy Council held in *Allen v. Kemble*[12] that a foreign drawer of a bill accepted in England could, in accordance with the foreign law, rely as against the holder in England upon a set-off available to the acceptor, which by the foreign (but not by English) law amounted to an extinction of the debt by the acceptor. This decision was approved and applied to cases of principal and surety, by the Court of Queen's Bench in *Rouquette v. Overmann*[13] upon the ground not that the foreign guarantor had a right to have it decided (conformably with the foreign law) that the principal debt had been paid within the meaning of the guarantee, but upon the ground that he had the right which the foreign law gave *him* as surety to take the benefit of a cross-claim by the principal against the creditor.[14]

Rouquette v. Overmann also addressed the position of the liability of the drawer in England of a bill in France to the person to whom he endorsed it in England. As the drawer was surety to the indorsee for the performance of the contract of the acceptor, "his liability was to be measured by that of the acceptor whose surety he was, and, as the obligations of the acceptor were to be determined by the *lex loci* of performance, so also must be those of the surety."[15] The court therefore held that a moratorium enacted by the French Government, of which the acceptor had the benefit, entitled the holder, as between himself and the drawer, to postpone presentment until it had expired.[16] **19–05**

The effect of the decision in *Rouquette v. Overmann* seems to be that the question whether the principal has performed his obligation and the question whether and at what moment there was a complete default by the principal (where the liability of the guarantor only arises upon such default) must be determined by the law governing that obligation.

---

[12] (1843) 6 Moo. P.C. 314.
[13] (1875) L.R. 10 QB 525 at 540.
[14] See *per* Cockburn C.J., in *Rouquette v. Overmann* (1875) L.R. 10 QB 525.
[15] *ibid.* at 537.
[16] *ibid.* at 537. A moratorium can be relied upon by the debtor if the relevant legislation is enacted according to the proper law of the contract.

CHAPTER 20

GUARANTEES AND UNFAIR CONTRACT TERMS

The Unfair Contract Terms Act 1977

20–01   There is no doubt that provided a creditor's rights and obligations arise in the course of a business and provided further that the contract is governed by English law, section 2(2) of the Unfair Contract Terms Act 1977 will not allow the creditor to restrict or exclude his liability for negligence unless the term or terms in question satisfy the requirements of reasonableness as set out in section 11 of the Act. The Act does not address itself to whether contract terms as a whole are unfair. By section 1(1) "negligence" is defined as including a reference to the breach of any obligations arising from any express or implied term of a contract to take reasonable care or to exercise reasonable skill in the performance of a contract as well as to any common law to take reasonable care or to exercise reasonable skill, but not to any stricter duty. Moreover, there is a general control in certain circumstances over certain contract terms not only which exclude or restrict liability for breach of contract[1] but also which purport to entitle one of the parties to render a contractual performance substantially different from that reasonably expected of that party or to render no performance at all.[2]

There also can be little doubt that the giving of a guarantee would in most cases be done in the course of a business,[3] even though the term "business" is not defined by the Act, provided that the provision of guarantees is an integral part of that business[4] and that the parties to the contract, and particularly the guarantor deal as "consumer".[5] A bank or similar lending institution would qualify but guarantees entered into as between trading companies or firms would probably not be covered.

The most obvious case of a provision which would seek to limit liability for negligence in a guarantee is where it is provided that the creditor is not to be liable with regard to the possible impairment of any security granted in support of the guarantee.

20–02   Section 2(2) provides that the requirements of reasonableness must be complied with. Similar requirements exist with regard to

---

[1] s.3(1), (2)(a).
[2] s.3(1), (2)(b).
[3] See s.1(3).
[4] See, *e.g. R. & B. Customs Brokers Co. Ltd v. United Dominions Trust Ltd* [1988] 1 W.L.R. 321.
[5] See s.12(1)(a) and (b).

the exclusion or limitation of liability arising for breach of contract.[6]

There is no English reported decision specifically considering the application of these provisions to a guarantee and particularly a bank guarantee, even though it has been stated that the 1977 Act does apply.[7] One of the requirements which may cause particular difficulties is whether the customer knew or ought reasonably to have known of the existence and extent of the term having regard in fact to the custom of the trade. This would seem to favour the individual guarantor in relatively medium sized transactions, *e.g.* with regard to property purchases. However many other considerations would enter into the equation with regard to large scale lendings involving corporate and individual guarantees. In any event, the evolving law regarding unconscionable bargains in the wake of *Barclays Bank v. O'Brien*[8] would in many cases provide greater protection than would the Act.

At least one type of provision normally found in a guarantee will not attract the operation of the Act, namely a provision that denies a guarantor discharge in the event of conduct by the creditor since such provisions are not breaches of a contractual undertaking but merely descriptions of a situation in which the surety would be discharged.

The Unfair Terms in Consumer Contracts Regulations 1994

The Unfair Terms in Consumer Contracts Regulations imple- **20–03** menting the E.U. Council Directive 93/13 which was adopted in April 1993 for implementation by member states by December 31, 1994, to be applicable to all contracts after that date,[9] came into force as from September 1, 1995.[10]

Unlike the position under the 1977 Act, the Regulations apply to any relevant contract which contains a choice of law clause which applies or seeks to apply the law of a non-Member State if the contract has a close connection with the territory of the Member State.[11]

The Regulations apply in general to any term in a contract concluded between a seller of goods or supplier of goods or services (in either case acting in the course of a business) and a consumer where that term has not been individually negotiated.[12] The first question is whether the Directive and the Regulations

---

[6] See generally s.3 and the guidelines in Sched. 2 of the Act: the guidelines are not exhaustive.
[7] *Standard Chartered Bank v. Walker* [1982] 1 W.L.R. 1410 at 1416 *per* Lord Denning M.R.
[8] See generally Chap. 6.
[9] Art. 10.
[10] It is unclear what the relationship between the Regulations and the Unfair Contract Terms Act 1977 is intended to be, suggesting that both regimes will co-exist.
[11] Art. 7: This prevents the circumvention of the Regulations in the case of a contract which has a close connection with England by the insertion of a non-English choice of law clause.
[12] reg. 7.

apply at all to guarantees and related contracts. The Regulations adopt definitions of "consumer", "seller" and "supplier",[13] and it may be argued that the provision of a third party guarantee does not necessarily extend to the supply of services, except possibly in the case of banks and lending institutions whose business customarily involves the taking of security. The principal contract of loan would clearly be the provision of a banking service and it seems unduly artificial not to extend the ambit of the Regulations to a related obligation such as a guarantee.

If applicable to guarantees, the Regulations apply to any term in a contract concluded between the supplier acting in the course of a business and a consumer, where the terms have not been individually negotiated.[14] Article 3(1) of the Directive and regulations 3 and 4 of the Regulations provide that a contractual term which has not been individually negotiated should be regarded as unfair if, contrary to the requirement of good faith, it causes a significant imbalance in the parties' rights and obligations under a contract to the detriment of the consumer. Terms in a standard form instrument will invariably constitute terms which have not been individually negotiated.[15]

20–04   If a term is found to be "unfair" within the meaning of regulation 4, the consumer will not be bound by that term, though the contract will behind the parties without such a term.

Schedule 2 sets out four elements which are to be taken into account in assessing good faith, namely, the strength of the bargaining position of the parties, whether the consumer had any inducement to agree to the term, whether the services were supplied by special order of the customer and finally the extent to which the supplier has dealt fairly and equitably with the consumer. Regulation 4(2) ensures in effect that all the surrounding circumstances be taken into account, which means at least considering the terms of the principal contract itself.

The possible applicability of a "significant imbalance" in the rights and obligations of the parties in the context of standard terms of a guarantee is in theory very great. A number of situations immediately present themselves. A provision which sought to treat a failure to observe a term in the principal agreement as an event of default is potentially unfair. A consumer might have to rearrange fresh finance following even a minor breach of the overall arrangements. The guarantee, or more likely the principal contract, whose conditions might be reflected in the guarantee, could not only be terminated without notice but also be subject to altered interest rates

---

[13] *e.g.* a supplier is a person who "supplies . . . services".
[14] A consumer is a natural person and therefore professional and corporate sureties are excluded.
[15] reg. 3(3).

without notice. Schedule 3[16] of the Regulations preserves the latter entitlement but only at the cost of the lender informing the consumer at the earliest opportunity of the change and giving the consumer the right to dissolve the contract immediately. Schedule 3[17] illustrates that clauses which exclude or impede the customer's right to take legal action or exercise any other legal remedy especially in circumstances in which the burden of proof is placed on the consumer, are also likely to be viewed as unfair. This would seem to cover conclusive evidence clauses. More significantly perhaps, provisions which entitle the creditor to vary the principal contract without impinging upon the liability of the guarantor now seem open to question, as do clauses which prohibit the guarantor from praying in aid any set-off or counterclaim against the lender.[18] Other terms which appear liable to attack are claims which oblige the guarantor to pay the creditor's expenses often on the basis of preventing taxation of such costs, as well as so called "principal debtor" clauses.

Another example would be a clause which purportedly sought to limit or exclude a guarantor who has paid the whole of his part of a debt from sharing in any securities held by the creditor until all the principal debtor's obligations have been satisfied in full or so called non-competition clauses which again curtail a guarantor's ability to prove alongside a creditor once he has paid part or all of the sums due from him. **20–05**

It is not easy to predict how the good faith requirements will be implemented. A bank will in most cases be in a far stronger bargaining position than a surety: there may be no inducement upon a surety to agree the terms. There exists the obvious possibility of affording the widest discretion to the question of fair and equitable dealing. On the other hand, since the 1977 Act has been in force, its impact upon bank guarantees has been minimal. The challenge will be to lenders to reconsider the way in which individual negotiations should be undertaken with regard to some or all of the terms normally employed in a transaction, given the particular needs and requirements of the transaction concerned.

Finally the Regulations make it incumbent upon banks to ensure that their security documents are written in clear English or as it is put "in plain intelligible language" and "if there is doubt about the meaning of a written term, the interpretation most favourable to the consumer shall prevail".[19] Reference has already been made to the possible continued application of the contra proferentum

---

[16] para. 2(b).

[17] para. 1(q).

[18] Being specifically mentioned in Sched. 3. There are 17 examples given in the Schedule. Such clauses have been subjected to the regime applicable under the Unfair Contract Terms Act 1977: see generally *Stewart Gill Ltd v. Horatio Myer & Co. Ltd* [1992] QB 600.

[19] reg. 6. This is the only specified consequence of failure to comply with the drafting requirements proposed by the Regulations. However it remains to be seen how this regulation will be interpreted.

rule of construction to contracts of guarantee[20] which may well find some renewed vigour in this respect.

---

[20] See Chapter 4 above.

Appendix 1

DRAFT BID BOND

To: The Buyer

A–01

Dear Sirs,

At the request of   (hereinafter referred to as "X") We (insert name of Bank) .... of (insert Bank's address) .... hereby undertake to pay to you subject as hereinafter provided such amount as may be claimed by you in writing up to £ .... (insert maximum figure) in respect of X's tender dated .... for .... (insert description of project) valid for a period of ...... (insert number of days or months) (hereinafter referred to as "the Tender") on the occurrence of either of the following events:

(1) Where you have indicated in writing your willingness to enter into a contract with X (hereinafter referred to as "the Contract") either on the terms of the Tender or on such modified terms as may have been agreed between you and X and X has indicated to you that it does not wish to sign or otherwise enter into the Contract, or

(2) Where you have signed the Contract with X and where the Contract would have otherwise come into force except only for X's failure to provide any Performance Guarantee or Bond required in connection therewith by the times and on the conditions stipulated in the Contract.

Provided that no such amount shall become due and payable by us under this **A–02** Guarantee:

(1) Where the aggregate amount claimed exceeds £ ....

(insert maximum figure)

(2) More than one month after the validity period of the Tender has expired, unless we have been notified by X that the period of validity of the Tender has been extended.

(3) Unless your written claim shall have been received by us accompanied by the following documents:

(a) in the circumstances provided for under (1) above a copy certified by a Notary Public of your written indication to enter into the Contract with X together with evidence of X's indication not to sign or otherwise enter into the Contract.

(b) In the circumstances provided for under (2) above a copy, certified by a Notary Public, of the signed Contract together with evidence that you have fulfilled all your obligations precedent to the coming into force of the Contract and that the Contract would have come into force but for X's failure as aforesaid.

A–03 Our liability hereunder shall cease and terminate on whichever of the following events first occurs, upon which event this Guarantee shall be returned to us for cancellation:

(1) When we have paid to you the amount of £ ....

(insert maximum figure)

(2) when you have awarded the contract to another company or organisation or have indicated to X that the Tender will not be accepted or have otherwise indicated that no contract will be placed with any tenderer, whichever occurs the earlier.

(3) One month after the validity period of the Tender (including any agreed extension thereof) has expired unless before that time we have received your written claim satisfying the conditions set out above.

This Guarantee and any claims arising hereunder shall be governed in all respects by English law and any disputes in connection therewith shall be submitted to arbitration in accordance with the Rules of Conciliation and Arbitration of the International Chamber of Commerce in Paris.

Yours faithfully, etc.

DRAFT PERFORMANCE BOND

A–04 To: The Buyer

Dear Sirs

At the request of (hereinafter referred to as "X") We (insert name of Bank) of .... (insert Bank's address) hereby undertake to indemnify you against all claims, costs and damages which you have necessarily incurred as a direct consequence of failure by X to fulfil in accordance with its terms any of its obligations under the contract signed between yourselves and X dated .... (hereinafter referred to as "the Contract") by paying to you subject as hereinafter provided such amount as may be claimed by you in writing in respect thereof.

This Guarantee shall not become effective unless and until we have been notified by X in writing that all conditions precedent otherwise required to bring the Contract into force have been fulfilled.

This Guarantee shall not in any event exceed £ .... (insert maximum figure) and shall be reduced proportionately as follows upon completion of the following phases of the Contract as provided thereunder:

Table 1

Phase of Contract	Percentage Reduction in Guarantee
e.g. (Factory Acceptance)	
(Provisional Acceptance)	

A–05 Provided that no such amount shall become due and payable by us under this Guarantee:

(1) Where the aggregate amount claimed exceeds £ .... (insert maximum figure).

(2) Where notification of your intention to make a claim has been received by us later than .... or .... or .... (insert dates respectively one month after which a Factory Acceptance Certificate or Provisional Acceptance or Final Acceptance Certificate is required to be issued as appropriate) in respect of any amount exceeding £ .... or £ .... or £ .... (inserted reduced figures as appropriate).

(3) Unless your written claim shall be accompanied by one of the following documents:

    (a) A signed admission by X of its failure as aforesaid and agreement to the amount claimed, or

    (b) A copy, certified by a Notary Public, of a Court or Arbitrator's award in your favour made in accordance with accordance with Clause .... of the Contract.

Our liability hereunder shall cease and terminate on whichever of the following **A–06** events first occur, upon which event this Guarantee shall be returned to us for cancellation.

(1) When we have paid to you the maximum amount for which we are liable hereunder.

(2) If the Contract is terminated by you otherwise than for reasons of X's default.

(3) On .... (insert date), being one month after the date provided in the Contract for Final Acceptance) unless before that date we have received notification of your intention to make a claim.

This Guarantee and all claims arising hereunder shall be governed in all respects by English law and any dispute in connection therewith shall be submitted to arbitration in accordance with the Rules of Conciliation and Arbitration of the International Chamber of Commerce in Paris.

Yours faithfully, etc.

DRAFT ADVANCE PAYMENT BOND

To: The Buyer   **A–07**

Dear Sirs

In consideration of your paying to   (hereinafter referred to as "X") the sum of £ .... due to them under Clause .... of their contract with you dated .... (hereinafter referred to as "the Contract") We (insert name of Bank) of (insert Bank's address) hereby guarantee that in the event of any failure on the part of X to deliver the equipment or carry out the work for which they are responsible under the Contract in accordance with its terms we shall, subject as hereinafter provided, pay you the amount of all claims, costs and damages which you have necessarily incurred as a direct consequence of such failure up to but not exceeding the amount paid to X under the said Clause.

Provided that no such amount shall become due and payable by us under this Guarantee:

(1) Where the aggregate amount claimed exceeds £ .... (insert maximum figure).

(2) Where any shipments made or services rendered under the Contract exceed £ .... (insert maximum figure) and X has provided us with invoices or shipping documents, certified by a Notary Public, to that value;

(3) Where notification of your intention to make a claim has been received by us not later than .... (insert date one month after which shipments are to be made or services rendered as appropriate).

(4) Unless your written claim shall be accompanied by one of the following documents–

    (a) A signed admission by X of its failure aforesaid and agreement to the amount claimed.

    (b) A copy, certified by a Notary Public, of a Court or Arbitrator's award in your favour made in accordance with Clause .... of the Contract.

A–08 Our liability hereunder shall cease and terminate on whichever of the following events first occurs, upon which event this Guarantee shall be returned to us for cancellation:

(1) When we have paid to you the maximum amount for which we are liable hereunder.

(2) If the Contract is terminated by you otherwise than for reasons of X's default.

(3) On .... (insert date one month after which shipments are to be made or services rendered, as appropriate) unless before that date we have received notification of your intention to make a claim.

This Guarantee and all claims arising hereunder shall be governed in all respects by English law and any disputes in connection therewith shall be submitted to arbitration in accordance with the Rules of Conciliation and Arbitration of the International Chamber of Commerce in Paris.

Yours faithfully, etc.

Appendix 2

SELECTED STATUTES

Statute of Frauds 1677, s.4

Statute of Frauds Amendment Act 1828, s.6

Mercantile Law Amendment Act 1856, ss.3 & 5

Bills of Exchange Act 1882, s.56

Consumer Credit Act 1974, ss.8–13, 19, 105–109, 111, 113 & 189

Unfair Contract Terms Act 1977, ss.2 & 11, Schedule 2

Civil Liability (Contribution) Act 1978, ss.1, 2, 3 & 4

Unfair Terms in Consumer Contracts Regulations 1994

Statute of Frauds 1677

(29 Car. 2, c.3)

Promises and agreements by parol

4.—[. . .] no action shall be brought [. . .] whereby to charge the defendant **A–09** upon any special promise to answer for the debt, default or miscarriages of another person [. . .] unless the agreement upon which such action shall be brought, or some memorandum or note thereof, shall be in writing and signed by the party to be charged therewith, or some other person thereunto by him lawfully authorised.

Statute of Frauds Amendment Act 1828

(Lord Tenterden's Act)

(9 Geo. 4, c.14)

Action not maintainable on representations of character, etc., unless they may be in writing signed by the party chargeable

6.—No action shall be brought whereby to charge any person upon or by **A–10** reason of any representation or assurance made or given concerning or relating to the character, conduct, credit, ability, trade, or dealings of any other person, to the intent or purpose that such other person may obtain credit, money, or goods

273

upon, unless such representation or assurance be made in writing, signed by the party to be charged therewith.

Mercantile Law Amendment Act 1856

(19 & 20 Vict. c.97)

Consideration for guarantee need not appear by writing

A–11   **3.**—No special promise to be made by any person [. . .] to answer for the debt, default, or miscarriage of another person, being in writing, and signed by the party to be charged therewith, or some other person by him thereunto lawfully authorized, shall be deemed invalid to support an action, suit, or other proceeding to charge the person by whom such promise shall have been made, by reason only that the consideration for such promise does not appear in writing, or by necessary inference from a written document.

A surety who discharges the liability to be entitled to assignment of all securities held by the creditor

A–12   **5.**—Every person who, being surety for the debt or duty of another, or being liable with another for any debt or duty, shall pay such debt or perform such duty, shall be entitled to have assigned to him, or to a trustee for him, every judgment, specialty, or other security which shall be held by the creditor in respect of such debt or duty, whether such judgment, specialty, or other security shall or shall not be deemed at law to have been satisfied by the payment of the debt or performance of the duty, and such person be entitled to stand in the place of the creditor, and to use all the remedies, and, if need be, and upon a proper indemnity, to use the name of the creditor, in any action, or other proceeding, at law or in equity, in order to obtain from the principal debtor, or any co-surety, co-contractor, or co-debtor, as the case may be, indemnification for the advances made and loss sustained by the person who shall have so paid such debt or performed such duty, and such payment or performance so made by such surety shall not be pleadable in bar of any such action or other proceeding by him: provided always, that no co-surety, co-contractor, or co-debtor, shall be entitled to recover from any other co-surety, co-contractor, or co-debtor, by the means aforesaid, more than the just proportion to which, as between those parties themselves, such last-mentioned person shall be justly liable.

Bills of Exchange Act 1882

(45 & 46 Vict. c.61)

Stranger signing bill liable as indorser

A–13   **56.**—Where a person signs a bill otherwise than as a drawer or acceptor, he thereby incurs the liabilities of an indorser to a holder in due course.

Consumer Credit Act 1974

(1974 c.39)

PART II

CREDIT AGREEMENTS, HIRE AGREEMENTS AND LINKED TRANSACTIONS

Consumer credit agreements

8.—(1) A personal credit agreement is an agreement between an individual ("the debtor") and any other person ("the creditor") by which the creditor provides the debtor with credit of any amount. **A–14**

(2) A consumer credit agreement is a personal credit agreement by which the credit provides the debtor with credit not exceeding £5,000.

(3) A consumer credit agreement is a regulated agreement within the meaning of this Act if it is not an agreement (an "exempt agreement") specified in or under section 16.

Meaning of credit

9. (1) In this Act "credit" includes a cash loan, and any other form of financial accommodation.

(2) Where credit is provided otherwise than in sterling it shall be treated for the purposes of this Act as provided in sterling of an equivalent amount.

(3) Without prejudice to the generality of subsection (1), the person by whom goods are bailed or (in Scotland) hired to an individual under a hire-purchase agreement shall be taken to provide him with fixed-sum credit to finance the transaction of an amount equal to the total price of the goods less the aggregate of the deposit (if any) and the total charge for credit.

(4) For the purposes of this Act, an item entering into the total charge for credit shall not be treated as credit even though time is allowed for its payment.

Running-account credit and fixed-sum credit

10.—(1) For the purposes of this Act— **A–15**
- (a) running-account credit is a facility under a personal credit agreement whereby the debtor is enabled to receive from time to time (whether in his own person, or by another person) from the creditor or a third party cash, goods and services (or any of them) to an amount or valued such that, taking into account payments made by or to the credit of the debtor, the credit limit (if any) is not at any time exceeded; and
- (b) fixed-sum credit is any other facility under a personal credit agreement whereby the debtor is enabled to receive credit (whether in one amount or by instalments).

(2) In relation to running-account credit, "credit limit" means, as respects any period, the maximum debit balance which, under the credit agreement, is allowed to stand on the account during that period, disregarding any term of the agreement allowing that maximum to be exceeded merely temporarily.

(3) For the purposes of section 8(2), running-account credit shall be taken not to exceed the amount specified in that subsection ("the specified amount") if—

(a) the credit limit does not exceed the specified amount; or

(b) whether or not there is a credit limit, and if there is, notwithstanding that it exceeds the specified amount,—

    (i) the debtor is not enabled to draw at any one time an amount which, so far as (having regard to section 9(4)) it represents credit, exceeds the specified amount, or

    (ii) the agreement provides that, if the debit balance rises above a given amount (not exceeding the specified amount), the rate of the total charge for credit increases or any other condition favouring the creditor or his associate comes into operation, or

    (iii) at the time the agreement is made it is probable, having regard to the terms of the agreement and any other relevant considerations, that the debit balance will not at any time rise above the specified amount.

Restricted-use card and unrestricted-use credit

A–16   **11.**—(1) A restricted-use credit agreement is a regulated consumer credit agreement—

(a) to finance a transaction between the debtor and the creditor, whether forming part of that agreement or not, or

(b) to finance a transaction between the debtor and a person (the "supplier") other than the creditor, or

(c) to refinance any existing indebtedness of the debtor's, whether to the creditor or another person,

and "restricted-use credit" shall be construed accordingly.

(2) An unrestricted-use credit agreement is a regulated consumer credit agreement not falling within subsection (1), and "unrestricted-use credit" shall be construed accordingly.

(3) An agreement does not fall within subsection (1) if the credit is in fact provided in such a way as to leave the debtor free to use it as he chooses, even though certain uses would contravene that or any other agreement.

(4) An agreement may fall within subsection (1)(b) although the identify of the supplier is unknown at the time the agreement is made.

Debtor-creditor-supplier agreements

A–17   **12.** A debtor-creditor-supplier agreement is a regulated consumer credit agreement being—

(a) a restricted-use credit agreement which falls within section 11(1)(a), or

(b) a restricted-use credit agreement which falls within section 11(1)(b) and is made by the creditor under pre-existing arrangements, or in contemplation of future arrangements, between himself and the supplier, or

(c) an unrestricted-use credit agreement which is made by the creditor under pre-existing arrangements between himself and a person (the "supplier") other than the debtor in the knowledge that the credit is to be used to finance a transaction between the debtor and the supplier.

Debtor-creditor agreements

13. A debtor-creditor agreement is a regulated consumer credit agreement being—

(a) a restricted-use credit agreement which falls within section 11(1)(b) but is not made by the creditor under pre-existing arrangements, or in contemplation of future arrangements, between himself and the supplier, or

(b) a restricted-use credit agreement which falls within section 11(1)(c), or

(c) an unrestricted-use credit agreement which is not made by the creditor under pre-existing arrangements between himself and a person (the "supplier") other than the debtor in the knowledge that the credit is to be used to finance a transaction between the debtor and the supplier.

Linked transactions

19.—(1) A transaction entered into by the debtor or hirer, or a relative of his, **A–18** with any other person ("the other party"), except one for the provision of security, is a linked transaction in relation to an actual or prospective regulated agreement (the "principal agreement") of which it does not form part if—

(a) the transaction is entered into in compliance with a term of the principal agreement; or

(b) the principal agreement is a debtor-creditor-supplier agreement and the transaction is financed, or to be financed, by the principal agreement; or

(c) the other party is a person mentioned in subsection (2), and a person so mentioned initiated the transaction by suggesting it to the debtor or hirer, or his relative, who enters into it—

   (i) to induce the creditor or owner to enter into the principal agreement, or

   (ii) for another purpose related to the principle agreement, or

   (iii) where the principal agreement is a restricted-use credit agreement, for a purpose related to a transaction financed, or to be financed, by the principal agreement.

(2) The persons referred to in subsection (1)(c) are—

(a) the creditor or owner, or his associate;

(b) a person who, in the negotiation of the transaction, is represented by a credit-broker who is also a negotiator in antecedent negotiations for the principal agreement;

(c) a person who, at the time the transaction is initiated, knows that the principal agreement has been made or contemplates that it might be made.

(3) A linked transaction entered into before the making of the principal agreement has no effect until such time (if any) as that agreement is made.

(4) Regulations may exclude linked transactions of the prescribed description from the operation of subsection (3).

PART VIII

SECURITY

General

Form and content of securities

A–19   105.—(1) Any security provided in relation to a regulated agreement shall be expressed in writing.

(2) Regulations may prescribe the form and content of documents ("security instruments") to be made in compliance with subsection (1).

(3) Regulations under subsection (2) may in particular—

   (a) require specified information to be included in the prescribed manner in documents, and other specified material to be excluded;

   (b) contain requirements to ensure that specified information is clearly brought to the attention of the surety, and that one part of a document is not given insufficient or excessive prominence compared with another.

(4) A security instrument is not properly executed unless—

   (a) a document in the prescribed form, itself containing all the prescribed terms and conforming to regulations under sub-section (2), is signed in the prescribed manner by or on behalf of the surety, and

   (b) the document embodies all the terms of the security, other than implied terms, and

   (c) the document, when presented or sent for the purpose of being signed by or on behalf of the surety, is in such state that its terms are readily legible, and

   (d) when the document is presented or sent for the purpose of being signed by or on behalf of the surety there is also presented or sent a copy of the document.

A–20   (5) A security instrument is not properly executed unless—

   (a) where the security is provided after, or at the time when, the regulated agreement is made, a copy of the executed agreement, together with a copy of any other document referred to in it, is given to the surety at the time the security is provided, or

   (b) where the security is provided before the regulated agreement is made, a copy of the executed agreement, together with a copy of any other document referred to in it, is given to the surety within seven days after the regulated agreement is made.

(6) Subsection (1) does not apply to a security provided by the debtor or hirer.

(7) If—

   (a) in contravention of subsection (1) a security is not expressed in writing, or

   (b) a security instrument is improperly executed,

the security, so far as provided in relation to a regulated agreement, is enforceable against the surety on an order of the court only.

(8) If an application for an order under subsection (7) is dismissed (except on technical grounds only) section 106 (ineffective securities) shall apply to the security.

(9) Regulations under section 60(1) shall include provision requiring documents embodying regulated agreements also to embody any security provided in relation to a regulated agreement by the debtor or hirer.

Ineffective securities

106.—Where, under any provision of this Act, this section is applied to any **A–21** security provided in relation to a regulated agreement, then, subject to section 177 (saving for registered charges)—

(a) the security, so far as it is so provided, shall be treated as never having effect;

(b) any property lodged with the creditor or owner solely for the purposes of the security as so provided shall be returned by him forthwith;

(c) the creditor or owner shall take any necessary action to remove or cancel an entry in any register, so far as the entry relates to the security as so provided; and

(d) any amount received by the creditor or owner on realisation of the security shall, so far as it is referable to the agreement, be repaid to the surety.

Duty to give information to surety under fixed-sum credit agreement

107.—(1) The creditor under a regulated agreement for fixed-sum credit in **A–22** relation to which security is provided, within the prescribed period after receiving a request in writing to that effect from the surety and payment of a fee of 15 new pence, shall give to the surety (if a different person from the debtor)—

(a) a copy of the executed agreement (if any) and of any other document referred to in it;

(b) a copy of the security instrument (if any); and

(c) a statement signed by or on behalf of the creditor showing, according to the information to which it is practicable for him to refer,—

(i) the total sum paid under the agreement by the debtor,

(ii) the total sum which has become payable under the agreement by the debtor but remains unpaid, and the various amounts comprised in that total sum, with the date when each became due, and

(iii) the total sum which is to become payable under the agreement by the debtor, and the various amounts, comprised in that total sum, with the date, or mode of determining the date, when each becomes due.

(2) If the creditor possesses insufficient information to enable him to ascertain the amounts and dates mentioned in subsection (1)(c)(iii), he shall be taken to comply with that sub-paragraph if his statement under subsection (1)(c) gives the basis on which, under the regulated agreement, they would fall to be ascertained.

(3) Subsection (1) does not apply to—

(a) an agreement under which no sum is, or will or may become, payable by the debtor, or

(b) a request made less than one month after a previous request under that subsection relating to the same agreement was complied with.

(4) If the creditor under an agreement fails to comply with subsection (1)—

(a) he is not entitled, while the default continues, to enforce the security, so far as provided in relation to the agreement; and

(b) if the default continues for one month he commits an offence.

(5) This section does not apply to a non-commercial agreement.

Duty to give information to surety under running-account credit agreement

A–23   **108.**—(1) The creditor under a regulated agreement for running-account credit in relation to which security is provided, within the prescribed period after receiving a request in writing to that effect from the surety and payment of a fee of 15 new pence, shall give to the surety (if a different person from the debtor)—

(a) a copy of the executed agreement (if any) and of any other document referred to in it;

(b) a copy of the security instrument (if any); and

(c) a statement signed by or on behalf of the creditor showing, according to the information to which it is practicable for him to refer,—

(i) the state of the account, and

(ii) the amount, if any, currently payable under the agreement by the debtor to the creditor, and

(iii) the amounts and due dates of any payments which, if the debtor does not draw further on the account, will later become payable under the agreement by the debtor to the creditor.

(2) If the creditor possesses insufficient information to enable him to ascertain the amounts and dates mentioned in subsection (1)(c)(iii), he shall be taken to comply with that sub-paragraph if his statement under subsection (1)(c) gives the basis on which, under the regulated agreement, they would fall to be ascertained.

(3) Subsection (1) does not apply to—

(a) an agreement under which no sum is, or will or may become, payable by the debtor, or

(b) a request made less than one month after a previous request under that subsection relating to the same agreement was complied with.

(4) If the creditor under an agreement fails to comply with subsection (1)—

(a) he is not entitled, while the default continues, to enforce the security, so far as provided in relation to the agreement; and

(b) if the default continues for one month he commits an offence.

(5) This section does not apply to a non-commercial agreement.

Duty to give information to surety under consumer hire agreement

A–24   **109.**—(1) The owner under a regulated consumer hire agreement in relation to which security is provided, within the prescribed period after receiving a request in writing to that effect from the surety and payment of a fee of 15 new pence, shall give to the surety (if a different person from the hirer)—

(a) a copy of the executed agreement and of any other document referred to in it;

(b) a copy of the security instrument (if any); and

(c) a statement signed by or on behalf of the owner showing, according to the information to which it is practicable for him to refer, the total sum which has become payable under the agreement by the hirer but remains unpaid and the various amounts comprised in that total sum, with the date when each became due.

(2) Subsection (1) does not apply to—

(a) an agreement under which no sum is, or will or may become, payable by the hirer, or

(b) a request made less than one month after a previous request under that subsection relating to the same agreement was complied with.

(3) If the owner under an agreement fails to comply with subsection (1)—

(a) he is not entitled, while the default continues, to enforce the security, so far as provided in relation to the agreement; and

(b) if the default continues for one month he commits an offence.

(4) This section does not apply to a non-commercial agreement.

Duty to give surety copy of default etc. notice

111.—(1) When a default notice or a notice under section 76(1) or 98(1) is served on a debtor or hirer, a copy of the notice shall be served by the creditor or owner on any surety (if a different person from the debtor or hirer). **A–25**

(2) If the creditor or owner fails to comply with subsection (1) in the case of any surety, the security is enforceable against the surety (in respect of the breach or other matter to which the notice relates) on an order of the court only.

112. [. . .] regulations may provide for any matters relating to the sale or other realisation, by the creditor or owner, of property over which any right has been provided by way of security in relation to an actual or prospective regulated agreement, other than a non-commercial agreement.

Act not to be evaded by use of security

113.—(1) Where a security is provided in relation to an actual or prospective regulated agreement, the security shall not be enforced so as to benefit the creditor or owner, directly or indirectly, to an extent greater (whether as respects the amount of any payment or the time or manner of its being made) than would be the case if the security were not provided and any obligations of the debtor or hirer, or his relative, under or in relation to the agreement were carried out to the extent (if any) to which they would be enforced under this Act. **A–26**

(2) In accordance with subsection (1), where a regulated agreement is enforceable on an order of the court or the Director only, any security provided in relation to the agreement is enforceable (so far as provided in relation to the agreement) where such an order has been made in relation to the agreement, but not otherwise.

(3) Where—

(a) a regulated agreement is cancelled under section 69(1) or becomes subject to section 69(2), or

(b) a regulated agreement is terminated under section 91, or

(c) in relation to any agreement an application for an order under section 40(2), 65(1), 124(1) or 149(2) is dismissed (except on technical grounds only), or

(d) a declaration is made by the court under section 142(1) (refusal of enforcement order) as respects any regulated agreement,

section 106 shall apply to any security provided in relation to the agreement.

(4) Where subsection (3)(d) applies and the declaration relates to a part only of the regulated agreement, section 106 shall apply to the security only so far as it concerns that part.

(5) In the case of a cancelled agreement, the duty imposed on the debtor or hirer by section 71 or 72 shall not be enforceable before the creditor or owner has discharged any duty imposed on him by section 106 (as applied by subsection (3)(a)).

(6) If the security is provided in relation to a prospective agreement or transaction, the security shall be enforceable in relation to the agreement or transaction only after the time (if any) when the agreement is made; and until that time the person providing the security shall be entitled, by notice to the creditor or owner, to require that section 106 shall thereupon apply to the security.

(7) Where an indemnity is given in a case where the debtor or hirer is a minor, or is otherwise not of full capacity, the reference in subsection (1) to the extent to which his obligations would be enforced shall be read in relation to the indemnity as a reference to the extent to which they would be enforced if he were of full capacity.

(8) Subsections (1) to (3) also apply where a security is provided in relation to an actual or prospective linked transaction, and in that case—

(a) references to the agreement shall be read as references to the linked transaction, and

(b) references to the creditor or owner shall be read as references to any person (other than the debtor or hirer, or his relative) who is a party, or prospective party, to the linked transaction.

Definitions

A–27 **189.**—(1) In this Act, unless the context otherwise requires—

"consumer credit business" means any business so far as it comprises or relates to the provision of credit under regulated consumer credit agreements;

[. . .]

"creditor" means the person providing credit under a consumer credit agreement or the person to whom his rights and duties under the agreement have passed by assignment or operation of law, and in relation to a prospective consumer credit agreement, includes the prospective creditor;

[. . .]

"debtor" means the individual receiving credit under a consumer credit agreement or the person to whom his rights and duties under the agreement have

passed by assignment or operation of law, and in relation to a prospective consumer credit agreement includes the prospective debtor;
[. . .]
"executed agreement" means a document, signed by or on behalf of the parties, embodying the terms of a regulated agreement, or such of them as have been reduced to writing;
"exempt agreement" means an agreement specified in or under section 16;
[. . .]
"goods" has the meaning given by section 62(1) of the Sale of Goods Act 1893;
[. . .]
"hire-purchase agreement" means an agreement, other than a conditional sale agreement, under which—

   (a) goods are bailed or (in Scotland) hired in return for periodical payments by the person to whom they are bailed or hired, and
   (b) the property in the goods will pass to that person if the terms of the agreement are complied with and one or more of the following occurs
     (i) the exercise of an option to purchase by that person,
     (ii) the doing of any other specified act by any party to the agreement,
     (iii) the happening of any other specified event.

"hirer" means the individual to whom goods are bailed or (in Scotland) hired under a consumer hire agreement, or the person to whom his rights and duties under the agreement have passed by assignment or operation of law, and in relation to a prospective consumer hire agreement includes the prospective hirer;
"individual" includes—a partnership or other unincorporated body of persons not consisting entirely of bodies corporate;
[. . .]
"payment" includes tender;
[. . .]
"prescribed" means prescribed by regulations made by the Secretary of State;
[. . .]
"regulated agreement" means a consumer credit agreement, or consumer hire agreement, other than an exempt agreement, and
"regulated" and "unregulated" shall be construed accordingly;
"regulations" means regulations made by the Secretary of State;
"security", in relation to an actual or prospective consumer credit agreement or consumer hire agreement, or any linked transaction, means a mortgage, charge, pledge, bond, debenture, indemnity, guarantee, bill, note or other right provided by the debtor or hirer, or at his request (express or implied), to secure the carrying out of the obligations of the debtor or hirer under the agreement;
"security instrument" has the meaning given by section 105(2);
"supplier" has the meaning given by section 11(1)(b) or 12(c) or 13(c) or, in relation to an agreement falling within section 11(1)(a), means the creditor,

and includes a person to whom the rights and duties of a supplier (as so defined) have passed by assignment or operation of law, or (in relation to a prospective agreement) the prospective supplier;

"surety" means the person by whom any security is provided, or the person whom his rights and duties in relation to the security have passed by assignment or operation of law;

Unfair Contract Terms Act 1977

(1977 c.50)

Negligence liability

A–28   **2.**—(1) A person cannot by reference to any contract term or to a notice given to persons generally or to particular persons exclude or restrict his liability for death or personal injury resulting from negligence.

(2) In the case of other loss or damage, a person cannot so exclude or restrict his liability for negligence except in so far as the term or notice satisfies the requirement of reasonableness.

(3) Where a contract term or notice purports to exclude or restrict liability for negligence a person's agreement to or awareness of it is not of itself to be taken as indicating his voluntary acceptance of any risk.

[*Section 11 and Schedule 2 do not apply in terms to section 2. However, in considering the test of reasonableness for the purposes of section 2 it might be helpful to consider the guidelines set out in Schedule 2 by analogy.*]

The "reasonableness" test

A–29   **11.**—(1) In relation to a contract term, the requirement of reasonableness for the purposes of this Part of this Act, section 3 of the Misrepresentation Act 1967 and section 3 of the Misrepresentation Act (Northern Ireland) 1967 is that the term shall have been a fair and reasonable one to be included having regard to the circumstances which were, or ought reasonably to have been, known to or in the contemplation of the parties when the contract was made.

(2) In determining for the purposes of section 6 or 7 above whether a contract term satisfies the requirement of reasonableness, regard shall be had in particular to the matters specified in Schedule 2 to this Act; but this subsection does not prevent the court or arbitrator from holding, in accordance with any rule of law, that a term which purports to exclude or restrict any relevant liability is not a term of the contract.

(3) In relation to a notice (not being a notice having contractual effect), the requirement of reasonableness under this Act is that it should be fair and reasonable to allow reliance on it, having regard to all the circumstances obtaining when the liability arose or (but for the notice) would have arisen.

(4) Where by reference to a contract term or notice a person seeks to restrict liability to a specified sum of money, and the question arises (under this or any other Act) whether the term or notice satisfies the requirement of reasonableness, regard shall be had in particular (but without prejudice to subsection (2) above in the case of contract terms) to—

(a) the resources which he could expect to be available to him for the purpose of meeting the liability should it arise; and

(b) how far it was open to him to cover himself by insurance.

(5) It is for those claiming that a contract term or notice satisfies the requirement of reasonableness to show that it does.

SCHEDULE 2

"Guidelines" For Application of Reasonableness Test

The matters to which regard is to be had in particular for the purposes of **A–30** sections 6(3), 7(3) and (4), 20 and 21 are any of the following which appear to be relevant—

(a) the strength of the bargaining positions of the parties relative to each other, taking into account (among other things) alternative means by which the customer's requirements could have been met;

(b) whether the customer received an inducement to agree to the term, or in accepting it had an opportunity of entering into a similar contract with other persons, but without having to accept a similar term;

(c) whether the customer knew or ought reasonably to have known of the existence and extent of the term (having regard, among other things, to any custom of the trade and any previous course of dealing between the parties);

(d) where the term excludes or restricts any relevant liability if some condition is not complied with, whether it was reasonable at the time of the contract to expect that compliance with that condition would be practicable;

(e) whether the goods were manufactured, processed or adapted to the special order of the customer.

Civil Liability (Contribution) Act 1978

(1978 c.47)

Entitlement to contribution

1.—(1) Subject to the following provisions of this section, any person liable in **A–31** respect of any damage suffered by another person may recover contribution from any other person liable in respect of the same damage (whether jointly with him or otherwise).

(2) A person shall be entitled to recover contribution by virtue of subsection (1) above notwithstanding that he has ceased to be liable in respect of the damage in question since the time when the damage occurred, provided that he was so liable immediately before he made or was ordered or agreed to make the payment in respect of which the contribution is sought.

(3) A person shall be liable to make contribution by virtue of subsection (1) above notwithstanding that he has ceased to be liable in respect of the damage in question since the time when the damage occurred, unless he ceased to be liable

by virtue of the expiry of a period of limitation or prescription which extinguished the right on which the claim against him in respect of the damage was based.

(4) A person who has made or agreed to make any payment in bona fide settlement or compromise of any claim made against him in respect of any damage (including a payment into court which has been accepted) shall be entitled to recover contribution in accordance with this section without regard to whether or not he himself is or ever was liable in respect of the damage, provided, however, that he would have been liable assuming that the factual basis of the claim against him could be established.

(5) A judgment given in any action brought in any part of the United Kingdom by or on behalf of the person who suffered the damage in question against any person from whom contribution is sought under this section shall be conclusive in the proceedings for contribution as to any issue determined by that judgment in favour of the person from whom the contribution is sought.

(6) References in this section to a person's liability in respect of any damage are references to any such liability which has been or could be established in an action brought against him in England and Wales by or on behalf of the person who suffered the damage; but it is immaterial whether any issue arising in any such action was or would be determined (in accordance with the rules of private international law) by reference to the law of a country outside England and Wales.

Assessment of contribution

A–32   **2.**—(1) Subject to subsection (3) below, in any proceedings for contribution under section 1 above the amount of the contribution recoverable from any person shall be such as may be found by the court to be just and equitable having regard to the extent of that person's responsibility for the damage in question.

(2) Subject to subsection (3) below, the court shall have power in any such proceedings to exempt any person from liability to make contribution, or to direct that the contribution to be recovered from any person shall amount to a complete indemnity.

(3) Where the amount of the damages which have or might have been awarded in respect of the damage in question in any action brought in England and Wales by or on behalf of the person who suffered it against the person from whom the contribution is sought was or would have been subject to—

    (a) any limit imposed by or under any enactment or by any agreement made before the damage occurred;

    (b) any reduction by virtue of section 1 of the Law Reform (Contributory Negligence) Act 1945 or section 5 of the Fatal Accidents Act 1976; or

    (c) any corresponding limit or reduction under the law of a country outside England and Wales;

the person from whom the contribution is sought shall not by virtue of any contribution awarded under section 1 above be required to pay in respect of the damage a greater amount than the amount of those damages as so limited or reduced.

Proceedings against persons jointly liable for the same debt or damage

3. Judgment recovered against any person liable in respect of any debt or **A–33** damage shall not be a bar to an action, or to the continuance of an action, against any other person who is (apart from any such bar) jointly liable with him in respect of the same debt or damage.

Successive actions against persons liable (jointly or otherwise) for the same damage

4. If more than one action is brought in respect of any damage by or on behalf **A–34** of the person by whom it was suffered against persons liable in respect of the damage (whether jointly or otherwise) the plaintiff shall not be entitled to costs in any of those actions, other than that in which judgment is first given, unless the court is of the opinion that there was reasonable ground for bringing the action.

<hr/>

Unfair Terms in Consumer Contracts Regulations 1994

(S.I. 1994 No. 3159)

Whereas the Secretary of State is a Minister designated for the purposes of **A–35** section 2(2) of the European Communities Act 1972 in relation to measures relating to consumer protection;
    Now, the Secretary of State, in exercise of the powers conferred upon him by section 2(2) of that Act and of all other powers enabling him in that behalf hereby makes the following Regulations—

Citation and commencement

1. These Regulations may be cited as the Unfair Terms in Consumer Contracts **A–36** Regulations 1994 and shall come into force on 1st July 1995.

Interpretation

2.—(1) In these Regulations— **A–37**
"business" includes a trade or profession and the activities of any government department or local or public authority;
"the Community" means the European Economic Community and the other States in the European Economic Area;
"consumer" means a natural person who, in making a contract to which these Regulations apply, is acting for purposes which are outside his business;
"court" in relation to England and Wales and Northern Ireland means the High Court, and in relation to Scotland, the Court of Session;
"Director" means the Director General of Fair Trading;
"EEA Agreement" means the Agreement on the European Economic Area signed at Oporto on 2 May 1992 as adjusted by the protocol signed at Brussels on 17 March 1993;

"member State" shall mean a State which is a contracting party to the EEA Agreement but until the EEA Agreement comes into force in relation to Liechtenstein does not include the State of Liechtenstein;

"seller" means a person who sells goods and who, in making a contract to which these Regulations apply, is acting for purposes relating to his business; and

"supplier" means a person who supplies goods or services and who, in making a contract to which these Regulations apply, is acting for purposes relating to his business.

(2) In the application of these Regulations to Scotland for references to an "injunction" or an "interlocutory injunction" there shall be substituted references to an "interdict" or "interim interdict" respectively.

Terms to which these Regulations apply

A–38   3.—(1) Subject to the provisions of Schedule 1, these Regulations apply to any term in a contract concluded between a seller or supplier and a consumer where the said term has not been individually negotiated.

(2) In so far as it is in plain, intelligible language, no assessment shall be made of the fairness of any term which—

   (a) defines the main subject matter of the contract, or
   (b) concerns the adequacy of the price or remuneration, as against the goods or services sold or supplied.

(3) For the purposes of these Regulations, a term shall always be regarded as not having been individually negotiated where it has been drafted in advance and the consumer has not been able to influence the substance of the term.

(4) Notwithstanding that a specific term or certain aspects of it in a contract has been individually negotiated, these Regulations shall apply to the rest of a contract if an overall assessment of the contract indicates that it is a pre-formulated standard contract.

(5) It shall be for any seller or supplier who claims that a term was individually negotiated to show that it was.

Unfair terms

A–39   4.—(1) In these Regulations, subject to paragraphs (2) and (3) below, "unfair term" means any term which contrary to the requirement of good faith causes a significant imbalance in the parties' rights and obligations under the contract to the detriment of the consumer.

(2) An assessment of the unfair nature of a term shall be made taking into account the nature of the goods or services for which the contract was concluded and referring, as at the time of the conclusion of the contract, to all circumstances attending the conclusion of the contract and to all the other terms of the contract or of another contract on which it is dependent.

(3) In determining whether a term satisfies the requirement of good faith, regard shall be had in particular to the matters specified in Schedule 2 to these Regulations.

(4) Schedule 3 to these Regulations contains an indicative and non-exhaustive list of the terms which may be regarded as unfair.

Consequence of inclusion of unfair terms in contracts

5.—(1) An unfair term in a contract concluded with a consumer by a seller of supplier shall not be binding on the consumer. **A–40**

(2) The contract shall continue to bind the parties if it is capable of continuing in existence without the unfair term.

Construction of written contracts

6. A seller or supplier shall ensure that any written term of a contract is expressed in plain, intelligible language, and if there is doubt about the meaning of a written term, the interpretation most favourable to the consumer shall prevail. **A–41**

Choice of law clauses

7. These Regulations shall apply notwithstanding any contract term which applies or purports to apply the law of a non member State, if the contract has a close connection with the territory of the member States. **A–42**

Prevention of continued use of unfair terms

8.—(1) It shall be the duty of the Director to consider any complaint made to him that any contract term drawn up for general use is unfair, unless the complaint appears to the Director to be frivolous or vexatious. **A–43**

(2) If having considered a complaint about any contract term pursuant to paragraph (1) above the Director considers that the contract term is unfair he may, if he considers it appropriate to do so, bring proceedings for an injunction (in which proceedings he may also apply for an interlocutory injunction) against any person appearing to him to be using or recommending use of such a term in contracts concluded with consumers.

(3) The Director may, if he considers it appropriate to do so, have regard to any undertakings given to him by or on behalf of any person as to the continued use of such a term in contracts concluded with consumers.

(4) The Director shall give reasons for his decision to apply or not to apply, as the case may be, for an injunction in relation to any complaint which these Regulations require him to consider.

(5) The court on an application by the Director may grant an injunction on such terms as it thinks fit.

(6) An injunction may relate not only to use of a particular contract term drawn up for general use but to any similar term, or a term having like effect, used or recommended for use by any party to the proceedings.

(7) The Director may arrange for the dissemination in such form and manner as he considers appropriate of such information and advice concerning the operation of these Regulations as may appear to him to be expedient to give to the public and to all persons likely to be affected by these Regulations.

SCHEDULE 1   **Regulation 3(1)**

CONTRACTS AND PARTICULAR TERMS EXCLUDED FROM THE SCOPE
OF THESE REGULATIONS

A–44   These Regulations do not apply to—

    (a) any contract relating to employment;

    (b) any contract relating to succession rights;

    (c) any contract relating to rights under family law;

    (d) any contract relating to the incorporation and organisation of companies or partnerships; and

    (e) any term incorporated in order to comply with or which reflects—

        (i) statutory or regulatory provisions of the United Kingdom; or

        (ii) the provisions or principles of international conventions to which the member States or the Community are party.

SCHEDULE 2   **Regulation 4(3)**

ASSESSMENT OF GOOD FAITH

A–45   In making an assessment of good faith, regard shall be had in particular to—

    (a) the strength of the bargaining positions of the parties;

    (b) whether the consumer had an inducement to agree to the term;

    (c) whether the goods or services were sold or supplied to the special order of the consumer, and

    (d) the extent to which the seller or supplier has dealt fairly and equitably with the consumer.

SCHEDULE 3   **Regulation 4(4)**

INDICATIVE AND ILLUSTRATIVE LIST OF TERMS WHICH MAY BE
REGARDED AS UNFAIR

A–46   **1.** Terms which have the object or effect of—

    (a) excluding or limiting the legal liability of a seller or supplier in the event of the death of a consumer or personal injury to the latter resulting from an act or omission of that seller or supplier;

    (b) inappropriately excluding or limiting the legal rights of the consumer vis-à-vis the seller or supplier or another party in the event of total or partial non-performance or inadequate performance by the seller or supplier of any of the contractual obligations, including the option of offsetting a debt owed to the seller or supplier against any claim which the consumer may have against him;

    (c) making an agreement binding on the consumer whereas provision of services by the seller or supplier is subject to a condition whose realisation depends on his own will alone;

    (d) permitting the seller or supplier to retain sums paid by the consumer where the latter decides not to conclude or perform the contract, without providing for the consumer to receive compensation of an equivalent amount from the seller or supplier where the latter is the party cancelling the contract;

(e) requiring any consumer who fails to fulfil his obligation to pay a disproportionately high sum in compensation;

(f) authorising the seller or supplier to dissolve the contract on a discretionary basis where the same facility is not granted to the consumer, or permitting the seller or supplier to retain the sums paid for services not yet supplied by him where it is the seller or supplier himself who dissolves the contract;

(g) enabling the seller or supplier to terminate a contract of indeterminate duration without reasonable notice except where there are serious grounds for doing so;

(h) automatically extending a contract of fixed duration where the consumer does not indicate otherwise, when the deadline fixed for the consumer to express this desire not to extend the contract is unreasonably early;

(i) irrevocably binding the consumer to terms with which he had no real opportunity of becoming acquainted before the conclusion of the contract;

(j) enabling the seller or supplier to alter the terms of the contract unilaterally without a valid reason which is specified in the contract;

(k) enabling the seller or supplier to alter unilaterally without a valid reason any characteristics of the product or service to be provided;

(l) providing for the price of goods to be determined at the time of delivery or allowing a seller of goods or supplier of services to increase their price without in both cases giving the consumer the corresponding right to cancel the contract if the final price is too high in relation to the price agreed when the contract was concluded;

(m) giving the seller or supplier the right to determine whether the goods or services supplied are in conformity with the contract, or giving him the exclusive right to interpret any term of the contract;

(n) limiting the seller's or supplier's obligation to respect commitments undertaken by his agents or making his commitments subject to compliance with a particular formality;

(o) obliging the consumer to fulfil all his obligations where the seller or supplier does not perform his;

(p) giving the seller or supplier the possibility of transferring his rights and obligations under the contract, where this may serve to reduce the guarantees for the consumer, without the latter's agreement;

(q) excluding or hindering the consumer's right to take legal action or exercise any other legal remedy, particularly by requiring the consumer to take disputes exclusively to arbitration not covered by legal provisions, unduly restricting the evidence available to him or imposing on him a burden of proof which, according to the applicable law, should lie with another party to the contract.

2. Scope of subparagraphs 1(g), (j) and (l) **A–47**

(a) Subparagraph 1(g) is without hindrance to terms by which a supplier of financial services reserves the right to terminate unilaterally a contract of indeterminate duration without notice where there is a valid reason, provided that the supplier is required to inform the other contracting party or parties thereof immediately.

(b) Subparagraph 1(j) is without hindrance to terms under which a supplier of financial services reserves the right to alter the rate of interest payable by the consumer or due to the latter, or the amount of other charges for financial services without notice where there is a valid reason, provided that the supplier is required to inform the other contracting party or parties thereof at the earliest opportunity and that the latter are free to dissolve the contract immediately.

Subparagraph 1(j) is also without hindrance to terms under which a seller or supplier reserves the right to alter unilaterally the conditions of a contract of indeterminate duration, provided that he is required to inform the consumer with reasonable notice and that the consumer is free to dissolve the contract.

(c) Subparagraphs 1(g), (j) and (l) do not apply to:
— transactions in transferable securities, financial instruments and other products or services where the price is linked to fluctuations in a stock exchange quotation or index or a financial market rate that the seller or supplier does not control;
— contracts for the purchase or sale of foreign currency, traveller's cheques or international money orders denominated in foreign currency;

(d) Subparagraph 1(l) is without hindrance to price indexation clauses, where lawful, provided that the method by which prices vary is explicitly described.

Insolvency Act 1986

(1986 c.45)

Application for winding up

A–48   **124.**—(1) Subject to the provisions of this section, an application to the court for the winding up of a company shall be by petition presented either by the company, or the directors, or by any creditor or creditors (including any contingent or prospective creditor or creditors), contributory or contributories, or by all or any of those parties, together or separately.

(2) Except as mentioned below, a contributory is not entitled to present a winding-up petition unless either—

(a) the number of members is reduced below 2, or

(b) the shares in respect of which he is a contributory, or some of them, either were originally allotted to him, or have been held by him, and registered in his name, for at least 6 months during the 18 months before the commencement of the winding up, or have devolved on him through the death of a former holder.

(3) A person who is liable under section 76 to contribute to a company's assets in the event of its being wound up may petition on either of the grounds set out in section 122(1)(f) and (g), and subsection (2) above does not then apply; but

unless the person is a contributory otherwise than under section 76, he may not in his character as contributory petition on any other ground.

This subsection is deemed included in Chapter VII of Part V of the Companies Act (redeemable shares; purchase by a company of its own shares) for the purposes of the Secretary of State's power to make regulations under section 179 of that Act.

(4) A winding-up petition may be presented by the Secretary of State—
    (a) if the ground of the petition is that in section 122(1)(b) or (c), or
    (b) in a case falling within section 440 of the Companies Act (expedient in the public interest, following report of inspectors, etc.)

(5) Where a company is being wound up voluntarily in England and Wales, a winding-up petition may be presented by the official receiver attached to the court as well as by any other person authorised in that behalf under the other provisions of this section; but the court shall not make a winding-up order on the petition unless it is satisfied that the voluntary winding up cannot be continued with due regard to the interests of the creditors or contributories.

Style and title of liquidators

163. The liquidator of a company shall be described—   **A–49**
    (a) where a person other than the official receiver is liquidator, by the style of "the liquidator" of the particular company, or
    (b) where the official receiver is liquidator, by the style of "the official receiver and liquidator" of the particular company;
and in neither case shall he be described by an individual name.

Preferential debts (general provision)

175.—(1) In a winding up the company's preferential debts (within the **A–50** meaning given by section 386 in Part XII) shall be paid in priority to all other debts.

(2) Preferential debts—
    (a) rank equally among themselves after the expenses of the winding up and shall be paid in full, unless the assets are insufficient to meet them, in which case they abate in equal proportions; and
    (b) so far as the assets of the company available for payment of general creditors are insufficient to meet them, have priority over the claims of holder of debentures secured by, or holders of, any floating charge created by the company, and shall be paid accordingly out of any property comprised in or subject to that charge.

Power to disclaim onerous property

178.—(1) This and the next two sections apply to a company that is being **A–51** wound up in England and Wales.

(2) Subject as follows, the liquidator may, by the giving of the prescribed notice, disclaim any onerous property and may do so notwithstanding that he has taken possession of it, endeavoured to sell it, or otherwise exercised rights of ownership in relation to it.

(3) The following is onerous property for the purposes of this section—

(a)   any unprofitable contract, and

(b)   any other property of the company which is unsaleable or not readily saleable or is such that it may give rise to a liability to pay money or perform any other onerous act.

(4) A disclaimer under this section—

(a)   operates so as to determine, as from the date of the disclaimer, the rights, interest and liabilities of the company in or in respect of the property disclaimed; but

(b)   does not, except so far as is necessary for the purpose of releasing the company from any liability, affect the rights of liabilities of any other person.

(5) A notice of disclaimer shall not be given under this section in respect of any property if—

(a)   a person interested in the property has applied in writing to the liquidator or one of his predecessors as liquidator requiring the liquidator or that predecessor to decide whether he will disclaim or not, and

(d)   the period of 28 days beginning with the day on which that application was made, or such longer period as the court may allow, has expired without a notice of disclaimer having been given under this section in respect of that property.

(6) Any person sustaining loss or damage in consequence of the operation of a disclaimer under this section is deemed a creditor of the company to the extent of the loss of damage and accordingly may prove for the loss or damage in the winding up.

Disclaimer of leaseholds

A–52   **179.**—(1) The disclaimer under section 178 of any property of a leasehold nature does not take effect unless a copy of the disclaimer has been served (so far as the liquidator is aware of their addresses) on every person claiming under the company as underlessee or mortgagee and either—

(a)   no application under section 181 below is made with respect to that property before the end of the period of 14 days beginning with the day on which the last notice served under this subsection was served; or

(b)   where such an application has been made, the court directs that the disclaimer shall take effect.

(2) Where the court gives a direction under subsection (1)(b) it may also, instead of or in addition to any order it makes under section 181, make such orders with respect to fixtures, tenant's improvements and other matters arising out of the lease as it thinks fit.

Land subject to rentcharge

A–53   **180.**—(1) the following applies where, in consequence of the disclaimer under section 178 of any land subject to a rentcharge, that land vests by operation of law in the Crown or any other person (referred to in the next subsection as "the proprietor").

(2) The proprietor and the successors in title of the proprietor are not subject to any personal liability in respect of any sums becoming due under the

rentcharge except sums becoming due after the proprietor, or some person claiming under or through the proprietor, has taken possession or control of the land or has entered into occupation of it.

Powers of court (general)

181.—(1) This section and the next apply where the liquidator has disclaimed **A–54** property under section 178.

(2) An application under this section may be made to the court by—
  (a) any person who claims an interest in the disclaimed property, or
  (b) any person who is under any liability in respect of the disclaimed property, not being a liability discharged by the disclaimer.

(3) Subject as follows, the court may on the application make an order, on such terms as it thinks fit, for the vesting of the disclaimed property in, or for its delivery to—
  (a) a person entitled to it or a trustee for such a person, or
  (b) a person subject to such a liability as is mentioned in subsection (2)(b) or a trustee for such a person.

(4) The court shall not make an order under subsection (3)(b) except where it appears to the court that it would be just to do so for the purpose of compensating the person subject to the liability in respect of the disclaimer.

(5) The effect of any order under this section shall be taken into account in assessing for the purpose of section 178(6) the extent of any loss or damage sustained by any person in consequence of the disclaimer.

(6) An order under this section vesting property in any person need not be completed by conveyance, assignment or transfer.

Effect of execution or attachment (England and Wales)

183.—(1) Where a creditor has issued execution against the goods or land of **A–55** a company or has attached any debt due to it, and the company is subsequently wound up, he is not entitled to retain the benefit of the execution or attachment against the liquidator unless he has completed the execution or attachment before the commencement of the winding up.

(2) However—
  (a) if a creditor has had notice of a meeting having been called at which a resolution for voluntary winding up is to be proposed, the date on which he had notice is substituted, for the purpose of subsection (1), for the date of commencement of the winding up;
  (b) a person who purchases in good faith under a sale by the sheriff any goods of a company on which execution has been levied in all cases acquires a good title to them against the liquidator; and
  (c) the rights conferred by subsection (1) on the liquidator may be set aside by the court in favour of the creditor to such extent and subject to such terms as the court thinks fit.

(3) For the purposes of this Act—
  (a) an execution against goods is completed by seizure and sale, or by the making of a charging order under section 1 of the Charging Orders Act 1979;

(b) an attachment of a debt is completed by receipt of the debt; and

(c) an execution against land is completed by seizure, by the appointment of a receiver, or by the making of a charging order under section 1 of the Act above-mentioned.

(4) In this section, "goods" includes all chattels personal; and "the sheriff" includes any officer charged with the execution of a writ or other process.

(5) This section does not apply in the case of a winding up in Scotland.

Interest on debts

A–56   **189.**—(1) In a winding up interest is payable in accordance with this section on any debt proved in the winding up, including so much of any such debt as represents interest on the remainder.

(2) Any surplus remaining after the payment of the debts proved in a winding up shall, before being applied for any other purpose, be applied in paying interest on those debts in respect of the periods during which they have been outstanding since the company went into liquidation.

(3) All interest under this section ranks equally, whether or not the debts on which it is payable rank equally.

(4) The rate of interest payable under this section in respect of any debt ("the official rate" for the purposes of any provision of this Act in which that expression is used) is whichever is the greater of—

(a) the rate specified in section 17 of the Judgments Act 1838 on the day on which the company went into liquidation, and

(b) the rate applicable to that debt apart from the winding up.

(5) In the application of this section to Scotland—

(a) references to a debt proved in a winding up have effect as references to a claim accepted in a winding up, and

(b) the references to section 17 of the Judgments Act 1838 has effect as a reference to the rules.

Preferences (England and Wales)

A–57   **239.**—(1) This section applies as does section 238.

(2) Where the company has at a relevant time (defined in the next section) given a preference to any person, the office-holder may apply to the court for an order under this section.

(3) Subject as follows, the court shall, on such an application, make such order as it thinks fit for restoring the position to what it would have been if the company had not given that preference.

(4) For the purposes of this section and section 241, a company gives a preference to a person if—

(a) that person is one of the company's creditors or a surety or guarantor for any of the company's debts or other liabilities, and

(b) the company does anything or suffers anything to be done which (in either case) has the effect of putting that person into a position which, in the event of the company going into insolvent liquidation, will be better than the position he would have been in if that thing had not been done.

(5) The court shall not make an order under this section in respect of a preference given to any person unless the company which gave the preference was influenced in deciding to give it by a desire to produce in relation to that person the effect mentioned in subsection (4)(b).

(6) A company which has given a preference to a person connected with the company (otherwise than by reason only of being its employee) at the time the preference was given is presumed, unless the contrary is shown, to have been influenced in deciding to give it by such a desire as is mentioned in subsection (5).

(7) The fact that something has been done in pursuance of the order of a court does not, without more, prevent the doing or suffering of that thing from constituting the giving of a preference.

Orders under ss.238, 239

241.—(1) Without prejudice to the generality of sections 238(3) and 239(3), an order under either of those sections with respect to a transaction or preference entered into or given by a company may (subject to the next subsection)— **A–58**

- (a) require any property transferred as part of the transaction, or in connection with the giving of the preference, to be vested in the company,
- (b) require any property to be so vested if it represents in any person's hands the application either of the proceeds of sale of property so transferred or of money so transferred,
- (c) release or discharge (in whole or in part) any security given by the company,
- (d) require any person to pay, in respect of benefits received by him from the company, such sums to the office-holder as the court may direct,
- (e) provide for any surety or guarantor whose obligations to any person were released or discharged (in whole or in part) under the transaction, or by the giving of the preference, to be under such new or revived obligations to that person as the court thinks appropriate,
- (f) provide for security to be provided for the discharge of any obligation imposed by or arising under the order, for such an obligation to be charged on any property and for the security or charge to have the same priority as a security or charge released or discharged (in whole or in part) under the transaction or by the giving of the preference, and
- (g) provide for the extent to which any person whose property is vested by the order in the company, or on whom obligations are imposed by the order, is to be able to prove in the winding up of the company for debts or other liabilities which arose from, or were released or discharged (in whole or in part) under or by, the transaction or the giving of the preference.

(2) An order under section 238 or 239 may affect the property of, or impose any obligation on, any person whether or not he is the person with whom the company in question entered into the transaction or (as the case may be) the person to whom the preference was given; but such an order—

- (a) shall not prejudice any interest in property which was acquired from a person other than the company and was acquired in good faith, for value and without notice of the relevant circumstances, or prejudice any interest deriving from such an interest, and

(b) shall not require a person who received a benefit from the transaction or preference in good faith, for value and without notice of the relevant circumstances to pay a sum to the office-holder, except where that person was a party to the transaction or the payment is to be in respect of a preference given to that person at a time when he was a creditor of the company.

(3) For the purposes of this section the relevant circumstances, in relation to a transaction or preference, are—

(a) the circumstances by virtue of which an order under section 238 or (as the case may be) 239 could be made in respect of the transaction or preference if the company were to go into liquidation, or an administration order were made in relation to the company, within a particular period after the transaction is entered into or the preference given, and

(b) if that period has expired, the fact that the company has gone into liquidation or that such an order has been made.

(4) The provisions of sections 238 to 241 apply without prejudice to the availability of any other remedy, even in relation to a transaction or preference which the company had no power to enter into or give.

Part VIII

Individual Voluntary Arrangements

Moratorium for insolvent debtor

Interim order of court

A–59 **252.**—(1) In the circumstances specified below, the court may in the case of a debtor (being an individual) make an interim order under this section.

(2) An interim order has the effect that, during the period for which it is in force—

(a) no bankruptcy petition relating to the debtor may be presented or proceeded with, and

(b) no other proceedings, and no execution or other legal process, may be commenced or continued against the debtor or his property except with the leave of the court.

Application for interim order

A–60 **253.**—(1) Application to the court for an interim order may be made where the debtor intends to make a proposal to his creditors for a composition in satisfaction of his debts or a scheme of arrangement of his affairs (from here on referred to, in either case, as a "voluntary arrangement").

(2) The proposal must provide for some person ("the nominee") to act in relation to the voluntary arrangement either as trustee or otherwise for the purpose of supervising its implementation.

(3) Subject as follows, the application may be made—

    (a) if the debtor is an undischarged bankrupt, by the debtor, the trustee of his estate, or the official receiver, and

    (b) in any other case, by the debtor.

(4) An application shall not be made under subsection (3)(a) unless the debtor has given notice of his proposal (that is, the proposal to his creditors for a voluntary arrangement) to the official receiver and, if there is one, the trustee of his estate.

(5) An application shall not be made while a bankruptcy petition presented by the debtor is pending, if the court has, under section 273 below, appointed an insolvency practitioner to inquire into the debtor's affairs and report.

Effect of application

254.—(1) At any time when an application under section 253 for an interim **A–61** order is pending, the court may stay any action, execution or other legal process against the property or person of the debtor.

(2) Any court in which proceedings are pending against an individual may, on proof that an application under that section has been made in respect of that individual, either stay the proceedings or allow them to continue on such terms as it thinks fit.

Cases in which interim order can be made

255.—(1) The court shall not make an interim order on an application under **A–62** section 253 unless it is satisfied—

    (a) that the debtor intends to make such a proposal as is mentioned in that section;

    (b) that on the day of the making of the application the debtor was an undischarged bankrupt or was able to petition for his own bankruptcy;

    (c) that no previous application has been made by the debtor for an interim order in the period of 12 months ending with that day; and

    (d) that the nominee under the debtor's proposal to his creditors is a person who is for the time being qualified to act as an insolvency practitioner in relation to the debtor, and is willing to act in relation to the proposal.

(2) The court may make an order if it thinks that it would be appropriate to do so for the purpose of facilitating the consideration and implementation of the debtor's proposal.

(3) Where the debtor is an undischarged bankrupt, the interim order may contain provision as to the conduct of the bankruptcy, and the administration of the bankrupt's estate, during the period for which the order is in force.

(4) Subject as follows, the provision contained in an interim order by virtue of subsection (3) may include provision staying proceedings in the bankruptcy or modifying any provision in this Group of Parts, and any provision of the rules in their application to the debtor's bankruptcy.

(5) An interim order shall not, in relation to a bankrupt, make provision relaxing or removing any of the requirements of provisions in this Group of Parts, or of the rules, unless the court is satisfied that that provision is unlikely to result in any significant diminution in, or in the value of, the debtor's estate for the purposes of the bankruptcy.

(6) Subject to the following provisions of this Part, an interim order made on an application under section 253 ceases to have effect at the end of the period of 14 days beginning with the day after the making of the order.

Nominee's report on debtor's proposal

A–63
256.—(1) Where an interim order has been made on an application under section 253, the nominee shall, before the order ceases to have effect, submit a report to the court stating—

   (a) whether, in his opinion, a meeting of the debtor's creditors should be summoned to consider the debtor's proposal, and
   (b) if in his opinion such a meeting should be summoned, the date on which, and time and place at which, he proposes the meeting should be held.

(2) For the purpose of enabling the nominee to prepare his report the debtor shall submit to the nominee—

   (a) a document setting out the terms of the voluntary arrangement which the debtor is proposing, and
   (b) a statement of his affairs containing—
       (i) such particulars of his creditors and of his debts and other liabilities and of his assets as may be prescribed, and
       (ii) such other information as may be prescribed.

(3) The court may, on an application made by the debtor in a case where the nominee has failed to submit the report required by this section, do one or both of the following, namely—

   (a) direct that the nominee shall be replaced as such by another person qualified to act as an insolvency practitioner in relation to the debtor;
   (b) direct that the interim order shall continue, or (if it has ceased to have effect) be renewed, for such further period as the court may specify in the direction.

(4) The court may, on the application of the nominee, extend the period for which the interim order has effect so as to enable the nominee to have more time to prepare his report.

(5) If the court is satisfied on receiving the nominee's report that a meeting of the debtor's creditors should be summoned to consider the debtor's proposal, the court shall direct that the period for which the interim order has effect shall be extended, for such further period as it may specify in the direction, for the purpose of enabling the debtor's proposal to be considered by his creditors in accordance with the following provisions of this Part.

(6) The court may discharge the interim order if it is satisfied, on the application of the nominee—

   (a) that the debtor has failed to comply with his obligations under subsection (2), or

(b) that for any other reason it would be inappropriate for a meeting of the debtor's creditors to be summoned to consider the debtor's proposal.

Summoning of creditor's meeting

257.—(1) Where it has been reported to the court under section 256 that a **A–64** meeting of the debtor's creditors should be summoned, the nominee (or his replacement under section 256(3)(a)) shall, unless the court otherwise directs, summon that meeting for the time, date and place proposed in his report.

(2) The persons to be summoned to the meeting are every creditor of the debtor of whose claim and address the person summoning the meeting is aware.

(3) For the purpose the creditors of a debtor who is an undischarged bankrupt include—

(a) every person who is a creditor of the bankrupt in respect of a bankruptcy debt, and

(b) every person who would be such a creditor if the bankruptcy had commenced on the day on which notice of the meeting is given.

Consideration and implementation of debtor's proposal

Decisions of creditors' meeting

258.—(1) A creditors' meeting summoned under section 257 shall decide **A–65** whether to approve the proposed voluntary arrangement.

(2) The meeting may approve the proposed voluntary arrangement with modifications, but shall not do so unless the debtor consents to each modification.

(3) The modifications subject to which the proposed voluntary arrangement may be approved may include one conferring the functions proposed to be conferred on the nominee on another person qualified to act as an insolvency practitioner in relation to the debtor.

But they shall not include any modification by virtue of which the proposal ceases to be a proposal such as is mentioned in section 253.

(4) The meeting shall not approve any proposal or modification which affects the right of a secured creditor of the debtor to enforce his security, except with the concurrence of the creditor concerned.

(5) Subject as follows, the meeting shall not approve any proposal or modification under which—

(a) any preferential debt of the debtor is to be paid otherwise than in priority to such of his debts as are not preferential debts, or

(b) a preferential creditor of the debtor is to be paid an amount in respect of a preferential debt that bears to that debt a smaller proportion than is borne to another preferential debt by the amount that is to be paid in respect of that other debt.

However, the meeting may approve such a proposal or modification with the concurrence of the preferential creditor concerned.

(6) Subject as above, the meeting shall be conducted in accordance with the rules.

(7) In this section "preferential debt" has the meaning given by section 386 in Part XII; and "preferential creditor" is to be construed accordingly.

Report of decisions to court

A–66 **259.**—(1) After the conclusion in accordance with the rules of the meeting summoned under section 257, the chairman of the meeting shall report the result of it to the court and, immediately after so reporting, shall give notice of the result of the meeting to such persons as may be prescribed.

(2) If the report is that the meeting has declined (with or without modifications) to approve the debtor's proposal, the court may discharge any interim order which is in force in relation to the debtor.

Effect of approval

A–67 **260.**—(1) This section has effect where the meeting summoned under section 257 approves the proposed voluntary arrangement (with or without modifications).

(2) The approved arrangement—

(a) takes effect as if made by the debtor at the meeting, and

(b) binds every person who in accordance with the rules had notice of, and was entitled to vote at, the meeting (whether or not he was present or represented at it) as if he were a party to the arrangement.

(3) The Deeds of Arrangement Act 1914 does not apply to the approved voluntary arrangement.

(4) Any interim order in force in relation to the debtor immediately before the end of the period of 28 days beginning with the days on which the report with respect to the creditors' meeting was made to the court under section 259 ceases to have effect at the end of that period.

This subsection applies except to such extent as the court may direct for the purposes of any application under section 262 below.

(5) Where proceedings on a bankruptcy petition have been stayed by an interim order which cases to have effect under subsection (4), that petition is deemed, unless the court otherwise orders, to have been dismissed.

Effect where debtor an undischarged bankrupt

A–68 **261.**—(1) Subject as follows, where the creditors' meeting summoned under section 257 approves the proposed voluntary arrangement (with or without modifications) and the debtor is in an undischarged bankrupt, the court may do one or both of the following, namely—

(a) annul the bankruptcy order by which he was adjudged bankrupt;

(b) give such directions with respect to the conduct of the bankruptcy and the administration of the bankrupt's estate as it thinks appropriate for facilitating the implementation of the approved voluntary arrangement.

(2) The court shall not annul a bankruptcy order under subsection (1)—

(a) at any time before the end of the period of 28 days beginning with the day on which the report of the creditors' meeting was made to the court under section 259, or

(b) at any time when an application under section 262 below, or an appeal in respect of such an application, is pending or at any time in the period within which such an appeal may be brought.

Challenge of meeting's decision

262.—(1) Subject to this section, an application to the court may be made, by any of the persons specified below, on one or both of the following grounds, namely— **A–69**

(a) that a voluntary arrangement approved by a creditors' meeting summoned under section 257 unfairly prejudices the interests of a creditor of the debtor;

(b) that there has been some material irregularity at or in relation to such a meeting.

(2) The persons who may apply under this section are—

(a) the debtor;

(b) a person entitled, in accordance with the rules, to vote at the creditors' meeting;

(c) the nominee (or his replacement under section 256(3)(a) or 258(3)); and

(d) if the debtor is an undischarged bankrupt, the trustee of his estate or the official receiver.

(3) An application under this section shall not be made after the end of the period of 28 days beginning with the day on which the report of the creditors' meeting was made to the court under section 259.

(4) Where on an application under this section the court is satisfied as to either of the grounds mentioned in subsection (1), it may do one or both of the following, namely—

(a) revoke or suspend any approval given by the meeting;

(b) give a direction to any person for the summoning of a further meeting of the debtor's creditors to consider any revised proposal he may make or, in a case falling within subsection (1)(b), to reconsider his original proposal.

(5) Where at any time after giving a direction under subsection (4)(b) for the summoning of a meeting to consider a revised proposal the court is satisfied that the debtor does not intend to submit such a proposal, the court shall revoke the direction and revoke or suspend any approval given at the previous meeting.

(6) Where the court gives a direction under subsection (4)(b), it may also give a direction continuing or, as the case may require, renewing, for such period as may be specified in the direction, the effect in relation to the debtor of any interim order.

(7) In any case where the court, on an application made under this section with respect to a creditors' meeting, gives a direction under subsection (4)(b) or revokes or suspends an approval under subsection (4)(a) or (5), the court may give such supplemental directions as it thinks fit and, in particular, directions with respect to—

(a) things done since the meeting under any voluntary arrangement approved by the meeting, and

(b) such things done since the meeting as could not have been done if an interim order had been in force in relation to the debtor when they were done.

(8) Except in pursuance of the preceding provisions of this section, an approval given at a creditors' meeting summoned under section 257 is not invalidated by any irregularity at or in relation to the meeting.

Implementation and supervision of approved voluntary arrangement

A–70   **263.**—(1) This section applies where a voluntary arrangement approved by a creditors' meeting summoned under section 257 has taken effect.

(2) The person who is for the time being carrying out, in relation to the voluntary arrangement, the functions conferred by virtue of the approval on the nominee (or his replacement under section 256(3)(a) or 258(3)) shall be known as the supervisor of the voluntary arrangement.

(3) If the debtor, any of his creditors or any other person is dissatisfied by any act, omission or decision of the supervisor, he may apply to the court; and on such an application the court may—

   (a) confirm, reverse or modify any act or decision of the supervisor,
   (b) give him directions, or
   (c) make such other order as it thinks fit.

(4) The supervisor may apply to the court for directions in relation to any particular matter arising under the voluntary arrangement.

(5) The court may, whenever—

   (a) it is expedient to appoint a person to carry out the functions of the supervisor, and
   (b) it is inexpedient, difficult or impracticable for an appointment to be made without the assistance of the court,

make an order appointing a person who is qualified to act as an insolvency practitioner in relation to the debtor, either in substitution for the existing supervisor or to fill a vacancy.

This is without prejudice to section 41(2) of the Trustee Act 1925 (power of court to appoint trustees of deeds of arrangement).

(6) The power conferred by subsection (5) is exercisable so as to increase the number of persons exercising the functions of the supervisor or, where there is more than one person exercising those functions, so as to replace one or more of those persons.

Effect of discharge

A–71   **281.**—(1) Subject as follows, where a bankrupt is discharged, the discharge releases him from all the bankruptcy debts, but has no effect—

   (a) on the functions (so far as they remain to be carried out) of the trustee of his estate, or
   (b) on the operation, for the purposes of the carrying out of those functions, of the provisions of this Part;

and, in particular, discharge does not affect the right of any creditor of the bankrupt to prove in the bankruptcy for any debt from which the bankrupt is released.

(2) Discharge does not affect the right of any secured creditor of the bankrupt to enforce his security for the payment of a debt from which the bankrupt is released.

(3) Discharge does not release the bankrupt from any bankruptcy debt which he incurred in respect of, or forbearance in respect of which was secured by means of, any fraud or fraudulent breach of trust to which he was a party.

(4) Discharge does not release the bankrupt from any liability in respect of a fine imposed for an offence or from any liability under a recognisance except, in the case of a penalty imposed for an offence under an enactment relating to the public revenue or of a recognisance, with the consent of the Treasury.

(5) Discharge does not, except to such extent and on such conditions as the court may direct, release the bankrupt from any bankruptcy debt which—

(a) consists in a liability to pay damages for negligence, nuisance or breach of a statutory, contractual or other duty, being damages in respect of persons injuries to any person, or

(b) arises under any order made in family proceedings or in domestic proceedings.

(6) Discharge does not release the bankrupt from such other bankruptcy debts, not being debts provable in his bankruptcy, as are prescribed.

(7) Discharge does not release any person other than the bankrupt from any liability (whether as partner or co-trustee of the bankrupt or otherwise) from which the bankrupt is released by the discharge, or from any liability as surety for the bankrupt or as a person in the nature of such a surety.

(8) In this section—

"domestic proceedings" means domestic proceedings within the meaning of the Magistrates' Courts Act 1980 and any proceedings which would be such proceedings but for section 65(1)(ii) of that Act (proceedings for variation of order for periodical payments);

"family proceedings" means the same as in Part V of the Matrimonial and Family Proceedings Act 1984;

"fine" means the same as in the Magistrates' Courts Act 1980; and

"personal injuries" includes death and any disease or other impairment of a person's physical or mental condition.

Disclaimer of onerous property

Disclaimer (general power)

315.—(1) Subject as follows, the trustee may, by the giving of the prescribed **A–72** notice, disclaim any onerous property and may do so notwithstanding that he has taken possession of it, endeavoured to sell it or otherwise exercised rights of ownership in relation to it.

(2) The following is onerous property for the purposes of this section, that is to say—

(a) any unprofitable contract, and

(b) any other property comprised in the bankrupt's estate which is unsaleable or not readily saleable, or is such that it may give rise to a liability to pay money or perform any other onerous act.

(3) A disclaimer under this section—

(a) operates so as to determine, as from the date of the disclaimer, the rights, interests and liabilities of the bankrupt and his estate in or in respect of the property disclaimed, and

    (b) discharges the trustee from all personal liability in respect of that
        property as from the commencement of his trusteeship,
but does not, except so far as is necessary for the purpose of releasing the
bankrupt, the bankrupt's estate and the trustee from the liability, affect the rights
or liabilities of any other person.

    (4) A notice of disclaimer shall not be given under this section in respect of
any property that has been claimed for the estate under section 307 (after-
acquired property) or 308 (personal property of bankrupt exceeding reasonable
replacement value), except with the leave of the court.

    (5) Any person sustaining loss or damage in consequence of the operation of
a disclaimer under this section is deemed to be a creditor of the bankrupt to the
extent of the loss or damage and accordingly may prove for the loss or damage
as a bankruptcy debt.

Mutual credit and set-off

A–73   **323.**—(1) This section applies where before the commencement of the bankruptcy there have been mutual credits, mutual debts or other mutual dealings
between the bankrupt and any creditor of the bankrupt proving or claiming to
prove for a bankruptcy debt.

    (2) An account shall be taken of what is due from each party to the other in
respect of the mutual dealings and the sums due from one party shall be set off
against the sums due from the other.

    (3) Sums due from the bankrupt to another party shall not be included in the
account taken under subsection (2) if that other party had notice at the time they
become due that a bankruptcy petition relating to the bankrupt was pending.

    (4) Only the balance (if any) of the account taken under subsection (2) is
provable as a bankruptcy debt or, as the case may be, to be paid to the trustee as
part of the bankrupt's estate.

Preferences

A–74   **340.**—(1) Subject as follows in this and the next two sections, where an
individual is adjudged bankrupt and he has at a relevant time (defined in section
341) given a preference to any person, the trustee of the bankrupt's estate may
apply to the court for an order under this section.

    (2) The court shall, on such an application, make such order as it thinks fit for
restoring the position to what it would have been if that individual had not given
that preference.

    (3) For the purposes of this and the next two sections, an individual gives a
preference to a person if—

    (a) that person is one of the individual's creditors or a surety or guarantor
        for any of his debts or other liabilities, and
    (b) the individual does anything or suffers anything to be done which (in
        either case) has the effect of putting that person into a position which,
        in the event of the individual's bankruptcy, will be better than the
        position he would have been in if that thing had not been done.

    (4) The court shall not make an order under this section in respect of a
preference given to any person unless the individual who gave the preference was

influenced in deciding to give it by a desire to produce in relation to that person the effect mentioned in subsection (3)(b) above.

(5) An individual who has given a preference to a person who, at the time the preference was given, was an associate of his (otherwise than by reason only of being his employee) is presumed, unless the contrary is shown, to have been influenced in deciding to give it by such a desire as is mentioned in subsection (4).

(6) The fact that something has been done in pursuance of the order of a court does not, without more, prevent the doing or suffering of that thing from constituting the giving of a preference.

Orders under ss.339, 340

342.—(1) Without prejudice to the generality of section 339(2) or 340(2), an **A–75** order under either of those sections with respect to a transaction or preference entered into or given by an individual who is subsequently adjudged bankrupt may (subject as follows)—

(a) require any property transferred as part of the transaction, or in connection with the giving of the preference, to be vested in the trustee of the bankrupt's estate as part of that estate;

(b) require any property to be so vested if it represents in any person's hands the application either of the proceeds of sale of property so transferred or of money so transferred;

(c) release or discharge (in whole or in part) any security given by the individual;

(d) require any person to pay, in respect of benefits received by hm from the individual, such sums to the trustee of his estate as the court may direct;

(e) provide for any surety or guarantor whose obligations to any person were released or discharged (in whole or in part) under the transaction or by the giving of the preference to be under such new or revived obligations to that person as the court thinks appropriate;

(f) provide for security to be provided for the discharge of any obligation imposed by or arising under the order, for such an obligation to be charged on any property and for the security or charge to have the same priority as a security or charge released or discharged (in whole or in part) under the transaction or by the giving of the preference; and

(g) provide for the extent to which any person whose property is vested by the order in the trustee of the bankrupt's estate, or on whom obligations are imposed by the order, is to be able to prove in the bankruptcy for debts or other liabilities which arose from, or were released or discharged (in whole or in part) under or by, the transaction or the giving of the preference.

(2) An order under section 339 or 340 may affect the property of, or impose any obligation on, any person whether or not he is the person with whom the individual in question entered into the transaction or, as the case may be, the person to whom the preference was given; but such an order—

    (a) shall not prejudice any interest in property which was acquired from a person other than that individual and was acquired in good faith, for value and without notice of the relevant circumstances, or prejudice any interest deriving from such an interest, and

    (b) shall not require a person who received a benefit from the transaction or preference in good faith, for value and without notice of the relevant circumstances to pay a sum to the trustee of the bankrupt's estate, except where he was a party to the transaction or the payment is to be in respect of a preference given to that person at a time when he was a creditor of that individual.

(3) Any sums required to be paid to the trustee in accordance with an order under section 339 or 340 shall be comprised in the bankrupt's estate.

(4) For the purposes of this section the relevant circumstances, in relation to a transaction or preference, are—

    (a) the circumstances by virtue of which an order under section 339 or 340 could be made in respect of the transaction or preference if the individual in question were adjudged bankrupt within a particular period after the transaction is entered into or the preference given, and

    (b) if that period has expired, the fact that that individual has been adjudged bankrupt within that period.

"Bankruptcy debt", etc.

A–76   **382.**—(1) "Bankruptcy debt", in relation to a bankrupt, means (subject to the next subsection) any of the following—

    (a) any debt or liability to which he is subject at the commencement of the bankruptcy,

    (b) any debt or liability to which he may become subject after the commencement of the bankruptcy (including after his discharge from bankruptcy) of reason of any obligation incurred before the commencement of the bankruptcy.

    (c) any amount specified in pursuance of section 39(3)(c) of the Powers of Criminal Courts Act 1973 in any criminal bankruptcy order made against him before the commencement of the bankruptcy, and

    (d) any interest provable as mentioned in section 322(2) in Chapter IV of Part IX.

(2) In determining for the purposes of any provision in this Group of Parts whether any liability in tort is a bankruptcy debt, the bankrupt is deemed to become subject to that liability by reason of an obligation incurred at the time when the cause of action accrued.

(3) For the purposes of references in this Group of Parts to a debt or liability, it is immaterial whether the debt or liability is present or future, whether it is certain or contingent or whether its amount is fixed or liquidated, or is capable of being ascertained by fixed rules or as a matter of opinion; and references in this Group of Parts to owing a debt are to be read accordingly.

(4) In this Group of Parts, except in so far as the context otherwise requires, "liability" means (subject to subsection (3) above) a liability to pay money or money's worth, including any liability under an enactment, any liability for

breach of trust, any liability in contract, tort or bailment and any liability arising out of an obligation to make restitution.

Insolvency Rules 1986

(S.I. 1986 No. 1925)

Section B: Quantification of Claim

Estimate of quantum

4.86.— (1) The liquidator shall estimate the value of any debt which, by **A–77** reason of its being subject to any contingency or for any other reason, does not bear a certain value; and he may revise any estimate previously made, if he thinks fit by reference to any change of circumstances or to information becoming available to him.

He shall inform the creditor as to his estimate and any revision of it.

(2) Where the value of a debt is estimated under this Rule, or by the court under section 168(3) or (5), the amount provable in the winding up in the case of that debt is that of the estimate for the time being.

Mutual credit and set-off

4.90.— (1) This Rules applies where, before the company goes into liquidation **A–78** there have been mutual credits, mutual debts or other mutual dealings between the company and any creditor of the company proving or claiming to prove for a debt in the liquidation.

(2) An account shall be taken of what is due from each party to the other in respect of the mutual dealings, and the sums due from one party shall be set off against the sums due from the other.

(3) Sums due from the company to another party shall not be included in the account taken under paragraph (2) if that other party had notice at the time they became due that a meeting of creditors had been summoned under section 98 or (as the case may be) a petition for the winding up of the company was pending.

(4) Only the balance (if any) of the account is provable in the liquidation. Alternatively (as the case may be) the amount shall be paid to the liquidator as part of the assets.

Provable debts

12.3.— (1) Subject as follows, in both winding up and bankruptcy, all claims **A–79** by creditors are provable as debts against the company or, as the case may be, the bankrupt, whether they are present or future, certain or contingent, ascertained or sounding only in damages.

(2) The following are not provable—
 (a) in bankruptcy, any fine imposed for an offence, and any obligation arising under an order made in family or domestic proceedings;
 (b) in winding up or bankruptcy, any obligation arising under a confiscation order made under section 1 of the Drug Trafficking Offences Act 1986.

"Fine", domestic proceedings" and "family proceedings" have the meanings given by section 281(8) of the Act (which applies the Magistrates' Courts Act 1980 and the Matrimonial and Family Proceedings Act 1984).

(3) Nothing in this Rule prejudices any enactment or rule of law under which a particular kind of debt is not provable, whether on grounds of public policy or otherwise.

"Debt", "liability" (winding up)

A–80   13.12.— (1) "Debt", in relation to the winding up of a company, means (subject to the next paragraph) any of the following—

    (a) any debt or liability to which the company is subject at the date on which it goes into liquidation;

    (b) any debt or liability to which the company may become subject after that date by reason of any obligation incurred before that date; and

    (c) any interest provable as mentioned in Rule 4.93(1).

(2) In determining for the purposes of any provision of the Act or the Rules about winding up, whether any liability in tort is a debt provable in the winding up, the company is deemed to become subject to that liability by reason of an obligation incurred at the time when the cause of action accrued.

(3) For the purposes of references in any provision of the Act or the Rules about winding up to a debt or liability, it is immaterial whether the debt or liability is present or future, whether it is certain or contingent, or whether its amount is fixed or liquidated, or is capable of being ascertained by fixed rules or as a matter of opinion; and references in any such provision to owing a debt are to be read accordingly.

(4) In any provision of the Act or the Rules about winding up, except in so far as the context otherwise requires, "liability" means (subject to paragraph (3) above) a liability to pay money or money's worth, including any liability under an enactment, any liability for breach of trust, any liability in contract, tort or bailment, and any liability arising out of an obligation to make restitution.

INDEX

(All references are to paragraph number)